ALL GLORY TO ŚRĪ GURU AND GAURĀṄGA

ŚRĪMAD BHĀGAVATAM

of

KṚṢṆA-DVAIPĀYANA VYĀSA

स्वस्त्यस्तु विश्वस्य खलः प्रसीदतां
ध्यायन्तु भूतानि शिवं मिथो धिया।
मनश्च भद्रं भजतादधोक्षजे
आवेश्यतां नो मतिरप्यहैतुकी ॥ ९ ॥

svasty astu viśvasya khalaḥ prasīdatāṁ
dhyāyantu bhūtāni śivaṁ mitho dhiyā
manaś ca bhadraṁ bhajatād adhokṣaje
āveśyatāṁ no matir apy ahaitukī (p.168)

BOOKS by
His Divine Grace A.C. Bhaktivedanta Swami Prabhupāda

Bhagavad-gītā As It Is
Śrīmad-Bhāgavatam, Cantos 1-5 (15 Vols.)
Śrī Caitanya-caritāmṛta (17 Vols.)
Teachings of Lord Caitanya
The Nectar of Devotion
Śrī Īśopaniṣad
Easy Journey to Other Planets
Kṛṣṇa Consciousness: The Topmost Yoga System
Kṛṣṇa, The Supreme Personality of Godhead (3 Vols.)
Transcendental Teachings of Prahlāda Mahārāja
Kṛṣṇa, the Reservoir of Pleasure
The Perfection of Yoga
Beyond Birth and Death
On the Way to Kṛṣṇa
Rāja-vidyā: The King of Knowledge
Elevation to Kṛṣṇa Consciousness
Kṛṣṇa Consciousness: The Matchless Gift
Back to Godhead Magazine (Founder)

A complete catalogue is available upon request.

The Bhaktivedanta Book Trust
3764 Watseka Avenue
Los Angeles, California 90034

TRANSFORMING
FREE SPEECH

TRANSFORMING FREE SPEECH

The Ambiguous Legacy of Civil Libertarianism

MARK A. GRABER

UNIVERSITY OF CALIFORNIA PRESS
BERKELEY   LOS ANGELES   OXFORD

University of California Press
Berkeley and Los Angeles, California

University of California Press, Ltd.
Oxford, England

© 1991 by
The Regents of the University of California

Library of Congress Cataloging-in-Publication Data

Graber, Mark A.
  Transforming free speech : the ambiguous legacy of
civil libertarianism / Mark A. Graber.
    p. cm.
  Includes bibliographical references (p.   ) and index.
  ISBN 0-520-06919-6 (alk. paper)
  1. Freedom of speech—United States—History. I.
Title
  KF4772.G73   1991
  342.73'0853—dc20
  [347.302853]   90-11066
                                                        CIP

Printed in the United States of America
1 2 3 4 5 6 7 8 9

The paper used in this publication meets the minimum requirements of American National Standard for Information
Sciences—Permanence of Paper for Printed Library Materials, ANSI Z39.48-1984.   ∞

To Lena Tobol and Frances Wine, My Favorite Readers

Contents

Acknowledgments

In Elie Wiesel's novel *Dawn*, the protagonist finds he has unusual company as he performs the central act of the work.

Ever since midnight the visitors had been pouring in. Among them were people I had known, people I had hated, admired, forgotten. As I let my eyes wander about the room I realized that all of those who had contributed to my formation, to the formation of my permanent identity were there. Some of them were familiar, but I could not pin a label upon them; they were names without faces or faces without names.

(Wiesel [1961], p. 75)

My room has been similarly crowded as I have researched, written, and thought about the subject matter of this book. Among the shadowy figures who flitted in and out as I was working were members of the student body and faculty of Dartmouth College, Columbia Law School, Yale University, and the University of Texas at Austin and several anonymous readers. Though I have rarely been able to recognize the specific influences that my colleagues, friends, and family have had on my work, their help made this project possible.

Fortunately, some characters remained in the room long enough to permit me to identify their contributions to *Transforming Free Speech*. Members of the Yale political science department, Texas government department, and University of Texas Law School were more than willing to share their thoughts on the nature of free speech and the relationship between ideas and interests. In particular, I thank Owen Fiss, Douglas Rae, Ian Shapiro, Steven Smith, David Plotke, Steven Skowronek, Leonard Levy, Jim Fishkin, Mike Munger, Brian Roberts, Jeff Tulis, Jay Budziszewski, Jack Balkin, Douglas Laycock, and David Rabban for their time and advice. I especially appreciate the efforts made by Sandy Levinson, David Mayhew, Wallace Mendelson, and Scot Powe, who read many frequently unintelligible versions of this manuscript. Lacking their insights, this work would have been significantly impoverished. I also thank those members of the Yale political science department, the University of Michigan government department, University of California at Los Angeles political science department, and the University of Texas government department who attended a number of talks in which parts of this manuscript were presented. I particularly acknowledge the helpful advice I received from Jeffrey Morris and Ronald Kahn when I presented a version of chapter 1 at the 1987 annual meeting of the American Political Science Association. Jon Cohen, Mike Klonsinski, David Anderson, Suzanne Colwell, and Corinne Hebda frequently went out of their way to assist me in my painful efforts to put the text of this work into the computer. Finally, Naomi Schneider, Amy Klatzkin, and Lisa Nowak Jerry of the University of California Press did a professional job of editing the manuscript and otherwise shepherding a nervous author through the publication process.

Rogers Smith and Julia Frank were almost always in the room whenever I worked. While any finite recounting of their help would only minimize the assistance that they gave me, I feel I owe a specific debt of gratitude to each person. Rogers Smith played the changing roles of adviser, friend, and colleague with his accustomed dexterity. Though the pages below echo with many of his suggestions and language, I am particularly grateful for his encouragement. His frequent exhortations that what I was saying was important (if said right) kept my enthusiasm far higher than the expected lot of a graduate student and member of the junior faculty. The other reason for my relatively high spirits was that I had the good sense to marry Julia Bess Frank. Beyond getting a good editor, I found a companion who could put up with my mood swings, create opportunities for work in the face of her own full-time job commitments, three pregnancies, and three babies, and generally at least feign interest when I repeated the same idea or problem for the fifth and sixth times.

In a less metaphorical sense, Naomi, Abigail, and Rebecca also frequently wandered into the room when I was working. Though their only direct contributions to this work probably consist of typographical errors, they are worth it.

Introduction

A Tradition and Its Consequences

Contemporary civil libertarians insist that their works preserve "a worthy tradition." The great figures of that tradition, they insist, both participated in the ongoing historical struggle to defend the free-speech rights of American citizens and agreed on the fundamental principles that justified their efforts on behalf of uninhibited public debate. Thomas Emerson claims that "the colonists viewed the essential functions of a system of freedom of expression much as we do today." Scot Powe speaks of "a print tradition . . . shared by both the framers of the First Amendment and the best of the scholars of freedom of expression." Legal historians similarly agree that the philosophical and constitutional defense of free speech has not changed significantly in the past two hundred years. Leonard Levy asserts that the libertarian principles underlying Justice William Brennan's opinion in *New York Times Co. v. Sullivan* had previously been articulated by opponents of the Sedition Act of 1798.[1] In "The First Amendment in Its Forgotten Years," David Rabban identifies a late nineteenth-century scholarly tradition that provided "the theoretical foundations for modern First Amendment doctrine." The "legal scholarship of that period," he concludes, "hardly seems the product of an earlier age."[2]

This book challenges both the existence and the value of this libertarian tradition. Contemporary libertarian arguments, I maintain, are neither traditional nor worthy. The understanding of expression rights that currently dominates scholarly debate is a product of the political and legal thought of the progressive era and was foreign to the conceptions advanced by earlier defenders of free speech. Zechariah Chafee, Jr., the early twentieth-century jurist most responsible for developing the modern interpretation of the First Amendment, deliberately manipulated history and theory by pretending that the liberty of discussion had always been derived from the major premises of John Dewey's pragmatism and Roscoe Pound's sociological jurisprudence. In fact, Chafee transformed the constitutional defense of free speech by treating expression as a functional requirement of democratic government, rather than as an aspect of a more general right of individual liberty. His works deliberately obscured earlier libertarian arguments that intimately connected the liberty of speech with the philosophical and constitutional principles underlying the liberty of contract. Furthermore, Chafee stunted the development of a more radical interpretation of expression rights, one that explored the ways in which the distribution of material resources affects the actual capacity persons have to articulate their opinions.

By inventing a mythical tradition that maintained that judges could adequately protect political and social commentary without exploring the manifold ways in which material inequalities might inhibit the efficient functioning of the marketplace of ideas, Chafee left expression rights enfeebled in a world where their exercise increasingly depends on the economic power to have one's voice heard. Contemporary libertarian theory largely ignores the mixed questions of expression and economics presented by such issues as campaign finance reform and access rights to mass media. Instead, free-speech debate in the 1980s and 1990s continues to emphasize such classic First Amendment questions as whether the Nazi party could march in Skokie, or, more recently, whether Americans have a constitutional right to burn the flag. This tendency shows little sign of abating even though these problems have an insignificant impact on the values that civil libertarians believe a system of freedom of expression should promote. Flag desecration seems particularly trivial when compared to such issues as the constitutionality of limiting candidates' spending in election campaigns, a matter rarely discussed at length by contemporary libertarian theorists. Even those jurists who recognize the threats that material inequalities present to a functioning system of freedom of expression encounter insuperable difficulties when they attempt to resolve the constitutional relationships between free speech and private property from within a model of constitutional discourse that absolutely divides the universe into democratic processes and governmental policies.

Recent works do not, of course, simply repeat Chafee's conclusions. Scholars have challenged his assertions about the relative acceptance of free-speech rights at various periods of American history and the precise standards that he thought were required by the democratic-process model of First Amendment adjudication. But contemporary thinkers share important understandings about the basic elements of First Amendment history and theory, understandings that first appeared in Chafee's writings. These beliefs and assumptions constitute the essence of what is perceived as the American libertarian tradition. They not only structure the works of such proponents of broad expression rights as Chafee, Alexander Meiklejohn, and Emerson, but they also provide starting places for other scholars concerned with some feature of this country's ongoing experience with the problems presented by free speech.

The Myth of the Worthy Tradition

Our libertarian tradition, most scholars claim, began with John Milton's fight against the royal licensing system. Inspired by John Trenchard, Thomas Gordon, John Wilkes, and other English radicals, Americans demanded that their new national government respect expression rights. Although historians debate whether the First Amendment was only intended to prohibit prior restraints on speech, they agree that political dissenters enjoyed much freedom in practice. Thus, the Federalist authors of the Alien and Sedition Acts of 1798 were swiftly punished by voters in the next election, even though the Federalist-controlled judiciary never declared those statutes unconstitutional.[3]

Unfortunately, the tradition maintains, most Americans soon forgot the principles that inspired the colonists' demand for broad free-speech rights. By the late nineteenth century, political and intellectual life in the United States was dominated by conservatives whose concern for liberty did not extend to the liberty of discussion.[4] Early twentieth-century progressives were similarly hostile to political dissent. Expression rights, they believed, should be restricted to those persons who spoke responsibly.[5] These repressive attitudes peaked during World War I and the red scare, when federal and state governments attempted to silence radical critics of American military and economic policies. Constitutional attacks on these speech limitations were rebuffed by conservative justices who declared that elected officials could regulate any published utterance with a bad tendency.[6]

Shocked by this heavy-handed censorship, some progressive and liberal thinkers sought to reinvigorate the principles that had inspired the First Amendment. Led by Zechariah Chafee, Jr., they developed constitutional arguments that incorporated and modernized the philosophical insights of early American libertarians and the libertarian standards proposed by a few prewar jurists. Chafee insisted that judges must protect those expression rights that Americans had traditionally enjoyed even if that meant expanding the previous legal definitions of permissible dissent. Justices Oliver Wendell Holmes, Jr., and Louis Brandeis adopted those arguments as their own when they declared that the Constitution protected all utterances that did not present a clear and present danger of some social evil.[7]

The conservative majority on the Supreme Court remained hostile to political dissent until 1937. Then, as part of the New Deal revolution, the justices stopped protecting property and began protecting speech. Although support for expression rights waned during the McCarthy era, judicial opinions in the 1960s and 1970s broadly interpreted the scope of the First Amendment. In such cases as *Brandenburg v. Ohio* and *New York Times Co. v. Sullivan*, the justices endorsed the principles and standards for which Chafee and his successors had fought. While many contemporary civil libertarians attack rulings of the Burger/Rehnquist Court on peripheral matters, such cases as *Hustler Magazine v. Falwell* (1988) and *Texas v. Johnson* (1989) demonstrate that a working majority on the conservative court remains committed to preserving the basic values underlying the modern constitutional defense of free speech.[8]

Proponents of this historical interpretation of the American libertarian tradition maintain that changes in First Amendment scholarship result from changes in the underlying threats to free speech. Like mainstream legal historians, they believe that constitutional arguments evolve in order to remain functional.[9] Thus, civil libertarians claim that external political conditions are the primary forces shaping the development of libertarian doctrine. For example, Chafee claimed that until World War I defenders of expression rights assumed that political dissent would be protected as long as juries resolved all issues in sedition trials. But the experience of World War I taught libertarians that juries would not protect unpopular speakers from government reprisals. Hence, the constitutional defense of free speech was updated to include rules that required judges to direct acquittals whenever the evidence did not demonstrate a substantial relationship between the utterance in question and some social evil.[10]

Although specific First Amendment standards change in response to social circumstances and can be the subject of some dispute, scholars working within this libertarian tradition see the foundations of the argument for free speech as timeless, transcending the particular intellectual fashions of any era. Chafee declared that the same basic principles "motivated each phase of the struggle" for expression rights. The leading proponents of civil libertarianism believe that uninhibited debate on matters of public importance primarily serves the interests of the audience rather than the speakers. They believe that social policy will neither be wisely made nor accurately reflect public sentiment unless citizens enjoy the full benefits of an unrestricted (or relatively unrestricted) freedom of expression. Judicial activism on behalf of free speech is usually justified by a more general judicial obligation to police the democratic process. Advocates of broad interpretations of the First Amendment believe that courts can only tolerate regulating opinions that are "the unmediated cause of fairly immediate improper action." Thus, they propose such standards of judicial protection as "clear and present danger," "incitement," "absolute protection," and "the speech/conduct distinction."[11]

Judicial solicitude for expression rights is closely connected to the judicial obligation to defer to the social and economic

policy decisions made by elected officials. Civil libertarians
claim that once they have assured themselves that free speech
has been permitted and other democratic procedures followed,
judges must allow the people of democratic societies to be governed in any way they see fit. In their view, courts can only review restrictions on inputs into the democratic process. The judiciary should not interfere with democratic outputs.

The above description of the development and nature of the
American libertarian tradition is a mainstay of scholarly popular
culture, handed down from author to author with little reexamination of the original sources. Inertia alone does not explain its
powerful influence. Those who have recently scoured historical
writings on free speech have, if anything, strengthened this belief in the constancy of libertarian argument over time. The ad-
mirable thoroughness of David Rabban and other academic
lawyers suggests that, if the tradition is an illusion, some force
must be actively generating that illusion. In fact, there are two
such forces.

First, Zechariah Chafee's writings remain the standard authorities on the history and theory of libertarian argument.
Chafee alleged that his only interest was promoting free speech,
and most scholars have taken him at his word. They assume that
Chafee designed his works on the evolution of the constitutional defense of expression rights to place that material in its best
historical light. Thus, previous academic critiques emphasize
those areas in which "Chafee allowed the passions of his personal commitment to a libertarian construction of the First
Amendment to overwhelm disinterested scholarship."[12] For example, Rabban demonstrates that Chafee misrepresented history when he ignored "the prewar tradition of hostility to free
speech" and asserted that Holmes "used the words 'clear and
present danger' in *Schenck [v. United States]* to make 'the punishment of words for their bad tendency impossible.' "[13] Chafee's admissions of weaknesses in the historical case for free
speech, however, are taken as dispositive, declarations against
interest. Recent studies never question Chafee's claim that
those who called for judges to protect private-property rights
were uniformly hostile to broad interpretations of constitutional expression rights.[14] Surely a person committed only to ex-

panding First Amendment freedoms would have said so if supporters of the freedom of contract had also supported the freedom of speech.

Second, previous scholarship on libertarian thought emphasizes the conclusions of legal arguments, the particular standards that various judges and scholars have thought the First Amendment required. The central question most historical works on First Amendment doctrine ask is, Under what conditions does a given thinker claim that government can regulate speech? From this narrow perspective all defenders of expression rights seem part of a common tradition. By definition, libertarians are persons who assert that government should rarely, if ever, regulate speech. Thus, it is hardly surprising that studies of free-speech argument in the late nineteenth and early twentieth centuries suggest that such libertarians as Thomas Cooley and Theodore Schroeder anticipated many of Chafee's conclusions.[15]

Superficial agreement over particular rules, however, may disguise other, more substantial disagreements over fundamental principles. Opposition to capital punishment, for example, may stem from religious convictions about human dignity or secular beliefs about the utility of executions. Similarly, the belief that government should rarely, if ever, regulate speech may be embedded in radically different and inconsistent world views. Persons opposed to state censorship may dispute the premises that support their mutual conclusions, the social institutions and policies necessary to promote and protect expression rights, and the other political positions that follow from the argument for free speech. Two libertarians may not even agree on what government actions restrict the liberty of discussion. In short, proponents of similar constitutional standards may conceptualize the system of freedom of expression differently.

The Perspective of Multiple Traditions

This book studies the broader political visions that have inspired libertarian interpretations of the First Amendment. My reexamination of the philosophical and jurisprudential foundations of American defenses of expression rights made from the

Civil War to the present emphasizes the reasons intellectuals have given for defending free speech, the policies and institutions they have thought necessary to protect free speech, and their larger understandings of a commitment to free speech. When these broader contexts are explored, the monolithic libertarian tradition disappears. Instead of a single conception of the system of free expression, we see two approaches: a conservative libertarian tradition dominated discourse from the Civil War until World War I; and a civil libertarian tradition has dominated twentieth-century argument.

The leading supporters of free speech in the late nineteenth century treated expression as one aspect of the personal liberty "to be free in the enjoyment of all faculties." Courts were expected to protect this freedom as part of their obligation to prevent untrammeled majorities from violating individual rights. The conservative libertarians who developed this interpretation of the First Amendment did not separate the system of free expression and the system of private property. Thomas Cooley and other treatise writers placed both the freedom of speech and the freedom of contract among the fundamental liberties protected by the due process clause of the Fifth and Fourteenth Amendments. John W. Burgess, a prominent political scientist of that era, claimed that constitutional protection of private property provided citizens with the resources and independence necessary for effectively exercising their free-speech rights.

Although early progressive-era libertarians discarded laissez-faire economics, they accepted the basic structure of the conservative libertarian constitutional defense of free speech. Theodore Schroeder and Ernst Freund claimed that expression rights were derived from the same general principle of equal liberty that was central to late nineteenth-century political and legal thought. They believed that individual speech rights were protected by the due process clause and that an independent judiciary should guarantee government's respect of a person's fundamental freedoms. However, Schroeder and Freund did not believe that the freedom of contract was another aspect of a citizen's liberty. Rather, these jurists suggested that a different set of substantive rights might follow from the general principle underlying the liberty of discussion.

The postwar generation of libertarians abandoned this "traditional" defense of free-speech rights. Chafee and others maintained that the Constitution emphasized the social interest in civic debate rather than the individual's right of self-expression. This social interest was the discovery of truth on matters of public importance. By safeguarding political dissent, courts ensured that legislatures making economic policies were well informed and democratically accountable. In contrast to conservative libertarians, civil libertarians claimed that the principles underlying the judicial protection of expression forbade judicial interference with economic and social policies. Judges protected democratic processes, not democratic policies. As Chafee noted, the "critical judicial spirit which gives the legislature a wide scope in limiting the privileges of property owners will also tend to allow speakers and writers a wide scope in arguing against those privileges."[16]

Civil libertarians do recognize that a functioning system of expression has certain economic prerequisites. The major figures of that tradition support welfare-state policies. They insist that government must regulate individual commercial activity in order to provide citizens with the resources and independence necessary for the effective exercise of their free-speech rights. Chafee and his followers, however, think that only elected officials should have the power to influence the economic and social environments in which speech takes place. In their view, judges must not concern themselves with the relationships between private property and political expression but should protect only those able to exercise their First Amendment rights.

Conventional functionalist accounts fail to explain this transformation of free-speech argument. The civil libertarian tradition was not a necessary response to changes in external political conditions. If anything, the earlier defense of expression rights afforded better protection to those radical critics of American war and economic policies who were punished during World War I and the red scare. Burgess, the last major conservative libertarian, argued that the entire federal suppression machinery (assembled by the "progressive" Wilson administration) was incapable of any constitutional application. This position was more protective of speech than that taken by any early proponent of the modern defense of free speech. Indeed, in its early formulations, Chafee's clear and present danger test only protected the rights of such relatively obscure speakers as Jacob Abrams and Benjamin Gitlow. Furthermore, conservative libertarian doctrine permitted judges to strike down legislation that they believed affected the actual capacity citizens had to express their opinions. Civil libertarians, however, tell judges that they must remain passive even when economic policies are distributing resources in ways that silence political dissent.

My research suggests a different explanation of the evolution of libertarian theory, one that emphasizes changes in the external intellectual environment. This intellectual environment consists of those modes of rhetorical justification that constrain political argument in any community. Every cultural language has legitimate first premises, rules for moving from these premises to others, and illegitimate conclusions.[17] Although external political conditions influence these ideological structures, recent scholarship suggests that ideas are "relatively autonomous." Quentin Skinner, among others, notes that the dominant belief systems of a given community influence not only what arguments are believed but also what arguments are made or even conceived.[18] Therefore, when broader patterns of social justification change, the structure of particular political arguments changes. Thinkers begin to ponder what was once inconceivable, advocates begin to assert what was once unsayable, and audiences begin to accept what was once unbelievable.

Such a structural change occurred in the early twentieth century. For reasons unrelated to expression rights, though clearly related to property rights, progressive thinkers rejected the concept of individual rights and the judicial obligation to protect those rights. Proponents of pragmatism and sociological jurisprudence instead contended that government should advance social interests and that these interests were best promoted by elected officials. The people's representatives, they argued, were inherently more qualified to resolve factual disputes underlying social conflict and democratically more accountable than life-tenured justices.

These ideological changes precipitated the first crisis of modern First Amendment theory. When early civil libertarians became interested in constitutional free-speech arguments during World War I, they discovered that they could not comfortably endorse the philosophical and jurisprudential premises of the then traditional defense of that right because that defense emphasized individual interests in expression. This forced Chafee and his allies to develop a new defense of expression rights consistent with the importance progressive thinkers placed on social interests. In other words, early twentieth-century libertarians were forced to change the premises, rather than the conclusions, of free-speech argument.

The principles of pragmatism and sociological jurisprudence did not logically entail any new defense of political dissent. Before World War I, most progressives endorsed a cultural nationalism or bureaucratic regimentation inconsistent with broad free-speech rights. Although some thinkers—most notably John Dewey, Jane Addams, and Louis Brandeis—believed that government should protect expression to foster diversity and mass participation in American life, they admitted that judicial activism on behalf of free speech was wrong for the same reason that judicial activism on behalf of private-property rights was wrong. Thus, early civil libertarians had to reshape the intellectual conventions of their day in the process of using them to justify judicial solicitude for First Amendment claims. Chafee developed such a principled, pragmatist constitutional defense of free speech by emphasizing the social function of political advocacy in the democratic process, the protection of which was central to progressive thought. This reinterpretation of constitutional free-speech guarantees enabled civil libertarians to distinguish expression from individual property rights, which remained subject only to the will of elected majorities. Indeed, as noted above, Chafee claimed that progressive thinkers had presupposed judicial protection of expression rights when they argued that courts should defer to the economic and social policy judgments of the elected branches of government. These assertions created a new understanding of the possibilities of sociological jurisprudence, one that permitted progressives to defend the freedom of speech while continuing to object to the freedom of contract.

The principles of early twentieth-century progressivism, however, could not justify everything that the principles of conservative libertarianism supported. The intellectuals who developed sociological jurisprudence wished to transfer economic power from the judiciary to elected officials. Hence, the legitimation structure of that approach to the legal problems was hostile to assertions that encouraged judicial activism of any kind. Moreover, as a result of such cases as *Lochner v. New York*,[19] progressives were unwilling to propound or accept arguments that permitted courts to make economic policies, even economic policies that they themselves supported. Judicial activism on behalf of property rights was an impermissible stopping place, even if reached by a series of legitimate moves.

To develop a defense of free speech consistent with the conventions of early and middle twentieth-century thought, Chafee sharply distinguished a judicially enforceable free-speech protection from the unquestioned and unquestionable legislative control of economic policy. In doing so, he became the first major libertarian to declare that courts had no power to provide citizens with the resources they would need to effectively use their free-speech rights. While Chafee continued to call for judicial protection of expression rights, he conceded that the courts could do little to bring about an environment in which that protection would actually advance the social interest in discovering truth on matters of public interest.

Chafee not only divorced free speech from private property, but he also retold the evolution of libertarian theory in a way that prevented reconciliation. He concocted a libertarian tradition in which there had never been intimate constitutional relations between expression and economic rights. Within the tradition Chafee created, his arguments were the only conceivable American constitutional defense of free speech, not merely the particular product of a particular era. Future civil libertarians who imbibed this history never realized that expression rights had been and could be defended in other ways. Instead, they devoted their efforts to perfecting the model of constitutional argument that Chafee and his progressive allies developed.

By teaching his successors to confuse one particular constitutional defense of free speech with *the* constitutional defense of free speech, Chafee precipitated the second crisis of modern libertarian theory. Today, the most important First Amendment issues facing American society concern the ways that disparities in economic resources affect access to the marketplace of ideas. Since 1973, major cases before the Supreme Court have explored the extent to which owners have a constitutional right to control the expressive uses of their holdings. Nevertheless, contemporary civil libertarians, working within the tradition invented by Chafee, continue to place these problems on the outskirts of theory. Such prominent defenders of free speech as Thomas Emerson and Norman Dorsen rarely discuss the constitutional status of campaign finance reforms, corporate speech, and speech rights that depend on access to private resources; for example, they only briefly analyze the right to hand out political leaflets in a privately owned shopping center otherwise held open to the public. Rather, their works and other contemporary discussions of the general theory of the First Amendment continue to emphasize the relationship between speech and lawless conduct, even though there has been little significant repression of this sort over the past twenty years.[20] The point, I should emphasize, is not that contemporary civil libertarians give wrong answers to questions about the constitutional relationships between expression and economics; rather, too often, they give no answer at all.[21]

A growing literature does specifically discuss whether money is speech. Participants in this debate propose solutions to the constitutional status of campaign finance reforms and access rights. Indeed, such scholars as Jerome Barron, Owen Fiss, and Scot Powe recognize that these issues are the most salient free-speech questions facing late twentieth-century America.[22] However, the rigid distinction civil libertarians draw between procedural inputs and substantive outputs permits only two extreme and unpalatable solutions to these problems. If money is speech, then government cannot remedy even the grossest inequalities in access to the marketplace of ideas. If money is not speech, then elected officials have virtually unlimited power to regulate all political uses of private property. No other solution seems possible because the free-speech tradition assumes that all constitutional problems can be neatly classified as affecting either democratic processes or substantive policies. Worse, civil libertarianism seems to be no basis for choosing between these positions. Its simplistic notions of political liberty and equality can be used both to support and oppose claims that money is speech.

In short, the modern constitutional defense of free speech again needs transformation, precisely because that defense is incapable of responding to a serious external threat to political dissent. Civil libertarianism consigns major hazards to the system of free expression to the periphery of theory, suggest unacceptable alternatives in response to those threats, and offers no basis for choosing among them. It may be the case, as many civil libertarians claim, that the average American has never been freer to speak. It is probably also the case that the average American has never had less opportunity to be heard.

The last chapter of this book briefly outlines a new libertarian theory that is both responsive to present conditions and consistent with important, though certainly not all, strains of contemporary philosophical and jurisprudential thought. Following a line of argument offered by Michael Walzer, I suggest that political power in a democracy should be distributed according to a person's rhetorical and organizing talents. The First Amendment, in this view, gives all persons the right to use their persuasive abilities in the public arena. The Constitution, however, does not protect efforts to magnify one's political capacities by taking advantage of superior material resources. This approach emphasizes the individual's right to seek political power. However, unlike those late nineteenth-century theorists who also emphasized individual free-speech rights, I believe we must be more sensitive to the threat that the economically powerful will invade the political sphere than to the significant threat that the politically powerful may invade the economic sphere.

The validity of this reinterpretation of expression rights, I should emphasize, does not follow from the expository arguments of this book. Indeed, the central theme of *Transforming Free Speech* is that history does not privilege any constitutional defense of free speech. Tradition cannot validate a particular libertarian argument because no single two-hundred-year-old tradition defends free speech in a particular way. Nor does the historical survival of civil libertarianism demonstrate that this mode of defending expression rights adequately advances libertarian purposes. Rather, I have sought to demonstrate that the modern constitutional defense of free speech has survived in spite of its consistent inability to respond to the main external threats to the system of freedom of expression. In short, contemporary libertarian doctrines must be evaluated on their own merits and not on their link to some mythical tradition.

Modern libertarian theory has undergone two major crises. The first occurred at the end of World War I when the philosophical and jurisprudential foundations of an earlier libertarian argument were undermined. Chafee's achievement, and that of the next generation of civil libertarians, was rebuilding First Amendment theory on foundations acceptable to the twentieth-century mind. Unfortunately, civil libertarianism is now strained to the breaking point, creating a second crisis. The structure of the modern constitutional defense of expression rights inhibits responses to the threats severe economic inequalities present to the marketplace of ideas. The purpose of this book is to show that just as free speech was once transformed, so can we transform it again.

Chapter One

The Conservative Libertarian Defense of Free Speech

In 1923 John W. Burgess asserted that all federal regulations that limited political dissent during World War I were unconstitutional and subversive of basic American liberties. "No man," he contended, "who does not recognize the complete freedom of individual thought and expression, . . . possesses the most essential qualification for citizenship of the republic or any other real republic." Public officials who supported suppressive measures "belong[ed] to the Orient with its doctrine of externally revealed truth to a privileged few, and its resultant stagnation, intolerance, persecutions, slaveries and cruel inhumanities."[1]

These were not the isolated utterances of an obscure pedant. Burgess was a founder of academic political science in the United States,[2] and he had defended expression rights for more than thirty years. Nevertheless, his works are ignored by scholars who celebrate the American free-speech tradition. Burgess's denunciations of state censorship cannot be found in any prominent discussion of the evolution of libertarian theory, and he is never included with Zechariah Chafee, Jr., Oliver Wendell Holmes, Jr., Louis Brandeis, Learned Hand, or Ernst Freund in the pantheon of American libertarian heroes. These omissions are not accidental. Burgess was not a founder of modern civil libertarianism; instead, he waooo551last prominent survivor of an earlier conservative libertarian tradition, a tradition that was being forgotten even as he spoke.

Philosophical Foundations

The doctrines of conservative libertarianism were propounded by the late nineteenth century's leading intellectual proponents of the night watchman state. Men like Burgess, Herbert Spencer, William Graham Sumner, E. L. Godkin,[3] Henry Adams,[4] Thomas Cooley,[5] Christopher Tiedeman,[6] John Randolph Tucker,[7] David Brewer,[8] and John Marshall Harlan[9] maintained that government existed only to protect "the property of men and the honor of women."[10] In their view, a legislature had no more business regulating expression than it had regulating property. In other words, these men were libertarians, at least with respect to state policies restricting the commercial and political relationships that adult males could form; as the above reference to "the honor of women" suggests, these thinkers did believe that government could regulate such speech and business practices as obscenity and the employment of women because a laissez-faire approach might weaken feminine moral standards.[11] Although there were some conservative elements in conservative libertarian thought, they are so described primarily because they frequently called themselves and have been called "conservative." As Richard Hofstadter noted, "We may wonder whether, in the entire history of thought, there was ever a conservatism so utterly progressive as this."[12]

This enthusiasm for change sharply distinguished conservative libertarians from previous conservative thinkers. Traditional conservatives, following Burke, emphasized the preservation of inherited social forms;[13] conservative libertarians claimed that progress was the first virtue of social institutions. They supported governmental policies that left individuals to their own devices because they believed such an approach would foster the most efficient, rapid, and dynamic improvements in the quality of public life. "Private activities and their spontaneous co-operation," Spencer claimed, "have done more towards social development than those which have worked through governmental agencies."[14]

Conservative libertarians insisted that increases in human capacity were the proper standard of social development. "The highest and ultimate purpose of institutional life," Burgess proclaimed, is "the fullest development of the individual." For this reason, most late nineteenth-century intellectuals maintained that every person should be allowed "to develop his unusual powers, tastes and ambitions." Spencer even spoke of a "duty to exercise [one's] faculties." The major judicial decisions that constitutionalized the freedom of contract relied on "the right of the citizen to be free in the enjoyment of all his faculties."[15]

The conservative libertarian defenses of both private property and free speech were derived from this interpretation of progress and human capacity. Sumner made two claims: that unrestricted use of private property led to "a higher order of society," and that "a society based on contract" would give "the utmost room and chance for individual development."[16] Intellectual development, his fellow conservative libertarians argued, was subject to the same natural forces as economic development and thus required the same laissez-faire policies. "The law of supply and demand," Spencer informed his contemporaries, "extends from the material sphere to the mental sphere." Therefore, "as interference with the supply and demand of commodities is mischievous, so is interference with the supply and demand of cultured faculty."[17] Henry Adams similarly claimed that human potential would be retarded if political discussion were restricted. John Stuart Mill, he asserted, had successfully demonstrated that societies could "only be sure of making the most of individuality if [they had] an atmosphere of freedom, encouraging free development and expansion."[18]

This commitment to individual freedom from state regulation inspired conservative libertarians to recognize a sphere of private mental conduct that was as inviolate as their cherished sphere of private commercial conduct. Government had, in their view, no more business interfering with a person's liberty to say and hear what he wished than with the liberty of a person to buy and sell what he wished. Burgess claimed that both free-speech and private-property rights followed from the general governmental obligation to mark out realms of individual autonomy once political order had been established. Sumner argued vigorously against those who would forbid the reading of certain books merely because they did not like how such books might affect the private emotional life of the reader. Referring in part to free-speech matters, future Supreme Court Justice George Sutherland worried about "the increasing disposition to give authoritative direction to the course of personal behavior."[19]

Conservative libertarian scholars also perceived empirical relationships between economic policies and expression rights. Like earlier Jeffersonian and Jacksonian thinkers, they argued that the system of private property was a necessary, if not a sufficient, condition of a functional system of free speech. In "Democracy and Plutocracy," Sumner claimed that "capital . . . emancipated slaves and serfs" and "set the mass of mankind free from the drudgery which . . . wears out the mind." Burgess, in particular, insisted that strict adherence to laissez-faire capitalism was the first prerequisite of an effective speech policy. By respecting and protecting private property, government ensured that private associations and individuals had both the independence and the resources necessary for intellectual pursuits. Burgess rejected economic regulation of private corporations in part because such regulation interfered with the freedom of speech. "Modern political science," he wrote, "absolutely demands that all institutions, through which new truth is discovered and the ideals of advancing civilization are brought to light and moulded into forms for application, shall be so far from governmental interference as to secure and preserve, at least, perfect freedom of scientific thought and expression." To maintain the intellectual independence of its citizens, government had to permit and protect even substantial accumulations of corporate wealth. Such fortunes were needed to finance the major projects necessary for realizing truth in the modern world.[20]

Although conservative libertarians primarily treated free speech as one of many individual liberties government was obligated to respect, they appreciated that expression also had a special relationship to the democratic process. Chief Justice Waite stated that free speech was implied in "the very idea of a government, republican in form." Prominent conservative treatise writers insisted that the American scheme of government required extensive advocacy rights. Christopher Tiedeman, for example, declared that "a popular government, and hence freedom from tyranny, is only possible when the people enjoy the freedom of speech and the liberty of press." Recognizing the role that the press played in providing political information to citizens, Supreme Court Justice David Brewer declared that newspapers must be permitted to "criticize without fear or favor."[21]

When discussing political speech, conservative libertarians frequently sounded like classical republicans. They did not promote a politically active state, but these thinkers highlighted the importance of a politically active populace. Sumner warned his contemporaries that they "must understand that it costs vigilance and exertion to be self-governing." Similarly, Cooley contended that persons had a "duty . . . to speak freely" on matters concerning public affairs.[22] This obligation to speak was most effectively exercised in small political communities. In *People v. Hurlbut,* Cooley declared that "the . . . precepts which . . . impelled" citizens "to summon the local community to redress local evils" were "the living spirit" of "our constitutional law." Speech in these intermediate associations also fostered the trust and common sentiment necessary for organized social life. Participation in local affairs, Burgess asserted, helped citizens "develop the capacity to view things from another's standpoint as well as from one's own."[23]

As chapter 3 details, progressives who defended free speech during World War I and its aftermath were similarly committed to the small community as the primary forum for democratic life. Their example suggests that American libertarians have historically shared something more than a mere devotion to expression rights. Proponents of a single free-speech tradition, however, have not emphasized this commitment to a decentralized politics. Rather, as noted in the Introduction, civil libertarians have claimed that defenders of advocacy rights have sharply distinguished those rights from laissez-faire private-property rights. Conservative libertarians made no such distinction; they claimed that the liberty of speech was the same sort of right as the liberty of contract and, indeed, that the system of freedom of expression could only function if the government also protected private property.

Practical Applications

Late nineteenth-century conservative libertarians were hardly the only Americans who waxed eloquent on the virtues of free speech. Unlike many Americans whose support for free speech rapidly diminishes when the setting moves from abstract principles to concrete cases,[24] they were willing to defend the speech rights of the most controversial political dissidents of their day. Significantly, conservative libertarians supported the right to advocate left-wing political doctrines that many progressive legislatures would outlaw in the early twentieth century.

In his article "Shall We Muzzle the Anarchists," Henry Adams condemned late nineteenth-century champions of repressive legislation. "The theory of free discussion," he contended, is "as fully applicable to the anarchists today as" it was "to those who dissented from the established order of society at any time in the past." In Adams's view, only radicals whose "avowed purpose" was inciting criminal conduct could be punished. Existing criminal statutes, such as conspiracy, already criminalized such speech. New legislation, he concluded, would probably prohibit some constitutionally protected speech and create sympathy for anarchists.[25] Forty years later, Burgess reminded a hysterical country that the followers of Lenin and Debs had the same free-speech rights as the followers of Wilson and Roosevelt.[26]

Conservative libertarians consistently refused to use war as an excuse for limiting expression rights. Indeed, virtually all major conservative libertarians opposed late nineteenth-century calls for the United States to enter the race for foreign colonies because they believed that such military force "meant the expansion of governmental powers at the expense of individual liberties." John Randolph Tucker, for example, described imperialism as "a course directly opposed to the spirit of our institutions," one that would "disturb the fundamental principles upon which these interests rest." "Expansion and imperialism," Sumner contended, would throw "away some of the most important elements of the American symbol."[27]

To prove that expansion abroad would cause repression at home, Edward Atkinson mailed several antiwar leaflets to

American military and civilian officials stationed in Manila during the Filipino insurrection of 1900.[28] Atkinson claimed that his only purpose was "to test the right of citizens of the United States to the free use of the mail," not to convince governmental officials to end the fighting.[29] When the McKinley administration failed this test by removing the leaflets from the mails on the grounds that they were "seditious,"[30] anti-imperialists announced that their case had been proved. E. L. Godkin's editorial in the *Nation* declared that any censorship "on American soil, all attempts to silence anything any man wishes to say, or to prevent any voter from seeing it and reading it in security and at his leisure, is treason of the worst kind, and any conqueror or President who orders it or sanctions it, worthy of impeachment." Godkin pointed out that any soldier in the army who voted was "entitled" to know what those critical of imperialistic policies had to say.[31] Two weeks later, the *Nation* accused President McKinley and Postmaster General Smith of introducing a new principle into American life: that "there can be no discussion of the expediency of a war once begun, or of the manner in which it is or has been conducted."[32]

Sumner supported this attack on the war policies of the government. In a series of anti-imperialist articles, he attacked "the doctrine that those who oppose a war are responsible for the lives lost in it, or that a citizen may criticize any action of his government except a war." In his view, the claim that opponents of the war were "rebels" or "traitors" was no more valid than the claim that opponents of a strike were "scabs." Like other conservative anti-imperialists, Sumner did not defend free speech because he wanted to attack the war; he attacked the war because he wanted to defend free speech. His fundamental claim was that imperialism would inevitably weaken American "national character and institutions," "political ideas and creed," and "temper in political discussions."[33]

Anti-imperialism, however, was the last hurrah for most conservative libertarians. By the time the United States entered World War I, Sumner, Cooley, Tucker, Godkin, Brewer, Harlan, and Atkinson were all dead, and the new defenders of free speech had discarded the principles of laissez-faire.[34] Only a few surviving dinosaurs continued to vehemently oppose federal and state efforts to silence wartime critics of governmental policies on traditional libertarian grounds. Burgess, for example, contended that the restrictions placed on free speech between 1917 and 1920 were as destructive to republican liberty as was the hated income tax.[35] The *Nation*, which was still dedicated to the principles of conservative libertarianism in 1917,[36] opposed all wartime limitations on rights of political dissent; by comparison, the progressive *New Republic* called for an intelligent censorship.[37] In an editorial written shortly after the Espionage Act of 1917 was proposed, Oswald Garrison Villard wrote, "Prussianizing is coming not only by statute but also by a change in the point of view. Those who preach the complete subordination of the individual to the state are the real Prussians and are more to be feared than any spy or careless editor or any commander of a Prussian U Boat."[38]

These examples are not intended to prove that conservative libertarians paid the same attention to the rights of political dissidents as they did to the rights of business entrepreneurs. Their work almost always emphasized political economy and the various threats to private property they saw in post–Civil War America. Many late nineteenth-century intellectuals devoted their lives to publicizing the evils they believed would result from social tampering with the free enterprise system. With the possible exceptions of Burgess and Cooley, conservative discussions of free-speech rights appear almost incidentally, other examples of appropriate limitations on governmental power.[39]

This lack of balance, however, partially reflected the low salience of First Amendment issues in the Gilded Age. Free-speech controversy in late nineteenth-century America tended to be of limited duration and national interest. The intense demands for repressing anarchism that resulted from the Haymarket Affair, for example, abated within a year and did not resume until the beginning of the twentieth century. No federal sedition laws were on the books in the late nineteenth century, and state sedition statutes were rarely enforced, short-lived, or nonexistent. As a result, the Supreme Court heard no major free-speech cases, and state cases normally concerned local officials and local affairs.[40]

Although governmental officials seldom explicitly barred advocacy of specific doctrines, extensive political repression clearly took place during the late nineteenth century. In most instances, however, both conservative libertarians and radical activists interpreted oppressive practices as raising economic, not expression, issues. This was particularly apparent when repression was sponsored by private forces,[41] but it was even noticeable when government took steps that contemporary civil libertarians would regard as clear violations of free-speech rights. For example, in *In re Debs*,[42] Clarence Darrow failed to argue that a court order enjoining leaders of the Pullman strike from urging workers to leave their jobs constituted a prior restraint or some other unconstitutional abridgment of the First Amendment. Darrow, a future member of the Free Speech League, pointed out that Eugene Debs and the other defendants were charged with persuading others to join the strike, but his defense was limited to the claim that there was a constitutional right to strike. At no point did he suggest that persuasion had a higher constitutional status than other forms of conduct.[43]

Similarly, although the right to speak on public property was fairly controversial in the late nineteenth century, all partisans to the debate treated that issue as a question of the power of municipal corporations rather than of free speech. Would-be speakers typically claimed that states or municipalities had no right to forbid actions traditionally permitted on public property. State or local statutes vesting one person with absolute discretion to determine who would be allowed to speak on public property were attacked as unconstitutionally arbitrary under the Fourteenth Amendment.[44] Most conservative jurists supported this right of free-speech access. Christopher Tiedeman's treatise on *Municipal Corporations*, for example, declared that "any ordinance, which commits to the will of a single official, unrestrained by charter or otherwise, the practically absolute power of prohibiting the use of some well known means of commercial or social activity, not a nuisance—as, or for example, a steam engine, or street processions,—is prima facie unreasonable and oppressive and hence unconstitutional and void."[45]

Living at a time of few publicly acknowledged threats to expression rights, conservative libertarians concluded that the fight for freedom of speech had already been won. They believed, with some justification, that the rights of political dissidents had already been secured; hence the task of their generation was to fight the same battle on behalf of the freedom of private property. As George Sutherland told the American Bar Association, "in the old days it was the liberty of person, the liberty of speech, the freedom of religious worship, which were primarily threatened. Today, it is the liberty to order the details of one's daily life for oneself—the liberty to do honest and profitable business—the liberty to seek honest and remunerative investment that are in peril."[46] Thus, conservative thinkers justified their disproportionate attention to questions of political economy by insisting that they merely wished to demonstrate that certain private-property rights should be as uncontroversial as they thought free-speech rights already were. William Ramsey, a prominent Ohio attorney, stated, "I believe in freedom of contract . . . as fully as in freedom of thought and speech touching all questions as to which the opinions of men are divided."[47]

Constitutional Protections

Conservative libertarians believed that the fundamental freedoms they valued could be secured in practice only if placed in a constitution whose final interpreters were an unelected judiciary. "Unless the domain of individual liberty is protected by an independent unpolitical department," Burgess asserted, "government degenerates first into majority absolutism and then into Caesarism."[48] Both bar and bench had to be vigilant in light of the threats presented by what Tiedeman described as "the extraordinary demands of the great army of discontents, and their apparent power, with the growth and development of universal suffrage, to enforce their views of civil polity." If conservative jurists relaxed their guard, the law would soon "reflect the popular sentiments of fanatics." Although proponents of laissez-faire constantly feared that electoral majorities would radically redistribute property, they expressed some concern that uncontrolled legislatures would also not tolerate political dissent. Sumner warned his contemporaries that "a democratic government . . . is excessive and pitiless against dissentients."[49]

The main principles of conservative jurisprudence were developed and popularized by a number of prominent legal treatises. The titles of the most influential works, *Constitutional Limitations* and *Limitations of the Police Power,* reflected their authors' hostile attitudes toward governmental regulation. Cooley wrote *Constitutional Limitations* in "full sympathy with all those restraints which the caution of the fathers had imposed upon the exercise of the powers of government"; Tiedeman's *Limitations of the Police Power* sought "to demonstrate that democratic absolutism is impossible in the United States."[50] Although the treatise writers were primarily interested in demonstrating the constitutional pedigree of laissez-faire private-property rights, they maintained that the Constitution also incorporated the basic principles of the conservative libertarian philosophical defense of expression rights. Their works asserted that the Constitution protected speakers who neither advocated criminal conduct nor intentionally uttered falsehoods. This right was explicitly protected against federal infringement by the First Amendment and was implicitly protected against state infringement by the Fourteenth Amendment, which forbade state actions that violated fundamental liberties. In addition to these specific guarantees of individual expression rights, some conservative jurists suggested that Congress was not constitutionally authorized to regulate any category of speech.

Constitutional Limitations: Sources

The treatise writers narrowly defined the constitutional powers of the national government. Congress, they claimed, could exercise only those few powers explicitly granted to it in Article I, Section 8. "The government of the United States is one of enumerated powers," Cooley stated, and can "pass no laws but such as the Constitution authorizes either expressly or by clear implication."[51] When federal officers exceeded their law-making authority, judges were obligated to declare their actions unconstitutional, even if no individual's constitutional rights had been violated. For example, because congressional domestic economic power was limited to regulating interstate commerce, conservatives maintained that the national legislature could not forbid the monopolization of local production; but an identical state law would not abridge economic freedoms.[52]

Speech had traditionally been considered an important area of federal impotence. Opponents of the Alien and Sedition Acts of 1798 emphasized that the people had not vested the national government with any right to regulate expression. In the Virginia and Kentucky Resolutions, Thomas Jefferson and James Madison insisted that "all lawful powers respecting [the freedom of speech] belonged to the States or to the people" because "no power over [them]" had been "delegated to the United States by the Constitution."[53] Justice Stephen Field reiterated this analysis of national authority in the late nineteenth century when discussing the federal postal power. Although Field recognized that Article I vested Congress with the right to regulate access to the mails, subject to the limits of the First Amendment, his unanimous opinion in *Ex Parte Jackson* maintained that the national government could not regulate the private distribution of printed material, even if the expression in question was not protected by the First Amendment. With specific reference to "newspapers and pamphlets," Field stated that he did "not think that Congress possesses the power to prevent the transportation in other ways . . . of matter it excludes from the mails."[54]

When the federal government began to combat political dissent during World War I, Burgess raised the traditional *ultra vires* argument. His analysis repeated the claim that Thomas Jefferson and James Madison had made more than one hundred years earlier: "the Constitution confers, neither expressly nor impliedly, any power upon the General Government to control the subjects of speech and press." The national legislature, Burgess declared, had "no power to infringe [expression] in the States either by way of censorship or by way of punishment for its use or *abuse*" (emphasis added). Thus, even though he claimed that the First Amendment did not protect libel and that it "would be an unendurable situation" for a society to permit libelous utterances, Burgess maintained that Congress was constitutionally "prohibited" from regulating such speech "in the states."[55]

Burgess admitted that a few constitutional provisions gave Congress some power to regulate political expression, the most important of which was the war power; Burgess also thought that as part of its power to make laws for the territories, Congress could prohibit speech unprotected by the First Amendment in those jurisdictions.[56] However, in his opinion, the war power could only be exercised "in case of actual invasion or rebellion," and then only "on the theater of actual conflict." In other words, the national government could not constitutionally prohibit criticism of a foreign war, even if the assertions in question were not otherwise protected by the First Amendment. Congress, Burgess concluded, was not authorized to restrict political dissent during World War I because no actual fighting took place in the United States and "national authority had not been overturned."[57]

Most conservative jurists, it should be noted, rarely discussed whether the federal government could regulate speech unprotected by the Constitution, in part because the issue was moot in the late nineteenth century. The dearth of federal speech restrictions noted above probably explains this dearth of judicial and legal commentary on the precise scope of federal power over speech.[58] Cooley, for example, noted that the constitutionality of the Alien and Sedition Acts had "always been disputed by a large party" but that it was unnecessary to discuss the merits of their claims because it was "impossible to conceive . . . of any state of things as would be likely to bring about its re-enactment."[59] The treatise writers did insist, however, that Congress could rarely use the war power to override an individual's constitutional expression rights. Cooley's *Handbook of Constitutional Law* condemned declarations of martial law in the North during the Civil War on the ground that there "can be no power to displace the guaranties and protections of the Constitution where the civil courts are discharging their functions." No treatise writer defended Lincoln's suppression of the antiadministration press, and John Randolph Tucker, a former Confederate general, declared those actions an unconstitutional usurpation of power.[60]

Conservative jurists were far more concerned with the constitutional limitations on state governments. These sovereignties were actively regulating individual behavior in the late nineteenth century, and several widely accepted principles of constitutional interpretation suggested their almost unlimited power to do so. In particular, the treatise writers admitted that local officials were not constrained by the doctrine of enumerated powers described above. The Constitution, Cooley observed, granted no power to the states but merely limited some of their earlier prerogatives. Hence, the local "legislature [had] jurisdiction of all subjects on which its legislation is not prohibited." This meant that states clearly had the power to regulate all expressive behavior not covered by constitutional free-speech guarantees.[61]

Furthermore, the pre–Civil War constitution did not seem to oblige states to protect free-speech rights or any other essential individual right. In *Barron v. Baltimore* (1833), Chief Justice Marshall had declared that state governments did not have to respect any liberty stated in the Bill of Rights or any fundamental freedom not clearly enunciated in the original Constitution. If local officials were taking private property without compensation or repressing political dissent, citizens could either throw the rascals out of office or amend state law.[62] Although conservatives thought this rule pernicious, they considered it the correct interpretation of the antebellum Constitution.[63]

Fortunately, the treatise writers argued, this last deficiency was remedied by the post–Civil War amendments. Shortly after the Fourteenth Amendment was proposed, John Norton Pomeroy asserted that its passage would give "the nation complete power to protect its citizens against local injustice and oppression."[64] Justice Field claimed that the new constitutional requirement that "no State shall make or enforce any law which shall abridge the privileges and immunities of citizens of the United States" placed "the natural and inalienable rights which belong to all citizens" under national protection. These rights were, of course, those individual liberties that conservative libertarians thought essential to a free government. Both "the right to acquire and possess property" and "the right of free speech" were included in Justice Bradley's catalog of the free-

doms protected against hostile state action by the new, improved constitution.[65]

Indeed, some conservative jurists indicated that the status of
expression rights in the amended constitution was far more secure than the status of economic rights. When questions concerning the scope of the Fourteenth Amendment first reached
the Supreme Court in the *Slaughter-House Cases* of 1873, proponents of the freedom of contract claimed that the new constitutional status of that right could be derived from the more obvious, new constitutional status of the freedom of speech. Former
Justice John Campbell, the lawyer for the petitioners, asked his
previous associates on the Court, "Can a state legislature say
that religion, speech, publication and invention shall be carried
on and employed in designated limits and under the superinten-
dence of the seventeen persons, and in their houses, yards or
pens?" "The same law," he insisted, "that protects them protects their personal right to labor. The constitution declares that
none of these privileges can be abridged by State laws."[66]

By the beginning of the twentieth century, the overwhelming majority of conservative jurists had endorsed the proposition that state governments were constitutionally obliged to respect the expression rights of their citizens. Even those
proponents of the freedom of contract who had little interest in
noneconomic liberties acknowledged that the freedom of
speech was also a Fourteenth Amendment right, although, as
noted below, some narrowly defined the scope of that right.
This agreement on the new status of speech rights did not, however, reflect a universally accepted interpretation of the post–
Civil War amendments. Instead, conservatives offered several
different explanations of the source of this newly limited state
power.

Many conservatives asserted that the Fourteenth Amendment
incorporated all the liberties stated in the Bill of Rights. Pomeroy urged his fellow citizens to pass that amendment on the
ground that it would overturn the "harmful" rule of *Barron v.
Baltimore.* "If history has taught us anything," Burgess stated,
"it is that civil liberty is national in origin, content and sanc-
tion." His three-volume history of the United States attempted
to demonstrate that the constitutional framers made a grave

mistake when they entrusted the states with the protection of
fundamental freedoms and that their blunder was only correct-
ed after the Civil War, when the restrictions on governmental
power stated in the first ten amendments were nationalized.[67]

Although the Supreme Court rejected this position in *Slaughter-House* and subsequent cases, many conservatives continued
to insist that the provisions of the Bill of Rights were among the
privileges and immunities of United States citizens. In *Spies v.
Illinois* (1883), John Randolph Tucker asked the Court to reverse those earlier rulings. If the Court would not overrule
precedent, he suggested that the justices at least recognize that
those provisions in the first eight amendments "of a fundamental nature and of common law rights" could no longer be violated
by state governments. Freedom of speech, Tucker maintained,
was one such right.[68] As late as 1898, William Guthrie was still
contending that previous judicial discussions of the privileges
and immunities clause were mere obiter dicta,[69] without precedential value.[70]

Two of the Supreme Court's most influential advocates for
the freedom of contract endorsed this version of the incorporation doctrine. Justice Harlan, who wrote several opinions that
helped constitutionalize the various economic liberties favored
by conservative libertarians, frequently asserted that all the liberties mentioned in the Bill of Rights were privileges and immunities of United States citizens.[71] Justice Brewer, a leading defender of laissez-faire property rights both on and off the
Court, signed one of Harlan's dissents on this point; and in *Patterson v. Colorado* he argued that state limitations on political
speech presented federal constitutional questions under the
Fourteenth Amendment.[72]

In his *Handbook on Constitutional Law*, Henry Black offered a
variation on this theme. Although he did not think that the
Fourteenth Amendment incorporated any provision of the Bill
of Rights, Black maintained that the privileges and immunities
clause protected "the right of the people to assemble for the
purpose of petitioning Congress for a redress of grievances, or
for anything else connected with the powers or duties of the national government." His writings also suggested that states
could not restrict the right of citizens to discuss local matters

because that liberty was "so essential to a free government that it would probably be regarded as inherent in the nature of our republican systems, even if it were not expressly placed under the protection of the constitution."[73] In other words, Black believed that the post–Civil War amendments specifically protected free speech even though they did not specifically incorporate any particular provision of the Bill of Rights.

This view was partially endorsed by the Supreme Court in *United States v. Cruikshank* (1875). The Court held that states did not have to respect a citizen's right "to peaceably assemble for any lawful purposes," but the justices agreed that local officials now had a federal constitutional obligation to protect the right "to meet peaceably for consultation in respect to public affairs and to petition for a redress of grievances."[74] Thus, two years before the Court even implied that some economic rights might be protected by the Fourteenth Amendment,[75] the justices clearly limited state power to regulate political dissent.

The most prominent conservative treatise writers never accepted the incorporation doctrine and interpreted narrowly the privileges and immunities clause.[76] Rather, they maintained the Fourteenth Amendment's guarantee that no state could "deprive any person of life, liberty, or property, without due process of law" was the source of constitutional protections for the fundamental rights of the individual, rights that included both the freedom of speech and the freedom of contract. In their view, this clause restricted governmental power over life, liberty, and property and did not simply guarantee that certain procedures would be provided whenever states sought to infringe those individual rights. The most frequently cited passage in *Constitutional Limitations* was Cooley's assertion that whenever "government . . . interferes with the title to one's property" courts must judge validity by reference to "those principles of civil liberty and constitutional protection which have become established in our system of laws, and not generally by rules that pertain to forms of procedure only."[77] Cooley's definition of due process specifically pointed to both expressive and commercial activities as examples of rights encompassed by that phrase. "It would be absurd," he argued, "to say that arbitrary arrests were forbidden, but that the freedom of speech . . .

[or] the right freely to buy and sell as others may . . . found no protection here."[78] Justice Harlan similarly observed that "it would be impossible to conceive of liberty" as defined in the Fourteenth Amendment, "which does not embrace the right to enjoy free speech and to have a free press."[79]

The treatise writers contended that the phrase "due process" incorporated the central principles of conservative libertarian thought. Cooley claimed that the specific freedoms protected by the due process clause could be derived from Mill's *On Liberty*. Both the rights to free speech and private property, he argued, were aspects of harm principle. Thus, after the Fourteenth Amendment was passed, states could not restrict the "liberty of tastes and pursuits" or "the liberty . . . of combination" unless the exercise of those freedoms directly damaged others.[80] Tiedeman, whose influence was second only to Cooley's, maintained that "state regulation . . . which denied the right of the individual to publish what he pleases . . . would be unconstitutional," under the Fourteenth Amendment "on the general ground that [it] would involve the deprivation of liberty and the right to pursue happiness." Prominent legal treatises written by Burgess, John Minor, and Henry Brannon similarly treated free speech as one aspect of a more general principle of individual liberty that they believed was protected by the due process clause of the Fourteenth Amendment.[81]

The Supreme Court first declared that the due process clause protected substantive freedoms in the 1897 case of *Allgeyer v. Louisiana*,[82] when a state insurance law was held an unconstitutional violation of the freedom of contract. Eight years later, in the infamous *Lochner* case, the Supreme Court held that a law limiting the hours a person could be employed as a baker violated "the general right to make a contract in relation to [a person's] business" that was protected by the Fourteenth Amendment. The New York statute, Justice Peckham declared, was "an illegal interference with the rights of individuals, both employers and employees, to make contracts regarding labor upon such terms as they may think best."[83]

Significantly, the justices of the *Lochner* era proved equally willing to treat the freedom of expression as a due process right. At least seven justices who sat on the turn-of-the-century Court (five of whom were still sitting when *Lochner* was decided) publicly declared that the post–Civil War constitution obligated states to protect free-speech rights. In *Downes v. Bidwell* (1901), Justice White, speaking for Justices Shiras, McKenna, and Gray, asserted that the federal legislature had to honor the individual rights inherent in the due process clause of the Fifth Amendment when governing the overseas possessions of the United States and that free speech was one of those rights. Whenever the United States took possession of a territory, he claimed, "laws . . . abridging the freedom of the press . . . would at once cease to be of obligatory force" because they were "in conflict with the political character, institutions and constitution of the [United States]."[84] In a separate opinion, Justice Brown argued that natural law determined the rights of citizens in the territories and that free speech was one aspect of that law. His understanding of natural law, however, was identical to the prevailing analysis of the due process clause.[85] Because the dissenters in *Downes* maintained that every constitutional limitation expressed in the Bill of Rights and other constitutional provisions was in force in the territories,[86] they did not elaborate the meaning of due process. As noted above, however, Justices Harlan and Brewer had previously declared that free speech was a Fourteenth Amendment right.

The Court's treatment of free-speech issues at the turn of the century reflected this understanding that states were constitutionally obligated to honor expression rights. In the twenty-five years following *Allgeyer,* the justices heard five cases in which the petitioner asserted a Fourteenth Amendment due process free-speech right and adjudicated all of them on the merits, even when the state argument emphasized the alleged failure of the post–Civil War amendments to protect free speech.[87] The Fuller, White, and Taft Courts never dismissed a case on the ground that the Constitution did not restrict state power to regulate speech. This was in sharp contrast to the way in which the justices treated other late nineteenth- and early twentieth-century claims that state governments had violated provisions of the Bill of Rights. These claims were regularly dismissed as not presenting federal questions;[88] the one other exception was a claim based on the just compensation clause of the Fifth

Amendment, which was upheld.[89] Indeed, by 1910, state briefs in free-speech cases were no longer seriously contesting this point but spending their energy arguing that no free-speech rights had been violated.[90]

In 1925, the Court explicitly stated what past practice suggested. Justice Sanford's opinion in *Gitlow v. New York* recognized that the earlier cases in which free-speech claims had been raised and adjudicated stood for the proposition that "freedom of speech and of the press . . . are among the liberties protected by the due process clause of the 14th Amendment from impairment by the states."[91] The Court's opinion recognized the close connection between economic and expressive freedoms by citing *Coppage v. Kansas* in support of this ruling.[92] That 1908 case struck down a state law forbidding yellow dog contracts under the due process clause of the Fourteenth Amendment.[93] Eleven years later, Justice Sutherland declared that in *Gitlow v. New York* and *Allgeyer v. Louisiana* the Court had recognized that the freedom of speech and the freedom of contract were both aspects of the general due process right of a person "to be free in the enjoyment of all his faculties."[94]

Constitutional Limitations: Standards

There is, of course, considerable difference between maintaining that the Fourteenth Amendment protected free speech and broadly interpreting the scope of that protection. Significantly, in no free speech case decided between 1897 and 1925 did the Supreme Court ever support the merits of a free-speech claim. In *Fox v. Washington,* for example, the Court upheld the convictions of persons who had praised nudism and called for an end to prosecutions for indecent exposure. The defendants in that case had merely asked their fellow citizens to boycott the businesses of persons who were urging prosecution of a nudist colony "until these invaders will come to see the brutal mistake of their action." Without commenting on the legality of such a boycott, the Court's unanimous opinion stated that "by indirection but unmistakably" such language "encourages and incites a persistence in what we must assume would be a breach of the state laws against indecent exposure."[95]

Nineteenth-century conservative treatise writers made several suggestions that seemed to support the narrow reading their early twentieth-century judicial brethren gave to expression rights. Cooley stated that to find the law of free speech "we must look to the common-law rules which were in force when the constitutional guarantees were established."[96] Other authors maintained that "in the interpretation of constitutions" judges should "give effect to the intention of the people who adopted it."[97] As Leonard Levy has argued, the framers of the First Amendment may have accepted Blackstone's assertion that "the liberty of the press . . . consists in laying no previous restraints upon publications, and not in freedom from censure for criminal matter when published."[98] This illibertarian standard suggests that conservative libertarians authorized government to punish speakers for any reason as long as the speaker was permitted to speak.

In actual practice, however, when eighteenth-century law was inconsistent with the conservative libertarian philosophical defense of free speech, conservative libertarian jurists did not hesitate to develop new legal standards. Cooley, Tiedeman, Tucker, Black, Burgess, and Brewer broke with common law teachings in three areas that have become the subjects of ongoing debate in American constitutional law.[99] They argued that free speech meant more than the absence of prior restraints, that only speakers who advocated criminal conduct could be punished, and that to prevail in a libel suit, public figures had to establish that false defamatory utterances were made in reckless or intentional disregard of the truth.[100] Moreover, while other scholars have contended that the founding fathers accepted far broader standards of constitutional free-speech protection than Levy described,[101] the treatise writers did not ultimately justify their interpretations of constitutional guarantees on historical grounds. Rather, as the following discussion indicates, they derived their interpretation of the First Amendment from their libertarian philosophical principles.

In *Constitutional Limitations,* Cooley admitted that Blackstone had correctly stated the common law of free speech. But he argued that "the mere exemption from previous restraint could not be all that is secured by the constitutional provisions."

That doctrine erroneously interpreted the constitutional meaning of free speech, Cooley insisted, because it did not adequately protect expression rights. Not only could there "be no previous censorship . . . of words to be uttered orally," but also
that rule would make "the liberty of the press a mockery and a
delusion." "The phrase itself" would merely be "a byword,"
Cooley continued, "if, while every man was at liberty to publish
what he pleases, the public authorities might nevertheless punish him for harmless publications."[102] Black's *Handbook on Constitutional Law* agreed that no prior restraint was the common
law rule, but without citing historical evidence, he claimed that
such a narrow rule could not have been endorsed by the framers
of the Constitution, who had intended to form a republican government. Similarly, Tiedeman observed that the First Amendment was primarily "intended to prevent all such previous restraints on publication." He then noted, however, that there
were also constitutional limitations on governmental power to
impose postpublication sanctions on speech.[103] Tucker endorsed the free-speech views of Henry Hallam, who rejected
the rule of no prior restraint as not sufficiently protective of expression rights.[104]

Unlike Blackstone, the treatise writers believed that expression should be free both before and after publication. Government, they argued, could only prohibit speech under very specific and narrowly defined circumstances. The possibility that
an utterance might cause some social evil was not a constitutionally sufficient reason for governmental restriction. Black stated
that hostility to the "bad tendency" test was one factor that inspired the First Amendment.[105] Cooley argued that citizens
"must be left at liberty to speak with the freedom which the
magnitude of the supposed wrongs appears in their minds to demand." Though persons might "exceed all the proper bounds
of moderation," he concluded that "the consolation must be,
that the evil likely to spring from violent discussion will probably be less, and its correction by public sentiment more
speedy, than if the terrors of the law were brought to bear to
prevent the discussion."[106]

More specifically, the treatise writers claimed that the state
could constitutionally punish only speakers whose "intent and
purpose" was "to excite rebellion and civil war."[107] Citizens,

Black contended, had a right to criticize political measures "provided only that such criticisms are not made with a purpose of inciting the people to treason or rebellion."[108] This meant that "opinions hostile to our system of government and our institutions are allowed perfectly free expression." Black added that even speech having dangerous tendencies could not be suppressed if the speaker did not intend to cause illegal conduct. He insisted that "the anarchist is not punished for his incendiary utterances, nor subject to any restraint until he commits a breach of the peace." Tiedeman similarly maintained that "the newspapers of anarchists and nihilists cannot be subjected to a censorship, or be absolutely suppressed" unless "their columns publish inflammatory appeals to the passions of discontents, and urge them to the commission of crimes against the public or against the individual."[109]

Tucker went one step further and defended in the courtroom the right to espouse anarchy. In *Spies v. Illinois* (1887), he presented an appeal to the Supreme Court on behalf of the seven prominent radicals who had been convicted and sentenced to death for their role in instigating a bombing in Chicago's Haymarket Square. Tucker's petition for a writ of error asserted that his clients had been convicted in derogation of their free-speech rights. No one, he contended, could "be legally convicted of the commission of a particular crime on the ground of general speech, writing or publication by them, not having in contemplation 'the commission of the crime' charged against them."[110] When his friends asked why he argued the case, Tucker responded, "I do not defend anarchy, I defend the constitution."[111]

Forty years later, Burgess made similar claims on behalf of all persons who had been convicted for speeches opposing United States military policy during World War I. Americans, he argued, had previously recognized that speakers had a constitutional right to propose any political program to their fellow citizens, as long as they did not endorse criminal conduct. That constitutional right was based on a sharp distinction between "advocacy and advancement of any subject whatever according to constitutional methods" and "attempts . . . at its realization by modes and means violative of, contrary to, or unknown to, the Constitution." "No matter how radical or ultra-conservative, how excessively progressive or how intensely reactionary, how destructive or how harmfully preservative a proposition might appear to this mind or that," Burgess contended, "it was not regarded as disloyal or unpatriotic, but as the exercise of the most fundamental constitutional right of the citizen."[112]

Burgess considered the Espionage Act of 1917 a clear example of an unconstitutional infringement of the right to free speech. Although he was particularly incensed at the provision that punished persons who "use[d] any abusive language about the form of Government in the United States," Burgess contended that the act "left no point uncovered where the freedom of speech and of the press and of assembly to petition for redress of grievances could be employed in opposition to the will of the government." For these reasons, Burgess declared the Supreme Court's decisions, holding that law constitutional, violated "all preceding authoritarian interpretation" and were "in flat contradiction with the Constitution."[113]

At least one conservative on the federal bench expressed similar antipathy toward wartime speech restrictions. In one of the most publicized sedition trials of that era, Judge George M. Bourquin held that a charge of sedition could not constitutionally be sustained against a person who made several pro-German remarks during a heated dispute in a bar. Bourquin, a Taft appointee whose economic decisions espoused an individualistic approach to the law,[114] held that the defendant in *United States v. Hall* could not be convicted of a criminal offense in the absence of evidence that he "inten[ded] to interfere with . . . the military and naval forces" of the United States. "The genius of democracy and the spirit of our people," Bourquin commented, refused to tolerate "crimes" such as "slanders and libels of government and its officers."[115]

The examples of Burgess, Bourquin, and Tucker, in particular, belie the progressive/civil libertarian claim that traditional free-speech defenses had to be expanded to cover the new forms of repression that occurred during World War I and the red scare. By issuing opinions and commentary defending both the speech rights of opponents of the war and the right to espouse anarchy and other radical, left-wing doctrines, these conservative jurists demonstrated the functional adequacy of the conservative libertarian constitutional defense of free speech in the early twentieth century. Furthermore, conservative libertarians did not fail to develop speech-protective doctrines in other areas of First Amendment law that became the subject of public debate in the late progressive era. For example, as noted above, the treatise writers uniformly supported the right to speak on public property, although they did not do so on First Amendment grounds. Moreover, they developed a standard of protection in libel cases that most civil libertarians would not adopt until the 1960s.

The conservative libertarian position on libel is of particular importance because, until World War I, private libel suits provided the main arena for contests over the constitutional meaning of free speech. While late nineteenth-century judges and scholars were rarely called upon to delimit the precise relationship between expression and lawless conduct, libel cases were frequent enough to justify special treatises on the law of defamation. The central issue in these cases was whether, in the absence of actual truth, a good faith belief that one's criticisms were true precluded liability.[116] Although courts divided on this issue,[117] conservative libertarian treatise writers uniformly endorsed the alternative most protective of speech. In their works, one finds the origins of the standard the Supreme Court eventually adopted in *New York Times Co. v. Sullivan*.[118]

In *Constitutional Limitations*, Cooley stated that defendants normally had the burden of proving the truth of their injurious statements and that, if they failed to do so, their bad faith would be automatically presumed.[119] Thus, plaintiffs in ordinary libel suits could recover damages simply by proving the defendant's defamatory statements were false. However, Cooley claimed that some categories of speech were conditionally privileged. This meant that the plaintiff or state had the additional "burden of offering some evidence of [malice] beyond the mere falsity of the charge."[120] Cooley defined "legal malice" as "publish[ing] as true what [one] knows to be false or what by proper investigation he might have known was false." In other words, when speech was conditionally privileged, persons had a constitutional right to say anything they reasonably believed was true.[121]

Cooley claimed that all libels on government or criticism of governmental officials and would-be officials were conditionally privileged. Republican institutions required that political speech be so protected because of the "duty of every one to speak freely what he may have to say concerning public officers, or those who may present themselves for public positions."[122] Any less-protective interpretation of the First Amendment would unduly burden citizens' participation in politics. Holding persons "to the strict and literal truth of every statement, recital and possible inference," Cooley declared in *Atkinson v. Detroit Free Press,* made "any attempt at public discussion practically worthless."[123]

Cooley made little effort to demonstrate the common law pedigree of either his conception or his examples of conditionally privileged speech. His *Atkinson* opinion recognized that many decisions differed with his interpretation of libel law, but Cooley claimed that these precedents had been discredited by *Wason v. Walter.*[124] *Wason* was an English case decided only thirteen years earlier. Moreover, Judge Cockburn's opinion in that case recognized that the libel standard he announced modified the older rule.[125] Thus, the holding of *Atkinson,* clearly founded on the philosophical value Cooley placed on free speech, was not an example of the "common-law rules which were in force when the constitutional guarantees were established" from which he claimed to have derived his First Amendment doctrines.

In fact, Cooley's standards turned the common law upside down. Blackstone claimed that libels on private figures were harder to establish than libels on public figures because truth was available as a defense only in the former circumstances.[126] Cooley, however, argued that libels on public figures were harder to establish; only in the latter cases could the defendant rely on the good faith exception noted above. Indeed, in *Constitutional Limitations,* Cooley suggested that even comments on the private lives of public officials were conditionally privileged on the ground that the "private character of a public officer [is not] something aside from . . . his public conduct."[127]

Black, Tiedeman, and Brewer specifically endorsed Cooley's analysis of the law of libel. Tiedeman maintained that "any candid, honest, canvass of [an] official's or candidate's character or capacity would be privileged." An attack on these persons could "not be held liable, civilly or criminally, if it proves to be false." A more "narrow limit," Black added, would be inconsistent with "the public sentiment and the understanding of the people."[128] Although Tucker did not explicitly discuss libel law in his treatises, he argued that the Alien and Sedition Laws were unconstitutional,[129] and those statutes permitted truth as a defense. The good faith defense was also endorsed by E. L. Godkin, the editor of the *Nation*, the leading journal of conservative libertarians. "A man doing an important public act," he asserted, "has no right entitling him to shut the mouths even of harsh and severe critics" if they did not have "that vehement desire, or distinct consciousness of doing evil, which alone the law denounces."[130]

The Supreme Court waited until 1964 before considering the constitutional status of libel law. In that year, it held that the First and Fourteenth Amendments "[prohibit] a public official from recovering damages for a defamatory falsehood relating to his official conduct unless he proves that the statement was made with 'actual malice'—that is, with knowledge that it was false or with reckless disregard of whether it was false or not."[131] In keeping with American iconography on free speech, Justice Brennan quoted Justice Louis Brandeis, Judge Learned Hand, James Madison, and Thomas Jefferson at length in support of his conclusions,[132] even though none of these thinkers ever endorsed the actual holding of the *Sullivan* case. The court did not cite a specific source for that standard; however, the opinion did note that "an oft-cited statement of a like rule which has been adopted by a number of state courts is found in the Kansas case of *Coleman v. MacLenan*."[133] Although the *Coleman* opinion relied on a number of cases, including *Wason v. Walter*,[134] that opinion clearly stated that Cooley's treatises and opinions correctly defined the constitutional meaning of free speech. In particular, *Coleman* claimed that Cooley's writings were the source of two propositions: constitutional protection of free speech meant more than freedom from prior restraint; and the Constitution forbade civil or criminal punishment for false political statements unless those statements were known to be false or made in reckless disregard of the truth.[135] The *Sullivan* Court ignored this bit of constitutional history. The only reference any justice made to the late nineteenth-century conservative treatise writers, the first Americans to endorse and publicize the actual malice standard, was a bare citation to *Constitutional Limitations* buried in the middle of a long footnote.[136]

A Vanished Tradition

When Burgess died in 1934, the conservative libertarian tradition did not merely end; it largely vanished. American intellectuals had already forgotten that there had ever been thinkers concerned with both the freedom of speech and the freedom of contract. Led by Zechariah Chafee, the new generation of libertarians insisted that Americans had always premised their philosophical and constitutional defenses of free speech on principles hostile to the individualistic foundations of late nineteenth-century conservative thought. The new generation of conservatives exhibited little interest in rehabilitating their intellectual ancestors on this score. Although some contemporary proponents of laissez-faire economics, most notably Ralph Winter, have also actively promoted free-speech rights,[137] most twentieth-century conservatives have proved more concerned with finding fault with the new libertarian doctrine than with the new libertarian history.

In his histories of free-speech theory, Chafee contended that the main opponents of expression rights were conservatives "satisfied with the existing state situation and anxious to keep things as they are." These persons approved such decisions as *Lochner v. New York,* which struck down governmental economic regulations, and *Abrams v. United States,* which sustained governmental speech regulations.[138] Although Chafee claimed to have studied all the previous scholarship and cases on the right of free speech, his writings never hinted that from 1870 until 1900, the leading supporters of free speech were those intellectuals who were primarily responsible for developing the philosophical and jurisprudential underpinnings of the freedom of contract. Chafee noted that Cooley had discussed the nature of constitutional expression rights, but he claimed Cooley's conclusions were limited to the vague proposition that speech should be free "so long as it is not harmful in its character, when tested by such standards as the law affords."[139] Nowhere could Chafee's reader find evidence that Cooley had articulated more specific, libertarian standards, or that many other prominent conservative jurists believed that Cooley had properly defined the constitutional meaning of free speech.

In fact, even those twentieth-century justices who most outspokenly defended the freedom of contract were not as unremittingly hostile toward political dissent as Chafee suggested. In the nine free-speech cases decided by the Supreme Court between 1921 and 1937, Justices Sutherland, McReynolds, Butler, and Van Devanter unanimously voted in favor of the free-speech claim in four,[140] evenly divided in one,[141] and unanimously rejected the free-speech claim in the other four.[142] This was a far higher percentage of support than those conservatives gave to the freedom of contract claims.[143] In *Associated Press v. National Labor Relations Board*, the infamous Four Horsemen of the New Deal Court dissented on the basis of a free-speech claim ignored by the emerging liberal majority. A newspaper, Justice Sutherland asserted, had a constitutional free-speech right to fire an editorial writer who belonged to a union. Furthermore, Sutherland argued, the scope of constitutional protection for speech was even greater than the scope of constitutional protection for private property. "Deprivation of a liberty not embraced by the First Amendment, as for example the liberty of contract," his dissent noted, "is qualified by the phrase 'without due process of law.' " But, "those liberties enumerated in the First Amendment are guaranteed without qualification, the object and effect of which is to put them in a category apart and make them incapable of abridgment by any process of law."[144] Thus, while some social conditions justified regulating conduct protected by the liberty of contract, conduct protected by the First Amendment could never be regulated.

Nevertheless, Sutherland's *Associated Press* dissent is a misleading statement of the dominant twentieth-century conservative free-speech view. During World War I and the following red scare, Cooley's descendants introduced several new categories of speech that were beyond the pale of First Amendment protection. Proponents of domestic laissez-faire policies began to argue that governmental power should be interpreted more broadly and individual rights more narrowly when the subject matter was foreign relations. Sutherland, the leading spokesperson for this position, maintained that "in all matters of external sovereignty . . . a rule of constitutional construction obtains which is radically more liberal than that which obtains in the case of the domestic powers which are distributed between the general government and the state." Principles, he argued, "which would result in curtailing or preventing action on the part of the national government in the enlarged field of world responsibility . . . might prove highly injurious or embarrassing."[145]

The military needs of the state, in particular, required that the government be able to use the war power to curtail such personal freedoms as free speech when hostilities had been declared. Because the "power to declare war include[d] every other subsidiary power to make the declaration effective," Sutherland maintained that "individual right must yield to the general and superior right of national defense."[146] For this reason, Congress could restrict political dissent whenever war had been declared, not merely, as Burgess had asserted, in the case of foreign invasion.[147] Thus, the conservative justices on the Supreme Court consistently voted against assertions of free-speech rights during wartime. To their credit, however, these conservatives were consistent. Not only did they endorse the limits placed on free speech during the war, but Sutherland and the Supreme Court also affirmed wartime restrictions on the use of private property, in particular, regulations of hours and wages, "which in time of peace would be intolerable and inadmissible."[148]

Twentieth-century conservative thinkers also suggested that doctrines attacking the principles of republican government had no claim to free-speech protection. In *Gitlow v. New York*, Justice Edward Sanford stated that the freedom of speech "does not include the right virtually to destroy" those "free and constitutional institutions" that are "the very basis and mainstay upon which the freedom of the press rests."[149] In a 1919 article published in the *Journal of Criminal Law and Criminology*, G. P. Garrett claimed that only the "loyalist of independent mind" and the member of the "political minority" had full rights of political speech (as long as they did not advocate criminal activity).[150] The advocate of "heresy" was not given this protection.[151] A heretic was defined as a person like Eugene Debs who "found his doctrine opposed to the ruling influence of the American spirit."[152] Garrett recommended that the speech of these persons be absolutely prohibited: "without much need as to them for submitting the act to the test of constitutionality, we turn material of this kind into the jails."[153] In a speech given the same year, George T. Page, president of the American Bar Association, argued that the United States must not only insist that the citizen "renounce allegiance . . . to every foreign potentate and power" but the citizen should also be required to abandon "every foreign 'ism' and scheme of government not reconcilable with our own."[154]

The Supreme Court majority never adopted this stance, although Justice Butler's dissent in *Stromberg v. California* suggested that "the anarchy that is certain to follow a successful 'opposition to organized government' " might be "a sufficient reason to hold that all activities to that end are outside the liberty so protected."[155] Conservative opinions, however, indicated that advocacy of certain political programs automatically merged into some other, less controversial, basis for affirming governmental regulation of speech. For example, in several cases handed down immediately after World War I, the Court concluded that opponents of the war had intentionally uttered falsehoods when they asserted that the American people had been tricked into supporting the Allies by President Wilson and capitalistic bankers. Majority opinions held that Woodrow Wilson's analysis of the causes of World War I was a self-evident truth, that the war was fought "in vindication of the 'most sacred rights of our nation and our people.' "[156] No reasonable person could in good faith argue otherwise.[157] In *Pierce v. United States*, Justice Pitney hinted that economic radicals were also guilty of bad faith. Socialism, he suggested, was so evidently false that no person could advocate it on the basis of its merits.[158]

Justice Van Devanter's dissent in *Herndon v. Lowry* merged the categories of criminal and antirepublican advocacy. He claimed that persons who advocated the abolition of republican institutions in the United States were necessarily arguing for a revolution because the American people would never peacefully tolerate such changes.[159] Echoing Tiedeman's assertion that the First Amendment did not protect "inflammatory appeals to the passions of discontents,"[160] Van Devanter claimed that advocacy of communism and measures supported by communism could only influence those persons whose "past and present circumstances" disabled them from rationally recognizing the obvious fallacies of those policies.[161]

Although these modifications and perversions of earlier conservative libertarian positions clearly had repressive implications, twentieth-century conservatives never endorsed a bad tendency test. Indeed, in several cases, conservative judges voted to overturn convictions for which the evidence seemed to satisfy that standard. Judicial proponents of the freedom of contract supported the free-speech claims of a person charged with distributing International Workers of the World (I. W. W.) literature, a speaker who attacked police brutality during a meeting held under the auspices of the Communist party, and a radical who raised a red flag in a communist summer camp.[162] Indeed, as I note in chapter 3, until 1937, progressive and liberal libertarians relied on conservative libertarian positions when justifying judicial activism on behalf of free speech.

As chapter 3 further details, the bad tendency test was a progressive standard and was, in fact, the same rule that opponents of the freedom of contract would use to test the constitutionality of governmental economic regulations. Indeed, all specific opponents of free speech whom Chafee labeled as conservatives based their opposition to free-speech rights on the same grounds that they attacked the *Lochner* decision.[163] The progressive bad tendency test was not more restrictive that Justice Butler's claim that certain creeds were beyond the pale of discussion, but it was based on different premises. Whereas the conservative justification of suppression was based on the principle that the Constitution declared that certain fundamental substantive values could not be abridged by democratic majorities, the bad tendency test was based on the progressive belief that fundamental values should be chosen by the democratically elected branches of government.

In short, not only does the myth of the single civil libertarian tradition ignore the existence of the conservative libertarian philosophical and constitutional defense of free speech, but also that tradition mischaracterizes the arguments made by conservative opponents of free speech. In other words, what civil libertarians treat as the full spectrum of American views on free speech is merely the way that progressives and liberals have defended and opposed expression rights in the twentieth century.

Chapter Two

Transformation
Foreshadowed

The Progressive Era

The political status of expression rights slowly changed over the first fifteen years of the twentieth century, a period known as the progressive era. A series of free-speech fights orchestrated by the International Workers of the World and other radical organizations attracted national political attention.[1] Legislatures began to discuss proposals limiting the scope of legitimate political dissent.[2] State and federal courts adjudicated an increasing number of free-speech cases and issues,[3] in part because early twentieth-century litigants raised expression issues in such controversies as labor injunctions and the right to speak on public property, conflicts formerly adjudicated on other grounds.[4] The Free Speech League, the first American association specifically dedicated to defending the liberty of discussion, was organized in 1902.[5] Scholarship reflected this heightened interest in expression. By 1916, the editors of the *University of Pennsylvania Law Review* could declare that next to the Fourteenth Amendment, the First Amendment was "the most popular . . . of the constitutional guarantees."[6]

Nevertheless, partisan free-speech conflict remained latent during the progressive era. Although increasingly discomforted, militant union organizers and left-wing agitators still found numerous opportunities to present their views. Legislatures may have discussed proposals to restrict expression rights, but such measures were rarely passed; those few that did pass were rarely enforced. As a result, constitutional issues adjudicated by courts continued to be of only local importance. The most significant First Amendment question resolved by the Supreme Court in this era was whether the Colorado Supreme Court could issue a contempt citation to a local newspaper that criticized an ongoing judicial proceeding.[7] In short, while partisan forces on both sides of free-speech debates began to mobilize, the political circumstances of the first fifteen years of the twentieth century did not provoke the intense demand for restrictions on political dissent that would mark World War I and the red scare.[8]

The progressive era was also a transitional period for the constitutional defense of free speech. Two developments foreshadowed the transformation and constitutional crisis of American libertarian thought during World War I. First, as the conservative libertarian tradition waned, a new generation of libertarians assumed the leadership of the fight for free speech. Members of this new generation rejected the connections previously drawn between the liberty of discussion and the liberty of contract. Emma Goldman and Theodore Schroeder, the most active defenders of expression rights in the early twentieth century, were philosophical anarchists who maintained that state recognition of private property was inconsistent with the fundamental human freedom of self-expression. The only other prominent libertarian scholar of this era, Ernst Freund, was a mainstream progressive thinker who combined advocacy of free speech with calls for extensive governmental regulation of individual economic behavior.

Second, a new generation of intellectuals rejected the broader philosophical and jurisprudential foundations of conservative libertarianism. Led by John Dewey and Roscoe Pound, proponents of pragmatism and sociological jurisprudence attacked both the conception of individual rights and the notion that the judiciary and the bar were especially suited to defend the fundamental principles of American government. Instead, these leading progressive thinkers insisted that public policy should promote the social interests of the community and that these interests could best be determined by elected officials and social science experts.

Nevertheless, before World War I, developments in American libertarian thought were largely isolated from contemporaneous developments in American political and legal thought. The new generation of libertarians continued to work within the philosophical and jurisprudential parameters marked out by the older, conservative libertarian tradition. Conservative treatise writers and early twentieth-century philosophical anarchists (as well as Ernst Freund in this period) agreed that free speech was an individual right and emphasized the judicial obligation to protect such freedoms from majoritarian pressures for censorship. Schroeder and Freund endorsed judicial activism on behalf of free speech because they thought expression was an individual liberty protected by the First Amendment and the due process clause of the Fourteenth Amendment. There was only one significant difference between the libertarians of the late nineteenth and early twentieth centuries: the latter insisted that laissez-faire private-property rights were not included among the freedoms subsumed under the general "right of the citizen to be free in the enjoyment of all of his faculties."

Early twentieth-century progressive intellectuals, in contrast, were largely unconcerned with the constitutional status of free speech. Proponents of pragmatism and sociological jurisprudence were committed to devising arguments that would encourage governmental intervention in commercial life and transfer economic power from the courts to the elected branches of government. These issues provided the focus of intense partisan debate during the progressive era. Because of the continued low salience of expression rights prior to World War I, progressive intellectuals were not compelled to explore seriously the effects that their new arguments might have on the constitutional defense of free speech. Pound declared that his flat ban on judicial protection of individual liberties specifically covered the individual right of free speech. His writings, however, did not clearly indicate whether he believed that judicial activism on behalf of free speech was never justified or merely that the individualistic framework of conservative libertarianism did not justify such activism.

The New Libertarians

The most prominent libertarians of the early twentieth century shared many political attitudes held by their earlier, conservative counterparts. The spiritual leader of the fight for free speech in the progressive era called for "a society based on voluntary co-operation of productive groups" and proclaimed that persons must be "free to choose the mode of work, the conditions of work, and the freedom to work." She thought "Herbert Spencer's formula of liberty . . . the most important on the subject."[9] Indeed, the only significant difference between Emma Goldman and William Graham Sumner was that "Red Emma" did not think government should protect even "the property of men and the honor of women."[10]

Goldman was committed to the principles of anarchy, which she defined as "liberty unrestricted by man-made laws." In her view, government should never interfere with an individual's labor, intellectual, or love life. Persons had the right "to arrange at all times for . . . forms of work in harmony with their tastes and desires," to "say and write what [they] please[d]," and "to follow [their] love without let or hindrance from the outside world." Such "complete individual and social freedom" was the necessary condition for a "free display of human energy."[11] Goldman maintained that the beloved private-property rights of conservative libertarianism were anathema to individual liberty because governmental enforcement of private economic holdings left others lacking the necessary means to develop their faculties. When the state supported some persons' "dominion over things" and their power to "den[y] to others the use of those things," those without resources were unable to exercise their fundamental right to "the freest possible expression of all the[ir] latent powers."[12]

Goldman's political activities during the progressive era were frequently devoted to defending an "unlimited exercise of expression." She traveled around the country publicizing the rights of political dissidents and provoking free-speech fights.[13] Although her assertion that she organized the Free Speech League is debatable, the association was dominated by Goldman's personal and political associates.[14] Between 1902 and

1917, these activists fought obscenity prosecutions and defended the expression rights of many radical thinkers.[15] Several
of her friends, in particular Gilbert Roe and Harry Weinberger,
later played major roles in the fight for free speech during
World War I and the red scare.[16] Indeed, Roger Baldwin,
founder of the American Civil Liberties Union (ACLU), stated
that Goldman "aroused [him] to a sense of what freedom really
means." After listening to her speak in 1911 he began to dream of
"a world where all men and women should be free of compulsion, and free to join in a network of voluntary associations to
satisfy human needs." For the rest of his life, Baldwin "never
departed far from the general philosophy represented in libertarian literature."[17]

While Goldman, Baldwin, Roe, Weinberger, and others led
the fight for free speech in the field, they did not produce extensive academic writing on the subject. They were far more
interested in actually defending the rights of political dissidents
than in detailing the philosophical and jurisprudential foundations of their libertarian beliefs. This role was taken by Theodore Schroeder, a self-described philosophical anarchist and
member of the Goldman circle.[18]

Theodore Schroeder

Schroeder was by far the most important and prolific scholarly
defender of expression rights in the progressive era. In scores of
articles and several books, he argued that "every idea, no matter how unpopular, so far as the law is concerned, shall have the
same opportunity as every other idea no matter how popular, to
secure the public favor." The driving force behind the actual
operations of the Free Speech League, Schroeder spent more
energy defending the right to discuss sexual matters than the
right to discuss politics. This emphasis on obscenity, however,
partly reflected what speech was actively being censored in the
early twentieth century. Moreover, Free Speech Leaguers
were committed to gender equality, a commitment inconsistent
with the conservative libertarians' Victorian belief that women,
as wards of the state, needed special protection against speech
that might lower their moral standards. Schroeder's attacks on

obscenity restrictions also had an important political compo-
nent. He believed that lovers of liberty must seek to prevent the
establishment of principles that might be broadened in the future to limit the scope of legitimate political dissent. It was "of
infinite importance to destroy a precedent which implies the
admission of a power to wipe out any literature upon any subject, which, through popular hysteria or party passion, may be
declared 'against the public welfare.' "[19]

Schroeder was the first American thinker who devoted himself almost exclusively to the liberty of discussion. Conservative libertarians normally raised free-speech issues to illustrate
general political and legal principles. Schroeder raised general
political and legal principles only when they were relevant to
his discussion of free speech. His writings never discussed antitrust, unionism, immigration, imperialism, or any other major
issue of the progressive era. Indeed, Schroeder professed disin-
terest in the major political controversies and intellectual developments of the early twentieth century. In his view, the debates between progressive and conservative partisans and
thinkers were merely "contests between neo-maniacs and neo-
phobiacs." During World War I, he refused to join the National
Civil Liberties Bureau (later the ACLU) because he believed
that organization was also promoting pacifism and economic reform. Schroeder was only concerned with one political debate
—free speech.[20]

Nevertheless, a broader egalitarian social vision inspired this
single-minded devotion to expression rights. Schroeder wished
to ameliorate the evils generated by unrestrained economic
competition. However, like other philosophical anarchists, he
did not think that progressive governmental regulations could
achieve that end. Schroeder believed that state efforts to eradi-
cate economic domination merely caused power seekers to devise other means of subordinating people. "A psychologist," he
stated, "may well insist that to abolish monopoly-interest in natural resources will leave all the evil psychological imperatives
intact, to create new modes of satisfaction."[21] Only the instruments of public discussion could bring about those changes in
human nature that would end human exploitation. When expression rights were recognized, persons would naturally "out-

grow the desire for parasitic and aristocratic privileges," the underlying causes of social unrest.[22] No additional state action would be necessary because the system of freedom of expression could function under any conditions. Schroeder thought that social equality would be the consequence if free speech were permitted in any political, economic, or social circumstance. "Violence directed against exploitation and evil," he concluded, "does little more than to change its form. Unlimited intellectual freedom will some day destroy its substance."[23]

Schroeder claimed that free speech would be sufficiently protected if government tolerated all speech that merely threatened some harm, even if the threat took the form of a direct incitement. He would punish only those speakers whose utterances caused actual material injuries. "The words 'freedom of speech and of the press,' " he argued, "can only mean that a man shall have the right to utter any sentiment . . . so long as the mere utterance of his sentiments is the only factor in the case." An orator could be "punish[ed] for murder, arson or other actual and resultant injury," but only "for his contribution toward and participation in bringing about these injuries."[24] Thus, speakers had the right to convince their audiences of the merits of any political or social doctrine. Schroeder explicitly endorsed the right to propose violent resistance to the government (or any lesser crime), as long as no actual crime or violence could be directly and immediately traced to such advocacy.[25]

Schroeder's philosophical defense of expression rights demonstrated the continued vitality of conservative principles in early twentieth-century libertarian thought. His writings endorsed the conservative libertarian practice of treating the liberty of discussion as an aspect of the individual's more general right to be free from governmental regulation. Free speech, he declared, was "a special application of Herbert Spencer's formula of freedom," which asserted that "every man [has the] freedom to do all that he wills, provided he infringes not on the equal freedom of every other man."[26]

Schroeder maintained that the "actual material injury" standard followed from Spencer's egalitarian formula. Because "a secular state" could "deal only with material factors," persons could claim that their right of equal freedom was infringed only if they suffered a "demonstrable and ascertained material injury." Therefore, Schroeder concluded, secular states could never prohibit speech or any other exercise of individual liberty merely on the grounds that other people considered such behavior distressing, disgusting, offensive, or immoral. These were "mere psychologic crimes." Unless speakers caused actual material injuries, their right of equal freedom forbade punishment on the basis of the sentiments uttered.[27]

Although Schroeder's writings emphasized that free speech was an individual right, he recognized the social importance of uninhibited discourse. As conservative libertarians had previously insisted, Schroeder maintained that free speech was not simply "a matter of the personal liberty of the speaker or writer." The liberty of discussion was necessary for "racial intellectual development by keeping open all the avenues for the greatest possible interchange of ideas."[28] Schroeder insisted that John Stuart Mill's claim that free trade in ideas was the best way to discover the worth of intellectual products "never has been answered and never will be."[29]

Conservative libertarian principles similarly structured Schroeder's defense of judicial activism on behalf of free speech. Like the treatise writers, he maintained that the judiciary functioned to protect the fundamental personal rights of the citizen as those rights were set out in the Constitution. Courts were especially obligated to strike down statutes and governmental practices that infringed on free speech rights because "unabridged and unabridgable freedom of discussion" could not be limited by "a legislature of mediocre attainments." "If our constitutional guarantees declare and determine rights," he observed, "then these cannot be destroyed by the arbitrary decree of the legislature, even though done in the alleged interest of the public welfare."[30]

Schroeder sometimes suggested that supporters of broad free-speech rights were foolish to believe that actual judges would protect those rights. Nevertheless, he continually emphasized the legal system's responsibility for safeguarding expression. The courts, not the legislatures, "destroyed and evaded the constitutional guarantee of freedom of speech." Schroeder called for a public opinion that would support judicial

decisions "against the state and in favor of individual liberty."
He never suggested that the public attempt to repeal the original legislative decision that had restricted free speech.[31]

While Schroeder proclaimed that consistency "with the logical requirements of natural law" was one virtue of the actual
material injury test,[32] he did not think that judges should rely on
their notions of natural law when interpreting the positive law
provisions of the Constitution. Following the rules laid down by
the conservative treatise writers, he insisted that the role of the
court was "to discover, declare and enforce the prior existing
law, and never to construct or to create law."[33] This "prior existing law" was discovered by examining historical sources, not
by deducing eternal principles of truth. Whenever Schroeder
discussed the constitutional meaning of free speech, his analysis
emphasized his interpretation of the original meaning of the
First Amendment. His writings aimed at achieving "a new definition of 'freedom of the press' based upon the viewpoint that
the framers of the constitution intended by that clause to en-
large the intellectual liberty of the citizen beyond what it had
theretofore been under the English system." "The materials"
for this interpretation were "antecedent historical controversies, whose issues the Constitution was intended to decide."[34]
Unlike earlier libertarians, Schroeder actually discussed the
history of constitutional free-speech protections at length. As
my discussion suggests, however, he was far more interested in
presenting historical evidence that supported his philosophical
conclusions than in discovering the precise intentions of the
framers of the First Amendment.

Schroeder's works outlined three different methods of exploring constitutional history: the analytic, the historic, and the
synthetic.[35] Each relied on a different perspective to determine
the original intentions of those who framed the Constitution
and relevant amendments. The analytic method scrutinized the
particular words chosen by the constitutional framers. Its "object" was "to ascertain from the actual wording of the constitution . . . the exact meaning and application of its implicit or explicit general principles." Rights plainly guaranteed, Schroeder
argued, are constitutional rights because those who wrote the
document presumably meant what they plainly stated.[36] Thus,

he emphasized the framers' declaration that "Congress shall make no law abridging the freedom of speech." Anticipating an argument that Justice Hugo Black later made famous, Schroeder maintained that if the members of the First Congress had believed that individual expression rights could be sacrificed on general policy grounds, then the text of the First Amendment would have been "Congress shall make no law abridging the freedom of speech or of the press, except in the interest of the public welfare."[37]

The historical method analyzed the particular purposes of constitutional provisions. That approach inquired "into those issues of principle which were the essence of the antecedent agitation, which conflicts our constitution was designed to decide."[38] Because the hated licensing system had been outlawed in England in 1694, Schroeder argued that this practice did not threaten political dissidents one hundred years later when the First Amendment was being debated. Hence, there would have been little need to pass a constitutional amendment that only forbade prior restraints. Rather, constitutional proponents of free speech must have intended to prohibit postpublication restrictions. Although Schroeder recognized that late eighteenth-century libertarians had accepted some exceptions to unlimited free-speech rights, he maintained that the basic principles underlying their arguments supported "an unabridged freedom of utterance."[39]

The synthetic method, "the process by which alone the best intellectual results can be obtained," explored more general constitutional principles. Unlike analytic or historic approaches, this perspective treated the Constitution as a whole. Its purpose was to ascertain the aspirations common to every constitutional provision. All constitutional "limitations and guarantees," Schroeder argued, were "part of the general idea of liberty." Constitutional interpretation involved "understanding each part in relation to all other parts" so that the theorist could "arrive at an all-inclusive generalization thereafter to be applied deductively and decisively to each concrete problem of freedom and to each separate constitutional guarantee of a partial or particular liberty." Thus, constitutional liberties could not be explicated piecemeal. The meaning of any particular consti-

tutional clause was partially determined by what other rights
that document protected.[40] In his view, a wide variety of constitutional provisions required broad interpretations of constitutional free-speech rights. For example, he thought the right to
bear arms was constitutional recognition that "in order to maintain freedom we must keep alive both the spirit and the means
of resistance to government . . . [which] included the right to
advocate the timeliness and right of resistance." Similarly,
Schroeder regarded the equal protection clause as protecting
"equal intellectual opportunity," and he considered the constitutional definition of treason as limiting crimes against the government to actual acts of war, not antigovernment rhetoric.[41]
He also derived free-speech rights from the constitutional rules
of criminal procedure. In particular, Schroeder claimed that
persons had both a natural and a due process right to fair notice
of social rules and regulations. For this reason, he rejected any
interpretation of speech freedoms that was based on the mere
probability that a particular speech might cause lawless conduct
or material injury. Laws punishing speech that had a bad tendency violated the individual's liberty because a speaker had no
way of estimating how a judge or jury would evaluate the possible consequences of his utterances.[42]

More generally, Schroeder thought that the right of self-
expression was inherent in the single principle of individual liberty which animated the entire Constitution. Proper use of the
synthetic method, he claimed, demonstrated that the essence of
the document was its guarantee that all persons would have the
"right to freedom from all artificial interference or human penalty in pursuit of any course of action, except that which in its
necessary and most immediate result inflicts actual and material
injury upon someone other than a sane, normal adult, participant therein or consentant thereto and consciously assuming
the risk thereof." This fundamental principle was none other
than "Herbert Spencer's formula of freedom . . . the greatest
liberty consistent with an equality of liberty."[43] Because free
speech was logically entailed by that precept, government was
obligated to protect "the right to express with impunity any
idea whatever so long as its mere presentation is the only factor
involved."[44]

The post–Civil War amendments nationalized this conception of expression rights. In language that echoed the themes of conservative libertarianism, Schroeder proclaimed that "the fourteenth amendment to the federal constitution withdrew even from the states all authority to deprive anyone of 'liberty' without 'due process of law.' " First Amendment freedoms were clearly aspects of this new due process right for two reasons. First, Schroeder maintained that the Fourteenth Amendment incorporated all the provisions in the Bill of Rights. "In the fourteenth amendment," he stated, " 'liberty' can mean only those fundamental liberties . . . which by previous amendments had been deemed sufficiently important to be expressly withdrawn from federal authority." Second, the post–Civil War amendments also obligated state officials to respect any individual's exercise of his or her rights of equal liberty. "By virtue of the fourteenth amendment," Schroeder declared, "the above state criteria of constitutional liberty are controlling even as to the conflict of state legislation with the federal constitution."[45] In other words, passage of the Fourteenth Amendment meant that states could abridge neither any liberty stated in the Bill of Rights nor any liberty that could be validly derived from Spencer's formula of freedom (i.e., "the above state criteria of constitutional liberty"). Free speech qualified on both grounds.

Schroeder also endorsed the conservative claim that the Constitution was a grant of express and limited powers. Thus, like Burgess, he insisted that the federal government was not authorized to regulate constitutionally unprotected speech. Postal restrictions based on the content of mail were unconstitutional, in Schroeder's opinion, because such practices were "not within any expressed or implied power of the Congress to enact."[46]

Although Schroeder relied on the same constitutional arguments that conservative libertarians had used to defend free speech, he did not accept their most important conclusion: that the freedom of contract was another aspect of the general right of liberty found in the Fourteenth Amendment. While he implied that the post–Civil War amendments protected some economic and social rights not explicitly mentioned in the text of the Constitution,[47] Schroeder specifically rejected laissez-faire private-property rights as applications of constitutional liberty.

The Fourteenth Amendment, he asserted, did not render constitutional the economic assertions in Herbert Spencer's *Social Statics*. Schroeder questioned "if any sane man really believes that another's law-created property-right in bread is more sacred than is his own natural right to live." Cases like *Lochner v. New York* were wrongly decided because "Spencer's formula does not permit of application to cases wherein it becomes necessary to balance mere psychic factors against the material things of life."[48]

Nevertheless, in an important sense, Schroeder's attack on the freedom of contract did not put him outside conservative libertarianism. He only insisted that private-property rights could not be derived from the more general right of equal liberty. Unlike the progressive thinkers discussed in the next section, Schroeder never rejected the fundamental individual right of equal liberty. In short, while late nineteenth-century conservative libertarians and philosophical anarchists disagreed on applications, they shared common principles. Cooley and Schroeder, in particular, can be said to be part of a common libertarian tradition. Their defense of expression rights stemmed from shared beliefs that free speech was an individual right, that this right was one aspect of the broader right of equal liberty protected by the due process clause of the Fourteenth Amendment, and that federal courts were expected to protect such liberties from the whims of elected majorities.

Ernst Freund

Schroeder's understanding of the constitutional relationships between freedom of speech, freedom of contract, and due process was not idiosyncratic to philosophical anarchists of the early twentieth century. Ernst Freund, the other prominent theoretical defender of free speech in the progressive era, similarly attempted to distinguish the substantive due process defense of free speech from the substantive due process defense of laissez-faire private-property rights. Freund's writings are particularly interesting because, although he was a leading progressive jurist, "the father of American administrative law" according to his biographer,[49] his defense of free speech in the first decade of the twentieth century clearly fell within the conservative libertarian tradition. His early writings provide an important example of the constitutional arguments of a prominent progressive jurist in the years before sociological jurisprudence was developed and popularized.

In his 1904 treatise, *The Police Power*, Freund firmly rejected conservative libertarian claims that persons had a constitutional liberty to be free from government interference when deciding their terms of employment. Although he believed in private property, Freund claimed that governmental regulation of the economy was justified whenever laissez-faire policies left persons unable to exercise effectively their right of equal liberty. The liberty of contract, for example, was chimerical because one side to the bargain frequently had no practical alternative to accepting the terms dictated by the other party. State laws regulating the hours a person could work were constitutional, he declared, because private contracts inconsistent with such statutory requirements either "involve the waiver of valuable personal rights, or . . . are virtually imposed by one party without power of choice on the part of the other."[50]

Although Freund claimed that the liberty of contract was not an aspect of a person's liberty, he believed that the Fourteenth Amendment did assert a general principle of individual freedom. *The Police Power* endorsed the more general conservative libertarian claim that the due process clause gave courts the power to protect "the fundamental rights of the individual." One of those fundamental rights, Freund claimed, was "civil liberty," which included such individual liberties as the "freedom of entering into legal relations with others, and of appealing in any manner to public opinion or sentiment," "the liberty of private conduct," and "the liberty of social intercourse." From these premises, he deduced that the Fourteenth Amendment protected "the freedom of religion, of speech and press, . . . of assembly, . . . the freedom of migration, of occupation, and of association." States could not regard these "forms of activity . . . as elements of public danger" and thus subject to the police power.[51] Freund's constitution protected free speech for the same reason it protected the right to consume alcohol in private, the right to engage in a traditional occupation, and the right to associate voluntarily with members of other races.[52] All these rights were derived from the general principle of liberty that established a sphere of private conduct and association beyond the reach of governmental regulation.

Like the earlier conservative libertarian thinkers, Freund believed the Constitution protected any utterance that was not "agitation inviting the use of criminal methods for the attainment of political ends."[53] His writings endorsed the constitutional right to advocate any doctrine, no matter how inconsistent with established political ideas. "Freedom of political discussion," Freund stated, "is merely a phrase if it must stop short of questioning the fundamental ideas of politics, law and government." The assertion that "every government is justified in drawing the line of free discussion at those principles or institutions, which it deems essential to its perpetuation," was one to which he thought "the Russian government would subscribe."[54] For this reason, Freund maintained that "exposition of social wrong or injustice must be allowed"; speakers could not be punished merely because either their words might have some tendency to cause criminal actions or they appealed "to sentiment rather than reason."[55] He did think that states had the power to punish speakers who had not explicitly called for criminal conduct; however, he insisted that indirect appeals for criminal conduct could be constitutionally punished only if the state statute in question clearly declared such utterances illegal.[56]

The writings of both Schroeder and Freund raise important questions about the transformation of the modern constitutional defense of free speech. As was the case with the conservative treatise writers, their standards clearly would have protected those political dissidents arrested and convicted during World War I and the red scare. Indeed, Schroeder probably would have supported every major free-speech claim made in the twentieth century. It is even difficult to find scholarly writing that advocates a more libertarian standard of protection than his actual material injury test.[57]

Furthermore, Schroeder and Freund also demonstrated that progressives could rely on the conservative libertarian defense of free speech without committing themselves to the judicial protection of laissez-faire private-property rights. Although neither discussed the matter in detail, both jurists suggested that the due process clause of the Fourteenth Amendment guaranteed a different set of economic liberties than those advanced by conservative libertarians. Progressive intellectuals, following their analyses, could have developed constitutional arguments that protected the economic and social freedoms they believed necessary to a functional system of free speech.

Nevertheless, Schroeder and Freund represent a path not taken. Their prewar writings were ignored by those progressives who, in the years immediately before, during, and after World War I, attempted to derive their own constitutional defenses of free speech. Significantly, Schroeder's work was discussed only once by a thinker who defended free speech in the second and third decades of the twentieth century, and then it was used as an example of an overly broad interpretation of the constitutional guarantee of free speech.[58] As chapters 3 and 4 argue, progressive thinkers rejected both scholars' analyses because Schroeder and Freund based their constitutional arguments on conservative libertarian principles, not because the scope of protection they offered to expression rights was weak. By 1915, progressives were unwilling to derive free speech, or any other substantive freedom, from the general principle of liberty expressed by the due process clause of the Fourteenth Amendment, even when such an argument seemed necessary to protect political dissent. Indeed, although Freund in his wartime writings never wavered from his philosophical commitment to free speech, the broader currents of twentieth-century political thought led him to retreat from several *constitutional* claims in *The Police Power*.[59]

The New Intellectuals

Although the foundations of libertarian argument remained essentially unaltered in the years before World War I, dramatic changes in American political thought and jurisprudence occurred during the progressive era. Unlike Schroeder and Freund, prominent early twentieth-century thinkers did not simply reject judicial activism on behalf of laissez-faire private-

property rights. John Dewey and Roscoe Pound attacked conservative claims that the primary purpose of government was to
protect individual rights and that the judiciary should ensure
respect for the fundamental liberties of the citizen. Proponents
of pragmatism and sociological jurisprudence insisted that the
primary purpose of government was to advance social interests
and that legislators and executives were best able to fulfill this
function. Progressive intellectuals were primarily interested in
promoting various national and local economic reforms, but
their assertions undermined the earlier constitutional defense
of free speech as well as the constitutional defense of private
property. If Dewey and Pound were correct, then the individual's interest in expression was relatively unimportant, and its
precise weight was a matter to be determined by the elected
officials.

John Dewey's Pragmatism

Progressive hostility to the dominant elements of conservative
libertarian thought was informed by its philosophical attitude
toward the nature of truth. Truth, pragmatists declared, was
relative to the particular circumstances of a given society; it was
not an eternal object of reason. John Dewey, the most influential American thinker of the early twentieth century, asserted
that the nature of reality could be discovered not by abstract
contemplation, but only through empirical analysis. He argued
that "thinking and beliefs should be experimental not absolutis-
tic": intellectuals should treat "policies and proposals . . . as
working hypotheses" that were "subject to constant and well-
equipped observation of the consequences they entail when
acted upon, and subject to ready and flexible revision in the
light of observed consequences." "Confirmation, corrobora-
tion, verification," Dewey maintained, "lie in works, consequences."[60]

This interpretation of the nature of truth has been called "instrumentalism" because the validity of concepts are measured
by their observable consequences when applied to human
affairs, rather than by their logical structure. Thus, Dewey
claimed that "ideas, meanings, conceptions, notions, theories,

systems are instrumental to an active reorganization of the given environment." "The test of their validity and value lies in accomplishing this work." Ideas that "succeed[ed] in their office" were "reliable, sound, good, [and] true." Ideas that "fail[ed] to clear up the confusion, to eliminate the defects," were "false."[61]

Although virtually every major progressive thinker was a pragmatist, one could be a pragmatist without being a progressive. Late nineteenth-century intellectuals had also been interested in instrumental conceptions of truth. Indeed, the basic principles of American pragmatism had been developed and popularized by the beginning of the twentieth century. However, such thinkers as Charles Pierce and William James were primarily interested in exploring the "cash value" of different approaches to the philosophy of science and the philosophy of religion.[62] To the extent that James and Pierce were interested in public matters, they seemed to have been political conservatives. The originality of Dewey's works lay in his willingness to apply pragmatic epistemological methods to political philosophy and place them in the service of social reform.

In particular, Dewey insisted that the instrumental theory of truth was inconsistent with claims that justice consisted of adherence to a set of eternally valid, deductively derived individual rights. These "natural rights and natural liberties," he argued, "exist only in the kingdom of mythological social zoology." Dewey maintained that the conservative libertarian conception of justice was simply a political program that was once effective. When social conditions changed, this older conception of natural rights became obsolete. The "inherent theoretical weakness" of classical economics and Marxism, Dewey asserted, was the belief that observations supporting particular policies "at a particular date and place . . . can obviate the need for continued resort to observation, and the continual revision of generalizations in their office of working hypotheses." Thus, policies that failed to improve the human condition in the present had to be replaced, despite their past success. "Consequences in the lives of individuals" were "the criterion and measure of policy," not the neatness of its logical justification.[63]

Dewey also rejected the vision of social life underlying previous notions of individual rights. The identity of a society, he argued, was not a function of the individuals who lived in it. Because human beings were naturally associated, the identity of individuals was a function of the society in which they lived. Social forces, Dewey believed, powerfully influence every aspect of individuality. In his view, "the content of [an individual's] beliefs and intentions is a subject-matter provided by association." Persons were "social animal[s] in the make-up of [their] values, sentiments and deliberate behavior," and "not merely de facto associated."[64] Even matters as seemingly private as mental states were, in Dewey's view, social in nature. "Knowledge," he claimed, "depends upon tradition, upon tools and methods socially transmitted, developed and sanctioned."[65] Individual "faculties of effectual observation, reflection and desire" were "habits acquired under the influence of the culture and institutions of society," "not ready-made inherent powers."[66]

The moral priority of community followed from its epistemological priority. "Common good," Dewey declared, "is the measure of political organization and policy."[67] In his *Ethics*, Dewey asserted that "the only fundamental anarchy is that which regards rights as private monopolies, ignoring their social origin and intent."[68] The very idea of individual rights was a social conception and thus had to be interpreted in a manner consistent with social interests. "Individual right," Dewey wrote, "must yield to the general welfare."[69]

Dewey believed that social beings developed conceptions of individual rights because their protection was "positively in [society's] interest."[70] In most circumstances, policies that respected individual rights would foster improvement in human capacity, thereby improving the contributions that all persons could make to communal life. Only by granting a broad sphere of individual freedom could society satisfy "the moral criterion [of] . . . social institutions and political measures, . . . whether a given custom or law sets free individual capacities in such a way as to make them available for the development of the general happiness or the common good." In other words, Dewey sought institutions that would foster "the development of all the *social* capacities of every individual member of society" (emphasis added).[71]

Many progressive thinkers disagreed with the details of Dewey's analysis, but they endorsed his basic principles.[72] Although Herbert Croly is generally thought to represent the other, more nationalistic wing of progressive thought,[73] he also insisted that all political actions "must be justified by their actual or presumable functional adequacy" and that "an individual has no meaning apart from the society in which his individuality has been formed."[74] Like Dewey, Croly rejected unfettered recognition of individual rights as a basis for social life. In *The Promise of American Life,* he declared that "of all perverted conceptions of democracy, one of the most perverted and dangerous is that which identifies it exclusively with a system of individual rights." Croly claimed that individual liberty was "important, but more important still is the freedom of a whole people to dispose of its own destiny." Only those individual rights that "contribute to national perpetuity and integrity" should be protected by government.[75]

Roscoe Pound's Sociological Jurisprudence

The new generation of progressive legal scholars eagerly adopted these developments in political philosophy. Roscoe Pound, the most influential academic lawyer of the early twentieth century, described "the sociological movement in jurisprudence" as "a movement for pragmatism as a philosophy of law." A sociological jurisprudence, Pound declared, would adjust "principle and doctrines to the human conditions they are to govern rather than to assume first principles." The "human factor" would be "in the central place," and legal "logic" would be "relegated" "to its true position as an instrument."[76] Pound's writings criticized legal decisions that relied on "rigorous logical deduction from predetermined conceptions in disregard of and often in the teeth of actual facts."[77] In language harking back to Dewey, Pound asserted that law "must be judged by the result it achieves, not by the niceties of its eternal structure." Thus, he called for a "jurisprudence of ends" rather than a "jurisprudence of conceptions."[78]

Proponents of sociological jurisprudence endorsed pragmatism's rejection of individual rights. By the beginning of World War I, Pound could declare that "in jurisprudence . . . the whole doctrine of natural rights has been definitively abandoned." "All natural law theories," he argued, were "purely personal and arbitrary" because such a theory could never truly resolve social conflicts "except when all men are agreed in their moral and economic views."[79] Instead, he maintained that "the concern of the law" has always been "with social interests."[80] His writings sought to demonstrate that legal systems had historically recognized the moral priority of the community. "Certain great social interests," he argued, "have determined the growth of law from the beginning." For example, in primitive societies "injuries to the body" were "not thought of at first as infringements of an individual interest," but rather "as involving infringement of an interest of a group or kindred or of a social interest in peace and good order."[81] But, like Dewey, Pound recognized that "there is a social interest in the individual moral and social life." Thus, when "securing individual interests to this end, the law is securing a social interest."[82] In fact, Pound declared that legal doctrine should satisfy Dewey's test of political insitutions: whether they would "free individual capacities in such a way as to make them available for the development of the general happiness or common good."[83]

Sociological jurisprudence encouraged judicial activism and creativity in common law cases. In most circumstances, Pound argued, courts could achieve a "jurisprudence of ends" by devising legal doctrines that balanced the various social interests at stake in any case.[84] Just as Dewey argued that "knowledge of the past is significant only as it deepens and extends our understanding of the present," so Pound claimed that "the function of legal history [was] one of illustrating how rules and principles have met concrete situations in the past and of enabling us to judge how we may deal with such situations in the present." Precedents, he maintained, should not be understood as "furnishing self-sufficient premises from which rules are to be obtained by rigid deduction."[85] Thus, "the real genius of our common law" was its ability to "giv[e] a fresh illustration of [a] principle to a concrete case, producing a workable and just result."[86] On these grounds, Justice Benjamin Cardozo, another prominent proponent of sociological jurisprudence, stated that one of his rules for deciding cases was "when the social needs demand one settlement rather than another, there are times when we must bend symmetry, ignore history and sacrifice custom in pursuit of other and larger ends."[87]

However, progressive jurists insisted that courts assume a more restrained judicial stance when considering the constitutionality of a statute or governmental practice. Legislation, Pound argued, was increasingly the product of "long and patient study by experts, careful consideration by conferences or congresses or associations, press discussions in which public opinion is focused upon all important details, and hearings before legislative committees."[88] Judges should respect the balancing of social interests reflected in legislative output because the elected branches of government had the greater capacity for discovering and analyzing the relevant social science data underlying conflicting social claims. Courts, Pound observed, had "no machinery for getting at the facts." They did not "have the advantage of legislative reference bureaus, of hearings before committees, of the testimony of specialists who have conducted detailed investigations, as the legislature can address."[89] Furthermore, governance by elected officials was "the more truly democratic form of law-making." "Legislation," Pound insisted, was "the more direct and accurate expression of the general will."[90] When the representatives of the people, after evaluating current circumstances, enacted specific social and economic programs, judges had to be "willing to assume that the legislature did its duty and to keep its hands off on that ground."[91]

Historical knowledge of the original purposes of constitutional provisions was no substitute for judicial lack of social science expertise. Pragmatists insisted that past circumstances not dictate present policies. Judges, in their view, had no right to strike down legislation merely because some inconsistency was perceived with the intentions of the constitutional framers. The framers, Pound claimed, neither intended nor should have intended "to dictate philosophical or juristic beliefs and opinion to those who were to come after them." Instead, they should be interpreted as stating some general principles beyond the power of government to circumvent but leaving to future generations the power to interpret those principles in light of contemporary needs and circumstances. The authors of the consti-

tution "laid down principles, not rules." The particular rules
they favored were only "illustrations of these principles so long
as facts and opinions remain what they were when the rules
were announced."[92]

Pound aimed most of his fire at "the indifference, if not contempt" that many "courts and lawyers" showed to the economic regulations passed during the progressive era.[93] In particular, he held that decisions striking down legislation as
inconsistent with the freedom of contract were based on "rigorous logical deduction from predetermined conceptions in disregard of and often in the teeth of the actual facts."[94] Cases like
Lochner v. New York "exaggerate[d] private right at the expense
of public right" and were based on "ignorance of the actual situations of fact." As a result, these manifestations of "judicial
jealousy of the reform movement" "obstruct[ed] the way of social progress"; they provided "a fruitful cause of strikes, industrial discord, and consequent lawlessness."[95]

Pound believed that the original constitution, based on many
principles of natural law, probably protected certain individual
rights. Indeed, he claimed that some progressive economic legislation "might have been an unreasonable deprivation of liberty as things were even 50 years ago." However, as noted
above, he disagreed with such jurists as Cooley and Schroeder
who insisted that judges were obligated to protect the individual rights the framers had previously placed in the Constitution.
Pound maintained that courts had to consider the present implications of policies protecting those rights. The crucial constitutional question was whether regulations were "reasonable . . .
as things stand now."[96] Because courts only "have the experience of the past," but "not . . . the facts of the present," judges
were not "competent to formulate rules for new relations which
require regulation." "What court," Pound concluded, "that
passes upon industrial legislation is able or pretends to investi-
gate conditions of manufacture, to visit factories and see them
in operation, and to take the testimony of employers, employees, physicians, social workers, and economists as to the needs
of workmen and of the public, as a legislative committee may
and often does?"[97]

Although Pound's writings on constitutional theory were primarily intended to weaken the constitutional foundations of judicial activism on behalf of the individual's right to freedom of contract, said to be protected by the due process clause of the Fourteenth Amendment, Pound also believed that he successfully undermined claims that courts should strike down legislation inconsistent with the individual's right to freedom of speech. Pound made this clear in a 1915 article, "Interests of Personality." That essay recognized that the framers of the Constitution had intended to protect the individual interest in speech.[98] But Pound stated that under current circumstances that interest should have no more weight than "other individual interests of personality."[99] In free speech cases, Pound asserted, the individual's interest in free speech "must always be balanced" with those social interests threatened by the speech in question. "The social interest in the security of social institutions," "disturb[ances] to the public peace [and] shocks [to] the moral feelings of the community" were among the social interests that frequently outweighed the individual's interest in free speech. Thus, Pound endorsed Lincoln's Civil War restrictions on the press and various cases in which courts upheld restrictions on speech rights.[100]

Pound never suggested that the principles of sociological jurisprudence were hostile to every constitutional defense of free speech. In "Interests of Personality" he claimed that the social interest in open discussion provided a better ground for judicial activism on behalf of free speech. This "social interest in free belief and free expression of opinion" was one of the "guarantees of political efficiency and instruments of social progress."[101] Indeed, Pound added that past cases demonstrated "an over-insistence upon the countervailing interest of the state in its personality or over-insistence upon the social interest in the security of some particular social institution."[102]

Nevertheless, Pound did not give any examples of actual circumstances where the social interest in expression outweighed other social interests. Indeed, he *never* endorsed an opinion that protected free speech. Perhaps because "Interests of Personality" primarily discussed common law rules, Pound paid little attention to the problems that would arise when a legislature explicitly declared other social interests outweighed the social interest in free speech. Moreover, his other writings suggested that courts should give the legislature the same leeway to balance the social interest in free speech as he thought courts should give when balancing the interest in freedom of contract.

Prewar politics did not force Pound or other progressives to confront legislation that explicitly restricted free speech. For the first fifteen years of the twentieth century the elected branches of government were neither passing nor enforcing limitations on the scope of legitimate political dissent. Thus, before World War I, most progressives were unaware of the potential that pragmatism and sociological jurisprudence had for tolerating narrow interpretations of free-speech rights. The burning constitutional question of that period was the status of the freedom of contract. Pragmatism and sociological jurisprudence proved to be powerful rhetorical tools in the progressive fight for economic, political, and social reform. Because they "succeed[ed] in their office," progressives considered those ideas "reliable, sound, good, [and] true." Nevertheless, one important consequence of this wholesale adoption of pragmatism and sociological jurisprudence emerged: when federal and state governments began to pass legislation explicitly restricting political dissent, the dominant mode of legal argument in the United States was either actively hostile to the then "traditional" conservative libertarian defense of constitutional expression rights or, at best, silent about the nature of a sound constitutional defense of free speech.

Chapter Three

Progressive Responses to Free Speech Conflict, 1915–1927

During World War I and the red scare, free speech became the subject of significant national debate for the first time in modern American history.[1] Fearing national disunity and Bolshevism, Congress passed the Espionage Act of 1917 and the Sedition Act of 1918,[2] the first federal statutes to restrict the expression rights of American citizens since the Sedition Act of 1798.[3] More than two thousand people were charged with violating their provisions, and more than one thousand were convicted. Many states followed suit, passing new laws or enforcing older ones in ways that significantly curtailed radical critiques of American politics.[4] Political dissidents quickly challenged the constitutionality of these repressive practices. Appeals from adverse lower court rulings soon reached the Supreme Court, which proceeded to hand down its first major decisions on the constitutional meaning of free speech.[5]

Although, as noted in chapter 2, progressives had not seriously considered the appropriate scope of governmental power over expression before World War I, they were well prepared to examine the matter.[6] Throughout the previous fifteen years, intellectuals had developed a new philosophical language, pragmatism, and a new legal language, sociological jurisprudence, for discussing and resolving fundamental political and constitutional issues. Earlier controversies over the status of immigrants in American society anticipated questions about the place of diversity and participation in American democratic life, concerns central to wartime and postwar fights over free speech. When confronting these issues, prewar progressive reformers disputed whether the community would benefit from policies that discouraged foreign-born residents from expressing their opinions on various political and cultural matters. When the Wilson administration began arresting its left-wing critics, proponents and opponents of speech rights could rely heavily on positions they formulated in prewar debates.

Many progressives asserted that preserving social community under modern conditions required an individual conformity inconsistent with broad rights of political dissent. Immigrants had to be "Americanized," they claimed, and radical critics silenced. Others thought that only a few leaders had the social science expertise necessary to maintain social cohesion. In the eyes of Herbert Croly and Walter Lippmann, universal expression rights were unimportant, if not inefficient. Federal and state censorship was constitutional, opponents of broad advocacy rights argued, because the elected branches of government had the same, virtually unlimited power over expressive activity that proponents of sociological jurisprudence thought the people's representatives had over economic activity. In their opinion, government could regulate any form of economic or speech behavior that might adversely affect the public welfare.

Several prominent progressive thinkers, however, were committed to free-speech rights for everyone. In the early years of the twentieth century, John Dewey, Jane Addams, Louis Brandeis, and others interpreted pragmatism's emphasis on social experimentation and communitarianism as a call for social heterogeneity and an active citizenry. They first promulgated these values in the early twentieth century while defending cultural pluralism, educational reform, and industrial democracy. When proponents of cultural homogeneity moved to unify political opinion during World War I and the red scare, many reformers who identified with the more locally oriented wing of the progressive movement claimed that protection and promotion of expression was another important way to foster much needed diversity and participation.

Dewey, Addams, and Brandeis were the first representatives of an emerging civil libertarian tradition. They stressed the social interest in debate about matters of public importance and denigrated those purely personal benefits of self-expression that such earlier libertarians as Cooley, Burgess, and Schroeder had emphasized. More generally, the new generation of libertarians spoke of the ways in which free speech contributed to a democratic social life, a life infused by democratic social policies as well as democratic political procedures. While both civil and conservative libertarians claimed that democratic societies must protect expressive behavior, Dewey, Addams, and Brandeis contended that such associations also had to regulate economic activity to ensure that all citizens had the resources necessary to participate effectively in the public life of their communities.

At its inception, however, the new civil libertarian tradition faced a severe constitutional crisis. Although the philosophical advantages of open political debate could be both defended and attacked by arguments wholly derived from the fundamental concepts of pragmatism, the principles of sociological jurisprudence seemed to condemn unequivocally any judicial activism on behalf of constitutional expression rights. As noted in chapter 2, early twentieth-century reformers opposed legal claims that were based on abstract principles of individual right, and they thought that courts should not second-guess the ways in which the elected branches of government had balanced various social interests in political conflicts. More generally, progressive jurists asserted that no principled distinction existed between judicial activism on behalf of the freedom of contract and judicial activism on behalf of the freedom of speech. Any constitutional defense of the latter, they thought, would implicitly defend the former, and proponents of sociological jurisprudence were not prepared to advance any argument that implied that *Lochner v. New York* might not have been a gross abuse of judicial power. Early civil libertarians were as fully committed to these propositions as were the advocates of restrictions on speech. Thus, they had difficulty translating their philosophical claims into constitutional arguments. If progressive proponents of open discussion failed to convince legislatures that the social interest in free speech outweighed the potential costs of advocacy, then their democratic principles seemed to preclude the possibility of an appeal to the judiciary.

In spite of these obstacles, Oliver Wendell Holmes, Jr., Ernst Freund, Learned Hand, and Louis Brandeis all issued celebrated attacks on judicial opinions that affirmed the convictions of political dissenters arrested during World War I and the red scare. Contemporary libertarians typically treat those utterances as the foundations of modern judicial solicitude for the liberty of discussion. Nevertheless, although these progressive jurists effusively praised the philosophical virtues of free speech, their writings did not attempt to refute the new constitutional attack on expression rights. Rhetorical flourishes aside, Holmes actually protected only the rights of obscure speakers. Freund and Hand conceded that Congress had the constitutional power to prohibit verbal opposition to the war and war policies, but they interpreted the Espionage Act as not criminalizing such speech. Brandeis defended prominent radical activists but admitted that such protection was inconsistent with his conception of the judicial function. He confessed that he would have dutifully refused to protect the liberty of discussion had conservative justices correctly refused to protect the liberty of contract. However, the principle of stare decisis, Brandeis insisted, obligated his brethren to strike down state restrictions on political dissent because speech was another aspect of the mistaken conception of constitutional freedom that the Court was using to protect property rights. Although temporarily successful, this line of argument would leave the liberty of discussion bereft of constitutional foundation in that not too distant day when *Lochner* and similar cases were no longer usable precedents.

The New Attack on Free Speech

Few progressive reformers were troubled by the difficulty of constructing a constitutional defense of free speech that was consistent with the principles of sociological jurisprudence. Most prominent early twentieth-century proponents of federal and state economic regulations also supported federal and state speech regulations. As numerous scholars have noted, progressive efforts to "discipline American society" and the progressive "appetite for national unity" were responsible for the restrictions placed on political debate during the second decade of the twentieth century.[7] Theodore Roosevelt, whose presidency ushered in the progressive era, endorsed "legislation, no matter how extreme, that will reach men who vilify and defame America."[8] Progressive members of the Wilson administration wrote, proposed, and enforced the Espionage and Sedition Acts. The most notorious red-baiter of the postwar era, Attorney General A. Mitchell Palmer, was a nationally known political reformer in the prewar years.[9]

Cultural Nationalism

Progressive calls for state censorship stemmed from their particular sensitivity to the threats that industrialization, urbanization, and immigration presented to the socially homogeneous small rural communities of nineteenth-century America.[10] Prominent intellectuals claimed that only self-conscious governmental policies designed to promote national cultural uniformity could reproduce these communities under twentieth-century conditions. As part of their effort to create a shared national ethos, many reformers called for positive federal programs to prevent foreign-born residents from transplanting their political and cultural institutions to American shores. Immigrants had to be "Americanized" if they were to shed allegiances to foreign governments and ideas.

The Americanization movement's emphasis on active government intervention reflected its strong progressive tinge. Frances Kellor, the longtime head of the National Americanization Committee, was a former Roosevelt aide and a member of the National Committee of the Progressive party. Assimilation, she and her associates maintained, could be achieved only through social planning; new arrivals would not spontaneously acquire uniform characteristics and values as the older, conservative, laissez-faire image of the melting pot suggested.[11] Kellor endorsed governmental employment agencies and stricter federal control of interstate businesses in order to eliminate the "causes of disorder,

unrest and disloyalty" among aliens. If the economic carrot did
not induce cultural and political loyalty, she called for the censor's stick. A central part of any national immigration policy, Kellor insisted, had to be government regulation of speech designed
to "[stamp] out . . . sedition and disloyalty wherever found."[12]

Before World War I, Americanizers emphasized instruc-
tional programs. However, the threat of war brought out the
more coercive elements of this movement.[13] In 1916, the Democratic party platform attacked organizations whose object "is
calculated and tends to divide our people into antagonistic
groups and thus to destroy that complete agreement and solidarity of the people . . . so essential to the perpetuity of free
institutions." Woodrow Wilson spoke of the need to suppress
those aliens who, despite being "welcomed under our generous
naturalization laws to the full freedom and opportunity of America, . . . poured the poison of disloyalty into the very arteries of
our national life." Henry Clayton, the sponsor of the antitrust
bill that bears his name, asserted that immigrants who attacked
American institutions "should get off the face of the earth, or at
least go back to the country they left."[14]

The actual declaration of war heightened this concern for national solidarity. Wilson informed potential opponents of his
policies that "for us there is but one choice. . . . Woe be to the
man or group of men that seeks to stand in our way in this day of
high resolution."[15] Although no American was immune to this
pressure for conformity, progressive nationalists particularly
feared that first- and second-generation immigrants were not
sufficiently loyal to permit the unified effort necessary for martial triumph. These worries seemed confirmed when the heavily foreign-born American Socialist party refused to support the
war effort. In this atmosphere, many Americans confused suppression of the political dissident with suppression of the disloyal
immigrant. As William Preston observed, "a fateful and erroneous identification of alien and radical was firmly implanted in
the public mind."[16]

This misunderstanding was particularly evident in the events
surrounding *Abrams v. United States*. Jacob Abrams, an obscure
anarchist, was arrested after he scattered leaflets that called on

munitions workers to strike in protest of American interference with the Russian Revolution. During his trial, Federal District Judge Clayton repeatedly reminded the jury of the defendant's alien status and several times asked Abrams, "Why don't you go back to Russia?" When sentencing Abrams and his codefendants, Clayton informed those assembled in the courtroom that "you can never get the American idea into the head of an anarchist."[17] Proponents of Clayton's actions shared this belief that only foreigners could hold certain left-wing doctrines. John Wigmore, a prominent progressive legal reformer, determined that "there was nothing spontaneous, nothing American, in [the *Abrams* defendants]." Abrams and his cohorts were "alien agents, who relied primarily on an appeal to the thousands of alien-born and alien-parented of their own races earning a livelihood in this country."[18]

Xenophobia continued to be closely associated with censorship after the war. Federal speech policies during the red scare placed far greater emphasis on expelling alien radicals than on imprisoning native political dissidents. The Justice Department informed the Bureau of Investigation (soon to become the FBI) that surveillance "should be particularly directed to persons, not citizens of the United States, with a view of obtaining deportation cases."[19] Although the federal government did not force many dissidents to leave the country, Emma Goldman and the *Abrams* defendants were among the persons sent back to Europe.[20]

The American Legion, the leading postwar opponent of broad free-speech rights, grew out of the Americanization movement.[21] Echoing the concerns of many prewar progressive reformers, that organization promoted state regulations of both commercial and expressive behavior. Legion commanders in the 1920s supported many economic reforms, most notably child welfare legislation, called for a halt to all immigration, particularly of persons "loath to accept our institutions," and demanded restrictions on radical expression. When Legion lobbyists asked Congress to enact peacetime sedition statutes that would "rid our country of this scum who hate our country, our flag, and who refuse to perform their duties," the "scum" in question were typically thought to be the foreign-born. "Communist activities," National Commander Homer Chaillaux confidently asserted, "are led within the United States by those who are to a shocking degree aliens."[22]

The Administrative State

Although most early twentieth-century intellectuals did not share this overt hostility to aliens or free speech, several prominent progressive thinkers advanced a vision of American society that was largely indifferent to expression rights. Herbert Croly and Walter Lippmann believed that if, as pragmatism asserted, truths could be discovered only by thorough examination of social science data, then only social science experts were capable of making public policy. For this reason, the chief editors of the *New Republic* sought to redefine democracy in terms of an enlightened bureaucratic elite who would legitimate their power through providing material benefits to all citizens. Croly endorsed "a democracy . . . of selective individuals, who are obliged constantly to justify their selection" by being "devoted to the welfare of the whole people."[23]

In this new society, the opinions of the unenlightened masses were as relevant to the administrative expert as the opinions of those in Plato's cave were to the philosopher-king. Speech by uninformed laypersons did not contribute to and might even distract from the truth- or progress-seeking processes of the scientific method. *The Promise of American Life*, Croly's main opus, implicitly commented on the importance of free speech by ignoring the subject.[24] Walter Lippmann's *Public Opinion* contended that most people, incapable of developing "sound public opinions on the whole business of government," were far more concerned with government output than government input. Leadership that improved the quality and quantity of consumer goods available to the public, Lippmann claimed, could ignore the diffuse musings of public debate. Elites did not have to respond "to the self-centered opinions that happen to be floating around in men's minds." Lippmann implied that political leaders could restrict expression when doing so might raise the standard of living. Their performance was only judged by whether they were "producing a certain minimum of health, of decent housing, of material necessities, of education, of freedom, of pleasures, of beauty."[25]

Lippmann and Croly did oppose the excesses of government censorship during World War I, but they opposed the excesses, not the censorship. The *New Republic* did not object to restrictions on political dissent that were well-administered, presumably by impartial bureaucrats. Soon after war was declared, that journal proposed that "if we are to have censorship, let it be centralized in competent hands." Lippmann urged Wilson to appoint censors who had "real insight and democratic feeling."[26] Only when a number of "super-patriots" sought to repress advocacy of the position that the Allies should declare their war aims while fighting continued did the *New Republic* unambiguously defend free speech. Intelligent persons, the editors recognized, would never censor any position championed by the wise men at the *New Republic*.[27]

The Progressive Origins of the Bad Tendency Test

When speech restrictions were challenged in federal courts, proponents of cultural nationalism and the administrative state asserted that the national and state governments had broad constitutional power to regulate political dissent. Following Pound, they insisted speech be treated no differently than any other activity that might threaten the achievement of social goals. A note in the *Harvard Law Review* stated that it was "for Congress to judge, in the light of existing conditions, . . . as to the kind and amount of repression necessary." Progressive jurists noted that state power over advocacy, like state power over the economy, was not limited by the specific standards of protection favored by the framers of the First Amendment. That particular speech prohibitions might have been unconstitutional in the past did not affect the national legislature's capacity to respond to the changed circumstances of the present. Charles Warren, chief author of the Espionage Act, reminded Americans "that a course of conduct or acts, under modern conditions, may render vital aid and comfort to the enemy, where similar conduct would not have done so in earlier days." Because of improvements in communication technology, he claimed, the federal government had to have the power to punish persons who uttered "statements either true or false of existing conditions or facts, the knowledge or belief in truth of which . . . would tend to diminish the effective[ness] of the United States."[28]

Elected officials, many early twentieth-century jurists declared, were both authorized and best able to estimate the costs and benefits of permitting advocacy of particular doctrines. For this reason, progressive supporters of government censorship endorsed the bad tendency test, a standard permitting legislatures to regulate any speech that might cause some social harm. Day Kimball insisted that congressional decisions limiting political dissent "should be respected by the courts unless palpably unreasonable." Similarly, Wigmore maintained that "a statute does not abridge the constitutional freedom of speech if it forbids A's exhortation of B to do a specific act which would have consequences deemed by the legislature to be deleterious to the commonwealth."[29]

This interpretation of the constitutional meaning of free speech was most fully developed in the writings of Edward Corwin, a scholar committed to the proposition that the "first requirement of the Constitution of a progressive society is that it keep pace with that society."[30] In the *War Cyclopedia*, a pamphlet written to publicize the government's interpretation of the war and war measures, Corwin declared that the federal "power to pass all laws that are 'necessary and proper' " to achieve national purposes provided a sufficient constitutional foundation for the Espionage and Sedition Acts. "Freedom of the press in war time," he contended, "rests largely with the discretion of Congress."[31]

Unlike many early twentieth-century conservative thinkers, Corwin thought that Congress could also restrict speech in peacetime. The Constitution, he maintained, vested the national legislature with the general power to ban any utterance that might injure the public. In two articles published immediately after the war, Corwin asserted that "Congress . . . may forbid words which are intended to endanger [national] interests if in the exercise of a fair legislative discretion it finds it necessary and proper to do so."[32] Judges, he added, should not overturn legislative decisions on the ground that they believed the expression in question was not sufficiently dangerous. If a doctrine had some tendency to cause social evils, then the people had the constitutional right to forbid its advocacy. The relationship between a given speech and harmful social consequences, Corwin concluded, was "largely in the custody of legislative majorities and of juries, which . . . is just where the framers of the Constitution intended it to be."[33]

Corwin frequently pointed out that this bad tendency test was the same standard that proponents of sociological jurisprudence applied whenever litigants challenged the constitutionality of any governmental regulation. His contributions to the *War Cyclopedia* asserted that the "necessary and proper" clause vested Congress with broad power to interfere with both the liberty of speech and the liberty of contract. Courts, he maintained, must "sustain any legislation which is reasonably calculated to promote the general welfare, if there is no other objection to it other than its effect on private rights."[34] Indeed, the general progressive revulsion against all individual liberties was the first premise of Corwin's attack on constitutional free-speech rights. While under "the uncomplicated conditions of frontier life" one might have been able to talk meaningfully of "inalienable rights," he claimed that under modern conditions, "the pursuit of happiness has become a joint-stock enterprise in which the welfare of all is embarked."[35] Corwin opposed "the curtailment of legislative discretion by definitive, unbending constitutional limitations," whether in the name of an individual's expression or property rights.[36]

Virtually every progressive indictment of judicial activism on behalf of expression rights repeated this assertion that the freedom of speech had no higher constitutional status than the freedom of contract. J. P. Hall, dean of the University of Chicago Law School, claimed that "private property, liberty of contract, of occupation, free speech, even life itself, are not absolute goods to be preserved rigidly under all circumstances alike." "The value and the protection they receive," he insisted, "are always relative to the dominant social needs." In a frequently cited article, Warren maintained that the due process clause of the Fourteenth Amendment should be used only to protect an individual's procedural rights at trial. Judicial declarations that found personal economic and expressive freedoms in that provision "awaken serious thoughts as to whether there is not danger now that the 'liberty' of the states is being unduly sacrificed to this new conception of the 'liberty' of the individual." For these reasons, progressive defenders of Supreme Court opinions sustaining restrictions on political dissent concluded that those decisions were right for the same reason that the *Lochner* case was wrong. "Those who have often condemned judicial refusal to give effect to so called 'liberal' legislation, because the refusal seemed to them based upon individual opinions of desirability," Day Kimball declared, "should not reverse their position now that the shoe pinches the other foot."[37]

This progressive attack on judicial activism on behalf of expression rights not only struck at all the foundations of conservative libertarian jurisprudence, but it also seemed even to vitiate the limited speech-protective claims made by many early twentieth-century conservative opponents of free speech. As noted in chapter 1, such conservatives as G. P. Garrett, Pierce Butler, and Edward Sanford suggested that peacetime speech restrictions could only forbid the advocacy of doctrines attacking the principles of republican government. Corwin and others claimed that elected officials could forbid the advocacy of any doctrine that might have a bad tendency. Progressive opponents of expression rights did not think that states could bar antirepublican speech that lacked a bad tendency, but this concession was worthless in light of their claim that courts should rarely, if ever, challenge a legislative decision that advocacy of certain doctrines might threaten other social interests. Indeed, the greatest strength of the new attack on judicial activism on behalf of free speech was that the principles underlying the bad tendency test could be endorsed by persons opposed to the new philosophical attack on free speech. Whatever one considered the constitutional meaning of free speech, Corwin and others believed that such rights had to be vindicated in the legislature, not the courtroom.

The New Philosophical Defense of
Free Speech

Although the fundamental principles of progressive thought supported represssive doctrines and practices, they did not inexorably lead early twentieth-century reformers to propose or tolerate state censorship. Pragmatism also provided a foundation for a new, civil libertarian defense of expression rights. Long before the United States entered World War I intellectuals associated with the grassroots, communitarian side of progressivism had insisted that democratic societies must foster diversity and participation.[38] Addams, Dewey, Brandeis, and others maintained that the scientific method would not function efficiently and the community would not be fully unified unless the polity encouraged citizens to express a wide variety of opinions on matters of public interest.

The Nature of a Democratic Society

Figuratively speaking, September 18, 1889, might be considered the birth date of the civil libertarian tradition. On that day, Jane Addams moved into Hull-House. This famous settlement house was designed to facilitate dialogue between native-born Americans and recently arrived immigrants. "It was the function of the settlements," she declared, "to bring into the circle of knowledge and fuller life, men and women who might otherwise be left outside."[39] Unlike proponents of cultural nationalism, Addams believed that communities would profit if they promoted varied life-styles, customs, and cultures. She asserted that "the foundation and guarantee of Democracy" was "diversified human experience." "To continually suspect, suppress or fear any large group in a community," she insisted, "must finally result in a loss of enthusiasm for that type of government which gives free play to the self-development of a majority of its citizens."[40] Unlike proponents of the administrative state, Addams thought that citizens should not be passive consumers of material goods. In her view, "good government [was] no substitute for self-government," and "modern social science" had refuted the

notion "that the people must be led into the ways of righteous-
ness by the experience, acumen and virtues of the great man."[41]

Addams regarded "democracy" as "an attempt at self-expression for each man," which required at a minimum "that different
policies be freely discussed and that each party shall have an opportunity for at least a partisan presentation of its contentions."
Democratic societies, in her view, established and encouraged
citizens to take advantage of their broad free-speech rights. For
this reason, she preferred political bosses to impartial experts because "the former at least are engaged in that great moral effort
of getting the mass to express itself."[42] At Hull-House, every
radical in the city of Chicago was permitted to advocate his or her
particular programs, and the settlement sponsored various clubs
in which persons could learn about and discuss the political and
social issues of the day.[43]

Like other progressives, Addams was quite concerned with
the breakdown of traditional communal life. However, she
thought that in the twentieth century, expression of diverse
opinions was essential to the formation of lasting social bonds. "It
is difficult to see how the notion of a higher civic life can be fostered," she claimed, "save through common intercourse." These
frequent interactions created the mutual values necessary for
harmonious communal existence. When "men, however far
apart in outward circumstances . . . meet as individuals beneath
a friendly roof [and] open their minds to each," Addams declared, "their 'class theories' [will be] insensibly modified by
the kindly attrition of personal acquaintance."[44]

John Dewey shared this desire to create a political community
of active and diverse citizens. A democratic society, he proclaimed, was one that made "provision for participation in its
good of all of its members on equal terms" and encouraged the
"interaction of the different forms of associated life." Like Addams, he thought democracy meant "diversification" and called
for communal institutions that gave all citizens "a responsible
share . . . in shaping the aims and policies of the[ir] social
groups."[45] Diversity and participation were valuable because
they were necessary to the effective functioning of the scientific method, a method Dewey identified with both pragmatism
and the democratic process. With respect to both science and

politics, Dewey observed, "lack of the free and equitable intercourse which springs from a variety of shared interests makes
intellectual stimulation unbalanced. Diversity of stimulation
means novelty, and novelty means challenge." He insisted that
"every combination of human forces" has "its own unique and
ultimate worth."[46]

To reap the benefits of heterogeneity, both the technical and
democratic communities had to protect and encourage expression. "It is the nature of science," Dewey claimed, "not so much
to tolerate as to welcome diversity of opinion." He added that
"freedom of inquiry, toleration of diverse views, freedom of
communication" were "involved in the democratic as in the scientific method."[47] Believing that "the democratic method is persuasion through public discussion," Dewey continually stressed
the importance of a system of communication adequate to modern industrial society. "The essential need of modern life," he
argued, "is the improvement of the methods and conditions of
debate, discussion and persuasion." At the very least, advances in
speech technology would assist the "constant watchfulness and
criticism by citizens" that was necessary for "a state [to] be maintained in integrity and usefulness."[48]

Dewey agreed with those who thought that open public debate would eventually promote social consensus on fundamental principles. Persons, he argued, "must have an equable opportunity to receive and to take from others" if they were "to
have a large number of values in common."[49] However, in his
view, the real significance of the scientific method was its capacity to further civic unity by adjudicating the factual bases of
public controversies. "The importance of 'methods of inquiry,' "
Dewey observed, "is that they bring new facts to light and by doing so establish the basis for consensus of beliefs." Once the scientific method disclosed the probable consequences of various
policies, citizens could easily identify the measures that best advanced the welfare of the community. By "publically and scienti-
fically weigh[ing]" conflicting claims, civic discourse enabled
"the public interest [to] be disclosed and made effective." Empirical investigation would settle political disputes "in the interest of the widest possible contribution to the interests of all,"
rather than in the narrow interest of a particular social class.[50]

Louis Brandeis was the third prominent progressive to advance this pluralistic vision of American public life. His writings urged adherence to "the democratic principle" that "each people has in it something of peculiar value which it can contribute to that civilization for which we are all striving." "America," he claimed, "has believed that in differentiation, not in uniformity, lies the path of progress."[51] Throughout his life, Brandeis advocated policies that would best contribute to "the making of men and women who shall be free self-respecting members of a democracy." These self-respecting individuals actively participated in their governance and were not willing to defer to a bureaucratic elite that might supply them with more consumer goods. "Among a free people," he insisted, "there can be no self-constituted body of men possessing the power to decide what the action of the whole people shall be."[52]

Citizens of democratic societies enjoyed and frequently exercised broad expression rights. "Differences in opinions," Brandeis maintained, "are not only natural but desirable where the question is difficult; for only through such differences do we secure the light and fuller understanding which are necessary to a wise decision." For this reason, he urged communities to reserve public areas for speech making "in every park." Such policies would best unite American society. "Unity," Brandeis declared, "implies interest and participation, [not] absence of discord."[53]

Other important early civil libertarians contributed to this understanding of democratic society. Ernst Freund, for example, promoted administrative law standards that would prevent specialized agencies from choking off popular participation in politics. In contrast to Lippmann and Croly, he thought that bureaucratic expertise "ought to be confined to non-controversial matters of a technical character." "Had a commission of economy and efficiency presided over American government from the beginning," Freund observed, "it would tax the imagination to think of the millions that might have been saved from waste." But that benefit could have occurred only at the cost of "that spirit of individualism, that glamour of liberty, that made American institutions attractive to aliens coming to this country."[54]

Horace Kallen, one of Dewey's former students, declared that "democracy dares to endow each citizen with the task that Plato . . . left to heartily trained and expert few." As he noted elsewhere, "the factual equivalent for democracy is social heterogeneity and intellectual diversification." Randolph Bourne, another former student of Dewey, identified "all human progress" with "novelty and non-conformity." He deplored the "universal American practice of organizing our institutional life in every department with Boards of Governors, Directors, and Trustees" as demonstrating that the "spirit of American government" was "inherently oligarchic." "Democracy," Bourne feared, "may come to mean that the individual feels himself somehow expressed . . . in whatever the crowd chooses to do."[55]

The democratic vision of early civil libertarians preserved many insights of the conservative libertarian past. Both the civil and conservative libertarian traditions considered political and industrial paternalism as the greatest threat to human development. Sumner anticipated the gist of Addams's attack on the administrative state when he claimed that the way to be charitable was to "help a man to help himself, by opening the chances around him." Increasing participatory opportunities, he maintained, put persons "in a position to add to the wealth of the community by putting new powers in operation to produce."[56] No conservative libertarian would have objected to either Bourne's assertion that "the modern ethic demands the development of the personal potentialities of every human being" or Dewey's claim that "the supreme test of all political institutions and industrial arrangements shall be the contribution they make to the all-around growth of every member of society."[57] Late nineteenth-century intellectuals recognized the value of diversity as well. Spencer, for example, declared that "the entire assemblage of societies thus fulfills the law of evolution by increase of heterogeneity."[58]

Early civil libertarians also maintained the conservative libertarian tradition's affinity for the small community as the forum where citizens could most effectively express and govern themselves. Dewey contended that the system of freedom of expression would function only if "political organization" was "on the basis of small units, small enough so that all its members could have direct communication with one another and take care of all community affairs." "Democracy," he insisted, "must begin at home, and its home is the neighborly community." Kallen thought that "in the familial relations of the village community . . . there prevails a significant democracy which is the dimmed original and minatory criterion of all larger forms."[59] Brandeis particularly was known for his opposition to large organizations; his major work was appropriately titled *The Curse of Bigness*. In this and other writings he argued that large organizations necessarily outstripped the capacities of those who ran them, discouraged innovation, and failed to offer significant scope for mass participation.[60] Although Brandeis usually defended governmental efforts to regulate the economy, he supported the Court's decision to strike down the National Recovery Act because he felt that the early New Deal gave too much power to the national government. Brandeis told federal officials that such "broad powers cannot be centralized in the Federal Government." "As for your young men," he concluded, "tell them to go back to the States. That is where they must do their work."[61]

These similarities suggest that, contrary to the central theme of this book, American libertarians have historically shared a common vision of the nature of a democratic society. But proponents of the single free-speech tradition do not point to this mutual commitment to participation, diversity, and small communities when defending their monolithic interpretation of libertarian theory in the United States. Rather, as noted in the introduction, contemporary civil libertarians insist that all previous defenders of free speech shared their understanding of the nature of free-speech rights and the relationship between the systems of private property and free speech. In these areas, early civil libertarian thought represented a fundamental break with the conservative libertarian tradition.

Progressive thinkers refused to defend the freedom of speech "as a merely individual right." "Democratic ideals," Brandeis insisted, "cannot be attained through emphasis merely upon the rights of man."[62] Instead, the new generation of libertarians maintained that the proper foundation of the philosophical defense of expression rights was the social interest in the spread of public truth and intelligence. Addams asserted that it was necessary to abandon "the eighteenth century philosophy upon which so much of our democratic theory depends." Persons, she said, must look at "social matters from the social standpoint."[63] Dewey declared that "liberalism has to assume the responsibility for making it clear that intelligence is a social asset and is clothed with a function as public as its origin."[64] Indeed, Brandeis suggested that public discussion of diverse political opinions so benefited the community that expression was more a social obligation than a personal right. The "full and free exercise of [free speech] by the citizen," he maintained, "is ordinarily also his duty; for its exercise is more important to the nation than it is to himself."[65]

Early civil libertarians also offered a new interpretation of the economic prerequisites of a functioning system of free expression. Although the scientific method did not require that such a conclusion be drawn,[66] these supporters of expression rights asserted that government had to regulate economic life if it wished to protect and foster discussion of important public questions. Kallen thought that society must restrict commercial freedom "to provide the conditions under which actual cultural groups might attain . . . cultural perfection." His fellow progressive pluralists agreed that government should abandon laissez-faire economic policies that once promoted political equality because such practices no longer served that purpose. "It is sheer perversion," Dewey claimed, "to hold that there is anything in Jeffersonian democracy that forbids political action to bring about equalization of economic conditions in order that the equal right of all to free choice and free action be maintained." In his view, "socialized economy is the means of free individual development as the end."[67]

More generally, early civil libertarian reformers called for a new conception of positive liberty to replace the older idea of laissez-faire. "Mere negative freedom," Bourne declared, "will never do as a twentieth century principle." Dewey insisted that "organized society must use its powers to establish the conditions under which the mass of individuals can possess actual as distinct from merely legal liberty." Thus, government had to regulate commercial and educational institutions so that all citizens would be provided with the wherewithal necessary to use meaningfully their more fundamental liberties. Persons, Dewey contended, enjoyed "effective freedom" only if they had "(1) positive control of the resources to carry purposes into effect, possession of the means to satisfy desires; and (2) mental equipment with the trained powers of initiative and reflection requisite for circumspect and far-seeing desires."[68]

Early civil libertarians thought that several elements of unregulated industrial life threatened the functioning of democratic societies. In their view, modern industrial conditions created an economic dependence inconsistent with political freedom. Brandeis observed that a person cannot "be really free who is constantly in danger of becoming dependent for mere subsistence upon somebody and something else than his own exertion and conduct." "If the Government permits conditions to exist which make large classes of citizens financially dependent," then government should assume, "or cause to be assumed by others, in some form the burden incident to its own shortcomings."[69] Progressive defenders of free speech claimed that material deprivations left most persons "so overburdened with toil that there is no leisure nor energy left for the cultivation of the mind." "Freedom of thought," Dewey noted, is "next to impossible for the masses of men so long as their economic conditions are precarious, and their main problem is to keep the wolf from their doors."[70] Governmental oversight of business conditions was, thus, needed to ensure that persons had the time as well as the independence necessary for effectively exercising their free-speech rights. Brandeis claimed that in a democracy all persons had a right to "free time when body and mind are sufficiently fresh to permit of mental effort."[71]

Finally, early civil libertarians maintained that unmanaged economic inequality enabled well-off persons to monopolize the material and cultural resources necessary to effective freedom. Progressive intellectuals claimed that these goods were social in nature and should therefore be distributed equally. "The common stock of intellectual enjoyment," Addams declared, "should not be difficult of access because of the economic position of him who would approach it."[72] In the hands of one social group these assets could be used to shape the very preferences that persons brought into the marketplace of ideas. Dewey declared that in "back of the appropriation by the few of the material resources of society lies the appropriation by the few in behalf of their own ends of the cultural, the spiritual, resources."[73] Thus, progressive defenders of free speech insisted that, at the very least, government had to regulate economic life to keep both the press and the academy out of the exclusive control of one class.[74]

Early Civil Libertarian Activity

In spite of their call for greater public solicitude for expression rights, Addams, Dewey, Brandeis, and other early civil libertarians did not play an active role in local free-speech fights during the progressive era. However, these early civil libertarians articulated their speech-protective vision of democratic societies in several prewar national controversies. The political debate that most united them concerned the place of the immigrant in American society. While cultural pluralists did not explicitly claim that foreign-born residents had the right to free speech, a right that the Americanization movement did not question until World War I,[75] they maintained that communities would benefit from the presence of persons with different cultural attachments. Thus, civil libertarians involved in the settlement movement encouraged new arrivals to "preserve and keep . . . whatever of value their past life contained." "The problem," Dewey declared, "is not to reduce them to an anonymous and drilled homogeneity, but to see to it that all get from one another the best that each strain has to offer from its own tradition and culture." Addams asserted that "democratic government . . . should include the experiences and hopes of all the varied people among us."[76] Implicit in these claims was the premise that immigrants should be permitted and encouraged to express their distinctive political and cultural commitments. Americans, pluralists recognized, would only realize the benefits of heterogeneity if these diverse perspectives were made public.

The early American Zionist movement was another haven for cultural pluralists. Although many assimilated Jews believed that one could not be loyal to both an American and a Jewish state, progressive Zionists argued that an Israeli nation would encourage a flowering of Hebraic culture in the United States. Jews active in the Zionist movement would then contribute more to both nations.[77] Brandeis helped lead this faction of American Judaism. In a number of speeches he declared that his "approach to Zionism was through Americanism"[78] and Americanism meant cultural pluralism. Brandeis insisted that "America has believed that each race had something of peculiar value which it can contribute to the attainment of those high ideals for which it is striving." Hence, social institutions should "preserve for America the good that is in the immigrant and develop in him the best of which he is capable." "The new nationalism adopted by America," he concluded, "proclaims that each race or people, like each individual, has the right and duty to develop, and that only through such differentiated development will high civilization be attained."[79]

In the second decade of the twentieth century, Randolph Bourne and Horace Kallen contended that cultural pluralism should be the public philosophy of the United States. Their writings proposed that America consider itself the "orchestra of mankind," a "cosmopolitan federation of national colonies."[80] "Its form," Kallen declared, "would be that of a federal republic; its substance a democracy of nationalities." Such a society would achieve "the perfection of men according to their kind" by "cooperating voluntarily and autonomously through common institutions in the enterprise of self-realization."[81] These heterogeneous communities would significantly enrich their members' lives. "Meeting now with this common American background," Bourne envisioned, "all of them may yet retain that distinctiveness of their nature, cultures and their national spiritual slants. They are more valuable and interesting to each other for being different."[82]

Both younger and older cultural pluralists agreed that immigrants could best contribute to American society by retaining and contributing to their particular cultures. In contrast to their political opponents, who feared that such diverse expression would undermine the American way of life, early civil libertarians saw immigrant speech as a means for revitalizing or strengthening native institutions. Bourne maintained that "it is not the Jew who sticks proudly to the faith of his fathers and boasts of that venerable culture who is dangerous to America, but the Jew who has lost the Jewish fire." "To be good Americans," Brandeis told a Zionist group, "we must be better Jews."[83]

Early civil libertarians raised free-speech issues more straight-forwardly in other prewar reform efforts. Throughout his life, Dewey maintained that "it is through education in its broadest sense that the right of thought and sympathy become effective." The school, he stated, was where democratic citizens acquired the skills necessary "to judge men and measures wisely and to take a determining part in the making as well as obeying laws." Because students mastered these abilities by speaking freely in their classrooms, Dewey urged educators to discourage rote memorization of historical data and develop participatory activities that challenged their pupils' creative talents. "A spirit of free communication, of interchange of ideas, suggestions, results, both successes and failures of previous experiences," he asserted, "becomes the dominating note of the recitation."[84] Dewey's philosophical allies also endorsed educational policies that prepared students to express themselves in both the classroom and the broader community. Bourne, for example, declared that schools must encourage pupils to be "uneasy, restless, [and] questioning," in order to make "them fit . . . to administer a free society."[85]

Brandeis established his national reputation in the fight for free speech in the workplace. "Rule by the people," he contended, "involves industrial democracy as well as political democracy." Because "the greatest developer is responsibility," Brandeis insisted that the "aim" of working people should be "participation in responsibility for the conduct of business; and . . . the eventual assumption of full responsibility—as in co-operative enterprise."[86] For employees to realize these ambitions, their speech had to be effective as well as free. Brandeis argued that industrial democracy meant "not only a voice, but a vote,—not merely a right to be heard, but a position through which labor may participate in management."[87] Governance of the workplace was another of Dewey's major themes. In his "Freedom of Thought and Work," he declared that "freedom

of speech and of the franchise is now significant because it is
part of the struggle for freedom of mind in industry, freedom to
participate in its planning and conduct." Addams agreed. "The
democratic ideal," she added, "urges the workmen to demand
representation in the administration of industry."[88]

Early civil libertarians became directly involved in free-
speech conflict when the government began arresting political
dissidents in the summer of 1917. More than a year before Chafee
published his first thoughts on free speech, Dewey wrote a series
of articles for the *New Republic* attacking censorship laws and
practices. Although he did "not [question] the importance of social solidarity, of unity of action, in war times," Dewey "denied
. . . the efficacy of force to remove disunion of thought and feeling." Indeed, he charged that cultural nationalists who "permitted themselves such unbridled denunciation of our immigrant
population" during the war were guilty of obstructing the national unity they professed to foster. Americanizers, Dewey stated, "are not morally innocent of promoting disunion through the
distrust they have sown of all who dared to differ from them in
matters of policy."[89]

Dewey's *New Republic* articles rejected earlier claims that
personal expression rights could be maintained against the general welfare. There was "something rather funny," he thought,
"in the spectacle of ultra-socialists rallying to the banner of Elihu
Root with its inscription of individual rights and constitutional
guarantees." Instead, he emphasized the pressing social importance of political expression. "Attempts to repress discussion of
unpopular ideas and criticisms of governmental action foster[ed]
intellectual inertness," and this "absence of thought, apathy of
intelligence [was] the chief enemy to freedom of the mind."[90]

Dewey's first discussion of wartime censorship, published on
September 1, 1917, declared that he was not "specifically concerned lest liberty of thought and speech seriously suffer
among us." However, his attack on the spirit of repression,
quoted above, clearly demonstrated that Dewey never intended
to slight the value of free expression. Rather, he merely underes-
timated the likelihood that elected officials would seriously attempt to interfere with verbal opposition to war policies. "The

fight [for free speech]," that essay continued, "was carried against so much greater odds in the past and still made its way, so that I cannot arouse any genuine distress on this score."[91] Two months later, in light of subsequent events, Dewey declared that his comments seemed "strangely remote and pallid." He called on liberal supporters of the war "to be more aggressive than they had been" in defending the rights of political dissenters. Such action was necessary to preserve the momentum for progressive reform once peace returned. Those who "passively tolerated invasions of free speech and action," Dewey prophetically concluded, were "preparing the way for a later victory of domestic Toryism."[92]

Kallen and Bourne responded to wartime calls for repression by insisting that the argument for cultural pluralism was also the argument for free speech. "The contradictory philosophies of Americanism," Kallen wrote, created an environment in which "repression overruled reciprocity." Wartime censorship only exacerbated national divisions. As a result, Kallen observed, postwar America consisted of "great groups of people thrown back upon themselves, rendered fearful of their neighbors, fearful of each other, fearful of government."[93] Bourne opposed participation in World War I because he believed that "willing war means willing all the evils that are organically bound up with it."[94] Like earlier conservative anti-imperialists, he thought that war inevitably caused suppression of free speech. Bourne's famous phrase—"war is the health of the State"—meant that militarism created an environment wherein government could "coerc[e] into obedience the minority groups and individuals which lack the larger herd sense."[95] Although Bourne attacked most progressive intellectuals for their willingness to tolerate restrictions on political dissent during World War I, he also criticized Dewey's belief that Americans could fight a foreign war while maintaining domestic liberties. His mentor, Bourne claimed, had wrongly "assumed that the war-technique can be used without trailing along with it the mob-fanaticism, the injustice and hatreds, that are organically bound up with it."[96]

Brandeis did not speak on wartime censorship until the constitutionality of the Espionage Act reached the Supreme Court in

early 1919. At first he sustained decisions that affirmed the convictions of political dissenters, but he regretted those votes almost immediately. He privately told his daughter that the red
scare was a "disgraceful exhibition;—of hysterical, unintelligent
fear." Within a year, Brandeis had decided to "let the future
know what we were not allowed to say in the days of the war."[97]
"The fundamental right of free men to strive for better conditions though new legislation will not be preserved," he declared
in *Pierce v. United States*, "if efforts to secure it by argument to
fellow citizens may be construed as criminal incitements." Brandeis excoriated "those exercising judicial power" who were punishing expression "merely because the argument seems to [them]
to be unfair in its portrayal of existing evils, mistaken in its assumptions, unsound in reasoning or intemperate in language."[98]
Seven years later, he penned the most inspiring statement of the
fundamental principles of early civil libertarian thought. "Those
who won our independence," Brandeis declared,

believed that the final end of the State was to make men free to develop their faculties; and that in government the deliberative forces
would prevail over the arbitrary. They valued liberty both as an end
and as a means. They believed liberty to be the secret of happiness and
courage to be the secret of liberty. They believed that freedom to
think as you will and to speak as you think are means indispensable to
the discovery and spread of political truth; that without free speech
and assembly, discussion would be futile; that with them, discussion affords ordinarily adequate protection against the dissemination of nox-
ious doctrine; that the greatest menace to freedom is an inert people;
that public discussion is a political duty; and that this should be a fundamental principle of the American government.[99]

The *Whitney* concurrence was a brilliant exposition of the new
philosophical defense of political dissent. However, the famous
passages of Brandeis's opinion contained no original justifications for judicial activism on behalf of expression. While Brandeis waxed poetic on the virtues of free speech, he offered no
principled challenge to the new constitutional attack on public
debate. In particular, as the next section points out, Brandeis
failed to explain why judges in democratic societies could second-guess an elected legislature's decision that other social interests outweighed the social interest in free speech.

The Constitutional Dilemmas of
Early Civil Libertarianism

Beneath the brilliance of the *Whitney* concurrence lurked difficulties that haunted early civil libertarian efforts to develop a
new constitutional defense of free speech. The opinion began
not with bold assertions of what the constitutional framers
thought,[100] but with substantial reservations about judicial capacity to protect expression rights. In contrast to conservative
libertarian jurists, Brandeis did not think courts were authorized to safeguard individual freedoms. He specifically contended that the due process clause of the Fourteenth Amendment only limited the procedures that state governments could
use when they sought to deprive a person of life, liberty, or
property.[101] Moreover, after rejecting the traditional constitutional defense of free speech, Brandeis refused to articulate a
workable alternative. He merely proclaimed that speech was
the same sort of right the Court was now committed to protecting. The judicial obligation to respect precedent, he concluded,
overrode the otherwise superior logic of the new constitutional
attack on free speech.

"Despite arguments to the contrary which had seemed to me
persuasive," Brandeis declared, "it is settled that the due process clause of the Fourteenth Amendment applies to matters of
substantive law as well as procedure." For this reason, and this
reason only, he admitted that "all fundamental rights com-
prised within the term liberty are protected by the Federal
Constitution from invasion by the States." "The right of free
speech, the right to teach and the right of assembly," he added,
"are, of course, fundamental rights."[102] In other words, such judicial decisions as *Lochner v. New York* implicitly held that the
Fourteenth Amendment also safeguarded an individual's expression rights.

Brandeis recognized that various social interests might justify legislative restrictions of conduct protected by the due process clause. "The right of free speech and assembly," he noted,
"are not in their nature absolute." They were "subject to restriction . . . in order to protect the State from destruction or
from serious injury." Normally, he maintained, "the legislature

must obviously decide . . . whether a danger exists which calls for a particular protective measure." This was, as noted above, a basic principle of progressive legal thought, one by which Corwin and others had justified judicial deference to legislative judgments that commercial and speech restrictions were in the public interest. Brandeis proceeded, however, to claim that "the enactment of the statute cannot alone establish the facts which are essential to its validity"; judges had the right to make a de novo determination as to whether a particular regulation sufficiently advanced social interests to justify restraining an individual's freedom. "Prohibitory legislation," he observed, "has repeatedly been held invalid, because unnecessary, where the denial of liberty involved was that of engaging in a business." As authority for this proposition, he cited five decisions in which the Court struck down economic regulations: *Frost v. R. R. Comm. of California, Weaver v. Palmer Bros. Co., Jay Burns Baking Co. v. Bryan, Pennsylvania Coal Co. v. Mahon,* and *Adams v. Tanner.* Yet in each case Brandeis had issued or signed a blistering dissent attacking the majority opinion for failing to realize that the judicial "function" was only "to determine in light of all facts which may enrich our understanding . . . whether the measure . . . transcends the founds of reason," so that "legislators acting reasonably could not have believed it to be necessary or appropriate for the public welfare."[103] Thus, with studied irony Brandeis concluded the first part of the *Whitney* concurrence by noting that "the power of the courts to strike down an offending law is no less when the interests involved are not property rights, but the fundamental personal rights of free speech and assembly."[104]

In short, Brandeis's defense of constitutional speech rights rested on principles he believed to be false. The first passages of the *Whitney* concurrence endorsed the underlying premises of the new constitutional attack on expression rights. Brandeis agreed that courts should respect legislative judgments that the estimated costs of certain utterances outweighed their expected benefits, and he continued to believe that the due process clause should not protect substantive liberties. The only significant difference between the *Whitney* concurrence and Corwin's postwar essays was Brandeis's insistence that civil libertarians should not hesitate to rely on the conservative libertarian defense of free speech as long as proponents of laissez-faire continued to promulgate the conservative libertarian defense of private property. Brandeis might never have written his impassioned plea for tolerance had the Court recognized the force of his dissents in freedom of contract cases.

The ambiguity of the *Whitney* concurrence reflected the central dilemma of early civil libertarian constitutional thought. Dewey, Addams, Brandeis, and others argued that democratic societies would protect and promote free speech in order to encourage diversity and citizen participation. They also thought, however, that a society was democratic only if the people's elected representatives determined what social interests would be protected and promoted. "The community," Dewey declared, "is, through legislative action, the seat of social experimental stations."[105] Both at the bar and on the bench Brandeis demanded that constitutional issues be determined in light of the actual facts[106] and that courts, on the basis of those facts, should determine only whether the legislature's conclusions were minimally reasonable. His judicial opinions frequently declared that "there must be power in the States and the Nation to remold, through experimentation, our economic practices and institutions to meet changing social and economic needs."[107]

Because they shared Brandeis's understanding of institutional responsibilities in democratic societies, early civil libertarians experienced similar difficulties when defending judicial solicitude for expression rights. Jurists sympathetic to Dewey's vision of a democratic society were not simply troubled by the Fourteenth Amendment's failure to mention expression explicitly. They had the same difficulty defending judicial efforts to limit federal censorship even though the First Amendment specifically barred congressional abridgment of free-speech rights. Proponents of sociological jurisprudence opposed judicial activism on behalf of any individual right, even rights clearly guaranteed by the Constitution. As Brandeis implied in *Whitney*, federal and state elected officials should have the power to act when they determined that the exercise of free-speech rights threatened other important social interests. This premise would consistently derail early civil libertarian efforts to justify judicial solicitude for expression rights. Even when they supported claims made by convicted political dissidents, progressive jurists inevitably concluded that, if the citizens of democratic communities had really wanted to forbid the utterance in question, "the only meaning of free speech" seemed to be "that they be given their chance and have their way."[108]

Henry Schofield's Illibertarian Libertarianism

The work of Henry Schofield, a professor at Northwestern University Law School, foreshadowed the difficulties early civil libertarians faced in developing a constitutional defense of expression rights. At a 1915 conference promoting free speech sponsored by the American Sociological Association,[109] Schofield delivered a paper that asserted the First Amendment protected expressions of "truth . . . on matters of public concern" and "any allowable opinion on any matter of public concern which any fair-minded man could or might form from the facts."[110] Although he endorsed older claims that "judges only declare pre-existing law" and specifically asserted that the First Amendment should be interpreted in accordance with the "true view of the original declaration,"[111] Schofield imputed progressive understandings of constitutional theory to the framers. His was the first effort to construct libertarian constitutional arguments from the social interest in free speech.

Schofield recognized that government could ordinarily regulate such interests as property; they existed "for the private profit and benefit of the owner." He suggested, however, that speech merited different treatment because the freedom of speech and the freedom of contract were different kinds of rights. A person's expression rights, Schofield emphasized, existed as a "trust for the educational profit and benefit of the public," "not for his own private profit and benefit."[112] Thus, courts served public interests when they protected expression rights. In particular, free speech was an important element of the democratic process established by the constitutional framers. The "foundation stone of the law of the land," Schofield declared, was the principle "that the governed are the master and the governors the servants." In its role as servant, government had no power to limit either criticisms of its performance or suggestions of alternatives.[113] Not only did the Constitution bar federal attempts to limit the freedom of speech, but also "the right to publish the truth on matters of national public concern [was] one of the privileges and immunities of the citizens of the United States protected from abridgment by any state."[114]

Chafee declared that Schofield's analysis of expression rights was "the best [prewar] discussion of the legal meaning of that subject."[115] By relying on the social interest in open public debate, however, Schofield actually narrowed libertarian interpretations of First Amendment freedoms. Although his article was advertised and treated as a *defense* of expression, Schofield frequently rejected as too protective of speech the positions essayed by conservative libertarian treatise writers. For example, as noted in chapter 1, late nineteenth-century treatise writers claimed that persons had a constitutional right to make any political utterance they honestly believed was true. Schofield referred to this "judge-made liberty of the press to publish defamatory falsehood on matters of public concern" as "unauthorized judicial legislation destructive of men's reputations and property." In sharp contrast to Burgess, who declared that congressional speech regulations were ordinarily ultra vires, Schofield maintained that the Constitution vested the national government with substantial power to regulate political commentary. Indeed, he concluded his article by noting a number of social interests that made federal and state legislation curbing speech rights both "desirable and necessary."[116]

More ominously, Schofield failed to clarify the constitutional relationships between free speech and lawless conduct. He did declare that the First Amendment was intended to abolish the common law crime of seditious libel, which he interpreted as forbidding advocacy that was intended or had a tendency "to create and diffuse among the people an ill opinion of existing public officers, government, institutions, and laws."[117] He also asserted that speech could not be punished "till it issues in some overt acts against the public peace and order."[118] This standard of protection, however, proved illusory. Schofield thought that "all publications [were] overt acts."[119] "Anarchist publications teaching and advising the use of force," "publications teaching and advising the practice of polygamy," and "indecent, vulgar, and vile language concerning any religion" were all "overt acts against peace and good order."[120] Schofield endorsed statutes that criminalized all speech "seriously endanger[ing] the public peace."[121] His only clear restriction on state power was that "publication[s]" could not be considered "overt acts against peace and good order simply because of their bad tendency as opinion-makers."[122] In other words, Schofield believed that government had no right to forbid speech that merely affected political opinions; speech could be punished, however, if it had some vaguely defined tendency to cause various social evils.

Schofield never attempted to encourage judicial efforts to alter the scales after the legislature had determined that some other social interest outweighed the social interest in free speech. This oversight proved particularly important because wartime speech restrictions were ostensibly designed to further important government policies. Thus, the Espionage Act spoke of "interfere[nce] with the operation of the military or naval forces of the United States" and "obstruct[ion]" of "the recruitment or enlistment services of the United States." The Sedition Act barred speech that "promote[d] the cause of [American] enemies" or "advocate[d] any curtailment of production . . . of any thing . . . essential to the prosecution of the war."[123] These were just the sort of interests that progressive scholars like Schofield agreed warranted limiting expression rights. At least, this was the position taken by Justice Oliver Wendell Holmes, Jr., the jurist who most inspired sociological jurisprudence.

The Myth of Holmes

On March 3, 1919, the Supreme Court handed down its first major decision on the constitutional meaning of free speech. In *Schenck v. United States*, the justices unanimously held that the Espionage Act of 1917 was constitutional and that there were no valid First Amendment objections to the conviction of several socialists who had passed out leaflets protesting the draft. In his unanimous opinion, Justice Holmes declared that the Constitution did not protect words that might "cause a clear and present danger" of "substantive evils that Congress has a right to prevent."[124] The repressive implications of *Schenck* were confirmed a week later when the justices handed down their decision in *Debs v. United States*.[125] In that case, a united court held that speakers could be constitutionally punished under the Espionage Act for asserting personal opposition to the war and approving the actions of persons "who had been convicted of aiding and abetting another in failing to register for the draft." Justice Holmes again wrote for the Court: He declared that a jury could have found these sentiments had a "reasonable tendency and reasonably probable effect to obstruct the recruiting service."[126]

Chafee claimed that those "decisions . . . came as a great shock to forward looking men and women"; moreover, "they were especially grieved that the opinions . . . were written by the Justice who for their eyes had long taken heroic dimension."[127] Yet American libertarians had no reason for surprise. Holmes had always been the leading authority for the narrowest interpretations of the constitutional meaning of free speech. He wrote the Court's opinion in *Fox v. Washington*, which held that states could punish advocacy of nudism. In other cases, Holmes rejected the good faith defense in libel suits, insisted that persons had no right to speak on public property, and suggested that the First Amendment merely rendered constitutional Blackstone's rule of no prior restraint.[128] Furthermore, no progressive jurist had developed a broad constitutional defense of expression rights that was consistent with Holmes's dissent in *Lochner v. New York*, a dissent that claimed "the word liberty in the Fourteenth Amendment is perverted when it is held to prevent the natural outcome of a dominant opinion."[129] Perhaps Chafee hoped Holmes could do better.

In the fall of 1919, Holmes seemed to do better. Dissenting in *Abrams v. United States*, he demonstrated that the clear and present danger test could protect unpopular speakers.[130] "It is only the present danger of immediate evil or an intent to bring it about," his opinion declared, "that warrants Congress in setting a limit to the expression of opinion." Jacob Abrams's attack on national policy toward the Soviet Union did not satisfy this standard. Holmes did not "see how anyone [could] find the intent

required by the [Sedition Act] in any of [his] words." He interpreted that statute as only prohibiting efforts to "impede the
United States in the war that it was carrying on," and he argued
"it was evident that the only object of [Abrams's] paper [was] to
help Russia and stop intervention there."[131] More important,
after dismissing the particular case before him on this statutory
ground,[132] Holmes closed with a dramatic assertion of the fundamental status of expression rights in the American constitutional scheme.

But when men have realized that time has upset many fighting faiths,
they may come to believe even more than they believe the very foundations of their own conduct that the ultimate good desired is better
reached by free trade in ideas—that the best test of truth is the power
of thought to get itself accepted in the competition of the market, and
that truth is the only ground upon which their wishes safely can be
carried out. That at any rate is the theory of our constitution.[133]

Early civil libertarians cheered this burst of eloquence. Chafee
stated that it was a "magnificent exposition of the philosophic
basis" of constitutional protection for free speech.[134] Max Lerner
and others have described this passage as "the greatest utterance
on intellectual freedom by an American, ranking in the English
tongue with Milton and Mill."[135]

Unfortunately, upon close examination, virtually all of
Holmes's reputation as the great modern defender of civil liberty
rests on the last paragraph of the *Abrams* dissent.[136] Although
some scholars claim that Holmes was first convinced of the importance of broader constitutional protection for expression in
the summer of 1919[137] and others maintain that the circumstances of the *Abrams* case brought out the latent civil libertarian in him,[138] Holmes's behavior after *Abrams* was hardly that of
a person committed to judicial activism on behalf of free
speech. The only illibertarian pre-*Abrams* position that
Holmes ever retracted was the hint he dropped in *Patterson v.
Colorado* intimating that the Constitution only forbade prior restraints.[139] He insisted both publicly and privately that he "never [saw] any reasons to doubt that the question of law" in
Schenck and *Debs* "was rightly decided."[140] During the 1920s
this "great" civil libertarian never unambiguously supported a

free-speech claim. Holmes voted to affirm the convictions of political dissenters in *Gilbert v. Minnesota* and *Whitney v. California*.[141] He seriously considered rejecting the free-speech claims made by Jacob Abrams and Benjamin Gitlow. In letters to Sir Frederick Pollak, Holmes stated that he might have been "wrong in thinking that there was no evidence on the Fourth Count" in *Abrams v. United States* and that "conscience and judgment are little in doubt" as to the correct decision in *Gitlow v. New York*.[142] Holmes indicated to others that Brandeis had persuaded him to dissent in *United States ex. rel Milwaukee Social Democratic Publishing Co. v. Burleson*, and he conceded that in *Pierce v. United States* he might not have been willing to be the only dissenter.[143] "The argument for free speech," Holmes elsewhere insisted, "is not easy."[144]

Holmes's reluctance or unwillingness to offer free speech any substantial or wholehearted protection followed from his fundamental political belief that "the proximate test of good government is that the dominant power has its way," a maxim he reiterated in the crucial passages of both the *Lochner* and *Gitlow* dissents.[145] Dominant power, he stated, was established by "physical power," not by elections or persuasion. "Truth was the majority vote of that nation that could lick all others."[146]

Because Holmes considered force the basis of sovereignty, he maintained that the dominant forces of any community had the "right" to remove any obstacle in the way of the present attainment of their goals. Holmes thought that "no society has ever admitted that it could not sacrifice individual welfare to its own existence." "Whenever the interest of society, that is, of the predominant power in the community, is thought to demand it," he declared, "the most fundamental right of the supposed preexisting rights—the right to life—is sacrificed without a scruple."[147] In contrast to early civil libertarians, who consistently emphasized that more speech would ameliorate social conflicts, Holmes seemed to regard expression as ultimately worthless. "When men differ in taste as to the kind of world they want," he wrote, "the only thing left to do is to go to work killing."[148]

The only limit on community power, Holmes apparently concluded, was that the dominant forces of the community could only prohibit present threats. In *Northern Securities Co. v. United States*, he declared that "not every act done in furtherance of an unlawful end is an attempt contrary to the law. There must be a certain nearness to the result." Societies, he frequently asserted, could only punish "act[s] . . . done of which the natural and probable effect under the circumstances is the accomplishment of a substantive crime." Thus, the law of criminal attempt, Holmes insisted, emphasized the dangerousness of a person's actions rather the moral value of the actor's motives. Deeds were evaluated "by their tendency under known circumstances and not by the actual intent that accompanies them." Judges should look to a person's state of mind only when that person's actions were "not sufficient in themselves to produce a result which the law seeks to prevent." In such cases, "an intent to bring it to pass" might be sufficient "to produce a dangerous probability that it will happen." Law had no legitimate interest in persons who hoped to impede the achievement of communal goals but lacked the power to do so.[149]

Holmes specifically declared that his interpretation "of [criminal] attempt in *[The] Common Law*" was the source of the clear and present danger test.[150] This meant that for all practical purposes, prominent spokespersons for left-wing views had no constitutional speech rights. These radical critics threatened the present objectives of the community's dominant forces, even when they did not intentionally advocate criminal conduct or utter falsehoods. Thus, Holmes consistently sustained the convictions of influential political dissidents. Charles Schenck was the secretary of the Socialist party in Philadelphia. Eugene Debs would receive over a million votes when he ran as the Socialist party candidate for president. Joseph Gilbert was a prominent official in the Non-Partisan League, an organization that achieved several major electoral successes in the Midwest, including a gubernatorial victory in South Dakota. Anita Whitney was a nationally known reformer and president of the California Civic League.

Under Holmes's interpretation of the law of criminal attempt, however, government could not punish speakers incapable of interfering with the dominant forces of contemporary American politics. This theme of impotence dominated the substantive portions of Holmes's famous free-speech dissents. His *Abrams* opinion declared that "nobody [could] suppose that the surreptitious publishing of a silly leaflet by an unknown man . . . would present any danger . . . or have any appreciable tendency to do so." In *Gitlow*, Holmes stated that "the redundant discourse before us has no chance of starting a present conflagration." Even if the prosecutor had demonstrated that Gitlow intended to bring about an immediate revolution, he insisted that the utterance before the Court might be "futile and too remote from possible consequences" to support a constitutional conviction.[151] Civil libertarians were inspired by Holmes's assertion that, "if in the long run the beliefs expressed in proletarian dictatorship are destined to be accepted by the dominant forces of the community, the only meaning of free speech is that they should be given their chance and have their way." But they overlooked that for Holmes it was at least as important that the "belief expressed in proletarian dictatorship" was not likely to have any short-term effect as that it should not be barred from influencing conduct in the unforeseeable future.[152]

The facts of *Gitlow* and *Gilbert* clearly illustrate the crucial role of a speaker's actual influence on Holmes's First Amendment votes. The texts of the relevant speeches suggest that *Gilbert* clearly presented the stronger libertarian case. Benjamin Gitlow, at the very least, implicitly called for violent revolution. He "repudiate[d] the policy of introducing Socialism by the means of legislative measures" and called for "class action of the proletariat in any form having as its objective the conquest of the power of the state." Joseph Gilbert, by comparison, was arrested for giving a speech that did not even hint at the desirability of illegal conduct; he merely declared that "if this is such a great democracy, for Heaven's sake why should we not vote on conscription of men."[153] Moreover, as noted below, Gilbert's lawyers claimed that federal speech restrictions preempted the Minnesota statute under which their client had been convicted. This matter was not raised in *Gitlow*.

The relative prominence of the defendants was the only difference between the two cases that could explain why Holmes supported only Gitlow's free-speech claim. Gilbert, a leader of the major opposition party in Minnesota, was a person who inspired actions. Gitlow was a relatively obscure radical. Holmes described him as "an ass [who] drool[ed] about proletariat dictatorship." Although Holmes observed that Gitlow's speech was not likely to start "a present conflagration," Robert Morlan's standard history of the Non-Partisan League is entitled *Political Prairie Fire*.[154]

As this comparison suggests, Holmes not only failed to solve the constitutional dilemma of early civil libertarian thought, but he was also never interested in the problem. One searches his writings in vain for any expression of concern for diversity and participation, the values that inspired other progressive defenders of free speech. Instead, Holmes frequently insisted that virtuous citizens assisted the dominant forces of their community and did not take part in the formation of its goals. He claimed to be a committed proponent of "my country right or wrong." In a speech before his old Civil War regiment, Holmes praised the soldier who would "throw away his life in obedience to a blindly accepted duty, in a cause he little understands, in a plan of campaign of which he has no notion, under tactics of which he does not see the use."[155] When asked to contribute to a Harvard Liberal Club meeting that was protesting censorship, Holmes did not deliver a ringing endorsement of the virtues of public debate. He merely noted that "with effervescing opinions, as with not yet forgotten champagnes, the quickest way to let them get flat is to let them get exposed to air."[156]

The First Crisis of Civil Libertarianism

While Holmes offered expression rights little constitutional protection, other libertarian jurists did not do much better. Although they denounced the new philosophical attack on free speech, early civil libertarians confessed that the new constitutional attack on those rights was sound. Repeatedly they admitted that if elected officials really wanted to restrict the liberty of discussion, judges committed to the principles of sociological jurisprudence should not prevent them. Indeed, at least one progressive defender of expression rights claimed that Holmes had, if anything, gone too far in favor of free speech.

In an article published in the *Michigan Law Review*, Herbert Goodrich claimed that Holmes's dissent in *Abrams* was wrong for the same reason that his dissent in *Lochner* was right. "The same kind of argument and the same line of thought which upholds a law which restricts a man in the contracts he may make," he asserted, "upholds a law limiting the exercise of his tongue when the majority wills it."[157] Goodrich, a law professor at the State University of Iowa, emphasized that his criticism of Holmes did not stem from any enthusiasm for the underlying merits of wartime censorship. He condemned the Espionage Act as "an effective silencer of all but the most polite discussion" and called the *Abrams* verdict a "great injustice."[158] But Goodrich insisted that courts had no constitutional authority to remedy those wrongs. Because "the question of freedom of speech is one of social values," "the advocates of free speech, as the champions of minimum wage laws, have to convince their fellow citizens that their cause is righteous, that the benefits outweigh the dangers." "If unrestricted speech cannot win in [that] field," he concluded, "we will probably have to get along without it."[159]

Ernst Freund's wartime and postwar writings likewise illustrated how adherence to the principles of sociological jurisprudence could significantly inhibit the development of constitutional defenses of free speech. One rallying cry of progressive jurists was Holmes's declaration that "the prophecies of what the courts will do in fact, and nothing more pretentious, [is] what I mean by the law." Freund similarly identified law with the actual decisions of courts. "The Constitution," he declared, "is an excellent weapon in legislative controversies before the courts have spoken." However, it was "a poor one afterwards" because "the conclusiveness of judicial interpretation is part of [our constitutional system]."[160] For this reason, Freund could not sustain attacks on illibertarian decisions. If courts consistently rejected free-speech claims, then the Constitution did not provide broad protection for free speech. Thus, Freund almost immediately conceded that the Supreme Court's decisions in Espionage Act cases authoritatively determined the constitutional meaning of free speech. Although free speech was "a problem in constitutional law" in 1914, after the *Debs* decision, speech had "become a problem in practical legislation."[161] By comparison, as noted in chapter 1, some conservative treatise writers insisted that the Supreme Court had systematically misinterpreted the privileges and immunities clause for more than thirty years.[162]

Freund also concluded that political as well as judicial reality made it "useless to over-emphasize the substantive limitations of the constitution." Communities inevitably forbade dissent, he confessed, in certain circumstances. Thus, in 1921 Freund suggested that the "cause of free speech gains if a constitution frankly provides for modification or even suspension of the right under the exegesis of war." By explicitly permitting government to limit public debate in wartime, society avoided establishing precedents that might linger after hostilities ended. Even in peacetime, the status of expression rights ultimately depended on public support. "Congress," Freund claimed, could "render the free expression of opinion harmless . . . by denying mail facilities."[163]

Nevertheless, Freund still found reason to criticize judicial decisions affirming the wartime convictions of political dissidents. Although his famous attacks on *Debs v. United States* in the *New Republic* did "not attempt to determine what in the way of restraint is possible under the First Amendment," Freund objected to the way that the justices interpreted the Espionage Act. The fault of Supreme Court opinions rejecting appeals of persons opposed to the war, he claimed, was that "the restraint of speech . . . [was] made to rest on judicial interpretation rather than upon legislation." In his opinion, the federal government in 1917 had recognized the social interest in free expression of criticisms of the war or war policies. Freund insisted that the Espionage Act did no "more than punish attempts to cause military insubordination or willful obstruction of the recruitment service." Therefore, the Supreme Court decision in *Debs*, which "construed the act as making agitation against the war criminal," was not "sound law." Indeed, this overly broad interpretation of federal sedition legislation amounted to unwarranted judicial policy making. "Had such a measure been deemed legitimate and necessary," Freund insisted, "it should have come from Congress."[164]

Judge Learned Hand's celebrated opinion in *Masses Pub. Co. v. Patten* was a similar exercise in statutory interpretation. That decision held that the postmaster general could not forbid the mailing of a publication that opposed the war effort because the Espionage Act only forbade "direct incitement to violent resistance."[165] Hand conceded that elected officials had the constitutional power to shut down antiwar publications. "The peril of war," he wrote, might "justif[y] any measure of compulsion, and measure of suppression, which Congress deems necessary to its safety." However, Hand did not think *Masses* raised issues that required him to consider the constitutional meaning of free speech. The statute before the Court "presented solely the question of how far Congress after much discussion has up to the present time seen fit to exercise a power which may extend to measures not yet considered." If persons believed that the direct incitement test permitted too much disloyal speech, Hand suggested they convince their elected representatives that present circumstances demanded further restrictions on public debate.[166]

In his early opinions, Brandeis demonstrated other ways in which judges could reverse the convictions of political dissenters without explicitly limiting the constitutional prerogatives of the national legislature. He admitted that "the power to suppress exists" when Congress "faced with a clear and present danger . . . conclude[d] that suppression of divergent opinion is imperative." However, in *Gilbert v. Minnesota*, Brandeis argued that the Constitution vested the federal government with "exclusive power over enlistments in the Army and Navy of the United States and the responsibility for the conduct of war." For this reason, only Congress could determine when circumstances justified restricting criticisms of national policies. States, Brandeis insisted, could restrict "free discussion in relation to [these functions] . . . only under the express direction of Congress." No such permission was given to local officials during World War I. Because "it was the established policy of the United States" that "enlistment should be the result of free, informed and deliberate choice," Brandeis contended that states could not constitutionally punish a person who urged others not to volunteer for the armed services. Indeed, Brandeis indicated that the national legislature had preempted all state sedition acts enacted during the war. By passing the Espionage Act, Congress "necessarily exclude[d] all" state restrictions on expression rights, even those purportedly "in aid of congressional action." "When the United States has exercised its exclusive powers," he declared, "the States can no more supplement its requirements than they can circumvent them."[167]

Brandeis voted to reverse several federal wartime speech convictions on the ground that the trial judge should not have let the jury decide whether a particular speech was of the sort that Congress had forbidden because there was insufficient evidence that the speaker had violated the Espionage Act. In *Schaefer v. United States*, Brandeis declared that judges had an obligation "to withdraw the case from the consideration of the jury" if "men, judging in calmness, could not reasonably say that they created a clear and present danger that [a particular utterance] would bring about the evil which Congress sought and had a right to prevent."[168] To rule otherwise, he wrote, would result in political dissidents being punished for utterances that elected officials had not intended to prohibit. In *Pierce v. United States*, he insisted that the trial court should have directed a verdict in favor of defendants who had expressed honest opposition to the war because the provision of the Espionage Act under which they were charged prohibited only willful misrepresentations.[169]

The libertarian claims made by Freund, Hand, and Brandeis were consistent with several strands of sociological jurisprudence. As noted in chapter 2, progressive jurists encouraged judges to develop legal doctrines that would protect vital social interests in cases not clearly governed by existing legislation. Because the Espionage Act did not declare the advocacy of any specific doctrine unlawful, Hand and Freund did not have to confront an explicit legislative judgment that the social interest in successfully fighting a war outweighed the social interest in permitting verbal opposition to the draft. For this reason, they could maintain that the social interest in free speech was sufficiently weighty to require clear evidence that the legislature had, in fact, intended to restrict "traditional" freedoms of speech. As Hand asserted in *Masses*, "the power to repress such opinion . . . is so contrary to the use and wont of our people that only the clearest expression of such a power justifies the conclusion that it was so intended.[170] Similarly, sociological jurisprudence never insisted that courts defer as readily to the findings of lay jurors as they did to legislative and administrative experts. "The unchecked discretion of juries," Pound declared, "is worse than the . . . rigid mechanical application of law" because verdicts were likely to be "influenced by emotional appeals, prejudices, and the peculiar personal ideas of individual jurors."[171] Hence, Brandeis was well within the mainstream of progressive legal thought when he argued that cases should not go to juries if, in the trial judge's expert and unbiased opinion, there was no evidence that the defendant had spoken in a manner prohibited by the people's elected officials.

Unfortunately, these doctrines did not protect political dissidents from postwar state and federal legislation that specifically banned promulgation of certain political doctrines. For example, the New York statute at issue in *Gitlow* prohibited the advocacy "of overthrowing or overturning organized government by force or violence."[172] Furthermore, as was the case with the Smith Act of 1940, the elected branches of government frequently engaged in substantial fact finding before banning the expression of particular beliefs. Thus, even if a court accepted the clear and present danger test, cases like *Gitlow v. New York* and *Dennis v. United States* forced libertarian jurists to substitute their opinion for an informed legislative judgment that certain utterances were dangerous. This was precisely the sort of judicial conduct that Pound and other proponents of sociological jurisprudence condemned in cases like *Lochner v. New York*. When the legislature determined that the advocacy of a specific doctrine presented a clear and present danger to some social interest, progressive jurists insisted that the judiciary defer to the superior fact-finding abilities of the elected branches of government.

This argument eventually proved compelling for virtually every prominent early civil libertarian. Although Learned Hand continued to proclaim the philosophical value of free speech in a democracy, his postwar writings opposed special judicial solicitude for expression rights. Hand confessed that the commands of the First Amendment were "not jural concepts at all," but "no more than admonitions of moderation." In *The Bill of Rights* he admitted that he "did not think that the interests men-

tioned in the First Amendment are entitled in point of constitutional interpretation to a measure of protection different from
other interests."[173] Felix Frankfurter, another prominent defender of free speech during World War I, later wrote influential opinions deferring to the federal government's judgment
that the communist threat was sufficient to justify prohibiting
such speech. His concurring opinion in *Dennis* claimed that
"free speech cases are not an exception to the principle that we
are not legislators." "How best to reconcile competing interests
is the business of the legislatures," Frankfurter declared, "and
the balance they strike is a judgment not to be displaced by
ours, but to be respected unless outside the pale of fair
judgment."[174]

Brandeis took a different tack. By 1922, he had decided that if
conservatives on the Court were going to abuse the power of
judicial review to advance their political agenda, he too was going to abuse that power to advance his own political agenda. Although he privately favored repealing the Fourteenth Amendment as a means of ending judicial protection for laissez-faire
property rights, Brandeis told Frankfurter that if the due process clause "must be applied to substantive laws," he was going
to apply it to "things that are fundamental." Under the heading
of "things that are fundamental," he listed "right to speech,
right to education, right to choice of profession, [and] right to
locomotion."[175] Brandeis was also prepared to limit the circumstances elected officials could use to justify restricting civic debate. As noted above, Brandeis stated he would review legislative judgments that a particular class of utterances presented
a clear and present danger with the same scrutiny which conservative justices applied in freedom of contract cases. If he did
not find enough evidence to justify restricting speech in the
public interest, Brandeis would declare that a conviction violated First and Fourteenth Amendment expression rights.[176]

Moreover, Brandeis sharpened Holmes's clear and present
danger test by requiring that the threatened harm be substantial. In order to meet First Amendment standards, he declared,
"it must be shown either that immediate serious violence was to
be expected or was advocated, or that past conduct furnished
reasons to believe that such advocacy was then contemplat-

ed."[177] This "immediate serious violence" standard was both more and less protective than that criminal advocacy test advanced by conservative libertarians. Brandeis thought that the Constitution permitted states to punish speakers who did not advocate lawless conduct or cause an actual material injury, as long as their utterances threatened vital social interests. Government, he asserted, could restrict speech that "would produce, *or* is intended to produce a clear and imminent danger of some substantive evil which the State constitutionally may seek to prevent" (emphasis added).[178] However, unlike previous libertarians, Brandeis sharply distinguished incitement and advocacy of illegal conduct. He thought incitement could always be punished, but "advocacy of law-breaking" that "falls short of incitement" could be punished only if the evidence demonstrated that "the advocacy would be clearly acted upon" and threatened severe injuries. Thus, persons could abstractly call for violating certain minor laws as long as they did not insist on immediate criminal conduct. In *Whitney*, Brandeis insisted that no person could be punished who only advocated that "pedestrians had the moral right to cross unenclosed, unposted wastelands . . . , even if there was an imminent danger that advocacy would lead to trespass." "The fact that speech is likely to result in some violence or in destruction of property," he declared, "is not enough to justify its suppression. There must be the probability of serious injury to the State."[179]

The most intriguing aspect of Brandeis's constitutional defense of expression rights was his assertion that the Constitution protected the entire social and economic program that early civil libertarians thought necessary to ensure a functional system of free speech. In 1914, before he joined the bench, Brandeis suggested that the due process clauses of the Fifth and Fourteenth Amendments obligated elected officials to pass the favorite measures of progressive reformers. "The 'right to life' guaranteed by our Constitution," he declared,

is now being interpreted according to the demands of social justice and of democracy as the right to live and not merely to exist. In order to live men must have the opportunity of developing their faculties; and they must live under conditions in which their faculties may develop naturally and healthily.

In the first place, there must be abolition of child labor, shorter hours of labor, and regular days of rest, so that men and women may conserve health, may fit themselves to be citizens of a free country, and may perform their duties as citizens. In other words, men and women must have leisure, which the Athenians called "freedom" or liberty. In the second place, the earnings of men and women must be greater, so that they may live under conditions conducive to health and to mental and moral development.[180]

Eight years later, Brandeis repeated his claim that the basic institutions of positive liberty were aspects of the general principle of liberty protected by the Fourteenth Amendment. He explicitly added that judges could enforce those constitutional guarantees. The "right to education and the right to choice of profession" were among the fundamental rights that Brandeis claimed he was going to use the Fourteenth Amendment to protect.[181] Although Brandeis never wrote a judicial opinion detailing the full scope of those rights, he voted to strike down state laws that forbade the teaching of German, required all children to attend public schools, and unduly regulated private schools because they interfered with the freedom of education protected by the Fourteenth Amendment; Brandeis also cited those cases in *Whitney* supporting his interpretation of the due process clause.[182]

Brandeis's willingness to rely on the conservative libertarian constitutional defense of free speech became the norm on the Taft and early Hughes courts. From 1927 to 1937, progressive and liberal supporters of expression rights unanimously voted to strike down state restrictions on expression rights without offering any novel justification for such judicial activism. As one of Justice Stone's clerks observed, libertarians on the bench were content to claim "that liberties enshrined in the Bill of Rights deserved as much protection as did 'liberty of contract' and that sauce for the goose should be sauce for the gander."[183] In *Near v. Minnesota*, for example, Chief Justice Hughes merely declared that "it was found impossible to conclude that this essential liberty of the citizen was left unprotected by the general guaranty of fundamental rights of person and property."[184]

Nevertheless, this practice was marked by another dilemma. If the *Whitney* concurrence and the *Lochner* majority stood and fell together, then civil libertarians could constitutionally protect speech only if they conceded that legislatures had no constitutional power to establish what they believed were the economic and social prerequisites of a functional system of freedom of expression. If early civil libertarians ever staged a judicial revolution that freed legislative activity on behalf of the necessary conditions of effective expression, that rebellion would also destroy the only extant basis for judicial activism on behalf of free speech.

Chapter Four

Zechariah Chafee's
Achievements

Zechariah Chafee, Jr., is the seminal figure in the development of the modern constitutional defense of free speech.[1] His friend Felix Frankfurter declared that Chafee's influence on "that pervasive area of national life known as civil rights has no match in the legal professorate." Chafee's *Freedom of Speech* (1920), which he updated in 1941 as *Free Speech in the United States*, has been described as the "Bible on civil liberties questions," "a landmark in the literature on the subject," and the "piece of writing" that did the most "to define the nature of personal liberty." "Two generations of free-speech advocates," Jonathan Prude observed, "looked to the work as the starting point for all their discussions and debates." Indeed, contemporary libertarian theory and history is still largely a series of responses to the problems Chafee addressed and the solutions he offered. Chafee's writings, his biographer recently concluded, have "set the agenda for the continuing dialogue on the meaning of 'Congress shall make no law abridging the freedom of speech or of the press.' "[2]

From the passage of the Espionage Act in 1917 until his death in 1957, Chafee, a professor at Harvard Law School, repeatedly contended that government could only constitutionally punish those rare instances of speech that threatened immediate harm. Justice Holmes, he claimed, correctly interpreted the Constitution in *Schenck v. United States* when he declared that the First Amendment protected debate over matters of public importance unless there was "a clear and present danger" that advocacy would "bring about the substantive evils that Congress has a right to prevent." Chafee maintained that Holmes's standard drew "the boundary line very close to the test of incitement at common law and clearly ma[de] the punishment of words for their remote bad tendency impossible."[3] Judicial adoption of the clear and present danger test would prevent critics of American policies from being imprisoned merely because they challenged cherished political values.

Chafee frequently insisted that his free-speech writings promoted traditional understandings of expression rights. A libertarian renaissance was necessary, he argued, only because Americans had forgotten the underlying principles of an inherited libertarian theory and their accepted standards of judicial protection had become outdated. In particular, Chafee claimed that the legal safeguards favored by eighteenth- and nineteenth-century libertarians proved inadequate in the face of novel repressive practices during World War I and the red scare. Hence, *Freedom of Speech* and other writings outlined two tasks for twentieth-century proponents of free speech. First, they had to remind Americans of the historical principles that provided the foundations for free-speech rights. Second, they needed to devise a new legal standard—the clear and present danger test—enabling courts to secure the advocacy rights that critics of domestic and foreign policy had previously enjoyed. By publicizing and updating what he claimed was a traditional libertarian doctrine, Chafee purportedly sought to ensure that the system of freedom of expression would continue to function in the face of contemporary threats to advocacy rights.

The testimonials in the first paragraph of this chapter demonstrate that Chafee successfully promoted a constitutional defense of free speech. But his alleged attempt to expand traditional libertarian standards of judicial protection was both an unnecessary measure and a failure. In 1917 the interpretations of the First Amendment that previous libertarians had offered did not need expanding. As noted in chapter 1, judicial adoption of conservative libertarian understandings of constitutional expression rights would have protected virtually every political dissident convicted during and immediately after World War I. Indeed, Chafee's version of the clear and present danger test actually offered less protection to twentieth-century political dissenters than the standards proposed by earlier speech advocates. Whereas Cooley and other late nineteenth-century treatise writers had declared that the Constitution affirmatively protected all speakers who did not advocate crimes or intentionally utter falsehoods, Chafee assumed that Congress could forbid any advocacy that significantly threatened any of numerous public interests. In sharp contrast to the conservative libertarian jurist John W. Burgess, who declared that wartime federal legislation restricting expression rights was incapable of any constitutional application, Chafee thought that the Espionage Act was a constitutional exercise of national power, and constitutionally applied in *Schenck v. United States* to speakers who attacked the constitutionality of the draft.[4]

The relative inadequacies of the clear and present danger test as a libertarian standard suggest that Chafee had motives other than his expressed desire to develop constitutional doctrines that would provide more protection to unpopular speakers. In fact, Chafee was as concerned with the premises of the constitutional defense of free speech as he was with its conclusions. He rejected the principles underlying the "traditional" conservative libertarian defense of expression rights because, although he sometimes pretended otherwise, he was a mainstream progressive who insisted that judges had no business protecting their idiosyncratic notions of individual rights. Like other civil libertarians, whose vision of a diverse and participatory society he shared, Chafee believed that majorities in democratic societies should be able to govern themselves as they saw fit. Thus, he was not willing to let an unelected judiciary determine the fundamental values of his community, even when doing so might successfully defend the expression rights he cherished.

Chafee's primary achievement, chapter 4 argues, was his construction of the first defense of judicial activism on behalf of expression rights that was consistent with the basic principles of early civil libertarianism. Chafee's writings successfully transformed the bases of the constitutional defense of free speech from the political and legal principles of conservative libertarianism to pragmatism and sociological jurisprudence. In his writings, free speech was no longer an individual right like the liberty of contract; now it was a procedural prerequisite of any democratic society. The guarantee of free speech, in other words, enabled people to choose democratically whether they also wished to enforce a guarantee of free contract. Once public discourse was conceptualized in this way, judges in democratic societies could consider themselves as obligated to protect expression as they were obligated to defer to the policy decisions made by elected officials.

Chafee's new constitutional tradition differed from conservative libertarianism in several important ways. First, following Pound and Schofield, Chafee insisted that the Constitution primarily protected the social interest in free speech, rather than the individual's interest in self-expression. Second, Chafee endorsed the claim of sociological jurisprudence that constitutional standards should be responsive to changing social conditions, not simply reflective of their framers' intentions. However, in contrast to such progressive opponents of speech rights as Edward Corwin, Chafee pointed out that this canon of interpretation sometimes required broader rather than narrower readings of constitutional guarantees. In his opinion, the same circumstances of twentieth-century life that justified limiting the economic rights stated in the Constitution necessitated expanding constitutional expression rights.

Third, Chafee inspired and then defended Justice Stone's claim that judicial activism on behalf of free speech was based on a judicial obligation to police the democratic process, rather than a judicial duty to protect fundamental rights from majoritarian tyranny. Legislatures, both contended, could make intelligent substantive policies and respond to the wishes of democratic majorities only if full and unrestricted debate on matters of public interest was assured. Thus, properly understood, sociological jurisprudence entailed judicial solicitude toward speech rights but judicial deference to the economic and social policy choices of elected officials.

Finally, as a consequence of this sharp distinction between expression and economic liberties, Chafee became the first American libertarian to renounce judicial protection of the economic rights that he believed were necessary to exercise speech rights effectively. Like other early civil libertarians, Chafee believed that democratic societies regulated economic life to ensure that all citizens could take part in public decision making. Indeed, he insisted that the First Amendment required legislatures to take into account the effect that various economic and social programs had on the system of free expression. This requirement, however, was not to be enforced by the judiciary. Decisions allocating material resources were substantive policies and, hence, matters to be decided by elected officials, even when the distribution of those resources obstructed the fair functioning of the democratic process. Thus, although advertised as an attempt to make free-speech standards more responsive to twentieth-century conditions, the new constitutional defense of free speech would be structurally insensitive to the economic inequalities that most civil libertarians now consider the main threats to a functional system of freedom of expression.

In promoting this new constitutional defense of free speech, Chafee gave civil libertarianism a new historical status. Previous progressive defenders of expression rights had correctly understood themselves as breaking with an earlier individualistic conception of free speech. As noted in chapter 3, John Dewey and others urged libertarians to abandon inherited understandings of expression rights.[5] Chafee, however, claimed merely to be popularizing traditional arguments. His historical discussions of libertarian theory maintained that the constitutional defense of expression had always been based on certain universal political and legal principles. These principles were, in fact, peculiar to pragmatism and sociological jurisprudence. Through this distortion of the libertarian past, Chafee could ground his clear and present danger test in historical precedent while avoiding comparisons with the more speech-protective, conservative libertarian tradition. In short, in transforming the constitutional defense of free speech, Chafee invented the civil libertarian tradition.

The Tactics of Transformation

Chafee openly admitted his willingness to sacrifice disinterested scholarship when promoting free speech. He avoided making legal claims that were "bound to be useless in the practical task of opposing current suppressive measures." "I have tried," he stated, "to argue about things to which I have some chance of winning."[6] However, Chafee did not regard the popularizing of speech-protective interpretations of the First Amendment as the sole aim of libertarian doctrine. He was as interested in promoting a particular approach to expression rights as he was in developing standards judges might use to safeguard political and social commentary. Thus, although he sometimes manipulated historical facts to buttress his conception of constitutional speech rights, Chafee suppressed or distorted evidence that strengthened the conservative libertarian interpretation of the liberty of discussion, even when that evidence supported expansive readings of First Amendment rights. By so perverting the history of libertarian theory, Chafee presented as the traditional constitutional defense of expression rights an original argument based entirely on the philosophical and jurisprudential principles of early civil libertarian thought.

Many of Chafee's tactics resembled those of ordinary legal advocates defending a client's advocacy rights. Lawyers normally tailor their arguments to suit the particular court before which they appear. Chafee similarly confessed that he occasionally concealed his personal preferences and promoted the libertarian standards he thought judges were more likely to adopt. "The clear and present danger test," he admitted, was "not the best possible formulation of the line between constitutionally protected speech and speech which is punishable," but only "the best which has yet been authoritatively laid down." Chafee privately favored the expression "direct incitement to violent resistance," which Learned Hand coined in *Masses,* or the phrase he used in 1918 that "speech should be free, unless it is clearly liable to cause direct and dangerous interference with [other social interests]."[7] Indeed, the two articles he published in 1919 declared that "direct provocation" was the correct standard of First Amendment protection.[8] Chafee only asserted that the clear and present danger test "mark[ed] the true limit of governmental interference with speech and writing under our constitution" after the Supreme Court's decision in

Abrams, when Holmes and Brandeis first used that standard to protect specific political utterances.[9]

Chafee's historical writings were no more objective than the discussion of precedent in most legal briefs. Important passages in *Freedom of Speech* exaggerated the historical foundations of Chafee's interpretation of constitutional free-speech guarantees. As many scholars have demonstrated, Chafee clearly invented history when he declared that Holmes used the phrase "clear and present danger" in *Schenck* to make "the punishment of words for their bad tendency impossible."[10] In fact, Chafee's 1919 *Harvard Law Review* article, "Freedom of Speech in War Times," marked the first time that "clear and present danger" was used as a speech-protective standard. When Holmes and Brandeis later decided to support the claims of political dissenters, they proceeded to accept "as their own the libertarian meaning Chafee erroneously read into their words."[11]

Chafee similarly minimized the import of precedents that narrowly interpreted the constitutional meaning of free speech. His works ignored the generally illibertarian nature of many pre–World War I free-speech decisions. Although recent scholarship has demonstrated that free-speech claims were frequently litigated and usually denied in the fifty years before World War I, Chafee claimed that such cases were "too few [and] too varied in their character . . . to develop any definite boundary between lawful and unlawful speech."[12] Chafee may have correctly asserted that the authors of the Bill of Rights "intended to wipe out the common law of sedition." However, he never discussed the evidence that others use to prove that the framers intended only to abolish prior restraints.[13]

Obscuring Conservative Libertarianism

While Chafee presented what was, at best, a wildly optimistic reading of the historical evidence favoring his conception of the constitutional meaning of free speech, his interpretation of the historical pedigree of conservative libertarian arguments was remarkably pessimistic. In works that purported to give a complete history of free-speech law and theory, Chafee never discussed the speech-protective doctrines offered by late nineteenth-century legal treatise writers. "During the whole of the nineteenth century," he falsely asserted, "the philosophical and political principles which underlay the constitutional guarantees [of free speech were] forgotten for lack of constant assertion and examination of them." Similarly, he ignored such libertarian utterances as Cooley's majority opinion in *Atkinson v. Detroit Free Press* and Harlan's dissent in *Patterson v. Colorado.* Without referring to any case by name, Chafee merely commented that earlier judicial opinions broadly interpreting constitutional expression rights were "precedents of very dubious value" because they "seem to ignore so seriously the economic and political facts of our time."[14]

Indeed, Chafee maintained that late nineteenth-century treatise writers and their philosophical allies opposed broad interpretations of First Amendment guarantees. As noted in chapter 1, Chafee declared that the historical opponents of broad free-speech rights had always been those conservatives who were willing to use the power of judicial review to strike down progressive and New Deal economic reforms.[15] Scholars reading Chafee's works were told that they would not find an alternative to civil libertarianism in the nineteenth century, particularly in the writings of late nineteenth-century conservative thinkers.

Not only did Chafee obscure the existence of conservative libertarians, but he also ignored the role they had played in developing the foundations for incorporating free speech into the Fourteenth Amendment. As noted in chapter 1, virtually every prominent conservative libertarian jurist insisted that free speech was a Fourteenth Amendment right. Furthermore, in the first twenty years of the twentieth century, the Supreme Court consistently adjudicated the merits of claims that state governments had violated free-speech rights. Chafee, however, did not present any of this evidence. *Free Speech in the United States* gave the impression, now shared by most contemporary scholars, that in *Gitlow* the Court's holding that states had to respect constitutional free-speech rights was a surprising reversal of doctrine, not merely an announcement of a previously established policy. Before 1920, Chafee declared, "no thoughtful lawyer would have dared make a firm assertion that the United States Constitution protects liberty of discussion against the states."[16]

Chafee similarly misrepresented the historical relationships between the freedom of contract and the freedom of speech. He maintained that defense counsel in *Gitlow* relied exclusively on *Meyer v. Nebraska* and *Pierce v. Society of Sisters* in support of their claim that the due process clause protected free speech;[17] these cases, respectively, held that the Fourteenth Amendment protected the right to teach a foreign language and the right of parents to send their children to private school.[18] In fact, the defense brief submitted in *Gitlow* made no mention of those authorities.[19] Instead, Gitlow's attorneys argued that a Fourteenth Amendment right of free speech was inherent in the holdings of *Allgeyer v. Louisiana* and *Coppage v. Kansas*, two cases decided on freedom of contract grounds.[20] Chafee never informed his readers that the *Gitlow* opinion indicated that these latter cases provided the precedential support for its holding, and he ignored other cases that explicitly connected constitutional free-speech and private-property rights.[21]

Underlying Chafee's slight of the historical evidence supporting the conservative libertarian assertion that free speech was a due process right was Chafee's hostility to the substance of that claim. One looks in vain through his writings for any historical, theoretical, or functional defense of the individual's Fourteenth Amendment right of self-expression. Although he explored the original purpose of the First Amendment at length, Chafee never discussed whether the framers of the post–Civil War amendments intended to protect expression rights against hostile state action. Similarly, his discussions of the constitutional meaning of free speech focused almost exclusively on the proper interpretation of the First Amendment. Chafee did claim that in *Gilbert v. Minnesota* "Justice Brandeis gives very interesting reasons for his position that freedom to discuss national affairs is one of the 'privileges and immunities' of citizens of the United States, which no state can abridge,"[22] but he refused to elaborate or endorse Brandeis's arguments.[23] In private correspondence, Chafee attacked those intellectuals whose "love for the privileges and immunities clause" inspired their constitutional defenses of free speech.[24]

Chafee's public discussions of the Fourteenth Amendment further revealed his distaste for the conservative libertarian tradition's use of the due process clause to protect expression rights. His analysis of *Gitlow v. New York* encouraged readers to peruse Charles Warren's article, "The New 'Liberty' under the Fourteenth Amendment," for an "able discussion of the background and implications of th[e] holding" that free speech was a Fourteenth Amendment right.[25] As noted in chapter 3, the Warren article attacked this decision on the ground that no principled distinction existed between economic substantive due process and due process protection of free speech.[26] Long after the Supreme Court had established otherwise, Chafee continued to suggest that "freedom of speech is too precious to be left altogether to the vague words of the due process clause."[27]

Although Chafee denied that conservative libertarians were interested in expression rights, he insisted that a second group of American conservatives played vital roles in the struggle for free speech. His "conservative libertarians" were persons who favored laissez-faire economic policies but recognized that the elected branches of government had significant constitutional power to regulate commercial life and, as such, did not call on judges to protect the freedom of contract.[28] Chafee insisted, however, that these conservatives offered no distinctive defense of free speech. Rather, in his account, these "conservative libertarians" and progressive thinkers agreed on a common constitutional defense of expression rights. To further this impression, Chafee successfully pretended that he was a conservative without interest in the reform movements of his day. Thus, those following in his footsteps assumed that Chafee presented the traditional interpretation of American advocacy rights. As Donald Smith recently stated, "his great defense of free speech was, in a significant sense, a reflection of his conservatism."[29]

The Illusion of Nonpartisanship

Jerold Auerbach observed that Chafee "labored strenuously to make his argument palatable to those who too eagerly assumed that civil libertarianism and radicalism were indistinguishable."[30] As part of this effort to distinguish his defense of the right to express radical opinions from a defense of the soundness of radical beliefs, Chafee constantly claimed that libertarian arguments transcended partisan political debate. The defense of free speech, he argued, was consistent with the justifications for any social or economic policy. Thus, proponents and opponents of the liberty of contract could agree on the value of uninhibited debate on the merits of that dispute. The "principle" underlying advocacy rights, Chafee declared, "may be invoked just as eagerly . . . by conservatives" as by left-wing critics of governmental policies. Chafee further insisted that the philosophical foundations of the system of freedom of expression were timeless, transcending the particular intellectual fashions of any era. In his view, libertarians had historically shared a common understanding of the foundation of expression rights. All proponents of free speech from Milton to Mill to Holmes, he contended, valued public debate for the same reasons. Disputes among libertarians were historically confined to questions over the best means of protecting free speech from particular repressive policies. Thus, developments in libertarian theory reflected only differences in the "machinery considered essential at the time to achieve this continuing purpose, whose great and permanent significance is triumphantly proclaimed in the opening clauses of our federal Bill of Rights."[31]

Chafee maintained that the leading proponents of expression rights had recognized that their arguments for expression rights were independent of those supporting partisan politics. The most important contributors to libertarian theory, he insisted, were persons who successfully divorced their attitudes toward economic and social policies from their attitudes toward free speech. *Free Speech in the United States* was a celebration of Justice Holmes,[32] whom Chafee observed was "much out of patience with the radicalism which judicial opinions placed under the protection of the Constitution," yet "reluctant to stop other men from trying to make things better" because he was "not sure enough of [his] own ideas to be certain that the reformers are wrong."[33] If anyone played the second lead in Chafee's modern history of free speech, that person was Charles Evans Hughes, whom Chafee claimed shared Holmes's attitudes toward economic and social reform. "Under [Hughes's] leadership," he wrote, the "inspiring proclamations of this great

American tradition of freedom of speech . . . became part of the majority of the Court."[34]

By comparison, Chafee was not nearly as effusive in his praise of Justice Brandeis, whom he saw as one of those partisan reformers "who are very much dissatisfied with existing conditions and anxious to change them."[35] Chafee never asserted that Brandeis made any significant contribution to First Amendment theory. Although most scholars consider the *Whitney* concurrence one of the most important free-speech opinions ever written by a Supreme Court justice because it added a requirement of seriousness to the clear and present danger test, Chafee implied that Brandeis was merely repeating Holmes's views. When, at the end of his life, Chafee reviewed the development of the constitutional defense of expression, he did not even mention Brandeis's name.[36]

Chafee emphasized that he "adhere[d] to traditional political and economic views" of the sort espoused by Justices Holmes and Hughes.[37] In the opening paragraphs of both *Free Speech in the United States* and *Freedom of Speech,* Chafee asserted, "I have no sympathy myself with the views of most of the men who have been imprisoned since the war for speaking out."[38] "The idea that government should support the people," he declared elsewhere, "is off my beat."[39] Chafee stated that he opposed "the ideal of social equality" that would "entrench without limit upon savings and business enterprise," was indifferent to the demands of labor unions, and regarded much of the New Deal as "too hastily" implemented. He expressed empathy with "the irritation which . . . businesses feel under the governmental state" and worried about "the coming epoch where education and everything else will be operated solely by a bureaucratic state." "Socialists," Chafee thought, "assume that human beings who dislike being ordered around by people who are better born or richer than themselves are going to relish being ordered about by people who are cleverer than they are."[40]

Although his efforts on behalf of free speech were devoted to defending persons who attacked the institutions of private property, Chafee claimed that he was "sufficiently convinced of the value of property to spend most of [his] time studying how the law can adequately protect it." Indeed, he asserted that his work on insurance problems was his most valuable contribution to public law.[41] Chafee reiterated this devotion to traditional economic policies during his famous trial at the Harvard Club. In response to conservative alumni of the Harvard Law School, who demanded that he be fired because of the political implications of his article attacking the verdict in *Abrams v. United States*,[42] Chafee emphasized that he had "no sympathy with the political and economic doctrines of these prisoners." "My sympathies and all my associations," he informed his accusers, "are with the men who save, who manage and produce. But I want my side to fight fair."[43]

As the testimony of many acquaintances attests, these professions of conservatism were partially true. Chafee did reject radical social visions. Like many other progressive thinkers, he opposed some aspects of the New Deal and hoped to restore an older community rather than create a new one. He certainly would have joined neither the Students for a Democratic Society nor the Critical Legal Studies Conference. Nevertheless, while he may have been a conservative in these senses,[44] Chafee was also a mainstream progressive thinker. He rejected both the policies advanced by conservative libertarians and the reasons they gave for advancing those policies. Instead, he was a firm proponent of pragmatism and sociological jurisprudence. Furthermore, he identified with the views of early civil libertarian thinkers and, in particular, endorsed the Dewey/Addams/Brandeis vision of the democratic society.

Chafee frequently declared that Spencer's formula of freedom and Mill's harm principle were outdated because "very few acts are wholly self-regarding." "The old-fashioned liberties," he argued, "are as precious as ever, but they are no longer enough. A man left alone cannot save himself. He would merely be out of a job, starve because meat and grain are not transported, freeze because coal and oil do not arrive in his city." Like other progressive thinkers, Chafee maintained that changing social conditions justified more governmental intervention than had been necessary in the past. "Our people," he maintained, "have put too much trust in the automatic tendencies of our society to right itself." In his view "the duties of government have ceased to be merely negative—to protect citizens from enemies foreign and domestic, including tyrannical officials." Social obligations were "also affirmative—to help keep running the thermodynamic machine of each human being and the equally complex interadjustments of a great aggregate of human beings."[45]

Most regulations of commercial activity enacted in the early twentieth century had Chafee's firm support. When Chafee questioned New Deal policies, he did so by contrasting them with welfare legislation passed in the progressive era.[46] Although opposed to their specific demands, he believed that radicals frequently pointed to areas where more moderate changes were necessary.[47] In "Prosperity," written just three months before the stock market crash of October 1929, Chafee challenged Americans to "employ" their largess "in planning and making secure a better world."[48] That article endorsed federal programs designed to alleviate unemployment and protect the environment.[49]

Chafee sided with such early civil libertarians as Dewey, Addams, and Brandeis when their values diverged from progressive opponents of free speech. He thought that the end of government was "to make men free to develop their faculties," that "the right of every individual to develop his mind and his soul in the ways of his own choice" was the meaning of "self-government and freedom." "The development of mind and spirit, and the search for truth," he insisted, are "the best things men stand for."[50] This human development would best be fostered in a diverse, participatory society. Chafee valued "the ideal of Roger Williams," who believed that the United States should be a land of small heterogenous communities, rather than one large homogenous community.[51] "If Americanization means anything concrete," he argued, "it certainly means tolerance for opinions different from our own, however objectionable they seem to us." "Diversity in the effective communication of facts and opinions" was "a fundamental presupposition of the self-righting process."[52] Echoing Brandeis, Chafee spoke of "the curse of bigness—big corporations, big unions, big government agencies." Large organizations, he claimed, encouraged a sluggishness inconsistent with a free citizenry. "Whenever I see a big enterprise," he declared, "I want to knock it into smaller pieces because the centralization of power seems dangerous and dull."[53] To combat bigness, Chafee urged that the majority of governmental functions be handled by local agencies so that "the public would have a fairly direct share in the functions of government that intimately affect their own life." By structuring the community in this way, society could best ensure the "abundance of inquiring minds among the people" that was necessary to maintain a democratic society.[54]

Chafee endorsed civil libertarian positions on industrial democracy and educational reform. His father approved of his decision to teach law because he could not tolerate his son's belief that senior employees in the family business should have a say in company policy and a share in company profits.[55] Like Dewey, Chafee argued that the function of a school "is to supply [students] not so much knowledge as power, power to understand the universe and the social order in which they exist now and the different social order of a quarter century hence when they will be in the lead. They must not regard the principles of today as eternal truths."[56]

Most important, Chafee shared the vision of a democratic society that inspired the new philosophical defense of free speech. Persons in the good society, he claimed, developed their powers and advanced the common good by actively participating in public debates over vital social questions. Chafee insisted,

A community is a universe of discourse in which the members participate by speaking and listening, writing and reading. In a free community the members establish and re-establish, examine and re-examine, in response to one another, their formulations of man's ultimate ends, the standards of their behavior, and their application to concrete issues. Thus, the society in a continuous enterprise of inquiry and discussion gropes its way through changing tasks and conditions; the individual, even if not free from the pressures of his own circumstances, can feel "free" by participating in that enterprise.[57]

In this democratic society, "speech" had to "be fruitful as well as free." "Experience," Chafee declared, "introduces this qualification into the classical arguments of Milton and John Stuart Mill, that only through open discussion is truth discovered and spread.''[58] Chafee endorsed civil libertarian demands for governmental economic regulations that would provide all persons with the resources necessary for meaningful input into the marketplace of ideas. He condemned "unmanaged processes, whether in economics or in communication.''[59] Legislation, Chafee insisted, had to ensure "the widespread distribution of the material things which make for a happy and fruitful life" and could not be "content with adjusting the negative forces which restrain liberty.''[60] In his "Liberty and Law" essay, Chafee argued that elected officials had to "consider the development of positive forces which will encourage [liberty] and remove the sluggishness of thought into which we all easily lapse even without any prohibitions upon opinion." "We cannot afford," he concluded, "to neglect methods for obtaining livelier oral discussion and places available for it, and for encouraging fuller presentation of all sides of international and industrial controversies in the press and over the radio.''[61]

Finally, like other early civil libertarians, Chafee recognized that threats to the meaningful exercise of free-speech rights were "just as great where the interference comes from corporations as when it comes from government." The most significant obstacle to an effective system of free expression, he insisted, is "the increased tendency for the most effective instrumentalities of communication to be bounded and shaped by persons who are often on one side of many public questions.''[62] Although Chafee did not believe that government should aggressively police the communications industry,[63] he called for government to provide free public facilities for speakers, improve the quality of education, and require commercial news organizations to sell their services to all those willing to pay the price.[64]

Chafee's attitude toward law was as partisan as his attitude toward politics. Like other progressives, he rejected conservative approaches to legal interpretation in favor of the more pragmatic method of sociological jurisprudence. Indeed, Chafee was at the center of early twentieth-century movements for legal reform. He first became interested in the philosophy of law when he attended one of Roscoe Pound's courses at Harvard Law School, an experience Chafee later described as "one

of the decisive influences on my life because it excited me about
the possibilities of doing something to make the law better."[65]
He accepted Pound's offer of a teaching position at Harvard
Law School because he wanted to "share in the modernizing of
American law."[66] When asked what books his law students
should read, Chafee nominated William James's *Pragmatism*
because that book was "an exposition of the philosophy which is
most influential upon the thinking of our time."[67]

Chafee's writings on other legal subjects promoted the basic
principles of sociological jurisprudence. Like Pound, Chafee
believed that judges should resolve cases by examining actual
social conditions, not by relying on a theory of natural rights.
"It is the judge's duty," he claimed, "to test a proposed rule by
its effect upon the welfare of those whom it concerns."[68] Natural rights were merely "lovely label[s] to be attached to the
ideas a particular person would like to have prevail."[69] Chafee
similarly asserted that contemporary legal problems could not
be solved by deductive processes or mechanical interpretations
of past decisions. "Logic," he insisted, "does not lead inevitably to a single sound rule of law for every conceivable legal
problem."[70] Judges should rely on precedents only when they
help advance contemporary social interests. "The teaching of
the past," he opined, "is of little use unless it emphasizes its
similarity to the present." Jurists had to have "the training and
ability to distinguish rules workable today from the unworkable." In this way, "the principles of the past" could be "used
and gradually extended to solve the complex problems of the
judge's own time."[71]

Constitutional interpretation was also a process of making legal principles serve social interests. Judges, Chafee claimed,
could not and should not rely on the intentions of the constitutional framers. In many cases, efforts to discover "the pre-existing will of the people" only revealed that "the people probably
never thought about the matter one way or the other when they
voted for the constitution."[72] Even if the framers' intentions
could be determined, those intentions were not dispositive of
constitutional questions. An evolving society might require new
interpretations of constitutional provisions. Chafee defended
the Supreme Court's eventual ratification of the New Deal on

the ground that "wider powers" of economic regulation were "appropriate to the new needs although inappropriate to the old needs."[73]

In keeping with sociological jurisprudence, Chafee declared that the judiciary had no business determining what economic regulations were necessary under contemporary social conditions. Making such choices was the function of the elected branches of government. "The vote of the majority of the electorate or the legislature," he asserted, "is the best way to decide what beliefs shall be translated into immediate action."[74] Legislatures were not only more accountable to the will of the people than the courts, but also, as Pound had argued, the elected branches of government had greater institutional resources for determining and responding to public interests and needs.[75] For this reason, Chafee believed that the constitution should be interpreted as permitting government to experiment with diverse social programs. That document, he wrote, is "compatible with other types of economic organization, such as national ownership of all industries."[76] Court opinions that used the due process clause of the Fourteenth Amendment to limit the regulatory power of the elective branches of government were as much an abuse of judicial power as was the *Dred Scot* decision.[77]

Before Chafee, progressive jurists had assumed that these principles of judicial restraint should also govern freedom of speech cases.[78] Even Brandeis admitted that judicial protection of political dissenters was inconsistent with the judicial obligation to defer to the legislature's assessment of the appropriate balance of social interests. In spite of such claims, Chafee refused to abandon the principles of sociological jurisprudence when constructing his constitutional defense of expression rights. Instead, he asserted that, properly understood, Pound's legal philosophy required a broader interpretation of the constitutional meaning of free speech than early civil libertarian jurists had thought possible.

Nevertheless, this decision to rely on the premises developed by earlier progressive jurists limited the extent to which Chafee could translate the democratic aspirations of early civil libertarian thought into constitutional law. Although he sincerely hoped that the dominant voices in his community would demand the social and economic conditions that would enable all persons to exercise their expression rights effectively, Chafee insisted that the majority had the right to choose any social or economic policies they pleased. The principles of sociological jurisprudence, he confessed, would not tolerate judicial activism on behalf of economic rights, even though he recognized those rights as an integral part of a functioning system of free expression.

The New Constitutional Meaning of Free Speech

In 1919, Chafee published the first constitutional defense of free speech that thoroughly broke with the conservative libertarian tradition. Although major chunks of "Freedom of Speech in War Time" and his subsequent writings extended and elaborated, without much originality, claims made earlier by Pound and Schofield, Chafee expanded their understanding of constitutional advocacy rights in important ways. Unlike Pound, Chafee discussed at length the social interest in debate about matters of public importance. Unlike Schofield, he derived his standards of protection from the needs of a twentieth-century system of freedom of expression, not from the particular intentions of long dead framers of the Constitution. More important, Chafee was the first thinker to suggest that changing social conditions might require broadening constitutional protections. If the standards preferred by the authors of the First Amendment no longer served the function that speech served in democratic societies, then the Constitution commanded judges to devise standards that would.

Chafee's analysis of the constitutional meaning of free speech began in the traditional manner, with a discussion of the original purpose of the First Amendment. The framers, he stated, sought to guarantee "a wide and genuine protection for all sorts of discussion of public matters." They thought they could do so by outlawing the crime of seditious libel, which permitted persons to be punished for true utterances, and by allowing juries to determine the issue of truth.[79] Chafee admitted that the original rationale of constitutional free-speech guarantees governed their subsequent interpretation. However, future generations were bound only by the principles underlying constitutional provisions, not by the particular means the framers believed necessary or sufficient to realize those values in practice. "The meaning of First Amendment," Chafee declared, "did not crystallize in 1791." Constitutional protections had to continue fostering the unrestricted interchange of ideas that the framers had envisioned. Eighteenth-century standards, reflecting the political conditions of their day, were subject to revision in light of changing circumstances. Although "conditions in 1791 must be considered," Chafee would not have them "arbitrarily fix the division between lawful and unlawful speech for all time."[80]

This emphasis on changing social conditions was one standard convention of early twentieth-century political and legal argument. As noted in chapter 2, progressive jurists consistently pointed to new industrial developments when justifying a narrower scope of constitutional protection for economic rights. Pound similarly argued that novel features of contemporary life might justify modifying both the individual's right to self-expression and the traditional rule against prior restraint.[81] Chafee, however, devised a novel use of this mode of argument. He proposed that sociological jurisprudence's emphasis on keeping the law abreast of current events might occasionally warrant expanding constitutional freedoms. The framers' procedural devices, he contended, no longer adequately safeguarded the social interest in open discussion. Hence, early twentieth-century speakers required more extensive expression rights if the First Amendment was to fulfill its original purposes of promoting and protecting public debate.[82]

The framers of the Constitution, Chafee maintained, valued measures that put the protection of free speech almost entirely in the hands of juries because they had experienced royal policies that outlawed advocacy of widely held objections to English rule. Taking the issue of truth away from judges adequately protected majority opinions from suppressive measures be-

cause the average member of the community was likely to sympathize with common criticisms of elected officials and their
policies. "Juries," Chafee observed, "will safeguard the criticism of the government of views popular among the electorate." However, the experience of World War I demonstrated
that allowing juries to determine the truth of political utterances would not secure minority opinion from infringement by
the majority. As Chafee noted, randomly selected members of a
community "are far less likely to acquit men who hold unpopular opinions, which nevertheless for the public good ought to be
allowed expression." For this reason, he concluded that modern conditions required "a reformulation of the definition of
free speech," so that political dissenters could freely express
their beliefs. The meaning of the First Amendment had to be
expanded to "impose limits on legislation against speech, beyond which statutes become invalid and juries are not permitted to convict."[83]

Earlier chapters have demonstrated that the mere claim of
some "limits on legislation against speech" only seems to expand constitutional expression rights if one ignores the conservative libertarian tradition. Late nineteenth-century treatise
writers had already proposed various standards limiting majoritarian power over speech. When seen from the perspective of
the dilemma of early civil libertarian constitutional thought,
however, Chafee's claim appears as a dramatic step forward.
Unlike conservative libertarian claims, Chafee's call for new
speech protections could not easily be challenged within the
structure of sociological jurisprudence. Progressive opponents
of expression rights who asserted that changing social conditions never justified broadening constitutional rights could be
justly charged with advocating the sort of rigid, a priori rule
that pragmatism condemned. Moreover, rather than disguise
their policy preferences as interpretations of the precise standards the framers had intended, Chafee enabled civil libertarians to derive constitutional protections from their understanding of "the purpose free speech serves in social and political
life."[84] Thus, the new constitutional defense of free speech
could accurately reflect "the desires and needs of the individual human being who wants to speak and those of the great

group of human beings among whom he speaks," or what Pound called the individual and social interests in free speech.[85]

Individual Interest in Free Speech

As noted above, Chafee rejected previous notions that expression rights were best understood primarily as an aspect of some general principle of individual liberty. His hostility to the conservative libertarian tradition's individualist approach to free speech was so strong that, as previously documented, in works allegedly dedicated to the general promotion of expression rights, Chafee systemically omitted evidence supporting claims that the Constitution valued highly the individual's interest in expressing his opinions. In addition to his theoretical objections to the idea of natural law,[86] Chafee claimed it was "useless to define free speech by talk about rights." An individual rights approach, he declared, could not provide standards that would resolve First Amendment issues. For every person who claimed a personal right to free speech, another person would claim a personal right not to be harmed by the possible consequences of speech. "Each side," he argued, "takes the position of the man who was arrested for swinging his arms and hitting another in the nose, and asked the judge if he did not have the right to swing his arms in a free country. 'Your right to swing your arms ends just where the other man's nose begins.' "[87]

For these reasons, Chafee maintained that the Constitution offered the individual's interest in free speech the same limited protection he believed that document offered the individual's interest in free contract. Like other progressive thinkers, Chafee believed that individual economic and expressive interests were subject to regulation for the benefit of the public. "The need for many men to express their opinions on matters vital to them if life is to be worth living," he declared, "must readily give way like other personal desires the moment it interferes with the social interest in national safety."[88] Although the socialist Rand School's interest in "the teaching of academic subjects" was a "liberty" protected by "the Fourteenth Amendment to the United States Constitution," that concern was no different from another person's desire to run a barbershop, and it could constitutionally be forced to yield before any reasonable exercise of the police power.[89] Chafee believed that the government was free to regulate commercial speech and obscenity because only individual interests were significantly advanced by those forms of expression. "The First Amendment," he stated, "was not adopted to protect vehicles of advertising and entertainment." While these were "legitimate and beneficial activities," they were similar to "stock-broking and circuses, which receive no constitutional immunity."[90]

The Social Interest in Free Speech

The First Amendment, Chafee maintained, was designed chiefly to protect the "social interest in the gains from open discussion."[91] He insisted that the main fault of previous scholarship was its failure to recognize that these social interests were constitutionally more important than individual interests in self-expression.[92] Nevertheless, as most progressives explained, the individual interest of particular speakers corresponded to the social interest of the great body of potential listeners.[93] The Constitution might not give much weight to the individual interest of an alien who wanted to speak to an American citizen; however, the social interest in free speech required that citizens not be "denied the privilege of listening to and associating with a foreign thinker." Similarly, Chafee believed that while the individual interest of the Rand School in running their academy could be regulated, the social interest in promulgating their ideas could not.[94]

This social interest in expression was "the attainment of truth . . . as the basis of political and social progress."[95] Truth is important, Chafee declared, "so that the country may not only adopt the wisest course of action but carry it out in the wisest way."[96] Although "the value of open discussion is most frequently realized when it is preliminary to political action," Chafee did not believe it was "confined to governmental controversies." "The same policy," he argued, "extends to the making of sound decisions and value-judgments in other matters of public interest, such as art, literature, education, and the relations between men and women."[97] In his view, society benefited from discussions of all matters in which the public might have an interest. Moreover, citizens had a right to debate all cultural and moral subjects because discussion of those topics advanced the citizens' political understanding. "The truth," Chafee declared, "is that there are public aspects to practically every subject." Although "Shakespeare and Whitehead do seem very far away from the next election," "poems and plays and novels" contributed to "the satisfactory operation of self-government." Discussion of such matters enabled "the individual to develop fairness, sympathy, and understanding of other men, a comprehension of economic forces, and some basic purpose of life."[98]

Chafee recognized that "the attainment of truth is not the only purpose for which the community exists."[99] Maintaining order and morality, developing youth, protecting against external aggression, fostering public safety, and promoting the aesthetic sense of the community were other important social interests.[100] Legislatures were obligated to afford these social interests the same protection as free speech. Because "it is impossible to satisfy all of these claims, at least in their entirety," Chafee endorsed Pound's balancing test as a means of adjudicating among conflicting social interests. "We must allot a weight to each according to its social value," he claimed, "and then balance them against one another in order to determine how far each can receive legal expression."[101] Nevertheless, because free speech was as important as any other social interest, the First Amendment did not permit expression to be sacrificed every time some remote action merely threatened a competing social interest. Speech could be restricted only if it significantly and immediately threatened other social interests. In the passage of his argument that he described as "key,"[102] Chafee declared

the true boundary line of the First Amendment can be fixed only when Congress and the courts realize that the principle on which speech is classified as lawful or unlawful involves the balancing against each other of two very important social interests, in public safety and in the search for truth. Every reasonable attempt should be made to maintain both interests unimpaired, and the great interest in free speech should be sacrificed only when the interest in public safety is really imperiled, and not, as most men believe, when it is barely conceivable that it may be slightly affected. In war time, therefore, speech should be unrestricted by the censorship or by punishment, unless it is clearly liable to cause direct and dangerous interference with the conduct of the war.[103]

Courts applying this test had to give all speech on matters of public interest the same heavy weight. In contrast to Frankfurter, who once suggested that communist speech "ranks low" "on any scale of social values,"[104] Chafee contended that the most obscure members of fringe groups had valid criticisms of current policies. Furthermore, he claimed that restrictions on "insignificant" speech often silenced more significant speakers. "Pertinacious orators and writers who get hauled up," Chafee observed, "are merely extremist spokesmen for a mass of more thoughtful and more retiring men and women." When officials "put the hotheads in jail, these cooler people do not get arrested—they just keep quiet."[105]

This emphasis on the social interest in expression suggested a new justification for requiring states to respect free-speech rights, one that did not center on the individual rights protected by the due process clause of the Fourteenth Amendment. Chafee claimed that, although the text of the First Amendment only restricted federal efforts to regulate political dissent, that amendment declared the national interest in free speech. Thus, the federal government's failure to limit speech rights created a presumption that Congress believed the nation would best be served by unregulated debate on matters of public interest. Like the interstate commerce clause, the "negative radiations" of the First Amendment preempted most, if not all, state regulations of speech on matters of national concern.[106] State regulations were clearly preempted when, as in the case of World War I, the federal government adopted policies on what speech was and was not to be prohibited. In his analysis of *Gilbert v. Minnesota*, Chafee asserted that after the federal government "decides to allow a fairly wide range of discussion to the opponents of a war either as a safety valve for discontent or for the sake of obtaining the advantage of their opinions, such national policies will be very seriously blocked if the various states see fit to run amok and establish inconsistent limitations on dissent."[107] Thirty years after *Gitlow*, Chafee still claimed that the negative radiations of the First Amendment provided the main constitutional basis for restricting local power over speech. In 1956, he declared that "state legislatures" should "give up concerning themselves with subversive activities, and entrust the whole matter of the safety of the nation to the government of the nation."[108]

The New Scope of Constitutional Free Speech Protection

Chafee presented the clear and present danger test as an unambiguous expansion of the constitutional defense of free speech. Prior to World War I, he claimed, proponents of expression rights had only been concerned with preventing prior restraints and ensuring jury trials in sedition cases.[109] When compared with these standards, the clear and present danger test appeared to be a significant step forward in libertarian theory. In contrast to such persons as Corwin, who believed that having juries determine the truth of utterances significantly protected political expression,[110] Chafee supported all the free-speech claims raised in the cases from *Debs v. United States* to *DeJonge v. Oregon*.[111] However, as noted above, the clear and present danger test did not dramatically extend the constitutional meaning of free speech when compared to the standards proffered by either late nineteenth-century conservative treatise writers or transitional figures like Theodore Schroeder and Ernst Freund. These jurists claimed that advocacy of lawless conduct was the only form of speech that could be constitutionally restricted, and Schroeder claimed that even such advocacy could be punished only if an actual injury resulted.[112] They would protect all speakers who advocated change by lawful means, even if such speech presented a clear and present danger. These different standards did not simply reflect different attitudes toward the value of expression, but broader differences between conservative and progressive thought.

The direct incitement test favored by earlier libertarians reflected conservative beliefs that individuals were generally free to interact with each other on their own terms. As Abraham

Chayes has noted, "the basic conceptions governing legal liability [in the late nineteenth century] were 'intention' and
'fault.' "[113] Thus, government could only punish speakers who
had consciously abused their speech rights by either urging
criminal conduct or intentionally telling lies. Advocates were
judged by their intentions, not by the possible social consequences of their speech acts.

Sociological jurisprudence, however, maintained that legal
doctrines should be based on the social consequences of action.
As noted in chapter 3, Holmes insisted the law prohibit acts that
created a high probability of harm, rather than acts done with a
guilty state of mind.[114] Holmes and Chafee independently derived their versions of the clear and present danger test from
this reinterpretation of the common law of criminal attempt.[115]
Although he sometimes spoke as if the First Amendment required states to prove that a speaker had intended to cause illegal conduct,[116] Chafee explicitly referred his reader to
Holmes's opinion in *Peaslee v. Commonwealth* for the correct
definition of criminal intent. In *Free Speech in the United States*
he declared that "to establish criminal responsibility, the words
uttered must constitute dangerous progress toward the con-
summation of the independent offense."[117] Thus, abstract discussions of tyrannicide were sufficiently dangerous "to bring
such discussions within the range of legislative discretion,"
even when the speaker had no intention of actually threatening
the life of any state official.[118]

While Chafee offered prominent speakers more protection
than did Holmes, his emphasis on the consequences of expression had the same potential to curtail the speakers and speeches
that society has the greatest interest in hearing. Chafee's analysis of *Herndon v. Lowry* clearly illustrated the relatively narrow
scope of his version of the clear and present danger test.[119] That
case concerned the prosecution of a black communist organizer
under a Georgia statute that punished efforts to foment insurrection. Although he noted that Herndon did not advocate
lawless conduct, Chafee asserted that Herndon was the one
free-speech defendant who did not "seem . . . fairly harmless."
Herndon was dangerous because he advocated politically ex-
plosive doctrines. He insisted that racial justice could be

achieved only through broad remedial measures and basic institutional changes. "Given the unrest of Negroes, share croppers, mill-workers," Chafee claimed that this "demand for equal racial rights, lavish relief, and the virtual abolition of debts might have produced some sort of disorder in the near future." "Smoking is all right," he contended, "but not in a powder magazine."[120] Chafee recognized that institutionalized unconstitutional racism was the reason why even peaceful advocacy of civil rights created a clear and present danger of violence. However, while he noted that "the very conditions that cause the grievances render agitation to remove the grievances dangerous,"[121] this was not a reason to question the soundness of his version of the clear and present danger test. Chafee would have upheld the long prison sentence given to Herndon in the trial court had the Georgia statute in question specifically prohibited his speech.[122] He concluded that the only general lesson one could draw from *Herndon v. Lowry* was the lack of wisdom in sedition prosecutions in such circumstances, which were "only likely to make matters worse."[123]

This refusal to defend Herndon's rights cannot be explained by Chafee's insensitivity to racial matters.[124] Rather, this failure was rooted in the structure of the new constitutional defense of free speech. What mattered to Chafee was the actual threat presented by a speech, not the speaker's intention to present that threat. Chafee was equally "insensitive" to the advocacy rights of influential speakers who promoted other causes. For example, he asserted that "turbulent persons like Emma Goldman" were properly deported under a federal law that permitted federal officials to decide on the basis of Goldman's political beliefs.[125]

Chafee believed, however, that the Constitution protected speakers who intended to threaten clear and present dangers but lacked the influence to do so. Chafee never denied that Gitlow had advocated violent conduct, but, like Holmes, he believed that Gitlow had a constitutional right to speak because no one was going to listen. After examining the remarks that led to Gitlow's conviction, he commented, "an agitator who read these thirty-four pages to a mob would not stir them to violence, except possibly against himself."[126] This observation implies that Chafee believed the First Amendment did not protect speakers who might incite mobs to violence by expressing Gitlow's ideas more eloquently.

These difficulties with the scope of the new constitutional defense of free speech were compounded by the varied social interests Chafee was willing to balance against First Amendment interests. As noted above, Chafee believed that legislatures could consider such social interests as morality, the development of the young, and aesthetics when deciding whether to regulate political expression. When the failure of citizens to cooperate voluntarily with the government would result in "a serious injury," the government had the power to punish those who urged others to exercise their legal right not to cooperate.[127] Chafee endorsed the *Schenck* decision because, at the very least, the defendants in that case urged citizens not to assist governmental efforts to raise troops during World War I.[128] Indeed, *Free Speech in the United States* suggested that preventing litter would be a constitutionally sufficient reason to curtail advocacy rights. On these grounds, states could severely restrict, if not prohibit, peaceful leafleting.[129]

There were, however, circumstances where sociological jurisprudence should have expanded the scope of the constitutional defense of free speech. The conservative libertarian tradition, with the exception of Schroeder, regarded advocacy of any crime as outside the limits of First and Fourteenth Amendment protection. In *Whitney,* however, Brandeis suggested that the social interest in freedom of speech outweighed the social interest in preventing minor crimes. For this reason, he claimed that advocacy of trespass could not be constitutionally punished, "even if there was imminent danger that advocacy would lead to trespass."[130]

By relying on the law of criminal attempt, Chafee failed to take advantage of all the circumstances in which a balancing test protected speech that the inflexible direct incitement standard prohibited. One can attempt both major and minor crimes. If Holmes's definitions are used, then the persuasive advocate of trespass has committed a criminal attempt punishable by law. Although Chafee never explicitly stated whether any successful advocacy of crime was beyond the pale of the First Amendment's protection, his editing implies that he accepted this consequence of his version of the clear and present danger test. When he discussed the *Whitney* concurrence, he quoted almost the entire paragraph in which Brandeis asserted that the harm must "be relatively serious" to justify repression of speech. The only passage Chafee hid from his reader's view was the one where Brandeis claimed that certain violations of minor laws were examples of insufficient harms.[131]

Yet, as the difference between Brandeis and Chafee illustrates, one could clearly make more libertarian claims within the structure of Chafee's arguments than he in fact made. Future defenders of expression rights could and did maintain that Chafee gave insufficient weight to the social interest in debate about matters of public importance. Some civil libertarians would later claim that government would correctly balance social interests in the highest percentage of cases if officials always protected free speech.[132] Nevertheless, this civil libertarian constitutional defense had yet another problem to overcome. Whatever the proper evaluation of constitutional freedoms, the issue remained whether judges could recalibrate the scales after elected officials determined that other social interests outweighed the social interest in free speech.

Judicial Activism on Behalf of Free Speech

Although Chafee believed that clear and present danger marked the boundary between constitutionally protected speech and speech legislatures had the power to restrict, he remained troubled by judicial capacity to patrol the border. An ardent opponent of the freedom of contract, he was dedicated to the proposition that elected officials were both authorized and best equipped to determine what conduct should be regulated in the public interest. This position had always been thought to demand judicial restraint whenever the people's representatives voted to limit existing speech rights. Judicial protection of political dissent, progressive jurists agreed, was an illegitimate product of a judge's personal policy preferences disguised as an appeal to fundamental individual rights.

Chafee's initial free-speech writings did not explicitly consider whether courts could declare speech restrictions unconstitutional. Like other early civil libertarian jurists he maintained that the central issue in *Debs* was "the proper construction of the Espionage Act."[133] The First Amendment was relevant to that question, but only as a statement of the "policy to be observed by courts in applying constitutional statutes to utterances." Thus, Chafee endorsed Hand's assertion that federal decisions affirming the conviction of political dissenters were objectionable because the national legislature had not specifically prohibited verbal opposition to American war policies. Legislation, he insisted, "should not be construed to reverse this national policy of liberty of the press and silence hostile criticism, unless Congress had given the clearest expression of such an intention in the statute."[134]

When first confronted with explicit legislative prohibitions of specific political doctrines, Chafee tended to concede that elected officials had the constitutional power to suppress political debate if they believed that restrictions were necessary to avoid clear and present dangers. In 1920, he concluded that "Congress alone can effectively safeguard minority opinion in times of excitement."[135] Chafee later argued that the national legislature could forbid all discussions of tyrannicide, require union leaders to take loyalty oaths, and restrict speech during strikes if it thought such measures necessary.[136] Furthermore, he suggested that the federal government could require a less stringent connection between advocacy and action than that provided for by the law of criminal attempt. While "the ordinary tests punish agitators just before [the pot] begins to boil over," Chafee declared that "Congress could change those tests and punish it when it really gets hot."[137]

More generally, Chafee maintained that a constitutional gap separated the scope of First Amendment rights and judicial power to protect advocacy. "Our Bill of Rights," he insisted, "performs a double function." The first ten amendments "fix a certain point to halt the government abruptly with a 'thus no far and no farther,' " but "long before that point is reached they urge upon every official of the three branches of the state a constant regard for certain declared fundamental policies of American life."[138] This meant that courts could not strike down laws merely because legislators did not exhibit the high regard for free speech demanded by the Constitution. The people's representatives had the power to restrict much socially beneficial speech. "What is constitutional," Chafee frequently observed, "may be very unwise." For this reason, Chafee thought that libertarian efforts should be primarily directed at convincing elected officials to refrain from restricting expression. In these debates, public welfare considerations mattered more than abstract constitutional standards. Thus, "in endeavoring to oppose suppressive measures," Chafee "found it best to keep on the level of wisdom and policy as much as possible." In the 1950s, for example, he declared that libertarian objections to McCarthyism "should be put on the grounds of wisdom and American traditions, rather than on Constitutionality."[139]

Chafee's understanding of the nature and sources of legal doctrine supported this emphasis on public policy. Following Holmes, Freund, and other progressive jurists, Chafee identified law with the actual decisions of courts. "What a majority of the Supreme Court votes," he stated, "does have considerable bearing on truth in constitutional matters."[140] Thus, political dissenters had the right to say whatever a majority of justices were willing to protect. Narrow Supreme Court interpretations of the First Amendment, in his view, excluded broader libertarian standards from the constitutional meaning of free speech.[141]

Moreover, the events of World War I taught Chafee that public opinion was the crucial element in determining the constitutional standards actually applied by courts. If the people passed sedition laws, "trial judges will be found to adopt a free construction of the act so as to reach objectionable doctrines."[142] "Final limits upon government power over discussion," he learned, "are of comparatively small service in the almost total absence from the national consciousness of any genuine belief in the usefulness of the open expression of unpopular ideas."[143] In this environment, technical constitutional defenses of expression were useless; rather, a general effort to persuade the people of the value of public debate was needed. As Chafee noted in the conclusion of *Free Speech in the United States*, "in the long run the public gets just as much freedom of speech as it really wants."[144]

Chafee never disavowed his belief that an educated populace was the only permanent security for expression rights, but as he grew older he increasingly advocated more judicial activism on behalf of free speech. He began "to doubt whether Holmes was right" when that jurist maintained "that Congress is the guardian of the liberties of the people as well as the courts." Although Chafee declared that he would "like to have legislatures and other lawmaking bodies protecting our civil rights," he became convinced that "we must in times of pressure and not to say hysteria look to the courts to guarantee them for us."[145]

To convince his contemporaries that courts should protect expression rights, Chafee had to explain why speech differed from commercial behavior, which sociological jurisprudence insisted elected officials could freely regulate. Progressive jurists had previously recognized one important distinction between speech and property. Property, Pound and Schofield declared, was an individual interest; speech was a vital social interest. "Freedom of Speech in War Time" reiterated that point. "The Fourteenth Amendment and the obligation of contracts clause," Chafee declared, only protected "important individual interests." Expression, however, was a vital social interest and thus could not "readily give way like other personal desires the moment it interferes with the social interest in national safety."[146] However, neither Chafee nor any other progressive jurist thought the distinction between individual and social interests justified any special judicial solicitude for expression rights. The crucial question such a claim had to answer was why judges were entitled to second-guess legislative determinations that other social interests outweighed the social interest in free speech.

Chafee first suggested a distinction between judicial activism on behalf of expression and economic rights in a 1922 article attacking New York's effort to close the socialist Rand School. Legislators, he contended, "can be trusted to recognize dirt or discriminate between dangerous and harmless machinery." But in light of the human "tendency to regard what one dislikes as a menace to the social order," elected officials "cannot be trusted to discriminate between dangerous and harmless ideas."[147] In other words, because of biases unique to free-speech issues, legislators could not competently evaluate the factual disputes underlying First Amendment controversies. Hence, given sociological jurisprudence's insistence that social interests should be balanced by the institution most capable of doing so, courts were the appropriate forum for resolving free-speech conflicts.

In the 1920s and 1930s, Chafee's writings occasionally intimated that sociological jurisprudence's insistence on democratic governance might similarly justify special judicial solicitude for expression rights. Those in power, he contended, should not be allowed to ensure their reelection by muting criticism of their policies. "A freedom which does not yet extend to a minority," his 1920 analysis of *Abrams v. United States* noted, "would be a very partial affair, enabling the majority to dig themselves in for an indefinite future." Although he recognized that "the vote of the majority of the electorate or the legislature is the best way to decide what beliefs shall be translated into immediate action," Chafee maintained that it was "inadvisable for the government to seek to end a contest of ideas by imprisoning or exiling its intellectual adversaries."[148] In 1931 he suggested that those justices who typically voted to sustain economic regulations and strike down expression regulations wished to give "much of the control [of business] to the elected representatives of the multitude who are virtually affected by business."[149]

A number of early civil libertarians similarly distinguished free speech and economic policies. In *The Police Power*, Freund suggested that while "conditions which affect health and morality are primarily subject to the police power," "our constitutions proclaim the principle of individual liberty" for "moral, intellectual and political movements." Twenty years later, Dewey claimed that Holmes had voted to sustain economic regulations because he recognized that judges should defer "to the beliefs of others to the extent of permitting them a free competition in the open market of social life." Frankfurter similarly maintained that "Mr. Justice Holmes attributed very different legal significance to those liberties of the individual which history has attested as the indispensable conditions of a free society from that which he attributed to liberties which derived merely from shifting economic arrangements." Finally, in a student note, Karl Llewellyn insisted that while "the majority is to rule, and the minority is to obey . . . , the minority shall have reasonable opportunity to object before laws are passed, and to turn itself, by peaceful conversion, into a majority if so be it can."[150]

Nevertheless, in the two decades following passage of the Espionage Act, no one developed these insights into a full-blown theory of the judicial function. Rather, as noted in chapter 3, civil libertarians were content to piggyback judicial protection of expression onto judicial protection for economic rights. As long as conservative justices struck down laws that abridged the freedom of contract, liberal jurists unashamedly used those precedents to strike down laws that abridged the freedom of speech. Chafee accepted this practice. In 1928, he insisted that *Lochner v. New York* and other such cases should "at least . . . serve as precedents justifying similar protection for freedom of speech."[151]

The New Deal turnaround of 1937 dramatically foreclosed this manner of defending free speech. A Supreme Court increasingly dominated by jurists committed to sociological jurisprudence repudiated what Justice Black would later call the "*Allgeyer-Lochner-Adair-Coppage* constitutional doctrine."[152] In *West Coast Hotel v. Parrish*, a five-to-four majority began the process of overruling or discrediting those freedom of contract cases that had served as the only foundations for judicial activism on behalf of expression rights. Chief Justice Hughes's majority opinion declared that "liberty under the Constitution [is] necessarily subject to the restraints of due process, and regulation which is reasonable in relation to its subject and is adopted in the interests of the community is due process."[153]

This conception of constitutional rights and legislative power seemed to preclude special judicial solicitude for any individual freedom, but some civil libertarians refused to surrender their power to protect political and social commentary. Only one year after the Court had seemingly renounced judicial activism generally, Justice Stone suggested that the justices might only be changing emphasis. In *United States v. Carolene Products Co.*, he agreed that courts should sustain economic regulations that had any rational basis. However, in a footnote undoubtedly influenced by the previous speculations of Chafee and others, Stone recommended that "legislation which restricts those political processes which can ordinarily be expected to bring about the repeal of undesirable legislation" be subject "to more exacting judicial scrutiny." As examples of appropriate exercises of judicial power, he pointed to Brandeis's concurrence in *Whitney,* Holmes's dissent in *Gitlow,* and previous Supreme Court decisions that held state governments had violated constitutional free-speech guarantees.[154]

Chafee immediately seized upon the theory of judicial review hinted at in the *Carolene Products* footnote. Over the next five years, he used his position on the Bill of Rights subcommittee of the American Bar Association (ABA) to promote Justice Stone's interpretation of the judicial function. Chafee was particularly active in the fight to have mandatory flag saluting declared unconstitutional. Although the specific issue in *Board of Education v. Barnette* and *Minersville School District v. Gobitis* concerned religious freedom, [155] Chafee wrote those sections of the ABA's amicus brief that claimed compulsory saluting of the flag also violated constitutional expression rights. He urged the Court to recognize that a "more exacting test of validity" was necessary when judges reviewed policies that infringed on the freedom of speech.[156] "In the ordinary due process case," Chafee declared, "a presumption may properly be held to run in favor of the validity . . . of legislation" because courts must ensure that "the processes of government shall not be crippled but shall remain flexible to meet changing public needs." However, no such presumption was justified when First Amendment rights were restricted. In such cases, "the Court should itself be convinced of the existence of a public need" that outweighed the social interest in freedom. In other words, because there were reasons to think that elected officials had not responsibly balanced the social interests affected by restrictions on speech, judges had to independently determine whether particular instances of state censorship advanced the public good. In support of this position, Chafee quoted the relevant portions of the *Carolene Products* footnote and italicized Justice Roberts's assertion in *Schneider v. New Jersey* that "mere legislative preferences or beliefs respecting matters of public convenience may well support regulation directed at other personal activities, but be insufficient to justify such as diminishes the exercise of rights so vital to the maintenance of democratic institutions."[157]

When he updated *Freedom of Speech* in 1941, Chafee elaborated and improved Justice Stone's analysis of the judicial function. Rather than simply asserting that the freedom of speech could be constitutionally distinguished from the freedom of contract, Chafee insisted that the same principles justifying judicial deference to economic regulations demanded judicial activism on behalf of expression. "The critical judicial spirit which gives the legislature a wide scope in limiting the privileges of property owners," he contended, "will also tend to allow speakers and writers a wide scope in arguing against those privileges." Proponents of sociological jurisprudence, Chafee explained, recognized that "statutes to be sound and effective, must be preceded by abundant printed and oral controversy." Thus, if government refused to allow open political debate on the merits of legislative proposals, then courts had no reason to presume that elected officials had decided wisely or in a manner responsive to democratic sentiment. "Discussion," Chafee insisted, "is really legislation in the soft." For this reason, any restriction on the scope of political debate would be a de facto restriction on the legislature's substantive powers. Policies that could not be advocated would never be enacted. This inflexible limitation on legislative power to meet social needs was precisely the problem with the freedom of contract. "Drastic restrictions on speeches and pamphlets," Chafee maintained, "are comparable to rigid constitutional limitations on lawmaking. A statute which prevents an orator from questioning the present distribution of property tends to crystallize that distribution in somewhat the same way as a rigid interpretation of the due process clause."[158]

In other words, the guarantee of judicial activism on behalf of free speech justified judicial deference to social and economic policy choices made by the people's elected representatives. Courts could only defer to the policy decisions of elected officials if justices were prepared to protect speech rights; otherwise jurists could not honestly claim that those policies reflected an educated majoritarian opinion. "It is really not surprising," Chafee contended, "that Justice Holmes dissented in both *Lochner v. New York* and *Abrams v. United States.* Liberty for discussion which may lead to the formation of a dominant opinion," he concluded, "belongs side by side with the liberty of the lawmakers to transform the dominant opinion into the statute that is its natural outcome."[159]

Free Speech and Private Property

By distinguishing expression rights from economic rights, Chafee could defend judicial activism on behalf of free speech in a manner consistent with the basic tenets of progressive and liberal thought. However, that distinction inhibited efforts to develop constitutional arguments that would adequately promote debate on matters of public importance, the very goal Chafee claimed had motivated his efforts on behalf of First Amendment rights. Although, as noted above, Chafee insisted that democratic social and economic institutions were necessary elements of a democratic society, he maintained that judicial decisions promoting positive liberties undermined the democratic values supporting judicial activism on behalf of free speech.

This decision to divorce judicial protection for free speech from judicial protection for the other rights necessary to the effective exercise of expression rights represented a dramatic break in the American libertarian tradition. With the exception of Schroeder, American libertarians had historically agreed that both economic and expression rights were vital to a functioning system of freedom of speech. Conservative libertarians claimed that laissez-faire economic policies freed persons from a dependence on governmental largess that inhibited their efforts to express their opinions on matters of public interest. Hence, Burgess and other treatise writers believed that judicial decisions protecting the freedom of contract also implicitly protected the freedom of speech. Early civil libertarians insisted that democratic societies would establish democratic economic institutions so that individuals would have the independence, leisure time, and access to intellectual resources necessary for participating effectively in the marketplace of ideas. Thus, Brandeis suggested that, as long as judges were protecting individual economic rights, they ought to protect the individual economic rights that progressives thought would best promote public debate.[160] Chafee's new constitutional defense of free speech, however, sharply distinguished democratic inputs from democratic outputs. In his view, judges had no business promoting any economic liberty, even those liberties necessary to a functioning system of free speech.

Chafee's unwillingness to justify judicial solicitude for the liberties he considered the economic and social prerequisites of a functioning system of freedom of expression stemmed from the nature of the democratic process model of the judicial function. The rationale of the *Carolene Products* footnote depends on the assumption that substantive policies and political processes are independent of each other. Courts must be able to secure democratic processes without limiting elected officials' policy choices. If economic and social policies affect electoral outcomes, then the principled distinction Chafee and Justice Stone tried to make between judicial activism on behalf of free speech and judicial activism on behalf of economic rights breaks down. Elected officials could subvert democratic processes by either restricting political dissent or implementing policies that impoverished their political rivals. Under these conditions, the judicial obligation to police "those political processes which can ordinarily be expected to bring about the repeal of undesirable legislation" might obligate courts to regulate the distribution of economic resources to ensure that most persons have some meaningful access to the democratic process.

Thus, followed to its logical conclusion, the claim that judges should ensure that legislation respond to the needs and desires of democratic majorities could justify judicial activism on behalf of economic rights. That activism might seek to ensure that the social and economic policies enacted by elected officials provided all persons with the resources necessary to participate in the political life of their communities. The *Carolene Products* rationale might require, for example, that courts order state governments to provide all citizens with a minimum standard of living.

Unfortunately, even if such decisions were consistent with the underlying structure of sociological jurisprudence, judicial protection of positive liberties would have betrayed the original purpose of that approach to legal doctrine. Progressives developed sociological jurisprudence as a rhetorical weapon in their fight to return economic power to the elected branches of government. They were unlikely to accept or be interested in arguments that suggested their legal principles merely provided a different basis for judicial activism on behalf of economic rights or supported a different set of economic rights. In short, neither Chafee nor his audience was prepared to endorse any constitutional argument that explicitly permitted courts to protect specific economic rights. If the *Carolene Products* footnote justified such activism, then the democratic process model of the judicial function was not an acceptable basis for judicial activism on behalf of free speech.

To salvage some form of judicial activism on behalf of expression rights, Chafee made a fateful decision. The constitutional defense of free speech, he declared, would implicitly pretend that the distribution of economic resources did not affect the system of freedom of expression. Throughout his life Chafee insisted that "speech should be fruitful as well as free,"[161] but he firmly maintained that the project of making speech fruitful was "a problem, not for law" (i.e., the courts).[162] The First Amendment, he claimed, was "directed only at government impairment of discussion." Judges were not authorized to remedy those obstructions to "the open and effective discussion of public affairs" that were caused by inequalities in private resources.[163] While Chafee continually asserted that "the remedy for a restrictive law is in the Constitution," he simultaneously confessed that "the remedy for private restraints on fair discussion lies in an aroused public opinion and the enterprise of individuals and the community, with the possibility of affirmative governmental action in the background."[164] Speakers who were unable to rent private facilities for their discourse had no legal recourse, provided their inability was not caused by official action.[165] That and similar barriers to attaining truth on matters of public interest consequently followed those substantive policies that constituted the exclusive domain of the elective branches of government.

Chafee detailed this position in his last book, *The Blessings of Liberty.* In his "Does Free Speech Produce Truth?" chapter he noted various "obstacles to the automatic emergence of truth" from free speech, of which inequality of wealth was the most significant.[166] Maldistribution of economic resources, Chafee admitted, biased the democratic process because of "the increasing tendency for the most effective instrumentalities of communication to be bounded and shaped by persons who are often on one side of many public questions." However, courts could do nothing to ameliorate this consequence of material inequality. Chafee conceived of "the First Amendment and other parts of the law" as "a fence inside which men can talk." "Lawmakers," he insisted, had to "stay on the outside of that fence. But what the men inside the fence say when they are let alone is no concern of the government."[167] Although the end of the First Amendment was the attainment of truth, judges could contribute to this end only by striking down governmental actions that banned political dissent. Courts had no power to prevent other social actors from interfering with the efficient functioning of the marketplace of ideas. As a result, Chafee admitted that the freedom of speech might be fully protected in a situation where "not a mite of truth has been attained or communicated."[168]

To be sure, the new constitutional defense of free speech required that courts sustain economic legislation designed to make speech more fruitful. As noted above, Chafee endorsed legislative proposals that would make economic resources more available to potential speakers. In particular, Chafee thought that government should provide public forums where all speakers could air their opinions. Such policies would prevent ideas from going unheard merely because their adherents lacked the resources to promote them privately.[169] Furthermore, Chafee believed that elected officials had the power to remove some private economic obstructions to an effective system of free speech. He maintained that to the extent "the instrumentalities of communications are businesses, they must be expected to share the [statutory] burdens of other businesses." For this reason, the communication industry's "marketing transactions" were subject to the antitrust laws.[170] When the Associated Press sought to give one newspaper in every community the exclusive right to determine whether any other paper could use their news services, Chafee endorsed the government's effort to prosecute under the Sherman Act. He further suggested that the Associated Press be required by statute "to regard itself as a public service open to all reputable newspapers who would pay the regular price for its news services."[171]

Although Chafee thought that elected officials had a constitutional duty to create a social environment in which all citizens would have the independence and wherewithal necessary to express their opinions, he conceded that this obligation was not judicially enforceable. Judges, Chafee insisted, had to sustain whatever social and economic policies the legislature passed, even policies motivated by a desire to weaken the economic power of political dissidents, as long as such policies did not directly punish speech.

Moreover, Chafee believed that the First Amendment actually impeded state efforts to equalize access to the marketplace of ideas. Elected officials could provide resources that enable impoverished advocates to advance their ideals, but legislation that limited the expressive uses of private property violated the free-speech rights of economically privileged speakers. Governmental regulation of the communications industry, Chafee claimed, had to be strictly "confined to marketing transactions—selling news or radio programs and leasing films."[172] Once government attempted to regulate actual efforts to persuade, the judicial obligation to police the democratic process required that such legislation be declared unconstitutional, even if the statute in question was designed to remove an economic impediment to a more democratic society. An enterprise, Chafee asserted, must "be left completely free to make up its own package of news and ideas; but the package, once it was made up, would have to be marketed on fair terms."[173] This interpretation of the democratic process gave property owners the exclusive right to determine what opinions their holdings would promote. Statutes requiring newspapers to publish differing opinions, on this theory, unconstitutionally abridged speech, and the judiciary had to strike down such laws under the rationale set out in the *Carolene Product* footnote. Whether excluded speakers had other forums to express themselves was not constitutionally relevant. "Liberty of the press," Chafee wrote, "is in peril as soon as the government tries to compel what is to go into a newspaper."[174]

Chafee never considered other possible constitutional relationships between free speech and private property. Indeed, by dividing the constitutional universe into substantive policies and democratic processes, he contributed to an environment in which the empirical and ideological connections between free speech and the distribution of economic resources would be constitutionally imperceptible. From this perspective, the difficulty with Chafee's analysis is not simply that he opposed judicial activism that promoted the economic conditions necessary for effectively exercising free-speech rights. The merits of such activism is the subject of fair scholarly debate.[175] More disturbing about Chafee's writings is their provision of few, if any, standards for evaluating legislation that mixes questions of property and expression. Rather, his democratic process model of the judicial function assumes that such problems are trivial or nonexistent. The clear and present danger test, deliberately tailored to disregard economic structure, provides no meaningful assistance in resolving such modern problems as whether corporations have the same free-speech rights as individuals or whether a person can enter a shopping center, otherwise held open to the public, for the purpose of passing out political literature.

At this point, Chafee's expository and historical analyses of free speech merge to obscure the same questions. By ignoring all substantive due process defenses of free speech and presenting the progressive bad tendency test as the conservative challenge to libertarian constructions of the First Amendment, Chafee confined free-speech debate within the parameters marked by sociological jurisprudence while appearing to discuss the full spectrum of free-speech debate in the United States. Within these parameters, the defense of expression rights still had to answer the difficult question raised by Corwin concerning how constitutional protection of free speech could be consistent with majoritarian democratic principles. Chafee's historical writings, however, excluded from the realm of discourse the questions raised by late nineteenth-century conservatives, Schroeder, and early civil libertarians concerning the relationship between free speech and the economic system guaranteed by the Constitution.

Chapter Five

The Triumph and Tragedy of Civil Libertarianism

Chafee's writings established the framework within which the next generation defended free speech. Civil libertarians in the 1940s, 1950s, and 1960s derived expression rights from the instrumental value of debate on matters of public importance, rather than from a theory of individual liberty. They thought that correct standards of First Amendment protection should reflect present social needs, not the intentions of the constitutional framers. Finally, they maintained that the judiciary had both an obligation to protect political dissent in order to ensure the country would be governed democratically and a corresponding duty not to interfere with the substantive policy choices of the people's elected representatives.

The developing civil libertarian tradition benefited from the continued strength of progressive ideas in academic and political circles. Although New Deal thinkers frequently challenged Dewey's and Pound's particular assertions, they shared their functionalist and majoritarian attitudes. Mature societies and individuals, such legal realists as Jerome Frank and Thurman Arnold contended, did not base their actions on abstract speculations about the rights of man.[1] Instead, proponents of the emerging welfare state typically argued that their policies were the most pragmatic means of promoting the common good. Daniel Bell's widely acclaimed *The End of Ideology*, for example, concluded that "a utopia has to specify where one wants to go, how to get there, the costs of the enterprise, and realiza-

tion of, and justification for the determination of who is to
pay."[2]

By the eve of World War II, most American scholars thought
that the logical or practical necessity of majority rule could be
derived from the principle that no economic or social system
was intrinsically superior to all others.[3] Some thinkers endorsed
Dewey's claim that democratic processes could best determine
what substantive policies would produce beneficial social results at any given point. Sidney Hook rejected "totalitarian culture" because such states left "no room for . . . the scientific approach, with its critical probing of alternatives, when questions
arise concerning the social ends and values which guide major
national policies." Others maintained that in the absence of any
impartial criteria of truth, electoral majorities should be permitted to do what they pleased. As Martin Shapiro observed,
such thinkers as Robert Dahl and David Truman based their political science on the assumption that "in a world in which there
were no objective values, but only personal preferences, the
politically and legally 'right' or 'rational' could only be defined
as whatever the democratic process ground out."[4]

Proponents of this relativist defense of democracy strongly
supported pluralism and civil liberties. In their view all democratic communities respected expression rights. Seymour Lipset and Earl Rabb praised "a society which tends to protect and
nurture the independent coexistence of different political entities, ethnic groups, ideas." Bell spoke of "the verities of free
speech, free press, the right of opposition and of free inquiry."[5]
Indeed, influenced by T. W. Adorno's pathbreaking study of
authoritarian personalities, prominent scholars suggested that
many intolerant persons were suffering from mental illnesses or
other forms of social pathology. "McCarthyism," Talcott Parsons declared, was "primarily the expression of fear, secondar-
ily of anger, the aggression which is a product of frustration."[6]

Democratic relativists recognized the effects of social and
economic programs on a system of free expression. "Every
overt form of economic pressure," Hook wrote, "is an overt
challenge to democracy." Dahl criticized as "highly inegalitar-
ian and undemocratic" the manner in which "superior wealth
. . . greatly exaggerate[d] the power of the few" in "the social

processes leading up to the process of voting." Like early civil libertarians, most mid twentieth-century intellectuals believed that governmental regulation of commercial activity would foster a social environment conducive to healthy debate on matters of social importance. Indeed, Dahl's empirical studies of different countries concluded that democratic governments survived only when democratic economic and social institutions were supported. "You cannot maintain rule by the people," he insisted, "except in a society where resources are rather equally distributed."[7]

The nearly hegemonic influence of relativist conceptions of democracy in mid twentieth-century liberal circles contributed to the contemporaneous expansion of the civil libertarian constitutional defense of free speech. If passage by objectively valid democratic processes was a precondition of the legitimacy of any economic or social policy, then free-speech rights could never be balanced against other, more subjective, ends because of the crucial role public debate played in the democratic process. Thus, the leading members of the second generation of civil libertarianism proclaimed that government could never, or hardly ever, limit the scope of debate about matters of public importance. This absolute or nearly absolute ban on state regulation of public debate offered influential speakers the same protections that Holmes, Chafee, and other proponents of the clear and present danger test only gave to "poor and puny anomalities."[8] No longer could a Joseph Gilbert or an Angelo Herndon be imprisoned merely because his rhetoric excited his audiences. Judicial adoption of the standards proposed by such proponents of freedom of expression as Alexander Meiklejohn, Thomas Emerson, Hugo Black, and William O. Douglas would give Americans the right to listen to those speakers they were most interested in hearing.

Unfortunately, the principles of democratic relativism also accentuated Chafee's constitutional separation of economic and expression rights. Democratic theorists in the years after World War II sharply distinguished democratic processes whose value could be objectively demonstrated from substantive policies that simply reflected the preferences of different groups. Hence, most members of the second generation of civil libertarianism assumed that the system of freedom of expression, particularly in its legal manifestation, could be fully secured without any reference to economic and social institutions. Rarely did their work examine the constitutional relationships between free speech and private property. Instead, mid twentieth-century analyses of expression rights concentrated almost exclusively on delimiting governmental power to restrict the advocacy of specific doctrines and speech that might have dangerous tendencies.

Civil libertarians were apparently rewarded in *New York Times Co. v. Sullivan* (1964),[9] when the Supreme Court endorsed their linked interpretations of the First Amendment and ignored the contributions that conservative libertarian treatise writers made to the actual holding of the case.[10] Although no majority opinion in the following years adopted the absolutist approach urged by prominent libertarians, a uniform series of speech-protective decisions had substantially the same effect. Influential opponents of American military, economic, and racial policies were either not prosecuted, not convicted, or had their convictions reversed on appeal. In *Brandenburg v. Ohio* (1971),[11] the Court announced a particularly stringent version of the clear and present danger test, one that no subsequent state or federal prosecution has yet been able to meet.

These libertarian triumphs, however, were soon followed by a new challenge, one the modern constitutional defense of free speech was not designed to meet. Increased concern with the corrupting effect that concentrated wealth was having on the democratic process inspired legislation limiting the conversion of economic resources into political expression. The constitutionality of statutes regulating corporate speech, campaign finance reform, and access rights to mass media soon became the most important speech issues facing the Supreme Court.[12] The leading members of the civil libertarian tradition had said little about those problems. In the 1970s and 1980s, civil libertarians continued to say little about those problems, other than to emphasize their practical importance. Indeed, the difficulties encountered by recent efforts to discuss these problems suggest that little can be said about the constitutional relationships between free speech and private property from within a model of constitutional argument that divorces expression from questions of economic and social policy. The doctrines of civil libertarianism seem largely irrelevant, if not obstructive, to the goal of its founders—the spread of truth on matters of public importance.

Elaboration and Victory, 1937–1973
The Second Generation of Civil Libertarians

Alexander Meiklejohn and Thomas Emerson, the leading academic defenders of free speech in the 1950s and 1960s, clearly offered civil libertarian conceptions and justifications of freedom of expression. Neither jurist wholly endorsed Chafee's teachings, and both contributed significantly to libertarian theory. Nevertheless, while Meiklejohn, Emerson, and their contemporaries presented sophisticated variations on the themes of *Freedom of Speech* and *Free Speech in the United States,* their books are best understood as developments within civil libertarianism, rather than as distinctive defenses of expression rights. The leading members of the second generation of civil libertarianism accepted the basic premises and structure of Chafee's analysis of the constitutional meaning of free speech, even as they refined his analysis in many important areas.

Meiklejohn's *Free Speech and Its Relation to Self-Government* (1948) and Emerson's *Towards a General Theory of the First Amendment* (1963) both endorsed sociological jurisprudence's insistence that contemporary social conditions govern the interpretation of constitutional guarantees. Freedom of speech, Meiklejohn declared, "is not a Law of Nature or of Reason in the abstract." First Amendment analysis "requires careful examination of the structure and functioning of our political system as a whole to see what part the principle of free speech plays here and now in that system." Following Chafee, Meiklejohn asserted that Americans were only bound by the original principles that inspired passage of constitutional guarantees, not by the particular standards that eighteenth-century jurists thought would adequately protect those rights. He contended that the framers' "adoption of the principle of self-government . . . is still transforming men's conceptions of what they are and how they may best be governed." "It is not even required," Meiklejohn stated, "that the meaning of the Constitution shall be in the future what it has been in the past. We are free to change both by interpretation and by explicit amendment."[13]

Emerson similarly asserted that analysis of the First Amendment must reflect present social needs. "Any study of the legal doctrines and institutions necessary to maintain an effective system of freedom of expression," he asserted, "must be based upon the functions performed by the system in our society." While Emerson thought "historical evidence reveals that the colonists viewed the essential functions of freedom of expression much as we do today," he maintained that standards of constitutional protection must be adjusted to fit modern conditions. Contemporary legal analysis had to look "to the underlying principles sought to be achieved by the Constitution, in terms of their current applicability." Thus, Emerson concluded that "whether [the system of free expression] will continue to grow and adapt to new circumstances, or lose its stability and be abandoned, depends on whether we, like the colonists, are daring and have faith in our capacity for progress."[14]

Meiklejohn and Emerson shared the early civil libertarian vision of a democratic society. Both contended that democratic and economic institutions were essential components of a functioning system of free speech. Emerson asserted that state officials had "to maintain the basic conditions that a system of free speech requires in order, not just to exist, but to flourish." Echoing Dewey and others, he called for state promotion of the positive liberties that fostered healthy public debate. "Conditions in a modern democratic society," Emerson insisted, "demand that a deliberate, affirmative, and even aggressive effort be made to support the freedom of expression."[15] His works emphasized that the benefits of free speech would be realized only if "the economic structure . . . provide[d] a certain standard of material welfare, shared broadly by all elements of the population."[16] Meiklejohn urged government to "engage in that positive enterprise of cultivating the general intelligence upon which the success of self-government so obviously depends." Like Chafee, he maintained that elected officials were obligated to establish forums for persons to publicize their opinions. "In every village, in every district of every town or city," Meiklejohn declared, "there should be established at public expense cultural centers inviting all citizens, as they may choose, to meet together for the consideration of public policy."[17]

Meiklejohn and Emerson did challenge the particular standard that Chafee believed justices should apply in free-speech cases. Both rejected the clear and present danger test in favor of a rule that legislators could never regulate speech. "As makers of the law," Meiklejohn contended, citizens had "an absolute freedom" of speech.[18] This meant that no substantive policy goal could trump an otherwise valid assertion of a free-speech right. "When men decide to be self-governing," Meiklejohn declared, "the search for truth is not merely one of a number of interests which may be 'balanced' on equal terms, against one another." Rather, "the attempt to know and to understand has a unique status, a unique authority, to which all activities are subordinated."[19] Emerson agreed that maintaining the system of free expression was constitutionally more important than promoting any particular social or economic policy. "Individual and societal interests in freedom of expression," he argued, "must be preferred over other individual and societal interests."[20] Thus, First Amendment rights could not be sacrificed in the name of other public goods. Expression could "not be restricted either for the direct purpose of controlling it or as a method of obtaining other social objectives." "The attainment of such other objectives," he insisted, "is to be achieved through regulation of action."[21]

Although claims that speech can never be restricted seem inconsistent with pragmatism's insistence on always balancing competing social interests, both Emerson and Meiklejohn defended their principles on the same instrumentalist grounds that Chafee used to defend the clear and present danger test. Each jurist argued that absolutely protecting free speech was the best practical means of advancing the general social interest. Meiklejohn maintained that his absolute standard of judicial protection was not derived from "a sentimental vagary about the natural rights of individuals" but constituted "a reasoned and sober judgment as to the best available method of guarding the public safety." After "measur[ing] the dangers and the values of the suppression of the freedom of public inquiry and debate," he declared, Americans had decided that the "destruction of freedom is always unwise."[22] Emerson similarly derived his full protection doctrine from weighing social concerns. "The decision to put into operation a system of free expression," he contended, was based on "a major balancing of interests." Embodying the communal decision that social interests would best be furthered if speech were always protected, the First Amendment meant that judges deciding particular cases were "not free to reopen this prior balancing."[23]

Meiklejohn and Emerson also apparently challenged Chafee's belief that the First Amendment protected debate on matters of public interest. Meiklejohn seemingly narrowed the constitutional meaning of free speech. In his view, political commentary was the only form of expression that legislatures could not regulate. Constitutional advocacy rights, he declared, were limited to "the freedom of those activities and thought by which we govern." Meiklejohn proclaimed that "the First Amendment is concerned, not with a private right, but with a public power, a governmental responsibility." The function of free speech, he insisted, is "to give to every voting member of the body politic the fullest possible participation in the understanding of those problems with which the citizens of a self-governing society must deal."[24] Expression that merely promoted individual goals, however, was constitutionally indistinguishable from those activities legislatures could regulate as they saw fit. Speech "directed toward our private interests, private privileges, private possessions" was only protected by the Fifth Amendment's requirement that governmental actions respect due process.[25]

Emerson appeared to broaden Chafee's conception of the precise role free speech played in contemporary society. "Maintenance of a system of free expression is necessary," he declared, "(1) as a method of assuring individual self-fulfillment, (2) as a means of attaining the truth, (3) as a method for securing participation by the members of the society in social, including political decision-making, and (4) as a means of maintaining the balance between stability and change in the society."[26] While the last three values are aspects of the social interest in debate on matters of public importance, "self-fulfill-ment" seems to be a purely personal interest. In contrast to Chafee, who deemphasized purely individual interests in speech, Emerson specifically asserted that "the right to free-dom of expression is justified first of all as the right of an indi-vidual purely in his capacity as an individual."[27]

When examined closely, these disagreements are either se-mantic or well within the structure of civil libertarian argu-ment. Thus, while Chafee declared that "it is shocking" that Meiklejohn would "deprive [art and literature] of the protec-tion of the inspiring words of the First Amendment,"[28] Meikle-john actually offered the same analysis of literary speech that Chafee had previously presented; to be fair to Chafee, howev-er, Meiklejohn's earlier works did seem subject to his criti-cism.[29] Both thinkers emphasized the political function of many artistic forms of expression. Just as Chafee declared that "po-ems and plays and novels" contributed to "the satisfactory op-eration of self-government," so Meiklejohn proclaimed that "the people do need novels and dramas and paintings and po-ems, 'because they will be called on to vote.'" Because "litera-ture and the arts" provided persons with a "sensitive and in-formed appreciation and response to the values out of which the riches of the general welfare are created," Meiklejohn in-sisted that such works "must be protected by the First Amend-ment." These forms of expression, he concluded, "have a 'so-cial importance' which I have called a 'governing importance.'"[30]

The differences between Chafee and Emerson are also more apparent than real. As noted in chapter 4, Chafee thought that societies should protect individual rights because doing so was in the public interest; similarly, Emerson placed individual rights in a broader social context. Following Dewey and other early civil libertarians, he believed that societies would best prosper by adopting policies that fostered the development of each citizen. "The theory of freedom of expression," he de-clared, "is put forward as a prescription for attaining a creative, progressive, exciting and intellectually robust community."[31] Moreover, Emerson claimed that the four values served by free speech are "an integrated set."[32] Thus, every regulation of the individual interest in free speech affected the social interest in expression on matters of public interest.

Emerson's and Chafee's attitudes toward obscenity illustrate the largely illusory difference in their conceptions of expression rights. Chafee offered no protection to such speech because he thought obscenity only advanced individual interests.[33] Emerson declared that the right to publish pornography was guaranteed by the First Amendment. "Any communication," he declared, "containing erotic material is protected against any kind of abridgement by the government." Emerson, however, did not see this as an instance of constitutionally protecting a purely personal right. In his view "the judgment of whether any particular expression possesses social value or no social value is not for the government to make."[34] In other words, Emerson disagreed with Chafee about who decided whether obscenity might advance social interests, not whether an individual interest in speech should be given significant constitutional protection.

Meiklejohn, Emerson, and Chafee may have placed marginally different emphases on the functions of free speech, but each jurist advanced the same justification for judicial activism on behalf of expression. All three libertarians asserted judicial obligations to police inputs into the democratic process and to accept democratic policy outputs. Courts, they argued, were expected to protect free speech because expression was a procedural requirement of democratic government. Emerson, who offered the most individualistic conception of expression rights, never claimed that judges were empowered to protect purely personal desires to speak. When discussing "the specific function of the judiciary in supporting a system of free expression" he spoke solely in terms of a duty "to ensure that the basic mechanisms of the democratic process will be respected." *Towards a General Theory of the First Amendment* opposed judicial "supervision over the decisions reached or measures adopted as a consequence of employing democratic procedures." "Judicial institutions," Emerson insisted, "are here dealing with the methods of conducting the democratic process, not with the substantive outcomes of that process."[35]

Meiklejohn similarly distinguished judicial activism on behalf of expression from judicial activism on behalf of other rights. Although he recognized that legislatures "must be free in their use of their delegated powers," Meiklejohn insisted that "the people must be free in the exercise of their reserved powers of self-government." Elected officials, he proclaimed, were "authorized . . . to limit the freedom of men as they go about the management of their private, their non-political, affairs"; however, "the same men, as they endeavor to meet the public responsibilities of citizenship in a free society, are in a vital sense, which is not easy to define, beyond the reach of legislative control." Thus, Meiklejohn concluded that the Constitution "declares that with respect to political belief, political discussion, political advocacy, political planning, our citizens are sovereign, and the Congress is their subordinate agent."[36]

Working within the democratic process model of the judicial function, Meiklejohn and Emerson rigidly separated economic and expression rights. As noted above, although both scholars insisted that expression rights were meaningless in the absence of positive economic rights, they agreed that courts could not implement the economic and social policies that would make speech more fruitful. Like Chafee, they believed that the elected branches of government were responsible for such policies. Emerson explicitly placed the economic and social prerequisites of a system of free expression beyond the jurisdiction of "a perfect set of legal rules and an ideal array of judicial institutions."[37]

For this reason, Meiklejohn and Emerson rarely considered the constitutional relationships between free speech, considered to be democratic input, and economic and social policies, considered to be substantive outputs. The central meaning of the First Amendment, in their view, was its guarantee that government could never regulate speech merely because citizens felt that a particular doctrine was false or dangerous. Nearly all of Meiklejohn's writings and the bulk of Emerson's work, particularly before 1973, were devoted to detailing this interpretation of the constitutional relationship between free speech and lawless or socially threatening conduct. Mid twentieth-century

courts, these jurists indicated, would have performed their as-
signed function in the system of freedom of expression if they
ensured that all Americans had the right to advocate communism enthusiastically, vehemently oppose the Vietnam War,
and actively participate in the civil rights movement.

Although Meiklejohn and Emerson briefly discussed some
mixed questions of speech and property, they conceptualized
those issues in ways that enabled them to ignore the potential
impact of material inequalities on a system of freedom of expression. This selective blindness was particularly apparent
when both civil libertarians analyzed the constitutionality of
statutes regulating the burgeoning broadcast industry. Meiklejohn maintained that radio producers were best understood as
part of the entertainment business; as such, broadcasters were
subject to the same relatively unrestricted governmental regulation that democratically elected legislatures had over all other
commercial enterprises. Radio operators, Meiklejohn declared,
were "engaged in making money," and "the First Amendment
does not intend to guarantee men freedom to say what some private interest pays them to say for its own advantage."[38]

Emerson treated broadcast regulation as analogous to state
regulation of speech in parks and streets. Because both airwaves and public parks were publicly owned, elected officials
had the power to pass legislation ensuring equitable access to
those scarce forums. "The government," Emerson declared, "is
obliged by the First Amendment to permit citizens to use the
facilities without discrimination." Thus, when the people's representatives allowed some persons to broadcast over the public
airwaves, they could insist that such licensees grant access to
third parties to "assure a fair allocation of the limited facilities
both to users and listeners." Of course, legislatures could not
censor the contents of particular radio and television broad-
casts. However, governmental officials could compel "a licens-
ee to present varied points of view on controversial issues, or
. . . forc[e] him to grant access to persons whose interests are
affected by a broadcast."[39]

By emphasizing the natural scarcity of broadcast media, Emerson ignored the constitutionality of policies that, in effect,
made wealth a crucial feature in determining which persons

were able to take advantage of these new and powerful modes of communication. This issue does not arise in traditional parks and streets cases because virtually all citizens have the material resources necessary to make speeches in those forums. Significantly, Emerson maintained that identical restrictions on print journalism would be unconstitutional because publishing faculties were privately owned. Limited access to the press, he declared, was only a product of "economic factors," not of "characteristics inherent in the medium."[40]

The System of Freedom of Expression also briefly analyzed governmental regulation of campaign financing. Although Emerson's analysis was interesting and important, he again failed to explore seriously the constitutional relationships between free speech and private property. Emerson assumed that the First Amendment protected the right to purchase speech. "Funds expended for expression," he stated, had the same constitutional status as expression. For this reason, elected officials could rarely regulate campaign expenditures. Such legislation was constitutional only if "clearly necessary to correct a grave abuse in the operation of the system and [was] narrowly limited to that end." In particular, Emerson declared that restrictions on the money persons could spend to promote their ideas must "not limit the content of expression; . . . [must operate] equitably and with no undue advantage to any group or point of view; . . . [must be] in the nature of a regulation and not a prohibition; . . . [must] not substantially impair the area of expression controlled; . . . [must] be specifically formulated in objective terms and reasonably free of the possibility of administrative abuse." Legislation only satisfied this standard, if "limited to restrictions (1) on the candidate himself, (2) in an election campaign."[41]

Unfortunately, Emerson's discussion of campaign finance reform emphasized the social interest in preventing political corruption. That interest concerns the effect large political contributions have on political actions taken by elected political officials, but not the effect that large political expenditures have on the political preferences of the electorate. Although he suggested that his analysis "raise[d] questions that go beyond the corrupt practices area," such as whether "the government has almost unlimited power to allocate resources available for expression,"[42] Emerson did not indicate what other "grave ab-use[s] in the operation of the system" of free expression would justify campaign finance reform. In particular, Emerson never discussed whether states could regulate political expenditures that unduly influenced the marketplace of ideas.[43]

More generally, Emerson and Meiklejohn did not believe that courts had a significant role to play in maintaining demo-cratic social and economic institutions. The best courts could do, they argued, was to sustain legislation that provided citizens with the resources necessary to participate actively in public af-fairs. In other words, like Chafee, Meiklejohn and Emerson left the material prerequisites of the system of freedom of expres-sion in the hands of elected officials, the very elected officials that civil libertarians claimed could not be trusted to regulate political and social debate.

In spite of this weakness, the basic elements of civil liber-tarian thought were universally endorsed by the other major proponents of speech-protective doctrines who wrote in the 1940s, 1950s, and 1960s. The publication of and response to Leonard Levy's *Legacy of Suppression* (1960) best illustrated the continuing functionalist orientation of First Amendment analysis. That work advanced the controversial thesis that the framers of the Constitution intended only to abolish prior restraints. Significantly, however, Levy did not think that his historical conclusions in any way affected the proper standards for contemporary First Amendment adjudication. Following Chafee, Meiklejohn, and Emerson, Levy insisted that only "the principles and not their framers' understanding of them are meant to endure." Hence, his contemporaries were free to con-struct whatever standards they believed would best promote debate on matters of public interest. "That they were Black-sonians," Levy concluded, "does not mean that we cannot be Brandeisians."[44]

With the exception of Hugo Black, Levy's colleagues endorsed his claim that revisionist understandings of the fram-ers' intentions had little bearing on constitutional doctrine. Ed-mond Cahn praised *Legacy* as a "splendid book" while remind-ing readers that each generation and every era "must build their own path to enlightenment and develop the institutions that suit their own needs and ideals." Martin Shapiro simply described Levy's "historical evidence" as "irrelevant." The First Amendment, he maintained, "allows—indeed requires—new interpretations to fit new situations."[45]

Midcentury civil libertarians consistently reiterated Chafee's emphasis on the democratic function of expression rights. In *Freedom of Expression: The Supreme Court and Judicial Review,* Shapiro contended that "those silenced by speech regulation were cut off from the self-curative powers of the democratic process contained in the central institution of democracy, the communication of political ideas and claims." Harry Kalven declared that "in a free society, government may not use its legal sanctions to silence criticisms of its policies and officials." "Relying as it does on the consent of the governed," Cahn maintained, "representative government cannot succeed unless the community receives enough information to grasp public issues and make sensible decisions."[46]

Scholars who defended judicial activism typically argued that political expression was the most important right courts could legitimately protect. Following Justice (later Chief Justice) Stone, they claimed that federal courts should police the democratic process but not promote their particular notions of substantive policy. In an influential article, Eugene Rostow declared that "the freedom of legislatures to act within wide limits of constitutional construction is the wise rule of judicial policy only if the processes through which they act are reasonably democratic." Robert McKay maintained that "the legislative process is in general well-suited to an examination of competing values in connection with social and economic programs, where the essential balancing can take place within the legislature." He then cited Chafee in support of the proposition that "the situation is different when the opposing values are free speech and the danger of violent acts, or where the balance is between freedom of the press and censorship."[47]

With the exception of some discussions of broadcast regulation,[48] mid twentieth-century libertarians rarely confronted the possible existence of significant issues that could not neatly be categorized as affecting the democratic process or the distribution of social resources. Proponents of free speech implicitly assumed that the system of freedom of expression would function efficiently if only government would stop trying to interfere. In this atmosphere, only a few intellectuals actually insisted that there were no constitutional relationships between free speech and private property. Rather, working within the framework first set out in the *Carolene Products* footnote and later elaborated by Chafee, most libertarians never considered the matter.

The Judicial Triumph of Civil Libertarianism

The adjudicative climate of the mid twentieth-century rarely forced Emerson, Meiklejohn, or other civil libertarians to detail their understanding of the constitutional relationships between private property and free speech. Legal scholarship typically reflects the Supreme Court's agenda,[49] and in those years, the overwhelming majority of First Amendment claims heard by the justices raised issues that Chafee had fully discussed. Constitutional litigants usually debated the relationship between expression and lawless conduct or the circumstances under which speech on governmental property could be regulated. The central issue raised by the most publicized case of that era, *Dennis v. United States*,[50] was whether Communist party organizers could be charged with participating in a conspiracy to overthrow the United States government by force or violence.

When deciding such questions, the leading civil libertarians on the Court could reiterate the same themes being played by their counterparts in academia. Judicial supporters of broad expression rights typically emphasized the social and democratic functions of free speech. "Freedom of expression," Justice Frank Murphy wrote, "must embrace all issues about which information is needed or appropriate to enable the members of society to cope with the exigencies of their period." Justice Robert Jackson declared that "this liberty was protected because [the framers] knew of no other way by which free men could conduct representative democracy." Judicial opinions that supported the constitutional claims of political dissidents invariably pointed to the distinction between democratic processes and substantive outcomes. In *Thomas v. Collins,* for example, Justice Wiley Rutledge asserted that "the usual presumption supporting legislation is balanced by the preferred place given in our scheme to the great, the indispensable democratic freedoms secured by the First Amendment."[51]

Although the Supreme Court rejected important First Amendment claims in the 1950s and early 1960s,[52] Justices William Douglas and Hugo Black, the most rabid defenders of free speech on the Vinson and early Warren Courts, continued to emphasize the need for judges in democratic societies to offer special protection to expression rights. Justice Douglas's dissent in *Dennis v. United States* insisted that "free speech has occupied an exalted position because of the high service it has given our society. Its protection is essential to the very existence of a democracy."[53] Justice Black similarly "adhere[d] to that preferred position philosophy." "Free speech," he maintained, "plays its most important role in the political discussions and arguments which are the lifeblood of any representative democracy."[54]

Early in their careers Justices Black and Douglas supported the clear and present danger test, but both adopted more absolute standards of protection by the early 1960s. Echoing Emerson, Justice Douglas declared, "the only line drawn by the Constitution is between 'speech' on the one side and conduct or overt activities on the other." "That 'Congress shall make no law,'" Justice Black bluntly stated, "means Congress shall make no law."[55] This movement from a balancing test to an absolute prohibition on speech restrictions took place within civil libertarianism's functionalist perspective. As Scot Powe has demonstrated, Justice Douglas, in particular, concluded that given the actual practices of censorship in the United States and the human impulse to overestimate the dangers of permitting expression, judges would reach the appropriate balance of social interests in the most cases if they struck down all speech regulations.[56]

The Court had two opportunities to determine the constitutional relationships between free speech and private property in the 1940s and 1950s, but both cases were decided on other grounds. In *United States v. C.I.O.* (1948), the justices were asked to declare unconstitutional a federal statute barring any corporate or union "contribution or expenditure in connection with any primary election to political office." Although the Court concluded that the C.I.O. had the right to endorse political candidates in the literature it sent to members, the majority opinion avoided the First Amendment issue by holding that the statute in question did not prohibit the union's activity. Congress, Justice Stanley Reed wrote, had not "intended to bar a trade journal, or house organ or a newspaper, published by a corporation [or a union] from expressing views on candidates or political proposals in the regular course of its publication." Nine years later, in *United States v. International Union United Automobile Workers*, the Court again dodged considering the constitutionality of that law. The justices refused to decide whether Congress could bar efforts to use union dues to pay for campaign commercials because the federal district court below had erroneously interpreted the statute in question.[57]

Justice Douglas, however, would have dismissed the indictment on constitutional grounds. In a dissent signed by Chief Justice Warren and Justice Black, Douglas insisted that such restrictions on political expenditures violated the union's First Amendment right to convert its economic resources into speech. "The fact that it costs money to make a speech," he declared, does not "make the speech any the less an exercise of First Amendment rights." Justice Douglas did suggest that the right to purchase speech was not as absolute as the right to advocate specific doctrines. Congress, he asserted, had the power to prohibit large contributions if they "had an undue influence upon the conduct of elections." In a later talk, however, Douglas suggested that such regulations must "[penalize] corrupt practices." "Undue influence," he insisted, "cannot constitutionally form the basis for making it unlawful for any segment of our society to express its views on issues of a political campaign."[58]

In 1964, the defenders of free speech triumphed more fully than ever before. In *New York Times Co. v. Sullivan*, the justices held that the First Amendment protected speakers who defamed public figures, unless they spoke recklessly or intentionally disregarded the truth. Moreover, the Court's opinion suggested that the basic principles of civil libertarianism had become the law of the land. In words that "echoe[d] Dr. Meiklejohn," Justice Brennan stated that "speech concerning public affairs is more than self-expression; it is the essence of self-government. The First and Fourteenth Amendments embody our 'profound national commitment to the principle that debate on public issues should be uninhibited, robust, and wide-open, and that it may well include vehement, caustic, and sometimes unpleasantly sharp attacks on government and public officials.' "[59] Justice Black's concurring opinion asserted that Meiklejohn correctly understood that "an unconditional right to say what one pleases about public affairs is . . . the minimum guarantee of the First Amendment."[60] Justice Goldberg's concurrence invoked Chafee's distinctions both between social and individual interests in free speech and between democratic processes and individual rights in support of a special judicial obligation to ensure that state officials respected expression rights. "Freedom of press and of speech," he declared, "insures that government will respond to the will of the people and that changes may be obtained by peaceful means."[61]

The next ten years confirmed predictions that *Sullivan* marked a clear libertarian turn in the Court's jurisprudence.[62] For the first time in American history, the Supreme Court consistently supported the First Amendment claims of those who protested American involvement in a foreign war. A young Californian was judged to have a constitutional right to wear a jacket that proclaimed "FUCK THE DRAFT," the right of high school students to wear black arm bands in class signifying their opposition to the Vietnam war was upheld, and most significantly, the *New York Times* was permitted to publish the *Pentagon Papers*, a series of classified documents that indicated the federal government had not been truthful about the nature of the war and war policies.[63] Judicial free-speech decisions in the 1960s also gave First Amendment protection to most of the nonviolent protests organized by the civil rights movement. With some exceptions, the Court interpreted public forum doctrines in ways that upheld rights to hold political rallies on a wide variety of public properties.[64] Moreover, the *Sullivan* case reversed a huge libel award that an Alabama jury gave to a southern sheriff who was defamed by an advertisement purchased by supporters of Martin Luther King.

Judicial doctrine reflected the justices' libertarian commitments. In opinions handed down between 1964 and 1971, the
justices overruled decisions to which Chafee had objected during World War I,[65] and they affirmed free-speech claims in circumstances identical to those in which such claims were earlier
denied. *Bond v. Floyd*,[66] for example, held that expression of
sympathy for those who had resisted the draft—the sentiments
that had sent Eugene Debs to prison in 1918—could not be construed as an incitement to violating the law.[67] In *Brandenburg v.
Ohio*, a case that actually concerned the free-speech rights of a
white supremacist group, the Court abandoned *Whitney v. California* and endorsed a Brandeisian standard of First Amendment protection. The per curiam opinion asserted that government could not "forbid or prosecute advocacy of the use of
force or of law violation except where such advocacy is directed
at inciting or producing imminent lawless action and is likely to
incite or produce such action."[68] Although this standard suggests that states may still forbid narrowly defined categories of
advocacy, the Supreme Court has not sustained such speech restrictions in the last twenty years.

These rulings seemed to mark the fulfillment of civil libertarian efforts. Melville Nimmer observed that had he been alive in
1984 "George Orwell would have been pleased . . . that in the
United States today freedom of speech is alive and tolerably
well if not always thriving."[69] Although the defenders of free
speech may have quibbled with the doctrinal basis of some of
the Court's libertarian opinions, they heartily endorsed the results. In a conversation with Professor Harry Kalven, Meiklejohn called the *Sullivan* decision "an occasion for dancing in the
streets." As Thomas Emerson noted, "the distance traversed in
First Amendment interpretation is quite apparent."[70]

The Second Crisis of Civil Libertarianism,
1973 to the Present

As the Vietnam War wound down and protest movements
waned, new challenges confronted civil libertarians. The Court's
protective stance and the fall of the Nixon administration halted

systemic public efforts to punish unpopular speakers. As Archibald Cox observed, "by the 1970s, the prosecutions for words and political associations spawned by World War One . . . had faded."[71] Although many governmental practices still presented traditional First Amendment issues,[72] federal and state restrictions on political advocacy in the 1970s and 1980s did not seriously affect debate on matters of public importance, except in the important sense that any restrictive precedent can be expanded in the future. For example, opponents of a proposed Nazi party rally in a community of Holocaust survivors emphasized the unique vulnerability of the march's targeted victims and did not seriously challenge the right to espouse Nazism in other circumstances.[73] Similarly, supporters of constitutional amendments or legislation prohibiting flag desecration have asserted that they only wish to outlaw some forms of symbolic expression.[74] By comparison, early civil libertarians fought policies designed to prevent the spread of certain ideas by any means. Radical critics of American policy making during World War I were persecuted in many communities, not just in the very few where their opinions could cause severe emotional trauma.

Nevertheless, many contemporary Americans believe that significant reductions in traditional forms of repression do not demonstrate the health of the system of freedom of expression. Prominent journalists and intellectuals have insisted that material inequalities are threatening democratic processes. Of course, as chapter 3 demonstrated, this complaint is not unique to late twentieth-century society or scholarship. Such early civil libertarians as Dewey, Addams, and Brandeis had previously detailed ways in which economic disparities inhibited the efficient functioning of the marketplace of ideas.[75] Many political observers in the late twentieth century feel, however, that the baneful influence of money on politics has intensified. In their view, increasingly sophisticated and expensive technologies further limit the control most citizens can exercise over governmental policy.

Wealthier persons, these analysts claim, are more likely and better able to participate in the political process. Their superior resources determine which candidates are nominated and which win general elections. Campaign contributions influence both the policies advocated by political parties and the legislation passed by elected officials. The increasingly monopolized media, many charge, do not reflect the full spectrum of political opinion in the United States and do not provide citizens with all the information they need to make responsible choices. In short, disparate economic holdings are affecting the capacity of elected officials to deliver programs responsive to the needs and sentiments of a majority of Americans.[76]

Charles Lindblom's *Politics and Markets* acutely diagnoses the ills afflicting contemporary America. In that work, Lindblom asserts that "democratic theory needs to be extended to take into account of what we will call the privileged position of business." "Business[es]," he claims, "enjoy a triple advantage: extraordinary sources of funds, organizations at the ready, and special access to government." Wealthy interests use these advantages to manipulate public opinion. Through their domination of the media, "business[es] achieve an indoctrination of citizens so that citizens' volitions serve not their own interests but the interests of business." Consequently, elected officials are more likely to serve a few special interests than to develop policies that best advance the public good. "The private corporation," Lindblom argues, can "insist that government meet [its] demands, even if those demands run counter to those of citizens expressed through their polyarchal controls." For these reasons, he concludes, "the large private corporation fits oddly into democratic theory and vision. Indeed, it does not fit."[77]

Not all Americans share this pessimistic interpretation of the changing relationships between money and politics. A few contemporary holdovers from the conservative libertarian tradition claim that new campaign technologies make government more democratic. In their view, novel methods of financing ideas "perform functions indispensable to a free and stable political process." "Campaign money," Ralph Winter declares, "acts as an agent of change, permits citizens with little free time to participate in politics, is a vehicle of expression by which individuals seek to persuade others, serves as a barometer of intensity of feeling over potent political issues, and weeds out candidates with little public support."[78]

In spite of these differences, both proponents and opponents of campaign finance reform recognize that the relationship between money and politics has changed and that these new relationships have eclipsed the relationship between speech and action as the most important First Amendment question facing American society. A general theory of free speech that does not respond to these questions is, thus, of little use in the continued effort to maintain a functioning freedom of expression.

Judicial Responses to Questions of
Speech and Property

Civil libertarians have had ample opportunity to test how responsive their theoretical approaches are to these new threats to speech liberties. Heightened concern with the economic prerequisites of the system of freedom of expression has inspired novel First Amendment claims. The nature of contemporary First Amendment litigation was foreshadowed in 1968 by *Food Employees v. Logan Plaza*.[79] In that case, the Supreme Court held that a labor union had the right to enter a privately owned shopping center in order to picket a store that did not use union labor. *Logan Plaza* differed from traditional political advocacy cases because the "real issue" in that "free speech controversy" was not, as Chafee had written, "whether the state can punish all words which have some tendency . . . to bring about acts in violation of the law,"[80] but whether a state-granted power to forbid expression on one's property was an economic right of the owner or a violation of the speech rights of the would-be advocate. The parties to *Logan Plaza* recognized that the picketers' speech did not present a clear and present danger of lawless conduct; they disputed whether the owners of the shopping center could exercise their property rights in ways that effectively silenced the union.

As the differing votes of Justices Black and Douglas suggested, the civil libertarian tradition did not provide an unambiguous answer to this mixed question of speech and property. Justice Douglas regarded *Logan Plaza* as a traditional example of an unconstitutional speech restriction. His concurrence charged that failure to recognize a constitutional right of ac-

cess would "make 'private property' a sanctuary from which
some members of the public may be excluded because of the
views they espouse."[81] Justice Black, on the other hand, treated the shopping center's action as a lawful exercise of property
rights. He agreed that "pickets do have a constitutional right
to speak about [the defendants'] refusal to hire union labor."
But his dissent asserted that "they do not have a constitutional
right to compel [the defendants] to furnish them a place to do
so on [their] property." To do so, would be to "wholly [disre-
gard] the constitutional basis on which private ownership of
property rests in this country." "The right to freedom of expression," Black argued elsewhere, "is a right to express
views—not a right to force other people to supply a platform
or a pulpit."[82]

Academic libertarians similarly disputed whether speaking
on privately owned property otherwise held open to the public
is an exercise of an expression right that cannot be abridged or a
violation of an economic right that government may assign to
particular individuals. Emerson contended that because of the
"public nature of the function performed" by a "shopping center," the Constitution protected certain access rights. Shapiro
disagreed, insisting that "trespass is a criminal action which accompanying speech cannot excuse."[83]

From the mid-1970s on, the major First Amendment cases before the Supreme Court have presented issues similar to those
raised by *Logan Plaza*, rather than those raised by *Schenck,
Debs, Abrams, Gitlow, Whitney, Dennis*, and *Brandenburg*.[84]
Aware that modern polling and advertising techniques place a
premium on a candidate's financial resources and chastened by
the experience of the Nixon reelection campaign, federal and
state legislatures have sought to limit the effect of material inequalities on the democratic process. The statutes they have
passed include limitations on both personal contributions to political campaigns and a candidate's expenditures during political campaigns, as well as special restrictions on corporate
participation in electoral politics. In addition, the federal government and some states have given individuals the right to promote their political views on other persons' properties. Broadcasters, in particular, have been required to permit others to use

their faculties. Some utility and shopping center owners have been similarly obligated. Many citizens have challenged the validity of these measures, claiming that the constitution guarantees all persons the right to control the expressive uses of their economic resources. Thus, in cases concerning campaign financing and access rights, courts have been asked to determine the constitutional relationships between speech and property.

Although civil libertarians had consistently endorsed government policies that equalized opportunities for political participation, the Burger/Rehnquist Court has refused to constitutionalize their ideals. Instead, when adjudicating First Amendment issues, the justices emphasized the ownership of the property sought to be used for expressive purposes.[85] In a series of opinions, they have held that a person's abilities to exercise his or her expression rights may be limited to those speech acts that a person could afford to engage in. If wealthy interests threaten to dominate the marketplace of ideas, the Court has seemed to say that "the only meaning of free speech is that they should be given their chance and have their way." Chief Justice Burger, the most forceful proponent of this view, asserted that "there are many prices we pay for the freedoms secured by the First Amendment; the risk of undue influence is one of them."[86]

Guided by this maxim, the justices have held that expenditures for political purposes are constitutionally protected speech. "A restriction on the amount of money a person or group can spend on political communication during a campaign," they declared, "necessarily reduces the quantity of expression by restricting the number of issues discussed, the depth of their exploration, and the size of the audience reached."[87] Elected officials have been constitutionally barred from equalizing participation in the marketplace of ideas by limiting the economic resources persons can bring into that forum. "The concept that government may restrict the speech of some elements of our society in order to enhance the relative voice of others," the justices maintained, "is wholly foreign to the First Amendment."[88]

The Burger/Rehnquist Court has applied the principle that owners' rights to control the expressive uses of their property is an aspect of a person's right to control the content of his or her speech in two ways. First, because the state must advance a compelling justification to regulate a person's right to free speech, the state must advance a similarly strong interest to regulate efforts to convert economic resources into political speech. Second, because the right of free speech normally prevents government from compelling individuals to profess specific beliefs,[89] the state may not require owners to allow their properties to be used to advance political views they do not share.

The Supreme Court first dealt with an owner's right to convert property into expression in *Buckley v. Valeo* (1976), a case concerning the constitutionality of the 1974 amendments to the Federal Election Campaign Act (FECA).[90] The justices' per curiam opinion declared that the financing of debate on matters of public importance could be regulated, but only under those rare conditions that might justify more traditional restrictions on expression rights. Regulations limiting the political uses of material resources had to satisfy the same "exacting scrutiny applicable to limitations on core rights of political expression."[91] This standard, the Court insisted, was satisfied only by legislation that prevented political corruption or its appearance.[92] This interest in the integrity of the political process, the *Buckley* plurality held, was sufficient to sustain statutory limitations on the contributions individuals could make to candidates running for public office. Such restrictions were "a necessary legislative concomitant to deal with the reality or appearance of corruption inherent in a system permitting unlimited financial contributions."[93]

However, the justices struck down all federal limitations placed on individual expenditures made independently on behalf of a specified candidate, individual expenditures on behalf of family members running for elective office, and campaign expenditures by the candidate.[94] These restrictions, the per curiam opinion maintained, did not help prevent political corruption. In the case of independent expenditures, "the absence of prearrangement and coordination . . . alleviates the danger that expenditures will be given as a quid pro quo for improper commitments from the candidate." Similarly, "the primary governmental interest served by the Act—the prevention of actual and apparent corruption of the political process—[did] not support the limitation on the candidate's expenditure of his own personal funds." Any potential for corruption due to large campaign expenditures, the Court added, was substantially reduced by other provisions of the act providing for "contribution limitations and disclosure provisions."[95]

Federal efforts to justify campaign reform as a means of promoting political equality were illegitimate because, as noted above, the Court did not regard that goal as a constitutional reason to limit First Amendment rights. In response to arguments "that the ancillary government interest in equalizing the relative abilities of individuals and groups to influence the outcome of elections" justified the regulation of spending and contributions, the justices quoted *New York Times Co. v. Sullivan's* injunction that "the First Amendment . . . was designed . . . to assure unfettered interchange of ideas for the bringing about of political and social change." Hence, financially well-off Americans had a constitutional right to purchase unlimited amounts of speech as long as they retained control of how their money was spent. "The First Amendment's protection against governmental abridgment of free expression," *Buckley* ironically continued, "cannot properly be made to depend on a person's financial ability to engage in public discussion."[96]

In the following years, the Court expanded the protection the First Amendment gave to wealthy political activists. In 1978, the justices held that corporations had constitutional free-speech rights. Citing Meiklejohn and Emerson, Justice Powell's opinion in *First National Bank of Boston v. Bellotti* asserted that citizens had a constitutional interest in political expression from any source. "The inherent worth of the speech in terms of its capacity for informing the public," he insisted, "does not depend upon the identity of its source, whether corporation, association, union, or individual."[97] While Powell endorsed traditional strictures against corporate contributions to individual candidates,[98] he claimed that Massachusetts could not restrict corporate advocacy on matters of public interest. Two years later, in *Citizens Against Rent Control v. Berkeley,* Chief Justice Burger asserted that persons had a constitutional right to make unlimited contributions "to committees formed to favor or op-

pose ballot measures."[99] The Chief Justice's opinion maintained that legislatures could only restrict contributions that
might corrupt political candidates, a matter without bearing on
political referendums. He found "no significant state or public
interest in curtailing debate" on political subjects.[100] Finally, in
1985, a narrow majority declared that government could not
limit the amounts independent political committees spent on
behalf of specific candidates. *FEC v. National Conservative PAC*
held that the "collective action" of political action committee
members "in pooling their resources to amplify their voices" is
"entitled to full First Amendment protection."[101] Justice Rehnquist's opinion recognized that PAC money influenced elections and legislation, but he saw the influence as beneficial.
"Candidates and elected officials," he declared, "may alter or
reaffirm their own positions on issues in response to political
messages paid for by the PACs," but this "could hardly be
called corruption" because "one of the essential features of democracy is the presentation to the electorate of varying points
of view."[102]

The Burger Court was also solicitous of owners' rights to prohibit their economic resources from being used to promote opinions with which they disagreed. As noted above, the justices
saw this right as one aspect of the established right not to be
forced to utter sentiments one abhors. The Supreme Court did
hold that, because airwaves were scarce and publicly owned,
the federal government could require broadcasters to devote
some time to balanced presentation of public issues and grant a
statutory right of reply to individuals who were personally attacked during those programs.[103] In 1973, however, the Court
announced that absent legislation, persons had no constitutional
rights of access to mass media. *Columbia Broadcasting v. Democratic Comm.* rejected claims that the First Amendment required
radio and television stations to accept paid political advertisements. Chief Justice Burger's opinion held that a private broadcasting company's refusal to air campaign commercials could not
be attributed to the government. Because no state action was involved, the rights of those wanting to express their views were
not violated.[104] In a separate opinion, Justice Douglas claimed
that private broadcasting companies had a First Amendment

right to determine what political opinions they would present.[105]

One year later, the justices unanimously agreed that the Constitution prohibited legislative attempts to grant any access rights to print journalism. In *Miami Herald Publishing Co. v. Tornillo*, Chief Justice Burger declared that publishers had an absolute right to decide what political and social commentary they would print. The Court specifically pointed to the First Amendment liberties of property owners when striking down a Florida statute that forced newspapers to print replies from candidates attacked in their editorials. State laws that imposed obligations to present a more equitable representation of public opinion "exact[ed] a penalty on the basis of the content of a newspaper." That "penalty resulting from the compelled printing of a reply is exacted in terms of the cost in printing and composing time and materials and in taking up space that could be devoted to other materials the newspaper may have preferred to print."[106] In other words, statutory access rights to print journalism were unconstitutional because such legislation required publishers to use their resources to promote opinions they did not share.

In cases where no state law compelled access to other forms of private property, the Court ruled that owners' exclusionary decisions were not state action. Hence, the justices rejected claims that persons had a constitutional right to speak on private property otherwise held open to the public. Adopting the principle of Justice Black's dissent in *Logan Plaza*, a majority of the Supreme Court declared that "the Court has never held that a trespasser or an uninvited guest may exercise general rights of free speech on property privately owned and used nondiscriminately for private purposes only." Thus, the justices permitted shopping centers to exclude labor picketers and persons handing out leaflets protesting the Vietnam War.[107]

The word "nondiscriminately" in the *Lloyd Corp. v. Tanner* passage quoted above merely meant that owners could not deny access on the basis of race. The Burger Court permitted owners to discriminate among the various political groups that sought to speak in the shopping center. The Lloyd Corporation let some associations, but not others, make political appeals on their property.[108] Thus, central in these cases was the right not to have one's property used to promote other views, rather than the right to exclude all political uses of one's resources. "This principle," Justice Powell declared, "protects a person who refuses to allow use of his property as a marketplace for the ideas of others."[109]

The Court seemed to modify its stance on access rights in 1980. *Pruneyard v. Robins* suggested that only newspaper owners had a constitutional right to forbid undesired expressive uses of their resources. Justice Rehnquist's unanimous opinion declared that states could grant persons a statutory right to speak on private properties, provided that their speech did not "unreasonably impair the value or use of [that] property." Such a rule seemed to follow from the Court's view that access cases concern property, not speech rights. Under the rationale of the *Carolene Products* footnote, elected officials are responsible for distributing social and economic resources. Hence, the people's representatives seemingly have the power to decide whether the property rights they distribute will include the right to exclude unwanted speakers.[110]

Nevertheless, six years later, the justices clearly indicated that *Miami Herald* was the rule and *Pruneyard* the exception. In *Pacific Gas & Electric v. California,* they held that the people's representatives could not constitutionally grant a consumer group the right to include in the monthly billings of a utility company an insert disputing many of the corporation's claims. Writing for the Court, Justice Powell claimed that constitutional guarantees were violated by state practices that either forced owners to assist unwelcome speakers or burdened the owner's own expression by forcing him or her to disassociate from or reply to the third party's speech. The California regulation was unconstitutional because, among other things, the utility company was required to mail criticisms of its own policies. "Under these circumstances," he concluded, "appellant might well have concluded that . . . the safe course is to avoid controversy thereby reducing the free flow of information and ideas that the First Amendment seeks to promote."[111] Indeed, Justice Powell's opinion in *Pacific Gas* seemed to confirm his earlier suggestion that the result in *Pruneyard* could best be explained by the owner's failure to properly assert his First Amendment rights. Owners of shopping centers, he intimated, could resist state-mandated access rights by claiming that such legislation burdened their expression rights rather than merely affected those property rights conceded to be valid subjects of state regulation.[112]

The Burger/Rehnquist Court has also limited the expressive uses persons may make of public property. The Court did treat as binding precedent a 1939 case that held that all citizens had the right to speak in certain public forums. The use of "streets and parks for communication of views on national questions," Justice Roberts declared in *Hague v. C.I.O.*, was one of the "privileges, immunities, rights, and liberties of citizens."[113] However, recent decisions have confined the application of this principle to public streets, parks, and sidewalks. Speech access to publicly owned properties has been limited to property that either "by long tradition or by government fiat [has] been devoted to assembly and debate" (i.e., public streets, parks, and sidewalks) or "which the State has opened for use by the public as a place for expressive activity."[114] On all other governmental properties, including the public areas of military bases, federal workplaces, schools, private mailboxes, city buses, and lampposts, elected officials can restrict all or some political expression, provided only that such regulations are "reasonable in light of the purpose which the forum at issue serves."[115] Although the justices asserted that such legislation must be content-neutral, in several cases policies limiting speech rights favored a particular side to a partisan debate. Thus, the Court sustained regulations that permitted only a certified union to send messages to school teachers and that barred organizations advocating political change from the federal workers' charity drive.[116] Furthermore, by upholding prohibitions on placing unstamped mail in mailboxes, the Supreme Court further limited the capacity of persons without their own resources to participate effectively in the marketplace of ideas.[117]

By no means have all the justices on the Burger/Rehnquist Court shared this understanding of the constitutional relationship between free speech and private property. Many decisions have been closely divided, and others, *Buckley* in particular, clearly reflect compromises. With the exception of access

rights to governmental property, however, the divisions among
the justices have not reflected differences in support for traditional civil libertarian concerns or, for that matter, differences
in general judicial philosophy. Chief Justice Burger and Justice
Powell were the firmest supporters of an unlimited right to purchase political expression. "Congress," Chief Justice Burger
consistently maintained, "can no more ration political expression than it can ration religious expression." Justice Scalia
seems similarly opposed to campaign finance reforms. "The
premise of our system," he has asserted, "is that there is no such
thing as too much speech—that the people are not foolish but
intelligent, and will separate the wheat from the chaff."[118] Justice White, on the contrary, has been the leading defender of
legislation curtailing the conversion of money into speech. "It
is critical," he insisted in *Buckley,* "to obviate or dispel the impression that federal elections are simply a function of money,
that federal offices are bought and sold."[119] Justice Rehnquist
frequently voted with Justice White, but generally on idiosyncratic grounds. For example, he would have upheld the Massachusetts restriction on corporate speech challenged in *Bellotti*
because of his "views of the limited application of the First
Amendment to the States."[120]

Mixed questions of speech and property seem to confuse Justices Marshall and Brennan, whose opinions in libel, obscenity,
and public forum cases established them as the leading civil libertarians on the Burger Court.[121] Both justices consistently
voted to grant speakers access to private property when the
owner merely asserted a proprietary right in defense of an exclusionary policy,[122] but they did not define a clear position in
cases where owners asserted a First Amendment right to control the expressive uses of their economic resources. For example, although Justices Brennan and Marshall voted to sustain
a Massachusetts law that forbade corporate expenditures intended to influence the vote in referendums, they voted to
strike down a New York administrative ruling that forbade utilities from inserting a discussion of their views on energy policy
in their monthly bill. Apparently, corporations can participate
in public debate as long as the issues they discuss are not being
voted on directly. Similarly, Justices Brennan and Marshall

maintained that permitting a consumers' group to include a clearly identified statement of their views in a utility bill impermissibly burdened the speech of a utility company, but the justices did not think that permitting a union to picket a store in a privately owned shopping center impermissibly burdened the speech of the store owner.[123]

Justice Brennan, the author of *New York Times Co. v. Sullivan* and numerous other opinions on First Amendment rights, was unusually reticent in cases involving contemporary problems. He did not discuss the constitutional relationships between free speech and private property until *Federal Elections Commission v. Massachusetts Citizens for Life* (1986).[124] His majority opinion in that case held that certain restrictions on corporate campaign donations could not be applied to some nonprofit entities. More generally, Justice Brennan suggested that "corporate spending on political activity" could be regulated to ensure that "resources amassed in the economic marketplace" are not "used to provide an unfair advantage in the political marketplace." Thus, in *Austin v. Michigan Chamber of Commerce*, Justice Brennan voted to sustain a state statute barring nonprofit corporations that solicited funds from for-profit corporations from spending money on behalf of political candidates. That restriction, Justice Marshall's majority opinion held, "reduces the threat that huge corporate treasuries amassed with the aid of favorable state laws will be used to influence unfairly the outcome of elections."[125]

Curiously, Justice Brennan continued to believe that legislatures cannot constitutionally regulate individual expenditures on behalf of political candidates. The "relative availability of funds," he maintained, "is after all a rough barometer of public support."[126] Justice Brennan's distinction between corporate and individual expenditures, however, seems to have little constitutional or factual basis. Nowhere did he point to any empirical evidence supporting his claim that those who have substantial personal fortunes are politically more representative than those who control huge corporate wealth. Moreover, Justice Brennan has not explained why the state can restrict corporate expenditures "amassed with the aid of favorable state laws" but cannot restrict personal expenditures even though many feder-

al and state laws provide individuals with economic advantages
they can proceed to exploit in the political marketplace.[127]

Civil Libertarian (Non-)Responses

Late twentieth-century academic lawyers rarely provide Justice Brennan or his brethren with any guidance as to the correct
civil libertarian position on First Amendment spending rights.
Although general constitutional and free-speech theories have
been growth industries in the 1970s and 1980s, jurists continue
to treat content regulations as posing the paradigmatic First
Amendment questions and remain relatively unconcerned with
mixed questions of speech and property. Not surprisingly, most
scholars defend standards of judicial protection designed to resolve the various relationships between speech and crime or social harm. Rarely are such rules of adjudication germane to the
constitutional relationships between expression and economics.

John Hart Ely's renowned *Democracy and Distrust* (1980) exemplifies the continuing failure of the democratic process model
to deal with contemporary free-speech problems. Ely details a
theory of judicial review based explicitly on the rationale of the
Carolene Products footnote. The Constitution, Ely argues, "must
prescribe legitimate processes, not legitimate outcomes."[128] For
this reason, he believes that judges are obligated to respect the
social and economic policy choices made by the people's elected
representatives. Ely asserts that the Constitution left "the selection and accommodation of substantive values . . . almost entirely to the political process."[129] Nevertheless, because elected officials desire to remain in office, they cannot be trusted to regulate
democratic procedures. "Ins," Ely writes, "have a way of wanting to make sure the outs stay out." In his view, the Supreme
Court is the federal institution best able to "objectively assess
claims" about whether various regulations of political processes
serve the public interest. Hence, the Court should function to
keep "the machinery of democratic government running as it
should, [making] sure the channels of political participation and
communication are kept open."[130]

The civil libertarian's traditional justification for judicial activism on behalf of expression rights follows from this analysis

of the judicial function. Like Meiklejohn, Ely declares that courts should protect free speech because uninhibited public debate is one element of a self-governing society. Advocacy rights are "critical to the functioning of an open and effective democratic process."[131] Although he rejects claims that speech rights can never be sacrificed to achieve other social goals, Ely insists that legislatures should be allowed to regulate only a few narrowly defined categories of speech. Expression, he claims, must always be protected, unless a speaker has uttered an "incitement of immediate lawless conduct" or the speech presents a "specific threat" of some social "evil . . . that is independent of the message being regulated."[132] Thus, while persons should have the right to advocate communism, the government can punish persons who incite a lynch mob.[133]

Unfortunately, even though his work was written after *Buckley* and *Bellotti* were handed down, Ely does not analyze the constitutional status of the right to control the expressive uses of one's material resources. Like previous civil libertarians, his work implicitly maintains that the marketplace of ideas will function fairly and efficiently as long as persons are permitted to advocate almost any doctrine. *Democracy and Distrust* fails to explore such issues as campaign finance reform or access rights, and Ely does not discuss the effect that different social and economic policies might have on "an open and effective democratic process."[134] Nor is it at all clear how the "specific threat" test might be used to resolve the mixed questions of speech and property that have come before the Supreme Court in recent years.[135]

The works of those contemporary thinkers who have abandoned *Carolene Products'* democratic process model of the judicial function in favor of an approach that emphasizes judicial activism on behalf of the basic values of American society similarly neglect the constitutional issues posed by regulations of political contributions and mass media. Such theorists as Ronald Dworkin call on judges to enforce "the political morality presupposed by the laws and institutions of the community."[136] Many jurists who work within this constitutional framework support the early civil libertarian vision of a democratic society. Some even claim that the Constitution guarantees certain welfare rights. Indeed, Frank Michelman suggests that the right to a minimal standard of living is inherent in the democratic process presupposed by the Fourteenth Amendment.[137] Nevertheless, the leading proponents of the "substantive values" school of constitutional thought do not consider whether, in a society that does not directly provide citizens with the resources necessary to participate effectively in the marketplace of ideas, owners should have a constitutional right to control the expressive uses of their holdings. Dworkin and Michael Perry, for example, only explore traditional free-speech problems in their general discussions of constitutional adjudication. Like Ely, they treat content regulation as the central First Amendment problem that a general theory of the judicial function must resolve. Neither jurist explains how his approach would help justices decide such cases as *Buckley v. Valeo* or *Food Employees v. Logan Plaza.*[138]

Recent works on the constitutional meaning of free speech similarly examine only the questions that occupied Chafee in *Freedom of Speech.* Contemporary general theories of the First Amendment consistently place the problem of subversive advocacy at the heart of libertarian theory. This practice continues, even though no civil libertarian claims that such restrictions on speech currently present a serious threat to the system of freedom of expression. By comparison, mixed questions of speech and property typically appear under the heading, "Freedom of Expression in Some Special Contexts."[139] Virtually all recent discussions of the meaning of the First Amendment can be divided into three categories: those that briefly discuss the constitutional relationships between speech and property,[140] those that admit they did not resolve those constitutional relationships,[141] and those that ignore them.[142]

Vincent Blasi's "The Pathological Perspective and the First Amendment" (1985) exemplifies the priorities of most contemporary libertarian theorists. His article insists that all free-speech questions should be approached with an eye to how particular doctrines might influence judicial and public willingness to protect unpopular speakers in times of national hysteria. Intellectuals, Blasi claims, must "equip the first amendment to do maximum service in those historical periods when intolerance of unorthodox ideas is most prevalent and governments are most able and most likely to stifle dissent." For this reason, Blasi would not resolve speech/property relationships by exploring either the values underlying free speech or the function expression plays in our society. Properly resolving such matters as campaign finance reform, in his view, is relatively unimportant because those issues do not significantly affect the quality of debate on matters of public interest. Instead, Blasi asks which understanding of the constitutional relationship between expression and economics would leave the First Amendment best prepared for "the worst of times" when "the storms of pathology" cause political dissent to be punished.[143] In other words, Blasi sacrifices solutions to contemporary threats to expression in order to develop doctrine that is more responsive to past problems.

Most prominent civil libertarians are more sensitive to the ways that material inequalities threaten the democratic process. In "First Amendment Doctrine and the Burger Court" (1980), Emerson attacks the justices for "fail[ing] to develop innovative doctrine that will enable the system of freedom of expression to adjust to the changing conditions of the day."[144] In particular, he charges that the Supreme Court has been oblivious to the way debate on matters of public importance actually takes place in the late twentieth century. Expensive campaign technologies and oligarchic control of media resources, Emerson elsewhere claims, have caused a "failure of the marketplace of ideas to operate according to the original plan." Although these circumstances highlight the importance of "gain[ing] access to the marketplace of ideas," he thinks the justices have not confronted the implications of the new free-speech problems that recent cases present.[145]

Nevertheless, while painfully aware of the issues, Emerson offers no novel proposals that might reconcile contemporary life with the needs of a system of free expression. Like Blasi and the justices he criticizes, Emerson continues to place the relationship between private property and free speech at the periphery of his general theory of the First Amendment. Indeed, Emerson admits that his full protection doctrine does not respond to the challenge of late twentieth-century conditions,

that "various subsidiary doctrines are essential to round out the
legal foundations of [advocacy rights]."[146] Emerson places outside the scope of mainstream First Amendment theory such
mixed questions of speech and property as "problems [that] re-
late to the physical place in which the right of expression is exercised, or the allocation of scarce physical facilities," and
"questions of internal regulation of promotion of the system."[147] In other words, Emerson confesses that the basic principles of civil libertarianism have little to say about the constitutionality of campaign finance reform or regulating mass
media—the issues he believes are posing the most severe contemporary threat to a functional system of freedom of
expression.

Emerson does explore some constitutional relationships between free speech and private property in "The Affirmative
Side of the First Amendment" (1981). Following his previous
remarks and the remarks of earlier civil libertarians, Emerson
claims that elected officials have a constitutional obligation to
ensure that all citizens have sufficient opportunities to express
their opinions. "Governmental intervention" is justified, he
claims, if it provides "greater opportunity for expression" or
"increased diversity."[148] Thus, Emerson maintains that if their
measures are designed to increase the opportunities for poorer
citizens to speak, the people's representatives can regulate the
use of such public forums as "airwaves for radio and television
broadcasting" or "certain privately owned facilities that can be
considered quasi public in nature" such as shopping centers.[149]

Nevertheless, while Emerson insists that all persons should
have access to public or quasi-public forums, his work still does
not confront the larger relationships between expression and
economics raised by questions of access to mass media. For example, Emerson continues to consider scarcity the only legitimate basis for federal regulation of radio and television. Government, in his view, would no longer be able to regulate
broadcasting "if opportunities to seek an audience on cable become as open as opportunities to communicate by the use of the
streets."[150] This position ignores those inequalities that occur
because wealthier persons can better exercise their access
rights. In effect, Emerson contends that elected officials cannot
regulate persons who purchase two-minute spots during *The*

Cosby Show if everyone can do the same during reruns of *Stupid Turtle Tricks* on local cable channels.

Emerson still has not detailed his position on the constitutionality of contemporary limitations on campaign contributions and spending, but he is clearly uncomfortable with such legislation. In 1981, Emerson asserted that "the system of freedom of expression is by definition a laissez-faire system and must tolerate differences in the economic capacity of the various participants." "Any attempt to eliminate all differences based on economic factors," he added, "would involve governmental regulation and governmental domination on a scale that would destroy the system."[151] This may mean that Emerson thinks every restriction on campaign spending is unconstitutional; however, he may have intended only to imply that efforts "to eliminate *all* differences" are unconstitutional. Emerson never clarified this point or specifically discussed any of the major regulations before the Court in *Buckley* or *Bellotti*. Significantly, both proponents and opponents of campaign finance reform continue to cite Emerson in support of their opposite positions on the constitutionality of specific reforms.[152]

Prominent ACLU officials similarly recognize and then ignore the novel nature of many constitutional free-speech issues. Norman Dorsen's recent writings clearly demonstrate that he believes the nature of the marketplace of ideas is changing rapidly. "The healthy vision the framers of our Constitution had of a society of roughly equal yeomen," he observes, "has also been eroded in recent years by the conglomerate ownership of newspapers, radio and TV stations." Like Emerson, he thinks that the Burger Court did not adequately respond to these new threats to the system of freedom of expression. He and Joel Gora attack that Court's tendency to prefer protecting property interests to promoting free speech. The justices, they argue, have only "been respectful of free speech interests principally when those interests have coincided with or furthered the protection of property."[153]

Remarkably, however, Dorsen and Gora's alternative approach, which they call "maximum protection of speech," does not answer the very questions they find central to contemporary First Amendment litigation. Their theory has five major elements:

1. The content of communication is entitled to the fullest protection possible and can be restricted only where the identified harm resulting from such communication cannot be remedied, mitigated, or prevented by "more speech." . . .

2. Communication that surely will cause the harm sought to be averted can be restricted, but only if it comes within one of a few rigorously defined categories. . . .

3. Speech can be placed in such categories only upon the most demanding showing, comparable to that required to overcome the "heavy presumption against [the] constitutional validity" of prior restraints.

4. So-called time, place, and manner restrictions on speech are to be gauged by a rigorous form of the compelling interest test. . . .

5. First Amendment "procedural" rules—the presumptive invalidity of prior restraints, the doctrines against overbreadth and vagueness, and the requirements of scrupulous procedural safeguards—should remain firmly in place.[154]

These standards provide answers to the question, When can speech be restricted?—the issue at stake in traditional free-speech controversies. Indeed, each element of Dorsen and Gora's "maximum protection of speech" is a libertarian measure designed to prevent some content restriction. The central issue in such late twentieth-century cases as *Buckley v. Valeo* or *Pacific Gas & Electric v. California*, however, is What is speech? Clearly, repeated and more sophisticated assertions that government should rarely, if ever, regulate expression do not answer this question. Like Emerson's "full protection" standard, "maximum protection of speech" offers no guidelines that determine when the expressive use of property is constitutionally protected speech, when one has a First Amendment right to exclude others from making expressive use of one's private property, or when government can regulate the expressive use of private property for the purpose of reducing the effects that disparities in economic holdings have on the marketplace of ideas.

Other civil libertarian activists also fail to analyze these important constitutional issues. The ACLU's public pronouncements suggest that its leaders consider the problems raised by First Amendment property or spending rights to be peripheral to core civil libertarian concerns. Franklyn Haimen, a former president of the ACLU, did not discuss the relationship between economics and expression in his *Speech and Law in a Free Society*. When Burt Neuborne, a former legal director of the ACLU, reviewed his "career as a lawyer asking judges to intervene on the side of first amendment values," he did not include any case concerning rights to convert economic resources into political assets.[155]

Official publications similarly imply that the ACLU does not think that mixed questions of speech and property present important First Amendment problems. Both the most recent ACLU policy guide and its anthology on the rights of Americans provide readers with standards and commentary on traditional free-speech problems. Neither publication analyzes or discusses ACLU policy toward campaign finance reform.[156] One must look elsewhere to determine whether civil libertarians should believe that corporations have free-speech rights or that the dollar amounts of political contributions ought to be limited.

ACLU officials and publications do have one clear response to mixed questions of speech and property. Most contemporary proponents of expression rights maintain the democratic vision of early civil libertarianism. Both the anthology and policy guide emphasize that "the effective exercise of liberty . . . requires a degree of command over material resources."[157] In areas outside the First Amendment, the ACLU fights to establish democratic economic and social institutions. If governmental officials implemented the welfare rights that many civil libertarians advocate, the significance of questions concerning an owner's right to control the expression uses of material resources would be significantly reduced, though not altogether eliminated.[158]

Unfortunately, perhaps, the ACLU's campaign for welfare rights has not succeeded. Many Americans are still financially unable to participate effectively in the marketplace of ideas. Hence, some policy must address whether, under contemporary conditions of material inequalities, persons should have unlimited power to convert their economic advantages into political resources. So far, the ACLU has had little to say about the constitutionality of the choices currently available to U.S. citizens. That organization has taken no clear public position on the

actual constitutional relationships between expression and economics in contemporary democratic life.

Although this account suggests that the ACLU is relatively
uninterested in mixed questions of speech and property, its
members are, in fact, deeply troubled by these problems. The
issues raised in *Buckley* and related cases have been hotly con-
tested within that organization. Many local affiliates have taken
inconsistent positions. Indeed, this conflict explains the ACLU's
public reticence on the constitutionality of campaign finance
regulations. Its members can easily determine the correct civil
libertarian response to legislation prohibiting flag desecration,
but the principles they share do not clearly denote the correct
civil libertarian response to issues that concern the extent to
which owners can legitimately control the expressive uses of
their material resources. Indeed, as the following discussion
suggests, civil libertarians are not going to be able to resolve
those issues unless they abandon or modify some of their principles. A tradition founded on the pretense that substantive
policies do not affect democratic process simply does not have
the intellectual tools necessary to resolve the problems created
when one recognizes that the distribution of material resources
affects the distribution of political power.

Is Money Speech?

While the prevailing general theories of the Constitution and
First Amendment ignore the constitutional relationships between expression and economics, an increasing number of civil
libertarians have attempted to explore such questions in books
and articles specifically devoted to that subject. Accepting the
rationale of the *Carolene Products* footnote, these jurists agree
that limitations on a person's right to control the expressive uses
of economic resources are constitutional if they regulate property but unconstitutional if they regulate speech. Hence, those
scholars working within the democratic process model of the
judicial function inevitably perceive the relevant First Amendment question as Is money speech?

Unfortunately, this approach has proven unworkable. Candid representatives of each position admit that accepted First

Amendment values support both an affirmative and a negative answer.[159] Different elements of the civil libertarian tradition, they recognize, treat money as speech and not as speech. More significantly, each alternative subverts one aspect of the democratic vision shared by most contemporary speech advocates. The argument that money is speech makes unconstitutional the redistributive policies civil libertarians believe necessary to a functioning system of freedom of expression. The argument that money is not speech makes constitutional many state practices that civil libertarians believe violate core rights of political advocacy.

Proponents of the view that money is speech typically assert that elected officials are constitutionally barred from regulating expression. The government, in their view, has "no legitimate power to pass any law respecting [speech or] the press." "The First Amendment," Ithiel de Sola Pool declares, "excludes one kind of commerce, namely communication, from governmental activity." Harry Kalven observes that the "atmosphere of surveillance" created by government regulation "is destructive of the morale of a free press."[160] Opponents of campaign finance reform and access rights assert that the public interest is best served when there is unrestricted debate on matters of public importance. Scot Powe insists that all leading civil libertarians have recognized that "if only the government would cease interference in the marketplace of ideas, the system of freedom of expression would be a lot better." "The open marketplace," Joel Fleishman and Pope McCorkle state, "is the traditional means of control."[161]

If the central meaning of constitutional expression guarantees is that government cannot interfere with private efforts to influence the marketplace of ideas, then owners clearly have a constitutional right to control the expressive uses of their holdings. For this reason, C. Edwin Baker claims that "an individual's use of her resources to make or sponsor political communication is speech for first amendment purposes."[162] Thus, statutes regulating the political uses of private property are illegitimate efforts to affect public debate. In particular, because they are expressly designed to influence public discourse, campaign finance reforms and regulations of mass media are unconstitutional.

Proponents of First Amendment spending rights think that direct efforts to reduce the influence of money on politics cause social harms and violate fundamental democratic norms. In their view, restricting campaign spending reduces the variety of opinions available to the public, thus inhibiting a voter's "ability to hear a large quantity of political ideas from any position on the political spectrum." "If a candidate's expenditures are restricted," Martin Redish claims, "there will be a commensurate reduction in his ability to convey information to the public."[163] Powe argues that "the theory that a speaker has the right to choose his message and the intensity and frequency of its delivery reflects the recognition that a free-for-all on public issues serves both the ideals of self-government and those of maximizing individual choices."[164] Many observers contend that access rights have a chilling effect on public debate, causing stations to "avoid overly controversial or caustic commentary," which requires that the target of the attack be permitted to respond. Fleishman and McCorkle suggest that "rather than increasing the diversity of opinion on the airwaves, a right of reply may well restrain a broadcaster from engaging in any controversial discussion."[165]

Finally, jurists emphasize that elected officials should not be given control of the campaign process. Daniel Polsby concludes that "knowledge of the caliber of people who sometimes get their hands on our government" is the best reason not to tolerate restrictions on campaign financing. In *American Broadcasting and the First Amendment,* Powe points out that "the privilege to broadcast has been granted to friends of the government and withheld from its foes; efforts at censorship have been employed to back the political agenda of the party in power; and abuses have occurred with unfortunate frequency." After we examine contemporary experience, he observes, "the old-fashioned tradition of freedom won't look so bad."[166]

These civil libertarians recognize that private conduct may have as adverse an impact on the fairness of democratic processes as state regulation. "The wealthy," Powe asserts, "enjoy tremendous influence." Fleishman and McCorkle similarly admit that "the campaign finance process contributes to the existence of a marketplace where the rich get politically richer and the poor get politically poorer."[167] However, opponents of campaign finance reform believe that these ills must not be cured by restricting the opportunities for speech of well-off citizens. Baker maintains that the Constitution "rules out decisions to limit the effectiveness of some persons' advocacy by limiting their speech freedom." Rather, these commentators contend that the state should provide poorer citizens with better opportunities to speak. "The traditional solution," Powe states, is "more rather than less speech." Redish argues that "the public interest would be better served by increasing access for the less wealthy rather than by decreasing access for candidates with greater financial resources."[168] Thus, opponents of restrictions on campaign finance frequently endorse proposals to provide "significant additional public funding . . . for electoral campaigns, so that the advantages of wealth can either be eliminated or minimized."[169]

More important, those who claim that money is speech believe that economic inequality should be attacked at "its source rather than its consequences." If material inequalities are biasing the marketplace of ideas, then elected officials should implement more democratic economic and social policies. Such egalitarian redistribution of property rights seems consistent with the rationale of the *Carolene Products* footnote, which obligates judges to defer to the substantive policy choices of the people's representatives. "The permissible manner for the government to advance the egalitarian goal of more equal access to the political arena," C. Edwin Baker declares, "is to increase . . . the egalitarian nature of our society generally." Fleishman and McCorkle state that "by taxing and redistributing wealth itself" reformers avoid "the apparent first amendment obstacle of political equality."[170] Of course, everyone recognizes that these proposals are not likely to be enacted, and even if enacted they may not "usher in an ideal state of political equality." Indeed, their proponents confess that "most citizens will still be relegated to the more passive role of political consumer." Nevertheless, from the perspective of First Amendment values, the alternatives are functionally worse.[171]

On closer examination, however, the argument that money is speech undermines the practical and constitutional possibilities for those redistributive policies proposed by civil libertarian advocates of First Amendment spending rights. While opponents of "level-down" policies are quick to chide their rivals for naively believing that elected officials will fairly attempt to equalize political influence, they have not explained why legislators might be expected to behave better when implementing "level-up" policies serving the same purpose.[172] Experience suggests that both sorts of reform favor in-groups or well-established interests. For example, recent federal campaign restrictions were biased toward incumbents; likewise, recent federal campaign subsidies were biased toward the two major parties. Both Emerson and Chief Justice Rehnquist maintain that the current system of funding federal elections violates the constitutional rights of third-party candidates and their supporters.[173]

Moreover, if the Constitution prohibits state interference with private attempts to influence the marketplace of ideas, then the social and economic policies that civil libertarians assign to legislatures in democratic societies violate the First Amendment. By limiting the money a person can earn, elected officials restrict an individual's political behavior. For example, the maximum-hour law considered by the Court in *Lochner v. New York* prevented employees from working overtime to be able to contribute to a political campaign. Reformers could not argue that the ten-hour day was a labor regulation that incidentally affected expression rights. Civil libertarians insist that economic and social programs should be designed to affect the distribution of political resources. The major purpose of economic policies, these commentators state, is to increase the ability of some and decrease the ability of others to influence debate on matters of public importance. Thus, if money is speech, state efforts to regulate both the commercial marketplace and the marketplace of ideas are unconstitutional. This position is consistent with conservative libertarianism, but subversive of civil libertarianism's call for legislative activity to create the necessary economic prerequisites of a functional system of freedom of expression.

Proponents of campaign finance reform and access rights offer a different interpretation of the constitutional meaning of free speech. In their view, the First Amendment guarantees that all opinions shall have equal chances to gain the public's favor. "The kind of community process that is at the heart of the First Amendment," Judge Skelly Wright maintains, is one "wherein ideas and candidates prevail because of their inherent worth, and not because prestigious or wealthy people line up in favor." Archibald Cox declares that "liberty means the opportunity of the individual man or woman to express himself or herself in a society in which ideas are judged principally by their merit." Defenders of "money is not speech" think that freedom of expression functions best when widely diverse ideas are available for public consumption. Constitutional speech protections, in their view, are primarily concerned "with the variety of ideas rather than the absolute quantity of words." Judge Wright claims that the "core notion of the first amendment remains the protection of diverse, antagonistic, and unpopular speech." Expression rights, Stephen Carter maintains, are "intended to promote free discussion of public policy, not to permit special interests to manipulate that discussion or prevent it from taking place."[174]

If the central meaning of constitutional free-speech guarantees is that ideas should be judged on their merits, then money is not speech. "Spending money," Albert Rosenthal insists, "is not the same as speech-making, even if the former may foster the latter."[175] Proponents of campaign finance reform and access rights believe that the doctrine of "money is speech" inhibits fair public debate in two ways. First, unequal resources prevent ideas from competing on equal terms. Marlene Nicholson contends that unregulated campaign spending "gives some a special advantage in influencing the outcome of elections"; "some voters are denied an 'equal voice' and some candidates are denied an 'equal chance.' " Rosenthal and Judge Wright claim that "lopsided media spending . . . overwhelmingly and effectively blo[ts] out the messages of [a candidate's] opponents."[176] Second, lack of material backing may prevent worthy ideas from competing at all for public favor. "Concentrated wealth," many commentators allege, "reduces variety in the marketplace of political ideas." Owen Fiss points out that an unregulated marketplace of ideas will include "only those that are advocated by the rich, . . . those who can borrow from others, or

. . . those who can put together a product that will attract sufficient advertisers or subscribers to sustain the enterprise." "A
comparatively few private hands," Jerome Barron argues, "are
in a position to determine not only the content of information,
but its very availability." "The need for huge sums of money to
compete with well-financed candidates," Nicholson observes,
"deters those without ties to wealthy interests from even entering the fray." Indeed, this problem may affect more than would-
be candidates. Judge Wright suggests that the power of "the be-
hemoths of concentrated wealth" means that "voters are bound
to become disillusioned and apathetic."[177]

Proponents of "money is not speech" assert campaign finance reforms do not trench on core rights of public advocacy.
Judge Wright insists that "restrictions on the use of money
should be judged by the tests employed for vehicles—for
speech-related conduct—and not by the tests developed for
pure speech."[178] Opponents of First Amendment spending
rights frequently invoke Meiklejohn's image of a town meeting
where the moderator ensures "not that everyone shall speak,
but that everything worth saying shall be said."[179] Efforts to
regulate the private financing of debate on matters of public
importance, they argue, are similarly justified by the accepted
governmental practice of regulating the time, place, and manner of speech.[180] Paul Freund asserts that "just as the volume of
sound may be limited by law, so the volume of dollars may be
limited, without violating the First Amendment." "Certainly
the evils to be rectified through prohibition of large contributions," Nicholson argues, "are at least equal to the concerns
which were held to outweigh the use of loud, raucous, sound
trucks."[181]

Even if the analogy between decibels and dollars is sound,
the civil libertarian tradition still places significant hurdles in
the path of reforming campaign finance. Significantly, Justices
Black and Douglas both dissented from the Supreme Court's decision in *Kovacs v. Cooper,* which held that the First Amendment did not protect the right to broadcast one's message on a
sound truck. Justice Black declared that "laws which hamper
the free use of some instruments of communication thereby
favor competing channels." "The basic premise of the First

Amendment," he declared, "is that all present instruments of communication, as well as others that inventive genius may bring into being, shall be free from governmental censorship or prohibition."[182] This would seem to suggest that government should also not regulate expensive communication technologies, even if only a few people can afford them.

Black did recognize that states could, in principle, regulate loud noises without violating constitutional expression rights. Thus, "unreasonable use of public speaking devices could be prohibited." "A city ordinance, that reasonably restricts the volume of sound," he stated, "does not . . . infringe the constitutionally protected area of free speech." Civil libertarians, however, have traditionally placed a heavy burden on elected officials to prove that their time, place, and manner regulations do not unnecessarily trench on First Amendment rights. As noted above, Norman Dorsen claims that such "restrictions on speech are to be gauged by a rigorous form of the compelling interest test." Thus, in *Kovacs*, Black insisted that legislation regulating sound trucks had to be drafted so as to avoid "absolutely denying to the community's citizens all information that may be disseminated or received through this new avenue for trade in ideas."[183] Given the tendency of incumbents to favor their own speech, it is doubtful that actual attempts to regulate campaign finance would satisfy this standard.

More significant, if the First Amendment only prohibits legislation that restricts the variety of ideas available to the public or prevents those ideas from being judged on their merits, elected officials could ban speech that civil libertarians have traditionally protected. Decisions that speech is redundant are just as political and subject to abuse as decisions that speech is false. A moderator who believed that all versions of communism are substantially similar would have the power to silence a Marxist speaker on the ground that another Marxist had previously spoken, even if both dissidents claimed that the other's opinions are distinct and deluded. This problem cannot be resolved by providing more knowledgeable arbiters. Questions about what constitutes intellectual variety generate as much scholarly dispute as questions of intellectual truth (witness the heated debates over what appointments would best diversify an academic department).[184] Legislatures committed to exposing citizens to a variety of ideas could also silence unpopular speakers by proving that their presence drives persons away from the marketplace of ideas. Groups favoring Nazism, for example, could be barred from passing out leaflets in the parks if proponents of other ideas could establish that removing Nazi speech would encourage more speech in the park and make more persons willing to listen.

Finally, the case for "money is not speech" suggests that elected officials have the constitutional power to equalize other resources that may prevent ideas from being judged by their intrinsic merits. Such political resources as political expertise, free time, good looks, stamina, and eloquence are not equally distributed. As Ralph Winter has argued, "since some groups have more free time than others, it is wholly arbitrary to treat 'volunteer' services and money differently."[185] Hence, statutory limits on political volunteering might be constitutional. Such limits seem particularly appropriate if the volunteers have special expertise not available to the general public. If Congress can constitutionally make it a criminal offense for a friend of a candidate to contribute fifty thousand dollars so that the candidate can hire a speechwriter, then the national legislature should have the constitutional power to make it a criminal offense for that friend to donate fifty thousand dollars worth of services as a speechwriter. The mere fact that a candidate is a particularly effective speaker or has associates who are talented political organizers does not seem particularly relevant to the worth of the ideas he or she espouses. Elected officials might similarly ban campaign appearances by celebrities on the ground that such endorsements have little to do with underlying ideas. Indeed, if American politicians are frequently advised to "say not one single word about [their] principles,"[186] then the state could regulate virtually the entire political campaign. These regulations are subversive of the civil libertarian tradition's insistence that individuals should be able to present their ideas in the manner they find most persuasive.

In short, debate over whether money is speech has an illusory quality. The dispute appears to take place within the framework of the democratic process model of the judicial function. Both parties delineate a wide area of speech that government may not regulate and a wide area of property that government may regulate. In their view, they are simply debating on which side of the line mixed questions of speech and property fall. But we have seen that each answer to Is money speech? obliterates the distinction between democratic inputs and democratic outputs. If money is speech, then virtually everything turns out to be speech, and government can regulate nothing. If money is not speech, then hardly anything turns out to be speech, and government can regulate everything. Of course, most participants in the debate over speech/property issues do not go this far. The point is that, in principle, there seems to be no good place to redraw the line between political processes and substantive outputs within a framework that treats "yes" and "no" as the only possible answers to the question, Is money speech?

If this analysis is correct, then the civil libertarian tradition may be facing a terminal crisis. Contemporary defenders of free speech have successfully established that persons must be allowed to express their political views, except in certain narrowly defined and extreme circumstances. However, their constitutional arguments fail in a world where the major threat to meaningful debate on matters of public importance is not that many are prevented from speaking but that many do not have the resources necessary to be heard. Because they treat property and free speech as two distinct realms of constitutional discourse, the writings of Chafee, Meiklejohn, and Emerson ignore the issues presented by statutes regulating the expressive uses of private property. Those commentators who debate whether money is speech have reached conclusions that undermine democratic understandings of the system of freedom of expression. As a result, civil libertarians overlook, grudgingly accept, or ineffectively protest a series of Supreme Court decisions suggesting that the current constitutional meaning of free speech is that the First Amendment "in its majestic equality, allows the poor as well as the rich to form political action committees, to purchase the most sophisticated polling, media and direct mail techniques, . . . to drown out each other's voices by overwhelming expenditures in political campaigns,"[187] and to have the exclusive right to determine what political messages shall be included in the bills they mail to consumers.

Chapter Six

Toward a Somewhat New Constitutional Defense of Free Speech

This study demonstrates that philosophical and jurisprudential justifications of expression rights are not timeless verities but reflections of the unique political and legal climate of their era. Conservative libertarianism expressed the value that late nineteenth-century thinkers placed on individual rights. Civil libertarianism expresses the value that twentieth-century thinkers place on democratic processes. Zechariah Chafee and others emphasized the social importance of uninhibited debate on matters of public importance because they were committed to developing a philosophical and constitutional defense of free speech that was consistent with those principles of pragmatism and sociological jurisprudence that progressive thinkers considered the foundations for all sound arguments. The "worthy tradition" they founded is a product of the peculiar intellectual conditions of their times, not a position inherent in either liberalism or the constitutional history of the United States.

Placed in its proper historical perspective, the modern constitutional defense of free speech offers new opportunities and presents new challenges for those committed to a democratic society. Freed from the myth of the single civil libertarian tradition, theorists need not continue straining inherited principles to extract some answers to the pressing First Amendment issues raised by campaign finance reforms and access rights. Instead, the next generation of libertarians can develop original conceptions of advocacy rights that incorporate late twentieth-century intellectual developments in an effort to resolve late twentieth-century problems. Although their theories cannot ignore traditional free-speech problems, contemporary libertarians must explore the constitutional relationships between expression and economics with the same energy that they have heretofore devoted to the constitutional relationships between advocacy and lawless conduct.

The Lessons of the Past

Civil libertarian doctrine suggests that efforts to develop new constitutional defenses of expression rights present few challenging theoretical problems. Chafee, Meiklejohn, and Emerson agreed that the central task of libertarian scholarship is to discover the policies that best promote the values served by public debate.[1] Hence, once they recognize that a general theory of the First Amendment must address mixed questions of speech and property, third-generation civil libertarians apparently need only adjust the standards required by the democratic process model of free speech to ensure that libertarian theory keeps abreast of whatever threats material inequalities currently present to the system of freedom of expression. Like their distinguished ancestors, contemporary proponents of expression rights can then claim that the rules that best contribute to the discovery of truth on matters of public importance also define the scope of the constitutional meaning of free speech.

Most scholarly discussions share civil libertarianism's understanding of the actual relationships between political and legal arguments. Studies of the way constitutional doctrines evolve regularly assume that persons and groups do not experience serious difficulties when expressing their values in jurisprudential terms. Although identifying the practices that best promote private or public goals may be extremely complex, developing legal justifications of those practices, many intellectuals argue, is relatively easy. This belief that law is simply politics in another forum is particular prominent among those political scientists who, influenced by David Truman's *The Governmental Process*, regard constitutional discourse as the mere rationalizations of interest groups. Proponents of political jurisprudence typically assert that most advocates claim the Constitution either supports or requires whatever policies they believe best serve the public interest. Martin Shapiro, for example, argues that the "principle role" of legal argument, "like that of most lobbying, is not to persuade 'the guys on the other side' but to provide good arguments for 'our guys.' "[2]

For this reason, civil libertarians and students of American law frequently see a close correspondence between the legal doctrines a jurist espouses and that person's underlying political preferences. Chafee and others maintain that persons who broadly interpret First Amendment rights believe that government should rarely, if ever, restrict speech. Persons who narrowly interpret First Amendment rights believe that the liberty of expression ought to be limited.[3] On similar grounds, Shapiro suggests that the *Carolene Products* footnote is best understood as a general "blueprint for transferring Supreme Court political services from Republican to Democratic clienteles." The New Deal court, he further claims, protected free speech because its protection served the interest of members of the New Deal coalition, most notably intellectuals. Privacy and sociological jurisprudence did not, in this view, influence either the Court's decision to protect free speech or the nature of that protection.[4]

Unfortunately, examining the first transformation of the constitutional defense of free speech demonstrates serious flaws in this explanation of doctrinal development. Translating abstract libertarian commitments into constitutional argument has never been a simple task. Over and over again, civil libertarians have acknowledged that their constitutional arguments do not fully satisfy their political agenda. Although the leading figures of civil libertarianism demand that interpretations of the First Amendment respond to the major problems facing the system of freedom of expression, they admit that their proposals do not address serious threats to the attainment of truth on matters of public importance. As noted in chapter 3, some early civil libertarians conceded that the judiciary lacked the power to protect the expression rights they cherished. Chafee confessed that under the clear and present danger test judges would have to sustain speech regulations he thought were unwise.

Most significant, civil libertarians from John Dewey to Thomas Emerson have consistently asserted that material resources must be distributed equally if all persons are to have the actual capacity to exercise their expression rights, but they have proposed constitutional doctrines that they admit let wealthy political activists dominate the marketplace of ideas. This shortcoming does not result from cramped visions of civic life, a defect that can be repaired by greater appreciation of the nature of a truly democratic society. Chafee and his successors continually urged elected officials to pass economic and social policies that would enable every citizen to participate in public life. Civil libertarians, however, do not allow judges to take account of the relationships between speech and property, even though they recognize that these relationships adversely affect the functioning of the system of freedom of expression.

This study suggests that ideological obstacles confronted by all arguments explain why civil libertarians failed to develop constitutional doctrines that sufficiently promote their values. Scholars working from many perspectives realize that the dominant modes of argument in a given society affect the content of political advocacy. Quentin Skinner, perhaps the most forceful proponent of this view, insists that "the courses of action open to any rational agent must in part be determined by the range of principles which he can profess with plausibility." "To be understood," James Boyd White observes, a speaker "must use the language of his audience."[5] Thus, the intellectual climate of any particular historical period limits potential policy alternatives. As Skinner points out, because political actors "cannot hope to stretch the application of the existing principles indefinitely," they "can only hope to legitimate a restricted range of actions."[6]

Indeed, the intellectual climate of a given society affects conceivable policy alternatives. If, as many social scientists argue, "all aspects of social life are pervaded by decidedly non-neutral assumptions whose acceptance by a member of the culture define what is 'possible' for that person,"[7] then partisan activists may be incapable of conceptualizing the reforms that best advance their ends. Thus, the community's dominant patterns of justification constrain all efforts to improve the system of freedom of expression or resolve any other social problem. The broader ideological environment restricts both the arguments that libertarians choose to make and the arguments they are capable of choosing.

In this respect, doctrinal evolution resembles institutional development. In *Building a New American State*, Stephen Skowronek observes that political change is "mediated by the organization of the preestablished state."[8] Although existing state structures can be modified in many ways, they shape prevalent political reforms because the old forms must implement the new. Political and constitutional theories develop in a similar manner. When faced with new problems, scholars apply preexisting patterns of justification. "The terms used by the founders of a new form of cultural life," Richard Rorty points out, "will consist largely in borrowings from the vocabulary of the culture which they are hoping to replace."[9] Indeed, the ruling ideas of a culture can be thought of as among that society's central political institutions.[10]

Of course, as Skinner notes, intellectuals are "limited by the prevailing conventions of discourse," but they are not "limited only to following those conventions."[11] They may apply old principles in new ways and, in doing so, modify those principles for future users. Hence, the intellectual environment changes over time, and the struggle to influence those changes is one of the most bitterly fought contests of social and political life.

Nevertheless, the ideological institutions of a given society constrain the theoretical analysis of new problems. Political and constitutional theorists function within specific intellectual contexts and can deploy a limited set of intellectual resources. They do not create arguments ex nihilo or repeat timeless themes first given to Adam and Eve in the Garden of Eden.

By analyzing the institutional constraints that general developments in American political and legal thought place on efforts to justify particular policies, scholars can better explain the functional weaknesses of modern free-speech theory. Although conservative libertarian arguments were responsive to repressive practices during World War I, progressives rejected that conception of expression rights because it was premised on what they believed were logically and socially indefensible notions of individual rights. Early civil libertarians maintained that any sound philosophical or constitutional argument must be derived from the principles of pragmatism and sociological jurisprudence.[12] Relying on the works of John Dewey and Roscoe Pound, Chafee and others based a new defense of free speech on the social interest in debate on matters of public importance. Their clear and present danger test was initially less protective of political dissent than the incitement rule advocated by late nineteenth-century treatise writers, but this test was the only standard they could justify given the available intellectual resources.

Civil libertarianism was not, however, merely a mechanical application of early twentieth-century thought. Before Chafee published and popularized his arguments, progressive thinkers opposed all manifestations of judicial activism in constitutional cases. Judicial policy making, such progressives as Edward Corwin claimed, was inconsistent with the majoritarian premises of American government. Although Chafee had to work within the frameworks of pragmatism and sociological jurisprudence, he did not have to accept claims that these modes of argumentation could not constitutionally defend free speech. Like the founders of other traditions, Chafee used the materials of an inherited language in ways that offered new possibilities to his contemporaries. He did so by demonstrating that judicial solicitude for expression rights could be justified within the parameters of sociological jurisprudence. In particular, Chafee claimed that judicial activism on behalf of free speech purified the democratic process, thus strengthening progressive claims that courts should not second-guess the substantive outputs of the people's elected representatives. This modification of Pound's philosophy of law helped inspire a new form of legal discourse, one that permitted twentieth-century jurists to oppose both *Lochner v. New York* and *Abrams v. United States*.

While Chafee was able to defend more speech than many progressives had thought possible or desirable, civil libertarians were never fully able to escape the limitations of a political and constitutional theory originally designed to justify transferring economic power from the courts to the elected branches of government. Sociological jurisprudence insisted that judges had neither the right nor the competence to strike down policies chosen by the people's representatives. To stay within these limits, Chafee and his successors sharply distinguished laws affecting the democratic process from laws allocating economic and social resources. Although this division enabled them to increase judicial protection for minority opinions, the modern constitutional defense of free speech became oblivious to the manifold relationships between political expression and private property. Libertarians soon assumed that politics and economics had always been two autonomous realms within constitutional discourse. Alternative understandings of expression rights were no longer rejected; they were lost. As a result, contemporary free-speech argument continues to emphasize the relationship between words and harmful conduct at the expense of seriously analyzing an owner's right to convert material resources into political speech. While the ACLU and other sympathetic jurists recognize the substantial effect that economic inequalities have on a system of freedom of expression, they work within a model of the judicial function that consigns those problems to the periphery of First Amendment theory.

If this analysis is sound, then intellectuals committed to correcting civil libertarianism's failure to resolve mixed questions of property and speech will no more be able to write on a blank slate than was Chafee. Even if a given scholar transcends the conceptual institutions of his or her culture, effective advocacy must conform to the belief systems of the time. Theorists cannot create new interpretations of expression rights from nothing; rather, they must transform the ideological resources of present-day society. Unfortunately, contemporary modes of legitimation may not support all the reforms that would characterize a truly healthy system of freedom of expression. The best understanding of constitutional expression rights may be one that can be neither justified nor even imagined by persons who work and think within the framework of late twentieth-century American philosophical and jurisprudential thought.

Obviously, knowing that some arguments may be beyond our present conceptual powers is of little use in constructing a system of freedom of expression for our time, although one purpose of this study is to expand the conceptions of expression rights available to intellectuals. However, libertarians should take seriously the possibility that some valid philosophical or constitutional arguments may simply be unacceptable to the late twentieth-century American mind. Many aspects of progressive thought no longer constrain legal argument, but the present ideological climate imposes different limits on efforts to constitutionalize the democratic vision that first inspired the modern constitutional defense of free speech. A few respectable contemporary thinkers have suggested that judges should second-guess some substantive social policies made by elected officials.[13] Mainstream thought, however, is still hostile to claims that judges should declare that all citizens have constitutional welfare rights. For example, legal activists frequently ask courts to strike down state laws restricting abortion rights, but the constitutional attack on Reaganomics has been limited to a few law review articles. In this intellectual environment, it may not be possible to argue persuasively that judges should guarantee all persons the material prerequisites for effectively exercising their political rights.

The evolution of the last section of *Transforming Free Speech* illustrates the constraints that recent legal developments place on libertarian arguments. In an earlier version of this work, I claimed that all persons should have the right to the resources necessary to participate in their community's search for the public good.[14] Although I still maintain this as a valid political ideal, I am no longer sure it is a constitutional ideal,[15] and I seriously doubt whether such an argument can be made convincingly at present. Given the direction of the Rehnquist Court, the best libertarians can do, I believe, is strengthen the constitutional case for campaign finance reform while hoping to create an atmosphere more hospitable to welfare rights.

Advocating doctrines unlikely to be accepted immediately is still a worthwhile activity. A profound defense of the right to have the resources necessary to participate in the community's search for the public good may significantly influence the intellectual climate of the unforeseeable future. It is a truism that pundits celebrated in their time are soon forgotten, while more obscure thinkers gain future favor. Most civil libertarians, however, wish to influence the present operation of the marketplace of ideas. Thus, contemporary proponents of a democratic society may confront the same difficult decision faced by early civil libertarians. They will also have to choose between promoting speech-protective doctrines that may gain the public's favor and advocating speech-protective doctrines that, if accepted, would actually best enable the system of freedom of expression to function under contemporary conditions.

Persons committed to a democratic society will never be able to avoid these painful choices. Although this study has documented the weaknesses of civil libertarianism, its continued general appeal suggests that Chafee's arguments express something fundamental in contemporary American political and legal thought. A theorist who completely disregards that model of constitutional argument probably surrenders whatever power a scholar may have to affect the present course of First Amendment theory. The intellectual resources of the late twentieth century, however, can improve our theoretical understandings of expression rights. For this reason, rather than completely abandoning civil libertarianism, jurists can use certain developments in recent scholarship to amplify some of its themes in ways that ultimately transcend their limitations.

Future libertarians can be more self-conscious about the central issues their theories seek to resolve. Heretofore, most works on the First Amendment have attempted to answer the question, When can speech be restricted? Such an approach suffices if the main threat to the values underlying expression rights is government policies that directly silence political and social dissent. As Chapter 5 indicated, however, most social scientists and academic lawyers agree that the dominant free-speech issues currently being adjudicated concern control over the material resources necessary for effective speech. The central question raised by cases concerning the constitutionality of campaign finance reform or access rights is What is speech? Enlightening analyses of the circumstances when speech can be restricted do not necessarily explain when speech has occurred. Hence, new theoretical approaches should be explicitly designed to address the constitutional relationships between free speech and private property.

Of course, no general theory of the First Amendment can resolve all controversies over expression rights. Inevitably, libertarians will have to develop subsidiary doctrines for particular problems, but their discussions of the central meaning of the First Amendment should address those practices that presently threaten most directly the system of freedom of expression. If such cases as *Buckley v. Valeo* have had the most significant impact on the values free speech serves, then libertarians must treat the constitutional relationships between speech and property as a paradigmatic question that a general theory of the First Amendment must answer. Peripheral doctrines should only be devised to deal with peripheral matters.

This emphasis on actual threats to the system of freedom of expression requires some empirical research. Academic lawyers cannot assume the system of freedom of speech is healthy merely because the grandchildren of Eugene Debs and Joseph Gilbert are not being arrested. Established groups may have abandoned traditional forms of speech restrictions only because they have found more effective means of unconstitutionally biasing the marketplace of ideas. Nothing in *Transforming Free Speech,* I should emphasize, conclusively establishes this point. While many social scientists and civil libertarians claim that material inequalities significantly threaten the system of freedom of expression, other disagree. Some thinkers insist that the effects of money on politics are either trivial or beneficial.[16] If the constitutional relationships between free speech and private property do not significantly affect the functioning of the marketplace of ideas, then future libertarians can justifiably exile mixed questions of speech and property to the hinterlands of First Amendment theory. But given the emphasis that such civil libertarians as Chafee, Meiklejohn, and Emerson placed on developing doctrine that best promotes the values underlying expression rights, contemporary civil libertarians should not tolerate scholarship that asserts these problems are of great practical importance but little theoretical interest.

Future libertarians must also develop more sophisticated concepts of political liberty and political equality, ones that recognize (if this is empirically the case) that economic and social policies have significant impacts on democratic processes. Political liberty cannot simply mean that government cannot interfere with the operation of the democratic process because virtually all forms of state action affect the democratic process. Political equality cannot simply mean that all persons should have the same power to affect democratic outcomes because such an ideal would require that government equalize virtually every human difference. Indeed, as Douglas Rae and others have pointed out, the totally equal society presupposed by much advocacy of campaign finance reform is a practical, if not a logical, impossibility.[17]

To avoid these difficulties, general theories of the First Amendment must ask When is money speech? rather than Is money speech? More generally, libertarian theory needs to recognize that in representative democracies some persons will have more power than others. The decision to elect or appoint officials, rather than choosing them by lottery, indicates that a society believes certain inequalities—whether inequalities of wealth, popularity, wisdom, integrity, or eloquence—justify political inequalities. The next defense of free speech must specify which inequalities persons can exploit to achieve political power and which government can regulate.

This approach fits easily within the intellectual environment of late twentieth-century America. Such contemporary works of political philosophy as John Rawls's *A Theory of Justice* discuss the philosophical relationships between free speech and private property. Robert Dahl's *Democracy and Its Critics* similarly explores theoretical connections between material inequalities and democratic processes.[18] Future libertarians need only incorporate some of this scholarship into their general theories of the First Amendment; this is, after all, exactly what Chafee and his allies did seventy years ago.

In short, the main lesson the libertarian past teaches is that the system of freedom of expression does not stand apart from American political and intellectual developments. As we have seen, the evolution of the constitutional defense of free speech

cannot be fully understood without looking at broader developments in American political and legal thought. Furthermore,
the problems of contemporary free-speech theory cannot be resolved unless libertarians quite consciously incorporate these
broader political and jurisprudential themes in their works. If
the system of freedom of expression is to remain functional in
the twenty-first century, then future civil libertarians must explore the actual relationships between expression and economics and develop theoretical frameworks for evaluating the relationships they find.

A Theory for the Future?

This book could easily end here, but I am unable to resist the
temptation to slip in a preliminary sketch of a new general theory of the First Amendment. Over the next few years, I hope to
develop a political libertarian approach to free-speech problems. This conception of expression rights borrows heavily
from the writings of Michael Walzer, the contemporary political theorist who most closely identifies with the views of early
civil libertarians. In *Spheres of Justice* and other works, Walzer
analyzes problems that civil libertarianism neglects. He discusses the philosophical significance of various relationships
between political and property rights and explains which inequalities citizens should be free to exploit in the political marketplace. Although I do not agree with all his conclusions or
methods, I believe that Walzer's works provide a sound starting
place for a future libertarianism.

Walzer maintains that democratic societies prevent persons
better off in one sphere of life from dominating other spheres.
"Society," he argues, "enjoys both freedom and equality when
success in one institutional setting isn't convertible into success
in another."[19] Those who endorse this vision do not worry if
some persons have more money, more political power, or more
luck in love, as long as money, political power, and love are distributed according to social understandings about what those
goods are and the mere possession of one good does not enable a
person to possess all others. Proponents of "complex equality"
contend that just political and social institutions limit the goods

that unequally distributed resources can be used to obtain. For example, Walzer thinks that persons should be allowed to use monetary advantages to purchase more luxury goods than their neighbors but not better basic health care. Similarly, most people think that physically attractive adolescents should be allowed to exploit their looks at their high school prom but not in college applications.[20]

Walzer's writings have been justly criticized for ignoring communal disagreements over the meaning of many goods he discusses,[21] but American society has reached a partial consensus on the best means of apportioning political power. Elections and policies, we agree, should not be decided on the basis of the contending parties' wealth. *The Federalist Papers* called for a large republic where citizens would be more "capable of choosing a fit representative" because they were "less likely to be diverted [by] the bribes of the rich."[22] The Jacksonian crusade against the money power, Sumner's tirades against plutocracy, and Dewey's advocacy of positive freedom were similar efforts to prevent material advantages from being converted into political resources. Contemporary opponents of campaign finance reform argue that there are better ways of controlling the insidious effect that economic inequalities have on the political process or assert that the risk of undue influence is the unfortunate price we pay to enjoy the superior benefits of free speech. Rarely do persons explicitly claim that money should make a difference in the public sphere.[23]

Most Americans think that democratic societies should allocate "political power . . . by arguing and voting." Hannah Arendt, I believe, stated an American as well as a Greek ideal when she celebrated "a way of life that was based exclusively upon persuasion and not upon violence."[24] Scholars as diverse as James Boyd White, Jürgen Habermas, Woodrow Wilson, and Richard Rorty variously praise the virtues of "a world of equal speakers with each other." Some thinkers maintain that government by conversation is the best way of discovering truths about human nature and social life. Others insist that democratic cultures regard persuasion as the means by which human beings create truth. However, as Rorty recognizes, this dispute over the function of public debate on matters of public importance "concern[s] only the self-image which a democratic society should have, the rhetoric which it should use to express its hopes," and not the speech policies that such a society should pursue.[25]

Walzer shares these visions of the democratic community. In *Spheres of Justice* he insists that "democracy puts a premium on speech, persuasion, rhetorical skill." In this view, those persons best able to convince their contemporaries are entitled to the greatest share of political power. "Ideally," Walzer suggests, "the citizen who makes the most effective persuasive argument—that is, the argument that actually persuades the largest number of citizens—gets his way."[26] Walzer also maintains, correctly in my opinion, that the ability to manage a campaign or perform any needed role in it are skills that also entitle a person to a share of political power. If this is correct, then the integrity of the political sphere is preserved when inequalities in political power reflect differences in the "rhetorical skill and organizational competence" of those who seek that good.[27]

Tyranny occurs when persons with political power convert that good into some other social good or when persons who have unequal, though justifiable, shares of some other social resource convert that good into political power. Classical liberalism established limits on the former sorts of boundary crossings. The founding fathers fought to create realms of religion, property, and privacy that were immune to the vicissitudes of political power.[28] Thus, the establishment clause of the First Amendment prevents the electorally successful from also resolving debates over theological questions. The contract and just compensation clauses similarly prevent democratic majorities from negating some of the benefits enjoyed by economically successful citizens. However, Walzer notes, modern societies must be as sensitive to protecting the distribution of political power "from the new power that arises within civil society itself, the power of wealth." New rules are needed to prevent material inequalities from trumping inequalities of "rhetoric skill and organizational competence" in the political arena. "Citizens," Walzer concludes, should "come into the forum with nothing but their arguments. All non-political goods have to be deposited outside: weapons and wallets, titles and degrees."[29]

These principles suggest the following interpretation of the First Amendment. The Constitution gives all persons the right to use their persuasive and organizational abilities to obtain political power. Thus, expression rights are violated whenever legislatures attempt to alleviate the disparities that result when persons take advantage of their political talents in the marketplace of ideas, although judges may justifiably prevent the politically powerful from dominating other social goods. Democratic majorities can never, or hardly ever, ban any argument or any manner of presenting arguments on the grounds of persuasiveness. If persons think that a particular candidate or policy is shallow, ignorant, mendacious, or destructive, they must persuade the public that their alternative is better. Demagogues must be exposed; they cannot be censored.

Political libertarians think that persons have the right to choose the policies they advocate and the means they believe will communicate their opinions most persuasively. "Congress," Justice Holmes should have said, "cannot forbid *any* effort to change the mind of the country," as long as such effort relies exclusively on resources that belong in the political sphere. From this perspective, virtually all traditional restrictions on speech are unconstitutional. Individuals have the right to persuade their fellow citizens that an ongoing war should be abandoned or intensified, that a military draft is constitutional or unconstitutional, or that they ought or ought not volunteer for the armed services. The Constitution protects speakers who advocate or oppose communism. A young man who wishes to wear a jacket with the lettering "FUCK THE DRAFT" has the same First Amendment right that his parents had when they wore the more sophisticated "I LIKE IKE" button.[30] For similar reasons, persons have the constitutional right to burn the flag. Ineffectiveness is the only punishment prescribed for speech others find offensive or simplistic.

Elected officials theoretically have the power to punish those who seek political power through inciting illegal conduct. Crime, after all, can be understood as a way of redistributing rights without persuading the relevant members of the public. The thief, for example, convinces neither the lawful owner to hand over his or her belongings nor the legislature to change the law of property. However, the Constitution does protect speakers who merely advocate the desirableness of criminal conduct or whose condemnations of existing policy may inspire others to break the law. Indeed, speakers have the constitutional right to urge their fellow citizens to abandon government by persuasion. Until they are successful, however, only speech uttered for the purpose of causing criminal conduct is beyond the pale of the First Amendment.

Political libertarianism clearly protects the free-speech rights of such dissidents as Charles Schenck, Eugene Debs, Jacob Abrams, Joseph Gilbert, Anita Whitney, Angelo Herndon, and Eugene Dennis. These speakers all attempted to persuade their audiences to adopt superior alternatives to the status quo. In my opinion, Benjamin Gitlow was the one speaker surveyed in this work who may have attempted to incite criminal conduct;[31] if so, then the First Amendment does not protect his speech. Nevertheless, I believe that the Supreme Court should have reversed Benjamin Gitlow's conviction. Actual standards of judicial protection must consider the historical tendency of juries and judges to impute unlawful motives to speakers with whom they disagree. As Justice Douglas recognized, given the actual dynamics of repression, courts are likely to maximize the number of cases they decide correctly if they adopt a rule that absolutely bars convictions where the primary evidence of criminal intention is the text of the actual speech.[32]

This emphasis on rhetorical ability, I should emphasize, does not necessarily favor the interests of the so-called "new class" of intellectuals. Walzer recognizes that the philosopher "must live with the ordinary odds of democratic politics"; and in democratic politics "truth is indeed another opinion, and the philosopher is only another opinion-maker."[33] For better or worse, few scholars have successfully convinced their fellow citizens to adopt their preferred policy prescriptions. Although most intellectuals regarded Ronald Reagan as a lazy yahoo whose economic and military policies were dangerously simplistic, most Americans found our fortieth president a far more persuasive figure than their old government professors.

Because they are not entitled to any share of political power, corporations have no expression rights independent of the rights of their owners. Corporate speech may be restricted as long as legislation does not discriminate among different speakers who wish to use the corporate form. Corporate speech may not be different in kind from individual speech, but artificial entities are different in kind from actual persons. Hence, in *Bellotti*, the Supreme Court should not have struck down the Massachusetts ban on corporate contributions during referendum campaigns. General Motors and the Bank of Boston have no First Amendment rights for the same reason they can neither vote nor run for political office.[34]

When confronted with questions about the constitutional relationships between political expression and private property, political libertarians properly ask When is money speech? rather than Is money speech? Individuals have the constitutional right to convert their material resources into political expression as long as the average member of the community can afford to invest similarly in politics.[35] They are entitled to choose the medium of their communication as well as their mode of communicating. Persons who are better able to persuasively use any asset available to most members of the public gain political power by virtue of their political skills. For this reason, those who object to short political advertisements on television should not be able to forbid others from making fifteen-second spot commercials. They must either convince the public that such presentations are worthless or find more successful means of communicating their own messages.

Citizens also have the right to combine in order to afford more expensive means of communicating their political ideas. Legislatures cannot constitutionally limit the resources that can be used to convince the public of the merits of any political proposal. Less articulate persons may decide that they can most persuasively communicate their values if they assist other power seekers, even if they lose some control over the content of their speech in the process. This is a risk they are free to assume. Constitutional principles are not offended when candidates or political organizations amass and use funds contributed by citizens who share their goals, as long as any equally persuasive candidate or political organization would be capable of raising the same amount of money from an equal number of citizens. For this reason, although its reasoning was wrong, the Burger/Rehnquist Court correctly held that there can be no constitutional limits on the funds expended by candidates or political action committees as long as those funds were donated by many small contributors.[36]

Money ceases to be speech only when persons attempt to convert their material advantages into political expression. No one has a constitutional right to use economic privilege to magnify otherwise relatively weak political skills. Citizens must persuade others to contribute to their campaigns if they need more resources to promote their opinions than the average member of the community can afford to invest in politics. Affluent Americans have no First Amendment right that permits them to achieve political success through constant repetition of relatively unwanted ideas.

To ensure that political resources determine the allocation of political power, elected officials are constitutionally permitted to regulate the effect of material inequalities on the marketplace of ideas. First, legislatures can limit the money that persons can spend for political reasons, provided that such limits are pegged at a level above that which most citizens can afford. Thus, in *Buckley*, the Supreme Court should not have struck down the provisions of FECA that limited the money a candidate could spend on his or her behalf or that another individual could independently spend on behalf of a political candidate. Second, persons who attempt to take political advantage of their superior material resources can be forced to grant access rights to less fortunate political activists. Although a radio station supported entirely by small contributions from listeners would not have to grant a right of reply to those who disagreed with its editorial policies,[37] a station that depended on a few large donations from wealthy individuals, advertisers, or corporations would. Indeed, political libertarians should think seriously about treating commercial broadcasters as commercial speech.

These policies will admittedly inhibit some speech. The owners of Logan Plaza or other shopping centers might decide not to permit any expression on their properties rather than grant all speakers reasonable access to their customers. Nevertheless, this potential reduction of the ideas available to the public does not present serious First Amendment problems from a political libertarian perspective. Constitutional rights are threatened when persons do not participate in the marketplace of ideas for fear of being exposed to criminal or civil liability.[38] There is no similar "chilling effect" when persons refrain from speaking for fear of being refuted if others are given the same opportunity to present their views. Qualms about potential rebuttals should influence speech. Persons who do not want to have their opinions challenged should not seek political power. "If you can't stand the heat," Harry Truman said, "get out of the kitchen."

These observations, I should quickly add, present only a tentative and skeletal outline of how a new libertarian theory might resolve problems that civil libertarianism ignores. In my future work I hope to fully justify this conception of expression rights. Although that book will emphasize those relationships between speech and property that most affect the contemporary marketplace of ideas, it will not propose a timeless theory of expression rights. Political libertarianism, like civil libertarianism, is destined to be a product of its times. As Dewey correctly observed, the best that any theory can accomplish is to clarify and help resolve contemporary problems. Early civil libertarians recognized that scholars should not work within an inherited tradition that no longer served their purposes. Contemporary libertarians will be true to our actual First Amendment tradition only if we also transform free speech so that our theories reflect the values we cherish and respond to the threats we face.

Notes

Introduction

1. Kalven (1988); Emerson (1977), p. 740; Powe (1987a), p. 250; Levy (1985), p. xix; 376 U.S. 254 (1964).

2. Rabban (1981), p. 586, 579. See Chafee (1941), pp. 497–509; R. Smith (1985), pp. 92–119; Fiss (1986), p. 1405.

3. See especially Levy (1985), p. x ("the American experience with a free press was as broad as the theoretical inheritance was narrow"). For attacks on Levy's specific conclusions, see Rabban (1985); D. Anderson (1986).

4. See especially Rossiter (1962), p. 136 ("One may search their writings in vain for evidence of genuine concern for the freedom of religion and expression"). For a summary of previous scholarly accounts of conservative attitudes toward free speech, see Graber (1988), pp. 19–24.

5. See, e.g., Murphy (1979), p. 40.

6. See, e.g., Murphy (1979).

7. See especially Rabban (1983); Rabban (1981); Murphy (1972).

8. 393 U.S. 948 (1969); 485 U.S. 46, 99 L.Ed 2d 41; 491 U.S. ———,105 L. Ed. 2d 342; See especially Smolla (1988), p. 303 ("the Supreme Court's opinion in *Falwell v. Flynt* is a triumphant celebration of freedom of speech"); Loewy (1989), p. 175 ("the Supreme Court has struck a major blow for freedom in *Johnson*"); Nimmer (1984), p. vii; Kalven (1988).

9. See especially Friedman (1985), pp. 18–19. For a discussion of the influence of "evolutionary functionalism" in contemporary legal history, see Gordon (1984), pp. 59–67; Gordon (1981), pp. 1028–36.

10. Chafee (1941), p. 509. See Bollinger (1986), p. 144.

11. Chafee (1928b), p. 97; Nimmer (1984), pp. 1–20; Kalven (1988), p. 124. These points are discussed at length in chapters 4 and 5.

12. Rabban (1981), pp. 590–91 and n. 429 (citing other sources).

13. Rabban (1983), p. 1290; Rabban (1981), p. 590. See also Levy (1985), especially p. 9 (arguing that Chafee "anticipated the present" when he claimed that the framers of the Constitution intended to abolish the crime of seditious libel).

14. Chafee (1941), p. 359.

15. See especially Rabban (1981), pp. 559–79; A. Anderson (1980).

16. Chafee (1941), p. 360.

17. See J. White (1984), p. 6.

18. See Skinner (1974), pp. 299–300; Gordon (1984), p. 101; R. Smith (1988), pp. 88, 98; Tulis (1987), p. 15.

19. 198 U.S. 45 (1905) (declaring constitutional laws limiting the hours that bakers could work).

20. The claims made in this paragraph and the following one are discussed at length in chapter 5.

21. Melville Nimmer is the only major contemporary civil libertarian who devotes some attention to these problems in a treatise devoted to the general theory of the First Amendment. See Nimmer (1984), pp. 1—15–16.

22. See Barron (1967); Fiss (1987); Powe (1983).

Chapter One

1. Burgess (1923), p. 26.

2. See Crick (1959), pp. 26–29.

3. E. L. Godkin (1831–1902) was founder and editor of the *Nation*, a leading intellectual weekly in the late nineteenth century. Under Godkin's direction, the *Nation* held an unswerving allegiance to the principles of laissez-faire, sound currency, free trade, civil service reform, and anti-imperialism. See Grimes (1953), especially pp. v–vi, 13–36 (quoting Godkin's editorials on these subjects). Godkin is sometimes thought of as an English liberal. However, as Spencer's career illustrates, the beliefs of late nineteenth-century American conservatives were nearly identical to those of middle nineteenth-century English liberals.

4. Henry Adams (1838–1918) was a prominent conservative historian and social critic. Although he was far less concerned with laissez-faire economics than were his counterparts, he actively supported civil service and tariff reform, two major concerns of conservative intellectuals, who tended to be political Mugwumps. Furthermore, Adams frequently argued that citizens should not rely on the government to do anything and, at least in the late nineteenth century, believed that the only economic reform the country needed was a return to honest government. H. Adams (1918), p. 500; H. Adams (1968), p. 185; H. Adams (1958), pp. 326–31; H. Adams (1930), p. 357.

5. Thomas Cooley (1824–1898) was a professor of law at the University of Michigan, a judge on the Michigan Supreme Court, and the first chairman of the Interstate Commerce Commission. Cooley is best known for his *Constitutional Limitations*, first published in 1871; that

work was considered the standard authority on constitutional law in the late nineteenth and early twentieth centuries. Although scholars have questioned the older view of Cooley as an apologist for the rights of business enterprises, his works were frequently cited as establishing that the due process clause of the Fourteenth Amendment protected economic freedoms.

6. Christopher Tiedeman (1857–1903) was the author of several prominent treatises and a professor of law at the University of Missouri, the University of the City of New York, and the University of Buffalo. Tiedeman's most influential work, *Limitations of Police Power*, first published in 1886, argued that the Constitution limited the powers of government to those consistent with the Latin maxim, *sic utere tuo, ut alienum non laedas* (so use your own as not to injure another). See Tiedeman (1886), p. 2.

7. John Randolph Tucker (1823–1899) was a professor of law at Washington and Lee University, a six-term congressman who chaired the House Judiciary Committee, a prominent lawyer who numbered Jefferson Davis as one of his clients, and the author of a well-known constitutional law treatise. In *The Constitution of the United States*, Tucker argued that legislative power was limited by Herbert Spencer's social Darwinist principles of political economy. See Tucker (1899a), pp. 24, 45.

8. David Brewer (1837–1910) was one of the first Supreme Court justices to claim that maximum-hours laws violated the Constitution. See *Holden v. Hardy*, 169 U.S. 366 (1898); *Adkin v. Kansas*, 191 U.S. 207 (1903). Brewer's attitude toward economic regulations was best expressed in *Budd v. New York*, 143 U.S. 517, 551 (1892) when he declared that "the paternal theory of government is to me odious." See generally Rossiter (1962), p. 149; Gamer (1965); Curtis (1986), p. 191.

9. John Marshall Harlan (1833–1911) is rarely included in discussions of late nineteenth-century conservatism because of the support he gave to black civil rights in the *Civil Rights Cases*, 109 U.S. 3 (1883), and *Plessy v. Ferguson*, 163 U.S. 537 (1896). However, Harlan's status as a defender of the constitutional status of private property is second to none. Harlan wrote several major court opinions that struck down governmental economic regulations as violations of due process. See *Coppage v. Kansas*, 236 U.S. 1 (1915); *Adair v. United States*, 208 U.S. 161 (1908); *Chicago, Burlington and Quincy Railroad Co. v. Chicago*, 166 U.S. 226 (1897). Although he dissented in *Lochner v. New York*, 198 U.S. 45 (1908), his opinions in *Powell v. Pennsylvania*, 127 U.S. 678, 684 (1888), and *Mugler v. Kansas*, 123 U.S. 623 (1887), provided the basis for the central claim of Justice Peckham's majority opinion: the Su-

preme Court would closely scrutinize legislative means to ensure that the legislature had intended a legitimate end.

This chapter contends that a distinct group of nineteenth-century conservative thinkers were committed to both the rights of business enterprises and the broader issues of civil liberties. Although my subject matter is free speech, I should also note that both Oswald Garrison Villard and Moorfield Storey, two founders of the NAACP, were conservatives on economic matters. See Wreszin (1965); M. A. Howe (1932). In a similar vein, Tiedeman was one of the first American jurists who argued that the Fourteenth Amendment barred states from restricting interracial marriages. Tiedeman (1886), pp. 536–37.

10. Summer (1982), p. 98.

11. See *Muller v. Oregon*, 208 U.S. 412, 421 (1908) (states could protect a "woman's physical structure" by limiting the number of hours that she could be employed); Cooley (1878), p. 527 (states should have the power to censor indecent literature).

12. Hofstadter (1955b), p. 8. See McCloskey (1951), p. vii; Eric Goldman (1952), p. 67; Rossiter (1962), p. 131; Fine (1956), p. 31; Roche (1963b), p. 135; Hurst (1956), pp. 9–10; Parrington (1930), pp. 18–19; Lustig (1982), p. 83.

13. See especially Burke (1973), pp. 119–20. For a study of American conservative thought before the Civil War, see Rossiter (1962), pp. 97–127.

14. Spencer (1896), pp. 357–58.

15. Burgess (1934), p. 392; Spencer (1972), p. 15; Carnegie (1908), p. 145; *Allgeyer v. Louisiana*, 165 U.S. 578, 589 (1897); *Grosjean v. American Press Co.*, 297 U.S. 233, 244 (1936); *Butcher's Union Co. v. Crescent City Co.*, 111 U.S. 746, 757 (1884) (Field, J., concurring). See Tucker (1899a), p. 12; Sutherland (1917), p. 203; Judson (1891), p. 873.

16. Sumner (1982), pp. 60, 24.

17. Spencer (1902), p. 83. See Burgess (1927), p. vi (noting that political science would "not advance far except under the methods of fullest toleration of investigation or discussion").

18. H. Adams (1886), pp. 446–47 (citing John Stuart Mill). See also Cooley (1873), pp. 668–69, n. 1 (deriving constitutional protection for free speech and private property from the principles stated in *On Liberty*).

19. Burgess (1890a), pp. 86–87; Sumner (1982), p. 100; Sutherland (1917), p. 201. See Tiedeman (1886), p. 189 (deriving the right of free speech from the right of the private individual to pursue happiness).

George Sutherland (1862–1942) is generally considered the intellectual advocate for those conservative justices who sought to declare much of the New Deal unconstitutional. Chronologically Sutherland should be considered an early twentieth-century conservative, but he never wavered from the principles of late nineteenth-century conservatism that he learned as a law student. In opinions like *Home Building & Loan Association v. Blaisdell*, 290 U.S. 398 (1934) (Sutherland, J., dissenting) (moratorium on mortgage foreclosure violates the contracts clause), *Adkins v. Children's Hospital*, 261 U.S. 525 (1923) (minimum-wage laws violate the due process clause), and *Carter v. Carter Coal Co.*, 298 U.S. 238 (1936) (federal regulations of wages and prices in the production of coal are beyond the scope of the commerce clause), Sutherland sought to limit the power of the state and federal governments to regulate the economy. Before serving on the Supreme Court, Sutherland was a Republican senator from Utah, a president of the American Bar Association, and a prominent adviser to President Harding.

20. Sumner (1963), p. 145. Burgess (1898), p. 211; Burgess (1927), pp. 333–34. See Burgess (1895), pp. 413–16; Burgess (1934), pp. 384–85; Burgess (1915), p. 382. See also Burgess (1927), pp. 29, 142, 152–53. For a discussion of this theme in Jeffersonian and Jacksonian writings, see Lustig (1982), pp. 46–52, 79–83.

21. *United States v. Cruikshank*, 92 U.S. 542, 552 (1875); Tiedeman (1886), p. 189; Brewer (1886), p. 364. See Cooley (1878), p. 518; Tucker (1899b), p. 670; H. Brown (1900), p. 330. Many conservatives were critical of the way in which the press performed that function. See Rosenberg (1986), pp. 190–93. Nevertheless, although they occasionally proposed procedural devices to make libel suits easier to bring, conservatives endorsed a libertarian interpretation of the substantive law of libel. See chapter 1, nn. 117–137 and accompanying text.

22. Sumner (1982), pp. 93–94; Cooley (1878), pp. 540–41.

23. *People v. Hurlbut*, 24 Mich. 44, 107 (1871) (opinion of Cooley, J.); Burgess (1934), p. 388. See Pomeroy (1870), p. 108; Tucker (1899a), p. 106; Henry Black (1895), p. 373.

24. See McClosky and Brill (1983), pp. 48–58; McClosky (1964), pp. 365–67; Huntington (1981), pp. 18, 266, nn. 8–9 (citing surveys).

25. H. Adams (1886), pp. 446–51; Justice Henry Brown, a member of the *Lochner* majority, also pointed to the probability that "the abuses would soon outnumber the advantages" if statutes prohibiting certain forms of dissent were enforced. H. Brown (1900), p. 337.

26. Burgess (1927), pp. 334–35.

27. Burgess (1923), pp. 37–38; Tucker (1899c), p. 84; Sumner (1934), p. 266. The Democratic party platform in 1900 stated that "imperialism abroad will lead quickly and inevitably to despotism at

home." Faulkner (1959), p. 274. See Godkin (1893), p. 173; Brewer (1899), p. 15; King (1967), p. 270 (quoting John Marshall Harlan); Cooley (1893), p. 394.

In general, the opposition to imperialism was led by older Mugwumps, who had advocated laissez-faire economics and honest government for more than thirty years. See Beisner (1985), pp. 9–11; Tompkins (1970), pp. 148–51.

28. Edward Atkinson (1827–1905) was a prominent conservative pamphleteer and anti-imperialist leader. The most concise statement of his political beliefs is found in an 1871 essay, "Inefficiency of Economic Legislation," which declared, "it does not appear that any laws of this so-called 'protective' character have ever proven efficient in causing a more equitable division of labor or of product than might otherwise have been had. In the category of protective legislation attempted in this country may be included usury laws, eight and ten-hour laws for adults, and protective tariffs." Atkinson (1871), p. 1. For a full exposition of Atkinson's life and ideas, see Williamson (1934).

29. Tompkins (1970), pp. 207–8.

30. For a fuller summary of Atkinson's efforts to secure "a limited residence in Fort Warren" prison and the McKinley administration's response, see Tompkins (1970), pp. 206–8; Beisner (1985), pp. 98–101; Williamson (1934), pp. 227–29.

31. Godkin (1899a), p. 346.

32. Godkin (1899b), p. 388. For other editorial criticisms of the McKinley administration's handling of the Atkinson affair, see Faulkner (1959), p. 256.

33. Sumner (1901), pp. 10–11. For other conservative and anti-imperialist attacks on McKinley's policy of censoring news dispatches and letters sent by soldiers stationed in the Philippines, see Parker (1904), pp. 13–14; Schurz (1913), pp. 87, 101–2; Tompkins (1970), pp. 201–2, 246 (citing articles and newspaper editorials).

34. Beisner (1985), pp. 9–10 (noting the ages of the anti-imperialists in 1898), 17; Fine (1956), pp. 373–78; Hofstadter (1955b), p. 203.

35. Burgess (1923), pp. 42–54 (arguing that the income tax was the greatest threat to individual liberty passed between 1898 and 1914), 64–85 (arguing that the Espionage Act was the greatest threat to individual liberty passed between 1914 and 1918).

36. Several weeks before the first *Nation* editorial appeared attacking censorship legislation that journal charged the *New Republic* with believing "that an ounce of fresh experiment is worth at least a pound of experience, and that the day after tomorrow is better than a thousand yesterdays." Villard (1917a), p. 410. During the Wilson adminis-

tration, the *Nation* opposed the Clayton Act, the Federal Trade Commission, federal child labor laws, and the nomination of Brandeis to the Supreme Court. For examples of the *Nation*'s prewar conservatism, see Villard (1912); Villard (1916). See generally Grimes (1953), pp. 66–70. The *Nation* did take a sharp turn to the political left after the war. See Grimes (1953), pp. 93–94 (claiming that 1919 was the crucial year in the transformation of the *Nation*'s editorial policy); Wreszin (1965), pp. 15, 26–27, 30; Radosh (1975), pp. 67–71.

37. See chapter 3.

38. Villard (1917b), p. 482. See Villard (1917c) (endorsing a directed verdict in a sedition case because the defendant did not advocate illegal conduct); Villard (1917d) (endorsing Judge Hand's opinion in *Masses Publishing Company v. Patten*, 244 F. 535 [S.D.N.Y. 1917]); Villard (1917e) (opposing the Espionage Act of 1917); Villard (1918a) (opposing the Sedition Act of 1918); Villard (1918b) (attacking the conduct and verdict of the *Abrams* trial).

39. See Burgess (1923), pp. x–xi, 23–26, 64–85; Cooley (1878), pp. 518–73. Scholars who have studied Cooley's career claim that he was more interested in the liberty of speech than the liberty of contract. Jones (1967), p. 765; Hyman and Wiecek (1982), pp. 354–56.

40. Murphy (1979), p. 50 (until World War I political controversy did not lead to "sufficient demands for public attention to civil liberties questions to involve any substantial number of people in a serious consideration of civil liberties issues"); Murphy (1972), pp. 13–14, 18; Chafee (1941), p. 507; Goldstein (1978), pp. 68–69; Dowell (1939), pp. 13–14, 21; Keller (1977), p. 519.

41. See Goldstein (1978), pp. 23–60, 68–69; Whipple (1927), pp. 210–20; Chafee (1941), p. 507; Murphy (1972), pp. 16–17.

42. 158 U.S. 564 (1895).

43. Darrow (1895), pp. 64, 94–95.

44. James Pickering's defense of the right to speak on public property in *Davis v. Massachusetts*, 167 U.S. 43 (1897) was devoted to these claims. Pickering (1897), pp. 30–43, 47–61. Those state courts that upheld a right of access to public property also relied on these claims. For example, the Illinois Supreme Court declared unconstitutional an Illinois statute that required street demonstrations be licensed because "it merely leaves it to the discretion or caprice of the superintendent of police to imperatively prescribe who shall be permitted to gather together in such processions, and who shall not." *City of Chicago v. Trotter*, 136 Ill. 430, 433 (1891). See *In re Gribben*, 47 P.2d 1074, 1077 (Okla. 1897) (ordinance violated traditional uses of public property); *In re Garrabad*, 54 N.W. 1104, 1107–8 (Wis. 1893) (ordinance was

arbitrary and violated traditional uses of public property); *Anderson v. City of Wellington*, 40 Kan. 173, 179 (1888) (ordinance violated traditional uses of public property); *Frazee's Case*, 42 N.W. 72, 76 (Mich. 1886) (same); *In re Flaherty*, 38 P. 981, 984–86 (Cal. 1895) (Harrison, J., dissenting) (ordinance was arbitrary); *Rich v. City of Naperville*, 42 Ill. App. 222, 223–224 (1891) (ordinance was arbitrary and violated traditional uses of public property). Municipal ordinances were sometimes attacked on the ground that the municipality had no authority under state law to so regulate public property. See *Anderson v. City of Wellington*, at 173; Pickering (1897), pp. 23–28. See chapter 1, nn. 52–58 (noting that similar arguments were used to limit state regulatory power).

At times, courts used language that seemed to indicate judicial awareness that free-speech issues were at stake. One court declared, "Ever since the landing of the Pilgrims from the Mayflower the right to assemble and worship according to the dictates of one's conscience, and the right to parade in a peaceful manner and for the lawful purpose, have been fostered and regarded as among the fundamental rights of a free people." *Rich v. City of Naperville*, at 222, 223–24. Nevertheless, while the Court may have thought that political speech was a particularly good use of the streets, the actual holding of the case was that municipalities could not forbid any traditional use of public property. Illinois courts also held that citizens had a right to picnic and dance on public land. *Village of Des Plaines v. Boyer*, 123 Ill. 348 (1888). Furthermore, in support of the right to speak in the street, several courts and the Pickering brief relied heavily on *City of Baltimore v. Radecke*, 49 Md. 217 (1878). See *Garrabad*, at 1107; *Flaherty*, at 985 (Harrison, J., dissenting); Pickering (1897), at 4, 6, 58. That case concerned the right of city officials to restrict the use of a steam engine in the center of town.

45. Tiedeman (1894), pp. 268-69. See Cooley (1878), p. 289, n. 4. See also Henry Black (1895), p. 324; Dillon (1881), p. 657, n. 4 ("making a speech in a public street is not a nuisance 'per se' ") (John F. Dillon's treatise *Commentaries on the Law of Municipal Corporations* was a leading authority for the proposition that state regulations could be made only for a limited number of purposes). See Jacobs (1954), p. 121.

The leading nineteenth-century opponent of the right to make speeches on public property was Judge Oliver Wendell Holmes, Jr. In *Commonwealth v. Davis*, 162 Mass. 510 (1895), Holmes declared that persons had no more right to speak on public property than they had to speak on another person's private property. The Supreme Court endorsed this analysis in *Davis v. Massachusetts*. Tiedeman cited the holding of *Davis* in his analysis of free speech in a later edition of his work; however, he never integrated that decision into his more general analysis of constitutional free-speech rights. See Tiedeman (1900), p. 231.

46. Sutherland (1917), p. 198; Spencer (1896), pp. 284–96. See Sumner (1982), p. 85.

47. Paul (1960), p. 65.

48. Burgess (1895), p. 422. See Guthrie (1898), p. 49 ("the perpetuity of our institutions . . . depend[s] . . . upon the power given the judiciary to declare null and void all legislation that is clearly repugnant to the supreme law of the land"); Judson (1913), pp. 47, 94; Paul (1960), p. 27 (quoting Tiedeman), pp. 229–30; Sumner (1982), p. 95; W. Taft (1920), pp. 19–20; Skowronek (1982), p. 152 (quoting Brewer); American Bar Association (1918), pp. 403–4; Parrington (1930), p. 166 (quoting E. L. Godkin, 119).

49. Tiedeman (1886), p. vii; Shumate (1887), p. 106; Sumner (1982), p. 28. For other expressions of conservative fears of popular democracy, see Tucker (1899a), p. 82 ("the democratic patriarcha must, in order to retain its power, band the multitude in its support by profuse and extravagant largess"); Spencer (1896), p. 298 ("the authority of a popularly-chosen body is no more to be regarded as an unlimited authority than the authority of a monarch"). For conservative discussions of the proper role of attorneys, see Guthrie (1898), p. 32; Burgess (1890b), p. 365.

50. Cooley (1878), p. iii; Tiedeman (1886), p. vii. For more general discussions of the rise and influence of these treatises after the Civil War, see Hyman and Wiecek (1982), pp. 341, 511; Keller (1977), pp. 344–45; Jacobs (1954); Twiss (1962); Paul (1960).

51. Cooley (1878), pp. 209–10. See Tiedeman (1886), p. 604; Tucker (1899a), pp. 353–54; Burgess (1890a), p. 215; Burgess (1923), p. 6.

52. *United States v. E. C. Knight Co.*, 156 U.S. 1 (1895). See McCurdy (1979). For other cases in which the Court held that federal regulations exceeded the scope of the interstate commerce clause, see *Carter v. Carter Coal Co.; United States v. Butler*, 297 U.S. 1 (1936); *Hammer v. Dagenhart*, 247 U.S. 251 (1918).

53. Jefferson (1975), p. 282. See Madison (1973), pp. 301–28. For a discussion of the eighteenth-century origins of this claim, see Levy (1985), p. 304–8.

54. *Ex Parte Jackson*, 96 U.S. 727, 735 (1877). See Cooley (1878), p. 535 (noting that federal courts had no common law jurisdiction over sedition or libel).

55. Burgess (1923), pp. 65–68.

56. Ibid.
57. Ibid., pp. 65, 70, 79–80.
58. See chapter 1, n. 41 and accompanying text.
59. Cooley (1878), p. 536.
60. Cooley (1880), p. 87; Tucker (1899b), pp. 595–97. See Tiedeman (1886), pp. 631–32; Henry Black (1895), pp. 197–202.
61. Cooley (1878), pp. 209–10. See sources cited in chapter 1, n. 52.
62. *Barron v. Baltimore,* 32 U.S. 243, 249 (1833).
63. See Pomeroy (1870), p. 151; Burgess (1915), pp. 293–302; Burgess (1886), pp. 18–23.
64. John Norton Pomeroy (1828–1885) was a professor of law at the University of New York and the University of California. He wrote a number of influential legal treatises and was generally considered the foremost authority of his day on equity.
65. Pomeroy (1870), p. 151; *Slaughter-House Cases,* 16 Wall 36, 96 (1873) (Field, J., dissenting); *Slaughter-House Cases,* at 117–18 (Bradley, J., dissenting).
66. Campbell (1873), p. 12.
67. Pomeroy (1870), pp. 145–51; Burgess (1890a), p. 224. See Burgess (1902), p. 70 ("real civil liberty is always national"); Burgess (1895), pp. 409–10; Burgess (1890a), pp. 184–85; Burgess (1915), pp. 293–302; Burgess (1934), pp. 294–311; Burgess (1886), pp. 18–23.
68. *Spies v. Illinois,* 123 U.S. 131, 150–52 (1887). Tucker's treatise on constitutional law, published ten years later, stated that the privileges and immunities clause did not incorporate the Bill of Rights. Tucker (1899b), p. 854. However, as his private conversations demonstrate, his argument in *Spies* better represented his interpretation of the Fourteenth Amendment. See Curtis (1986), p. 186.
69. William D. Guthrie (1859–1935) was one of the most successful conservative lawyers of his time, a member of the Columbia Law School faculty, and the author of *Lectures on the Fourteenth Article of Amendment to the Constitution of the United States,* an influential legal treatise. Guthrie was active in the fight against child labor laws and was counsel to business interests in such cases as *Champion v. Ames,* 188 U.S. 321 (1903) (power of Congress to regulate interstate lotteries), *Pollock v. Farmers' Loan and Trust Co.,* 157 U.S. 429 and 158 U.S. 601 (1895) (the constitutionality of the income tax), and *Northern Securities Co. v. United States,* 193 U.S. 197 (1904) (constitutionality and interpretation of antitrust laws).
70. Guthrie (1898), pp. 62–65; see also pp. 21–23. For other conservative authors who claimed that the privileges and immunities clause forbade state violations of the liberties guaranteed by the Bill of Rights,

see Judson (1891), p. 880; Watson (1910), p. 1612. See generally Connor (1920), p. 230 (citing various sources who endorsed John Campbell's interpretation of that clause). See generally Curtis (1986), chapter 7.

71. *Twining v. New Jersey*, 211 U.S. 78, 122 (1908) (Harlan, J., dissenting); *Maxwell v. Dow*, 176 U.S. 585, 606–8 (1900) (Harlan, J., dissenting); *O'Neil v. Vermont*, 144 U.S. 277, 370 (1888) (Harlan, J., dissenting).

72. *O'Neil v. Vermont*, at 323 (1892); *Patterson v. Colorado*, 205 U.S. 454, 465–66 (1907) (Brewer, J., dissenting).

73. Henry Black (1895), pp. 481, 464.

74. 92 U.S. 549, 551–52 (1875). Rabban has argued that in *Spies v. Illinois* the Supreme Court dismissed a free-speech claim because it believed that no federal question was presented. This interpretation, however, is erroneous. The *Spies* decision held that the factual basis of the free-speech claim either did not appear on the record of the case or was not properly presented to the state court. Thus, the Court noted, but did not adjudicate, any of petitioner's free-speech claims. *Spies*, at 166–82.

75. See *Munn v. Illinois*, 94 U.S. 113 (1877).

76. See Cooley (1873), pp. 658–59; Tiedeman (1886), p. 15; Henry Black (1895), p. 268; Brannon (1901), pp. 63–66.

77. Cooley (1878), p. 441. See Willoughby (1910), p. 868; Watson (1910), p. 1451; Henry Black (1895), p. 418 ("That which the provision is intended to perpetuate is not remedies or forms of procedure, but the established principles of private right and distributive justice"). See also Jacobs (1954), pp. 32, 39–58 (noting the influence of Cooley's interpretation of the due process clause).

78. Cooley (1873), p. 668.

79. *Patterson v. Colorado*, at 454, 465 (Harlan, J., dissenting).

80. Cooley (1873), pp. 668–69, and n. 1. To the best of my knowledge, this is the first time that a prominent American legal scholar endorsed John Stuart Mill's defense of free speech.

81. Tiedeman (1886), p. 189; Burgess (1890a), pp. 86–87; Minor (1882), p. 80; Brannon (1901), p. 114. John Minor (1813–1895) was a professor at the University of Virginia and is best known for his influence on Justice James McReynolds. Henry Brannon (1837–1914) was a justice on the Supreme Court of West Virginia, where he influenced the rise of substantive due process.

82. 165 U.S. 578 (1897).

83. *Lochner v. New York*, at 45, 53, 61.

84. *Downes v. Bidwell*, 182 U.S. 244, 296, 298 (1901) (White, J., concurring). The precise issue of free-speech rights in the territories was

never adjudicated because Congress had by statute granted that right to the inhabitants of the territories. See *Kepner v. United States,* 195 U.S. 100, 123–24 (1903).

85. *Downes,* at 282–83 (opinion of Brown, J.). See *Rassmussen v. United States,* 197 U.S. 516, 531 (1905); *Hawaii v. Mankichi,* 190 U.S. 197, 217–18 (1903).

86. *Downes,* at 359 (Fuller, C. J., dissenting).

87. *Davis v. Massachusetts,* at 43; *Patterson v. Colorado,* at 454; *Mutual Film Corp. v. Industrial Commission of Ohio,* 236 U.S. 230 (1915); *Fox v. Washington,* 236 U.S. 273 (1915); *Gilbert v. Minnesota,* 254 U.S. 325 (1920).

88. See *Twining v. New Jersey,* at 78 (the Fourteenth Amendment did not incorporate the Fifth Amendment right against self-incrimination); *Maxwell v. Dow,* 176 U.S. 581 (1900) (the Fourteenth Amendment did not incorporate the Sixth Amendment right to a twelve-person jury; *Maxwell* also affirmed earlier cases holding that the Fourteenth Amendment did not incorporate rights stated in the Second, Fifth, Seventh, and Eighth Amendments); *West v. Louisiana,* 194 U.S. 258 (1904) (the Fourteenth Amendment did not incorporate the Sixth Amendment right to confront witnesses). For a comprehensive citation to turn-of-the-century cases in which the Supreme Court failed to incorporate provisions of the Bill of Rights, see Frankfurter (1965).

89. *Chicago, Burlington and Quincy Railroad Co. v. Chicago,* at 226.

90. In *Patterson v. Colorado* the state did submit a lengthy argument against incorporation. Dickson (1907), pp. 59–64. Other states briefs either only discussed the merits of the free-speech argument (Knowlton and Travis [1897]; Tanner and Remann [1915]) or baldly cited a few cases without any argument as to their meaning. Sherman, Wetherbee, and Dawes (1925), p. 7; Hilton and Markham (1920), p. 25; Dawson (1915), p. 45. The main brief for the state of New York in *Gitlow v. New York,* 268 U.S. 652 (1925), virtually conceded the issue. Sherman and Benton (1925), p. 9.

91. *Gitlow,* at 666 and n. 9 (citing these earlier cases). There is dictum in *Prudential Ins. Co. v. Cheek,* 259 U.S. 530 (1922) stating that the liberties protected by the Fourteenth Amendment did not include expression rights. However, the Court rejected this "incidental statement" at the next opportunity. *Gitlow,* at 666. Furthermore, the *Prudential Ins. Co.* case dealt with commercial speech. The Court had earlier held that only speech associated with educational or political purposes (i.e., speech that would help persons develop their faculties) was within the ambit of constitutional protection. *Mutual Film Corp.,* at 230, 244–45.

92. 236 U.S. 1 (1915).

93. *Gitlow*, at 666, n. 9.

94. *Grosjean v. American Press Co.*, at 233, 244.

95. *Fox v. Washington*, 236 U.S. 273, 276–77 (1915).

96. Cooley (1878), pp. 527–28. See Watson (1910), pp. 1402–3. See also Murphy (1979), p. 195 (interpreting Cooley as advocating those standards that were accepted when the Constitution was passed).

97. Henry Black (1895), p. 65. See Willoughby (1910), pp. 28–35; Guthrie (1898), pp. 38–39; Tucker (1899a), p. 351; Pomeroy (1870), p. 94; Tiedeman (1886), pp. 12–13; Judson (1913), p. 60; Cooley (1878), p. 212.

98. Levy (1985); Blackstone (1773b), p. 151.

99. The other treatise writers discussed in the first part of this section did not discuss specific free-speech standards.

100. By comparison, the leading intellectual contemporaries of late nineteenth-century conservatives took positions that were either explicitly or implicitly hostile to broad constitutional protections for free speech. For example, the prewar opinions of Oliver Wendell Holmes, Jr., argued that the constitutional guarantee of free speech only limited prepublication sanctions and that plaintiffs in libel suits did not have to prove actual malice in addition to falsehood. See *Patterson v. Colorado*, at 454; *Burt v. Advertiser Newspaper Co.*, 154 Mass 238, 242 (1891) (Holmes, J.). Holmes acknowledged that at the time of *Patterson* he believed that no prior restraint was the rule of the First Amendment. See Bogen (1982), p. 100 (quoting Oliver Wendell Holmes, Jr., to Zechariah Chafee, Jr. [June 12, 1922]). For discussions of Holmes's early free-speech decisions, see Bogen (1982), pp. 122–31; Rogat and O'Fallon (1984), pp. 1352–60. Holmes was, of course, an early opponent of late nineteenth-century jurisprudence. See especially Holmes (1920), pp. 167–202; *Lochner v. New York*, at 45, 74–76 (Holmes, J., dissenting).

James Bradley Thayer, another leading opponent of substantive due process, did not discuss free speech in his writings. However, his claim that courts should only strike down statutes whose unconstitutionality was "not open to rational question" was inconsistent with significant judicial protection of free-speech rights. Thayer (1893), pp. 143–52, especially p. 144. See Shattuck (1891) (prominent article claiming that neither the right to labor nor the right to free speech was protected by the due process clause of the Fourteenth Amendment). See also chapter 3 (claiming that progressives were responsible for increased interest in governmental regulation of speech in the early twentieth century); Rabban (1983), pp. 1215–16 (claiming that postwar progressive civil libertarians had little interest in free speech before the war); D. Johnson (1963), pp. 194–98.

101. Rabban (1985); D. Anderson (1986); D. Anderson (1983).

102. Cooley (1878), p. 527.

103. Henry Black (1895), p. 473; Tiedeman (1886), pp. 191–92.

104. Tucker (1899b), p. 670 (discussing Hallam [1847], p. 164).

105. Henry Black (1895), pp. 474–75.

106. Cooley (1878), p. 537.

107. Ibid., p. 536. See Tiedeman (1886), p. 192 (endorsing Cooley). In *The Principles of Constitutional Law,* Cooley claimed that political dissenters had the right "to bring the people to the point of consenting to any change short of the abolition of republican institutions." Cooley (1880), pp. 277–78. Although this standard would later be used to limit the scope of legitimate political dissent, Cooley never discussed what such advocacy might mean and indicated that efforts to forbid "condemnation of the government or Constitution" were probably beyond the pale of legislative authority. Cooley (1880), p. 277. *Constitutional Limitations,* which is essentially the unabridged edition of *The Principles of Constitutional Law,* never discussed this exception and endorsed an English case that held criticisms of democracy were within the right of free speech when made by persons who believed them true. Cooley (1878), pp. 538–41, n. 1 (endorsing *Respublica v. Dennie,* 4 Yeates 267 [1805]).

108. Henry Black (1910), p. 652.

109. Ibid., pp. 657–58; Tiedeman (1886), pp. 192–93. See H. Adams (1886); H. Brown (1900), p. 335 (arguing that Communists had the right to speak as long as they "did not directly incite to criminal acts").

110. Salomon et al. (1887), p. 21. In *Turner v. Williams,* Justice Brewer suggested that the federal government had no constitutional power to deport alien anarchists who rejected violence as a means of achieving their political ends. *Turner v. Williams,* 194 U.S. 279, 296 (1904) (Brewer, J., concurring).

111. Curtis (1986), p. 186. Tucker was one of many prominent conservative jurists who presented free-speech claims to the Supreme Court. Tucker was brought into the *Spies* case by Roger A. Pryor, a Wall Street attorney who helped defend the sugar monopoly against prosecution under the Sherman Anti-Trust Act in *United States v. E. C. Knight Co.* See Avrich (1984), p. 334. The main attorney for the E. C. Knight Company was John O. Johnson, who later sought to persuade the Court in *Twining v. New Jersey* that the Fourteenth Amendment incorporated all the provisions of the Bill of Rights. Johnson et al. (1908), p. 51. For a fuller discussion of Johnson's legal activities, which included constitu-

tional attacks on virtually every piece of commercial regulation passed by the federal government at the turn of the century, see Winkelman (1942). Alton B. Parker, the Cleveland Democrat who ran for president in 1904, was the first attorney who asked the Supreme Court to hold that a labor injunction violated the constitutional right of free speech. See *Gompers v. Bucks Stove and Range Company,* 221 U.S. 418, 430 (1911) (argument of the petitioner). While a judge in New York, Parker voted to uphold the New York maximum-hour law later invalidated by the Supreme Court in *Lochner v. New York,* but he endorsed the principles of economic substantive due process in his scholarly writings. See Parker (1914), pp. 631–32, 635–40. Parker became involved in the *Gompers* litigation as a result of his work with the National Civic Federation, a group of leading conservative industrialists who were seeking to compromise with less radical labor unions like the American Federation of Labor. Weinstein (1968), p. 16. Guthrie successfully argued *Pierce v. Society of Sisters,* 268 U.S. 510 (1925), before the Supreme Court. Although his brief primarily asserted that an Oregon law closing private schools violated the freedoms of contract and religion, Guthrie also claimed that the statute violated free-speech rights and quoted Justice Holmes's statement that the "ultimate good desired is best reached by free trade in ideas" in support of that point. Guthrie and Hershkopf (1925), p. 82 (quoting *Abrams v. United States,* 250 U.S. 616, 630 [1919] [Holmes, J., dissenting]).

112. Burgess (1923), pp. 75–76. In 1890, Burgess claimed that statutes punishing criticisms of the government or comments about the public character of state officials were examples of an "unusual law of libel and slander." Burgess (1890a), p. 192.

113. Burgess (1923), pp. 80–83.

114. Gutfeld (1968), pp. 165–66. See *In re Conciliation Commissioner for Sanders County, Mont.,* 5 F. Supp. 131 (D. Mont. 1933) (describing the New Deal as "government in defiance of the Constitution").

115. *United States v. Hall,* 248 F. 150, 152–53 (D. Mont. 1918). Judge Bourquin also delivered an important opinion that restricted federal power to deport alien radicals during the red scare. In *Ex Parte Jackson,* Bourquin freed an alien dissident who was being deported on the basis of illegally seized evidence. Referring to the broader violations of constitutional rights that he saw taking place in American society, Bourquin stated, "the inalienable rights of personal security and safety . . . are limited to no man, race or nation, to no time, place, or occasion, but belong to man, always, everywhere, and in all circumstances." *Ex parte Jackson,* at 110, 113.

116. Most nineteenth-century state constitutions asserted that truth (for good motives and good ends) was a complete defense. See Cooley (1878), pp. 518–22, n. 1. Conservative treatises rarely paid any attention to the limitations that good motives and good ends might have placed on the scope of constitutional free-speech protection; similarly, there seems to be no case law on what constituted good motives and good ends. Cooley's writings suggest that the duty to speak on public affairs created an irrebuttable presumption that true political statements were published for good motives and good ends. This qualification on truthful statements may have concerned revelations about private affairs and conduct. See chapter 1, n. 128.

117. For a good summary of the cases, see the addendum to Haig (1891). See also Haig (1891), p. 565 (noting that the cases are "hopelessly irreconcilable"). I have not determined whether the more conservative state benches took the most protective speech positions.

118. 376 U.S. 254, 279–80 (1964).

119. Cooley (1878), p. 528. See *Atkinson v. Detroit Free Press*, 46 Mich. 341, 375–76 (1881) (Cooley, J., dissenting).

120. Cooley (1878), p. 533.

121. Ibid., pp. 540–41; *Atkinson*, at 341, 377 (Cooley, J., dissenting). See *Miner v. The Detroit Post and Tribune Company*, 49 Mich. 358 (1883).

122. Cooley (1878), pp. 540–41.

123. *Atkinson*, at 379 (Cooley, J., dissenting). See *Miner v. The Detroit Post and Tribune Company*, at 358.

124. *Atkinson*, at 384 (Cooley, J., dissenting).

125. *Wason v. Walter*, 4 L.R. 73, 93–94 (Q.B. 1868).

126. Blackstone (1773a), p. 125; Blackstone (1773b), pp. 150–52.

127. Cooley (1878), p. 549. But see Tiedeman (1886), p. 51 (claiming that there was no constitutional right to discuss the private lives of public officials). This question was more recently left open by the Supreme Court in *Cox Broadcasting Corp. v. Cohn*, 420 U.S. 469 (1975).

128. Henry Black (1895), pp. 478–79, 483; Tiedeman (1886), pp. 45, 50–51, 54; Brewer (1886), p. 364. See also H. Brown (1900), p. 330 (claiming that some false speech was protected by the Constitution).

129. Tucker (1899b), p. 670.

130. Godkin (1890), p. 63.

131. *New York Times Co. v. Sullivan*, 376 U.S. 254, 279–80 (1964).

132. *Sullivan*, at 270, 274–77.

133. *Sullivan*, at 280.

134. *Coleman v. MacLenan*, 78 Kan. 711, 718 (1908).

135. *Coleman*, at 720, 733–36.

136. *Sullivan*, at 280, n. 20.

137. See chapter 5.

138. Chafee (1941), pp. 357–60.

139. Ibid., p. 13.

140. *Associated Press v. National Labor Relations Board*, 301 U.S. 103 (1937); *DeJonge v. Oregon*, 299 U.S. 242 (1937); *Grosjean v. American Press Co.*, at 233; *Fiske v. Kansas*, 274 U.S. 380 (1927). Conservative justices also voted to strike down state laws that limited the subjects school children could be taught or the forums in which they could be taught. See *Farrington v. Tokushige*, 273 U.S. 284 (1927); *Pierce v. Society of Sisters*, at 510; *Meyer v. Nebraska*, 262 U.S. 390 (1923) (Sutherland, dissenting).

141. *Stromberg v. California*, 283 U.S. 359 (1931) (Justices Sutherland and Van Devanter supported the free-speech claim; Justices Butler and McReynolds did not).

142. *Herndon v. Lowry*, 301 U.S. 242 (1937); *Near v. Minnesota*, 283 U.S. 697 (1931); *Whitney v. California*, 274 U.S. 357 (1927); *Gitlow*, at 652.

143. See Jacobs (1954), p. 224; R. Brown (1927), p. 945, n. 11 (citing statistics).

144. *Associated Press*, at 135 (Sutherland, J., dissenting).

145. Sutherland (1919), pp. 20–21.

146. Ibid., pp. 96–98.

147. Ibid., pp. 70–72. See H. Taft (1921), pp. 719–20; Wallace (1920), pp. 394–95 (I was unable to ascertain M. G. Wallace's general political convictions).

148. Sutherland (1919), pp. 98–99, 101–4, 111–15. See *Block v. Hirsh*, 256 U.S. 135 (1921); *Wilson v. New*, 243 U.S. 332 (1917). See also Siegan (1980), p. 168; Murphy (1979), p. 183; Paul (1960), pp. 228–29. For a fuller discussion of Sutherland's attitude toward the role of the Supreme Court in foreign affairs, see Paschal (1951), pp. 221–29. See also *United States v. Curtiss-Wright Export Company*, 299 U.S. 304 (1936) (Congress could grant the executive more discretionary power over foreign affairs than over domestic matters).

149. *Gitlow*, at 668 (quoting *Toledo Newspaper Co. v. United States*, 247 U.S. 402 [1917]).

150. Garrett endorsed Tiedeman's claim that the fundamental rule of constitutional interpretation was *alterum non laedere*. Garrett (1919), pp. 73–74.

151. Ibid., pp. 71–72, 75.

152. Ibid., p. 71.

153. Ibid.

154. Page (1919), pp. 537–39. For a discussion of the general tone of bar association statements on free speech, see Lawrence (1974), p. 71. Progressives, as well as conservatives, tended to identify radicalism and aliens. See Wigmore (1920), p. 543. See also Preston (1963); Higham (1978), pp. 194–263. This matter is discussed in chapter 3.

For contemporary conservative claims that the First Amendment does not protect the advocacy of "anti-American" doctrines, see Emerson (1970), pp. 48–49, n. 4 (citing sources); Jaffa (1970), pp. 221–38.

155. *Stromberg v. California*, at 359, 376 (Butler, J., dissenting).

156. *Gilbert*, at 333. For similar remarks, see *Pierce*, at 251; *Schaefer v. United States*, 251 U.S. 466, 481 (1920).

157. The Court permitted prosecutors to place President Wilson's "war message" into evidence in sedition cases and allowed federal officials to testify about the laudable purposes behind the war policies of the United States. *Pierce*, at 251; Carroll (1918), p. 645. In *Pierce*, Justice Pitney declared a prediction that the draft would become mandatory to be false, even though the prediction had been verified by the time the case came to the Supreme Court. *Pierce*, at 264 (Brandeis, J., dissenting).

158. *Pierce*, at 245.

159. *Herndon*, at 276 (Van Devanter, J., dissenting) ("for all know that such measures could not be effected otherwise").

160. Tiedeman (1886), pp. 192–93.

161. *Herndon*, at 276 (Van Devanter, J., dissenting).

162. See *Fiske*, at 384–85; *DeJonge*, at 358–62; *Stromberg*, at 365–67.

163. Chafee's examples of conservative articles on free speech were written by Edward Corwin, Day Kimball, and J. P. Hall. Chafee (1941), pp. 508–9. Corwin was one of the most influential opponents of conservative jurisprudence. See chapter 3. Kimball was a Frankfurter protégé (he clerked for Holmes, and Frankfurter supplied all of Holmes's clerks) (Holmes and Laski [1963a], p. 226). Hall, the dean of the University of Chicago Law School during the first quarter of the twentieth century, expressed his hope that *Lochner* and other such cases "will be abandoned by the courts." Hall (1917), p. 146. The only other articles Chafee cited that defended the constitutionality of wartime restrictions on political dissent were written by Herbert Goodrich and John H. Wigmore. Chafee (1941), pp. 108–9, n. 3. Goodrich claimed that *Abrams* was right because *Lochner* was wrong. Goodrich (1921), p. 500. Wigmore was an admirer of Justice Holmes, and the *Abrams* decision was one of only two times that the two ever disagreed on the correct outcome in a case. See Roalfe (1977), especially pp.

148–49. The progressive origins of the bad tendency test are discussed at length in chapter 3.

The only Supreme Court opinion Chafee analyzed at length was Justice Clarke's majority opinion in *Abrams*. Chafee (1941), pp. 128–36. Not only did Clarke believe that statutes should be sustained whenever the legislation might appear to be constitutional to a rational person, but he was also prepared never "to hold a statute unconstitutional whenever several of the Justices conclude that it [was] valid—by conceding that two or more being of such an opinion in any case must necessarily raise a 'rational doubt.' " Clarke (1923), p. 692.

Chapter Two

1. See Preston (1963), pp. 43–55; Drinnon (1961), pp. 121–42.

2. For discussions of legislative activity during the progressive era, see Whipple (1927), p. 263; Goldstein (1978), pp. 68–69; Preston (1963), pp. 21–34; Chafee (1941), pp. 506–8; Murphy (1972), p. 18.

3. See Rabban (1981).

4. See *Gompers v. Bucks Stove & Range Co.*, 221 U.S. 418, 436–39 (1911) (discussing the free-speech issues raised by a labor injunction); Shepard (1915); Chamberlain (1915) (treating the right to speak on public property as raising First Amendment concerns); Woods (1915); Brooks (1915). Progressive thinkers also believed that free-speech issues were raised whenever private force was used to curtail political dissent. See Whipple (1927), pp. 326–27 (citing the 1915 report of the Federal Industrial Relations Commission).

5. See Rabban (1987); Whipple (1927), p. 328 ("the third sign of the times was the appearance of pure libertarians—men and women who defended the principles of liberty for use by all people, yet without any special axe to grind themselves").

6. Note (1916), p. 170. For citations to this prewar literature, see Rabban (1981), pp. 559–60 and n. 235.

7. *Patterson v. Colorado*, 205 U.S. 454 (1907).

8. For summaries of the political status of free speech from 1900 to 1915, see Preston (1963), pp. 11–87; Higham (1978), pp. 106–93.

9. Emma Goldman (1982), pp. 68, 50, 49.

10. Sumner (1982), p. 98.

11. Emma Goldman (1982), pp. 64, 68, 55, 58; see especially pp. 150–57 (noting the connections between the freedom of speech and the freedom of intimate relations). See also Solomon (1987), p. 46 ("Goldman's anarchism was essentially libertarianism"); Shulman (1982), p. 43.

12. Emma Goldman (1982), pp. 49–50, 68.

13. Ibid., p. 55. For an account of Goldman's travails on behalf of expression rights, see Drinnon (1961), pp. 121–42.

14. Compare Emma Goldman (1932), p. 348, with Rabban (1987), p. 5.

15. For a general history of the Free Speech League, see Rabban (1987).

16. For discussions of the activities of Weinberg and Roe on behalf of free speech, see Polenberg (1986), pp. 75–81; Rabban (1987), pp. 9–10, 13.

17. Drinnon (1961), p. 140 (quoting Baldwin); Baldwin (1961a), pp. 265, 138. See Lamson (1976), pp. 58–65.

18. See Schroeder (1916), p. 8 (describing himself as an anarchist, but in the sense that Ralph Waldo Emerson, Thomas Jefferson, Herbert Spencer, and John Stuart Mill might also be anarchists); Emma Goldman (1932), p. 335 (describing Schroeder as a friend).

19. Schroeder (1910), p. 22; Schroeder (1911), p. 8. For Schroeder's role in the Free Speech League, see Rabban (1987), pp. 5–9.

20. Schroeder (1942), p. 14; Murphy (1972), p. 31 (quoting Schroeder's letters to Roger Baldwin). See Schroeder (1942), p. 11 (claiming that both the liberals and the conservatives of his day suffered from "feudal mindedness"); Rabban (1987), pp. 13–14. See generally Murphy (1972), pp. 20, 31–32; Whipple (1927), p. 327.

21. Schroeder (1942), p. 9. See Schroeder (1916), pp. 194–95.

22. Schroeder (1942), p. 9. See Schroeder (1916), pp. 73–74.

23. Schroeder (1942), pp. 7, 16–18; Schroeder (1916), pp. 194–95. Although Goldman also believed that "broad and wide education" would help "bring about social reconstruction," she maintained that "the most powerful weapon" in that struggle was "the conscious, intelligent, organized, economic protest of the masses through direct action and the general strike." Emma Goldman (1982), p. 60.

24. Schroeder (1911), p. 151; see also p. 13; Schroeder (1910), p. 22; Schroeder (1916), pp. 33–34.

25. Schroeder (1916), pp. 100, 105, 107.

26. Ibid., p. 94.

27. Schroeder (1911), pp. 350–51. See Schroeder (1916), pp. 39–42, 113.

28. Schroeder (1911), p. 153.

29. Schroeder (1916), p. 43 (quoting Cooper, "A Treatise on the Law of Libel and the Liberty of the Press," p. xxi); see also p. 3. The Free Speech League republished and circulated James Mill's similar defense of free speech; see Mill (1913).

30. Schroeder (1911), p. 212.

31. Schroeder (1916), pp. 80-81, 2. See Schroeder (1911), pp. 25, 161, 204.

32. Schroeder (1916), pp. 44.

33. Schroeder (1908), pp. 373. See Schroeder (1911), p. 32.

34. Schroeder (1911), pp. 142, 212; see also pp. 33–41. Schroeder (116), pp. 82–115.

35. Schroeder (1916), p. 82.

36. Ibid., p. 83. See Schroeder (1911), p. 148 (only if the wording of the text is ambiguous does historical evidence of the framers' intentions become relevant).

37. Schroeder (1911), p. 210.

38. Schroeder (1916), p. 86; see Schroeder (1911), p. 212.

39. Schroeder (1911), pp. 222, 210–30.

40. Schroeder (1916), pp. 90–91, 87. Of course, one had to examine historical sources when determining what the Constitution as a whole meant; see also pp. 91–111.

41. Schroeder (1916), p. 105.

42. Schroeder (1911), pp. 236–37; see also p. 150; Schroeder (1916), pp. 2, 91–101.

43. Schroeder (1916), pp. 113, 94.

44. Ibid., p. 112.

45. Ibid., p. 114.

46. Schroeder (1911), p. 11.

47. Harry Weinberger did maintain, however, that the liberty not to be vaccinated against smallpox was another aspect of the individual's Fourteenth Amendment rights. See Polenberg (1987), p. 78.

48. Schroeder (1916), pp. 13, 94; see also p. 80.

49. Kraines (1974), pp. 10–11. In the years following the publication of *The Police Power* (1904), Freund became an active participant in the movement for a sociological jurisprudence. See Brandeis (1934), p. 316 (claiming that Pound and Freund were the founders of sociological jurisprudence).

50. E. Freund (1904), p. 539.

51. Ibid., pp. 475–77.

52. Ibid., pp. 484–85, 531, 719–20.

53. E. Freund (1921), p. 345. See E. Freund (1904), p. 510. In 1904, Freund endorsed the traditional claim that constitutional history was the primary source of legitimate constitutional standards. E. Freund (1904), p. 504. He added that practice over time could substitute as a source for constitutional interpretation when the intent of the framers was unclear. See E. Freund (1973), p. 240.

54. E. Freund (1904), pp. 509–10. See E. Freund (1973), p. 242 ("a country can ill spare the men who when waves of militant nationalism run high do not lose the courage of their convictions"); E. Freund (1921), p. 345.

55. E. Freund (1904), p. 511.

56. E. Freund (1973), p. 239.

57. For example, although Alexander Meiklejohn claimed that the First Amendment provides absolute protection for political speech, he did not believe that the Constitution protects any other category of speech. Meiklejohn (1960), pp. 79–80.

58. See Schofield (1921), p. 528, n. 28. Chafee noted the existence of Schroeder's works but never discussed their merits. Chafee (1920), p. 378.

59. See chapter 3.

60. Dewey (1927), pp. 202–3; Dewey (1950), p. 128. See Dewey (1927), p. 34; Dewey (1935), p. 20; Dewey (1934), pp. 38–39. For Dewey's discussion of the logical and epistemological consequences of pragmatism, see Dewey (1950), pp. 77–130.

61. Dewey (1950), p. 128. See Dewey (1929b), p. 546; Dewey (1934), p. 71; Dewey (1927), p. 45. See generally Quandt (1970), pp. 110–11; Damico (1978), p. 24.

62. For a good discussion of pragmatism in the late nineteenth century, see J. Smith (1963), pp. 3–79.

63. Dewey (1935), p. 17; Dewey (1939), p. 87.

64. Dewey (1927), p. 25; see pp. 160–61; Dewey (1939), p. 21. See also Dewey (1927), p. 11; Damico (1978), pp. 30, 75.

65. Dewey (1927), p. 158.

66. Dewey (1934), p. 86. See Damico (1978), pp. 10–11; Quandt (1970), p. 121.

67. Dewey (1935), p. 24.

68. Dewey and Tufts (1913), p. 441.

69. Dewey (1935), p. 66.

70. Dewey and Tufts (1913), p. 440.

71. Ibid., pp. 482–83, 474. See also Noble (1981), especially p. x ("On the surface progressivism was a rejection of nineteenth-century competitive individualism in favor of an ideal of community. But most American progressives defined that ideal community as so spontaneous and natural that the individual would not have to sacrifice any of his autonomy and independence through participation in group endeavor").

72. See M. White (1957), especially p. 6 ("Pragmatism, instrumentalism, institutionalism, economic determinism, and legal realism ex-

hibit striking philosophical kinships. They are all suspicious of approaches which are excessively formal; they all protest their anxiety to come to grips with reality, their attachment to the moving and the vital in social life"); Wigdor (1974), pp. 209–13; Purcell (1973), pp. 3–113; Lustig (1982), pp. 109–226.

73. See Quandt (1970), p. 215, n. 1 (citing sources). See generally R. Smith (1985), p. 79; Thomas (1981), pp. 653–54. For a fuller discussion of the differences between Dewey and Croly, see chapter 3.

74. Croly (1965), pp. 278, 263; see also pp. 282, 288.

75. Ibid., pp. 81, 178, 190.

76. Pound (1908a), p. 609–10. See Wigdor (1974), p. 185 (quoting Pound). See also Commager (1950), p. 380; R. Smith (1985), p. 78; M. White (1957), p. 19.

77. Pound (1909), p. 463. See Pound (1910–11), p. 596; Pound (1908a), pp. 606–7, 622.

78. Pound (1908a), p. 611; see also p. 605. See Pound (1910–11), pp. 598, 140–41; Pound (1909), p. 463; Wigdor (1974), p. 162 (quoting Pound).

79. Wigdor (1974), p. 276 (quoting Pound); Pound (1908c), p. 393; Pound (1909), p. 457.

80. Pound (1915), p. 344; Pound (1910–11), p. 146.

81. Pound (1915), pp. 344, 356. See Pound (1954), pp. 33–34.

82. Pound (1915), p. 349. See Pound (1910–11), p. 143; Pound (1954), p. 44 ("compromises of conflicting human desires"). See also Wigdor (1974), p. 192; Commager (1950), p. 380.

83. Pound (1915), p. 347 (quoting Dewey and Tufts [1913], pp. 482–83). See Pound (1915), p. 349; Pound (1954), p. 37.

84. See, e.g., Pound (1915), p. 454–55.

85. Dewey (1935), p. 74; Pound (1910–11), pp. 146–47. See also Dewey (1935), p. 49; Pound (1910–11), pp. 161–62; Pound (1908a), p. 622.

86. Pound (1908a), p. 623.

87. Cardozo (1921), p. 65.

88. Pound (1908c), p. 384.

89. Pound (1909), pp. 469–70. See Pound (1908a), pp. 621–22. See also Wigdor (1974), pp. 176–77.

90. Pound (1908c), p. 406.

91. Pound (1909), p. 470. See Wigdor (1974), pp. 179–80.

92. Pound (1909), p. 457–58.

93. Pound (1908c), p. 383.

94. Pound (1909), p. 462. See Pound (1908a), pp. 615–16.

95. Pound (1909), pp. 457, 470; Pound (1908c), pp. 388, 384; Pound (1908a), p. 616.

96. Pound (1909), pp. 467, 469.

97. Pound (1908c), pp. 403, 405.

98. Pound (1915), p. 453.

99. Ibid.

100. Ibid., pp. 454–56. The two articles Pound wrote on specific free-speech issues supported legislative and judicial restrictions on expression. See Pound (1916), pp. 650–55 (Blackstone's rule of no prior restraint was an insufficient constitutional objection to an equitable decree restraining defamatory statements before publications); Pound (1908b) (endorsing restrictions on press coverage of trials). See Rosenberg (1986), p. 215 (noting Pound's relatively illibertarian positions).

101. Pound (1915), p. 453. The social interest in peace was also advanced by protection for free speech because "the individual will fight for his beliefs."

102. Ibid., p. 454.

Chapter Three

1. See Murphy (1979), p. 30; Donohue (1985), p. 128; Rabban (1981), p. 519.

2. The Espionage Act of 1917 declared:

Whoever, when the United States is at war, shall willfully make or convey false reports or false statements with the intent to interfere with the operation or success of the military or naval forces of the United States or to promote the success of its enemies and whoever, when the United States is at war, shall willfully cause or attempt to cause insubordination, disloyalty, mutiny, or refusal of duty, in the military or naval forces of the United States or shall willfully obstruct the recruiting or enlistment service of the United States to the injury of that service or of the United States, shall be punished by a fine of not more than $10,000 or imprisonment for not more than twenty years, or both.

(40 Stat. 219 [1917])

The Sedition Act of 1918 declared:

Whoever, when the United States is at war, . . . shall willfully make or convey false reports or false statements, or say or do anything except by way of bona fide and not disloyal advice to an investor or investors, with intent to obstruct the sale by the United States of bonds or other securities of the United States or the making of loans by or to the United States, . . . and whoever, when the United States is at war, shall willfully utter, print, write, or publish any disloyal, profane, scurrilous, or abusive language about the form of government of the United States, or the Constitution of the United States, or the military or naval forces of the United States, or the flag of the United States, or the uniform of the Army or Navy of the United States, or any language intended to bring the form of government of the United States, or the Constitution of the United States, or the military or naval forces of the United States, or the flag of the United States, or the uniform of the Army or Navy of the United States into contempt, scorn, contumely, or disrepute, or shall willfully utter, print, write, or publish any language intending to incite, provoke, or encourage resistance to the United States; or to promote the cause of its enemies, or shall willfully display the flag of any foreign enemy, or shall willfully by utterance, writing, printing, publication, or language spoken, urge, incite, or advocate any curtailment of production in this country of any thing or things, product or products, necessary or essential to the prosecution of the war in which the United States may be engaged, with intent by such curtailment to cripple or hinder the United States in the prosecution of the war, and whoever shall willfully advocate, teach, defend, or suggest the doing of any of the acts or things in this section enumerated, and whoever shall by word or act support or favor the cause of any country with which the United States is at war or by word or act oppose the cause of the United States therein, shall be punished by a fine of not more than $10,000 or imprisonment for not more than twenty years, or both.

(40 Stat. 553–54 [1918]).

3. For the full text of all federal speech restrictions passed during World War I, see Scheiber (1960), pp. 13–17.

4. See Scheiber (1960), p. 19; Dowell (1939); Chafee (1941), pp. 578–97. Harold Hyman argues that more than six thousand Americans were punished in some way for violating wartime sedition statutes; Hyman (1960), p. 268. For general discussions of state and federal repression in the years immediately after World War I, see Murray (1955); Murphy (1972), pp. 38–76; Goldstein (1978), pp. 137–91; Hilton (1951); Roche (1963a), pp. 50–75. In addition to official activity, federal and state government officials encouraged private groups, such as the American Protective League, which harassed political dissenters. See Jensen (1968); Hyman (1960), pp. 272–97.

5. See *Whitney v. California*, 274 U.S. 357 (1927); *Gitlow v. New York*, 268 U.S. 652 (1925); *United States ex. rel Milwaukee Social Democratic Publishing Co. v. Burleson*, 255 U.S. 407 (1921); *Gilbert v. Minnesota*, 254 U.S. 325 (1920); *Schaefer v. United States*, 251 U.S. 466 (1920); *Pierce v. United States*, 252 U.S. 239 (1920); *Abrams v. United States*, 250 U.S. 616 (1919); *Debs v. United States*, 249 U.S. 211 (1919); *Schenck v. United States*, 249 U.S. 47 (1919).

6. Strictly speaking, progressivism was a prewar reform movement or collection of movements. At some point between 1920 and 1940, persons who believed that the government needed to continue building upon previous political and economic reforms began to call themselves and to be called liberals rather than progressives; this is not to say that all or even most progressives supported the New Deal. See Graham (1967). While the early civil libertarians discussed in chapter 3 supported these liberal reforms, I believe that persons such as John

Dewey, Louis Brandeis, and Jane Addams are best described as progressives because they rejected many new intellectual trends of the 1920s and 1930s. For example, while Dewey, Addams, and Brandeis were proponents of sociological jurisprudence, they never became legal realists. See generally Purcell (1973), pp. 74–94 (noting the evolution of legal thought in the first third of the twentieth century); and pp. 42–43 (noting that Dewey objected to the ethical relativist strand of New Deal thought).

7. Wiebe (1967), pp. 287–88; Thomas (1981), p. 738. See Rosenberg (1986), p. 209; Rabban (1983), pp. 1213–14; Preston (1963), pp. 56, 143; Hilton (1948), pp. 357–58. See also Higham (1978), pp. 206–7. James Weinstein claims that progressive reformers favored limiting expression rights, but he identifies the leaders of progressivism as those big businessmen that other scholars treat as conservatives. See Weinstein (1968), p. 116. Paul Murphy argues that progressive reformers were hostile to free speech in the prewar and wartime years but that postwar reformers supported expression rights because they were "repelled by wartime excesses and abuses." Murphy (1972), pp. 18–19, 31; Murphy (1979), pp. 25–26. Although R. Jeffrey Lustig recognizes that many progressives were active in the fight for free speech, he claims that the philosophical basis of progressivism was more conducive to the suppression of political dissent. Lustig (1982), pp. 171–72, 260. See also Kennedy (1980), pp. 46–47, 88.

8. Polenberg (1987), p. 32 (quoting Roosevelt); see p. 57. See also Preston (1963), p. 31; Murphy (1972), p. 194. Roosevelt did oppose speech restrictions that he feared might curtail his activities during World War I. Polenberg (1987), p. 32.

9. For a discussion of the Wilson administration and civil liberties, see Scheiber (1960). For a discussion of Palmer's career, see Coben (1963), especially p. vii ("how can we reconcile the progressive reformer of pre-World War One years . . . with the militant Attorney General who violated civil liberties to an extent unprecedented in American history"). Conservative Republicans led the floor fight against the Espionage Act of 1917, but they seemed more concerned that Wilson would censor their speech than with broader libertarian concerns. For general discussions of the legislative debate, see Kennedy (1980), pp. 24–26; Murphy (1979), pp. 76–85; Livermore (1966), pp. 32–37; Rabban (1983), pp. 1217–27; Polenberg (1987), p. 32.

10. For discussions highlighting the importance of communal themes in progressive thought, see Wiebe (1967); Hofstadter (1955a), pp. 174–78; Price (1974); Noble (1981); Higham (1978), pp. 158–263; Roche (1963a), p. 25; Thomas (1981).

11. See Hofstadter (1955a), pp. 180–82; Higham (1978), pp. 235–42.

12. Kellor (1918), pp. 8–9. See Kellor (1916), pp. 14–15. For a general analysis of Americanization, see Higham (1978), pp. 204–7, 234–54; Gleason (1982), pp. 84–89.

13. Wartime efforts to achieve national unity continued to emphasize educational programs. The Wilson administration created a special agency, the Committee on Public Information, which produced propaganda intended to convince Americans that federal war policies were just. See Kennedy (1980), pp. 53–75.

14. Scheiber (1960), pp. 8–9; Lawrence (1974), pp. 37–38 (quoting Wilson); Polenberg (1987), p. 101 (quoting Clayton). See Murphy (1979), pp. 53–56; Scheiber (1960), pp. 7–9, 56; Kennedy (1980), p. 281 (noting Wilson's racism).

15. Scheiber (1960), p. 27. Wilson allegedly told a reporter that once war began the American people would "forget there was ever such a thing as tolerance"; however, this expression of sympathy for free speech seems to have been apocryphal. Auerbach (1967), pp. 611–12, 616. As Harry Scheiber has argued, from 1915 to 1919, Wilson consistently sought to suppress speech in the name of cultural uniformity and national unity. Scheiber (1960), especially pp. 52–53.

16. Preston (1963), p. 4. See Lawrence (1974), p. 107; Murphy (1979), pp. 46, 52–55; Roche (1963), pp. 26–75; Higham (1978), pp. 194–234; Scheiber (1960), pp. 59–60; Hofstadter (1955), pp. 180–82; Murphy (1972), p. 8; A. Anderson (1980), p. 74, n. 89; Keller (1977), pp. 559–60.

17. See Polenberg (1987), especially pp. 121, 142; Chafee (1920b).

18. Wigmore (1920), p. 543. For evidence of Wigmore's progressivism, see chapter 1.

19. Murray (1955), p. 196.

20. For general discussions of deportation during the red scare, see Murray (1955), pp. 190–209; Preston (1963), pp. 200–207; Polenberg (1987), pp. 323–45; Chafee (1941), pp. 196–240.

21. See Kennedy (1980), p. 218; Pencak (1989), p. 18.

22. Pencak (1989), pp. 18, 256, 157, 257. For a discussion of the Legion's related attitudes toward speech and immigration, see Pencak (1989), pp. 3–23, 144–69, 256–60.

23. Croly (1965), p. 214; Croly retreated somewhat from the elitism of *The Promise of American Life* in his second book *Progressive Democracy*. For a discussion of this aspect of progressive thought, see Lustig (1982), especially pp. 201–8 (discussing Woodrow Wilson); Thomas (1981), pp. 909, 920; Eric Goldman (1952), p. 156; Weinstein (1968), pp. xiv, 155; Kolko (1963), p. 76. Roscoe Pound also

promoted rule by an enlightened bureaucracy. See Wigdor (1974), pp. 198–200 (quoting Pound) ("exaltation of incompetency and distrust of special competency . . . seems to be an unhappy by-product of democracy").

24. Croly briefly noted that expression should be permitted unless it "made the excuse for personal injustice or national disloyalty." Croly (1965), p. 286.

25. Lippmann (1922), p. 197. See generally Lustig (1982), pp. 238–39.

26. Croly et al. (1917a), p. 316; Steel (1980), p. 125. See Croly et al. (1917d), p. 250; Croly et al. (1917b), p. 228; Croly et al. (1918a), p. 240 (objecting to postal censorship because administrative procedures in the postmaster general's office were inferior to those of the Justice Department).

27. See Croly et al. (1918b), p. 340 ("what our critics really demand is, not that a discussion of policy shall cease, but that any liberal contribution to it shall"); Croly et al. (1917e), p. 206; Croly et al. (1917c), pp. 255–57.

28. Kimball (1920), p. 447; Warren (1917), p. 341.

29. Kimball (1920), p. 447; Wigmore (1920), pp. 556–57. See Hall (1921), pp. 535–37.

30. Corwin (1934), p. 184. See Corwin (1941), pp. 112–13 ("the laissez-faire non-interventionist conception of governmental function [does not offer] a feasible approach to the problem of adapting the Constitution to the needs of the Twentieth Century. . . . The National Government is entitled to employ any and all of its powers to forward any and all of the objectives of good government"). For a brief discussion of Corwin's leading stature as an opponent of broad constitutional free-speech rights, see Vaughn (1979), pp. 116–17. For a summary of Corwin's scholarship and activities, see Crews (1985).

31. Paxson, Corwin, and Harding (1918), p. 101. Although the entries in the *War Cyclopedia* were not signed, Corwin must have written the selections on free speech and legal theory. Corwin's postwar writings repeated the same defense of congressional limitations on free speech. Furthermore, no other contributor to the *War Cyclopedia* was a specialist in constitutional law. For more evidence that Corwin wrote the particular passages quoted in the text, see Vaughn (1979), p. 118, and n. 79 (citing Corwin's correspondence).

32. Corwin (1920a), p. 55. See Corwin (1920b), pp. 657–58; Kimball (1920), p. 447, n. 35; Wigmore (1920), pp. 556–57. For conservative arguments that the war power was the source of congressional power over political dissent, see chapter 1.

33. Corwin (1920a), p. 55. See Corwin (1920b), p. 658; Corwin (1952), pp. 338–39, 357 (endorsing the majority opinion in *Gitlow v. New York*); Kimball (1920), p. 443; Hall (1921), p. 537. But see Hall (1921), p. 535 (suggesting that the bad tendency test only governed wartime legislation).

34. Paxson, Corwin, and Harding (1918), p. 218; see also pp. 82–83 (relying on the same argument to debunk the liberty of contract).

35. Corwin (1920), p. 55.

36. Ibid. See Kimball (1920), p. 447, nn. 32 and 34 (citing both Pound and Thayer in support of his defense of the majority opinion in *Abrams v. United States*).

37. Hall (1921), p. 537; Warren (1926), p. 462; Kimball (1920), pp. 447–48. See Corwin (1920a), p. 55; Hall (1921) (noting that judicial decisions sustaining legislation restricting speech were consistent with judicial decisions permitting legislative majorities to govern other areas of public life).

38. See Quandt (1970); Lustig (1982), p. 171.

39. Addams (1930), p. 404; see p. 380. See also Addams (1961), p. 40.

40. Addams (1964), pp. 6–7; Addams (1930), p. 401. See Addams (1945), p. 141 ("all other forms of growth begin with variation from the mass"); Addams (1907), p. 112; Addams (1930), pp. 88–89.

41. Addams (1945), pp. 21, 65; see also p. 58.

42. Addams (1930), p. 383; Addams (1961), p. 236; Addams (1964), p. 270. See Addams (1930), p. 40 (free speech is necessary to keep the community "better informed" on the political issues of the day); Addams (1964), pp. 170–71.

43. Addams (1930), p. 407. See Addams (1961), pp. 239–56.

44. Addams (1965), pp. 32, 60–61; see p. 40; see also Addams (1907), pp. 16–17.

45. Dewey (1916), p. 115; Dewey (1929b), pp. 559–60; Dewey (1950), p. 162. Dewey (1927), pp. 146–48, 203–9 (attacking Lippmann's elitist conception of democracy). See generally Damico (1978), pp. 107–8.

46. Dewey (1916), p. 98; Dewey (1950), p. 158.

47. Dewey (1939), p. 102. See Dewey (1927), p. 167; Dewey and Tufts (1913), p. 485 (a just social order will promote both diversity and free speech).

48. Dewey (1939), p. 128; Dewey (1927), p. 208. See Dewey (1927), pp. 142, 152 (better means of communication were "a prerequisite" to effective participation). Dewey (1950), pp. 20–21, 160–61; Dewey (1939), p. 175 (centrality of "extending the application of democratic methods, methods of consultation, persuasion, negotiation, communi-

cation, co-operative intelligence"). See generally Damico (1978), pp. 55, 103, 124.

49. Dewey (1916), p. 97. See Dewey (1939), p. 12.

50. Dewey (1939), p. 116; Dewey (1935), pp. 79–85. See Dewey (1969), pp. 72–73. See generally Lustig (1982), pp. 124–25; Quandt (1970), pp. 128–29; Damico (1978), pp. 49–50.

51. Brandeis (1934), p. 270; Brandeis (1942), p. 10.

52. Brandeis (1934), pp. 270, 233. See also Urofsky (1971), p. 154.

53. Brandeis (1934), pp. 233–34; Brandeis and Frankfurter (1986), p. 323. Brandeis did assert that discussion should cease in times of action, but at no point did he assert that such a cessation be coerced. See Brandeis (1934), p. 233; see also pp. 35–36 (need for a broad public debate over Zionist issues).

54. E. Freund (1928), pp. 220–21; E. Freund (1916), p. 2. See Kraines (1974), pp. viii, 88–90.

55. Kallen (1924), p. 186, nn. 1, 65; Bourne (1964), p. 73; Bourne (1977), pp. 242, 267.

56. Sumner (1982), p. 143.

57. Bourne (1977), p. 246; Dewey (1950), p. 147. For other early civil libertarian expressions of the value of individual development, see Dewey (1916), p. 142; Dewey (1935), pp. 25, 32; Dewey (1939), p. 129; Brandeis (1942), p. 11 ("each individual has the right and duty to develop"); *Whitney*, at 375 (Brandeis, J., concurring); Addams (1964), p. 178; Addams (1930), p. 383; Kallen (1924), p. 123 ("there are human capacities which it is the function of the state to liberate and to protect in growth").

58. Spencer (1972), p. 262. The racial beliefs of many conservative libertarians, however, limited their conception of diversity to behavior exhibited by Aryan, Nordic, or Teutonic types. See Burgess (1890a), pp. 44–45.

59. Dewey (1939), p. 159; Dewey (1927), pp. 211–13; Kallen (1924), p. 183. See Addams (1907), pp. 121–22; Addams (1945), pp. 104–5; Bourne (1964), pp. 75–76. See also Quandt (1970), pp. 36–50.

60. See Brandeis (1933), p. 223 ("man's work often outruns the capacity of the individual man"), p. 276; Brandeis (1934), pp. 196–97; Brandeis (1932), p. 151 ("a huge organization is too clumsy to take up the development of an original idea"); Brandeis (1934), 127 (large organizations "narrow the field of human effort by confining leadership to a comparatively few individuals").

61. Paper (1983), p. 351. See Brandeis and Frankfurter (1986), pp. 325–26, 337. Compare *New State Ice v. Liebmann*, 285 U.S. 262, 311 (1932) (Brandeis, J., dissenting); Brandeis (1934), p. 65.

62. Dewey (1935), p. 66; Brandeis (1941), p. 36.

63. Addams (1907), p. 28; Addams (1964), p. 160.

64. Dewey (1935), p. 67. See Dewey (1929b), p. 569.

65. *Gilbert*, at 338 (Brandeis, J., dissenting). See *Whitney*, at 375 (Brandeis, J., concurring) ("public discussion is a political duty"). See generally Brandeis (1941), p. 36 ("duty must be accepted as the dominant conception in life").

66. I do not believe that late nineteenth-century intellectuals were opposed to the empirical methods of progressive science, although they may have disputed some of its epistemological underpinnings. Sumner, for example, always claimed that an examination of actual facts would support laissez-faire policies. See Sumner (1982), p. 135; Purcell (1973), p. 9. Similarly, Justice Brewer was quite willing to take judicial notice of a fact-laden "Brandeis brief." *Muller v. Oregon*, 208 U.S. 412, 419–20 and n. 1 (1908). Roscoe Pound may have also thought that progressive science would support laissez-faire policies with some modifications. Wigdor (1974), p. 208.

67. Kallen (1924), pp. 120–21; Dewey (1939), p. 162; Dewey (1935), p. 90. Dewey did not specifically argue for "socialized economy" until the 1930s, but his earlier writings asserted that wide-ranging governmental intervention in economic life was necessary to establish the prerequisites of a functional system of free speech.

68. Bourne (1964), p. 46; Dewey (1935), p. 27; Dewey and Tufts (1913), p. 438. See Dewey (1928), pp. 249–50; Dewey (1927), p. 168; Addams (1907), p. 42 ("the whole situation is more industrial than political"); Brandeis (1933), p. 59; Brandeis (1942), pp. 5–7; Kallen (1928), pp. 15–16; Bourne (1977), pp. 216–18, 239, 243. See generally Murphy (1972), pp. 246–47; Lustig (1982), p. 130; Damico (1978), p. 89.

69. Brandeis (1933), p. 59. See Brandeis (1942), p. 7; Paper (1983), p. 132 (a financially dependent person is not "free to speak his mind").

70. Addams (1961), p. 193; Dewey and Tufts (1913), p. 447. See Addams (1907), p. 127; Brandeis (1942), pp. 5–6; Dewey (1935), p. 89.

71. Brandeis (1933), p. 33.

72. Addams (1961), p. 310.

73. Dewey (1935), p. 53.

74. See Dewey (1939), p. 149; Dewey (1929b), p. 519.

75. See chapter 4, nn. 11–18 and accompanying text.

76. Addams (1965), p. 50; Dewey (1929b), p. 467. Addams (1907), pp. 47–48; see pp. 409–10. See also Addams (1930), p. 410 ("we may get, and should get, something of that revivifying and upspringing of our culture from our contact with the groups who come to us from foreign countries"); Dewey (1927), p. 115; Dewey (1950), p. 53.

77. Brandeis (1942), pp. 28, 54. For a general summary of the debate over Zionism among American Jews, see Urofsky (1975).

78. Brandeis (1942), p. 49.

79. Ibid., pp. 10–11.

80. Kallen (1924), p. 124; Bourne (1964), pp. 117, 129. Although Kallen's *Culture and Democracy in the United States* was published in 1924, many essays in that work appeared in various journals during the 1910s.

81. Kallen (1924), p. 124. Dewey argued for a slightly different form of national pluralism, a federation of different types of associations. In his view, "the state remains highly important—but its importance consists more and more in its power to foster and co-ordinate the activities of voluntary groupings." Dewey (1950), p. 158. See Dewey (1929b), p. 430. For general discussion of cultural pluralism, see Gleason (1982), pp. 96–105.

82. Bourne (1964), p. 118; see also p. 122; Kallen (1924), pp. 184, 231.

83. Bourne (1964), pp. 113–14; Brandeis (1934), p. 209; Addams (1965), pp. 95–104. Brandeis, Kallen, and Bourne either actively participated in or endorsed the goals of the Zionist movement, which they believed would provide a bulwark against the destructive effects of the assimilation threatened by the breakdown of the ghetto walls in modern life. See Bourne (1964), pp. 128–33 (Zionism as "the purest pattern and most inspiring . . . [conception] of trans-nationalism"); Brandeis (1942), p. 30; Kallen (1977), p. 529.

84. Dewey and Tufts (1913), pp. 446–47; Dewey (1916), p. 120; M. White (1957), p. 97 (quoting Dewey). See Dewey (1916), pp. 162, 416. See generally Damico (1978), p. 36.

85. Bourne (1977), pp. 210, 207. For similar opinions, see Brandeis (1942), pp. 64 ("In a government where everyone is part sovereign, everyone should be competent, if not to govern, at least to understand the problems of government; and to this end education is essential") and 22 (education is necessary to develop individuality); Brandeis (1933), p. 32; Addams (1965), pp. 50, 178; Addams (1907), pp. 47–48; Addams (1930), pp. 409–10.

86. Brandeis (1934), pp. 73, 270. See Brandeis (1932), p. 208.

87. Brandeis (1934), p. 83. See Brandeis (1933), p. 11. Although Brandeis was an enthusiastic proponent of scientific management, he insisted that workers had the right to approve industrial changes in advance: "in a democratic community men who are to be affected by a proposed change of conditions should be consulted." Brandeis (1933), p. 54.

88. Dewey (1929b), pp. 524–25; Addams (1964), p. 139. See Addams (1964), pp. 143–45, 179–80; Addams (1907), pp. 168–69; Bourne (1977), pp. 202–4, 331–35.

89. Dewey (1929b), pp. 573, 567.
90. Ibid., p. 569; see generally, pp. 566–75.
91. Ibid., p. 569.
92. Ibid., pp. 571, 575.
93. Kallen (1924), pp. 144, 136.
94. Bourne (1964), p. 41.
95. Ibid., pp. 71, 65–91.
96. Ibid., p. 54. Jane Addams's similar fear of political oppression was one reason she opposed declaring war in 1917. See Addams (1945), pp. 174–75; Addams (1907), p. 220. Although Addams elected not to speak out against wartime repression until after the war, when the government threatened to confiscate the literature of left-wing organizations, she offered those organizations the use of the Hull-House Library. Addams (1930), pp. 140–43.
97. Brandeis (1975), p. 441; Brandeis and Frankfurter (1986), pp. 323–24 ("I have never been quite happy about my concurrence in the *Debs* and *Schenck* cases. I had not then thought the issues of freedom of speech out. . . . Not until I came to write the *Pierce* (&) *Schaefer* cases did I understand it").
98. *Pierce*, at 273 (Brandeis, J., dissenting). See *Schaefer*, at 495 (Brandeis, J., dissenting).
99. *Whitney*, at 375 (Brandeis, J., concurring).
100. See Blasi (1988), p. 671 ("Brandeis begins by invoking the authority of 'those who won our independence' ").
101. *Whitney*, at 373 (Brandeis, J., dissenting); Brandeis and Frankfurter (1986), pp. 320, 325.
102. *Whitney*, at 373 (Brandeis, J., concurring).
103. *Jay Burns Baking Co. v. Bryan*, 264 U.S. 504, 534 (1924) (Brandeis, J., dissenting). See *Weaver v. Palmer Bros. Co.*, 270 U.S. 402, 416 (1926) (Holmes, J., dissenting); *Frost Trucking Co. v. Railroad Commission of California*, 271 U.S. 577, 600–601 (1926) (Holmes, J., dissenting); *Pennsylvania Coal Company v. Mahon*, 260 U.S. 393, 418–19 (1922) (Brandeis, J., dissenting); *Adams v. Tanner*, 244 U.S. 590, 599–600 (1917) (Brandeis, J., dissenting).
104. *Whitney*, at 373–74 (Brandeis, J., concurring).
105. Dewey (1929a), p. 102; see also pp. 100–106. See Dewey (1929b), p. 479; Dewey (1935), pp. 5–6; Bourne (1977), pp. 238–39; Addams (1930), pp. 340–41.
106. The famous Brandeis brief in *Muller v. Oregon* consisted of 2 pages of legal argument and 110 pages of actual data. Brandeis (1908). See Brandeis (1933), p. 251; Brandeis (1934), pp. 321–22 ("no law, written or unwritten, can be fully understood without a full knowledge of

the facts out of which it arises, and to which it is to be applied"), 325; *Burns Baking Co.*, at 504, 520 (Brandeis, J., dissenting) ("unless we know the facts on which the legislatures may have acted, we cannot properly decide whether they were [or their measures are] unreasonable, arbitrary or capricious"); *Adams*, at 590, 600 (Brandeis, J., dissenting).

107. *New State Ice v. Liebmann*, at 262, 311 (Brandeis, J., dissenting); also at 284–87, 300. See *Burns Baking Co.*, at 534 (Brandeis, J., dissenting); *Adams*, at 600 (Brandeis, J., dissenting); Brandeis (1934), p. 65 ("when we know that the evil exists which it is sought to remedy, the legislature must be given latitude in experimentation").

108. *Gitlow*, at 673 (Holmes, J., dissenting).

109. Edward A. Ross, a prominent progressive sociologist, chaired the conference. See Ross (1915) (advocating broad rights of free speech).

110. Schofield (1921), pp. 526–27.

111. Schofield (1921), pp. 43, 526. Of course, like many before and after him, he found that in the case of free speech "the common sense of the community and the law of the land [were] in harmony." Schofield (1921), p. 728.

112. Ibid., p. 540.

113. Ibid., p. 521.

114. Ibid., p. 567.

Schofield's interpretation of the due process right of free speech is difficult to determine. In his essay on free speech, he reserved judgment on whether expression was a due process right. In another essay, he asserted that the Fourteenth Amendment restricted the power of state judges to alter common law doctrines, but he did not think that similar limits had been placed on state legislation. Schofield (1921), p. 34. Unfortunately, Schofield died before finishing a constitutional law treatise that might have clearly established his views on the scope of the Fourteenth Amendment.

115. Chafee (1919a), pp. 232–33, n. 1. See E. Freund (1921) ("excellent treatment").

116. Schofield (1921), pp. 569–71; see also pp. 536, 550–51. For a general discussion of the weaknesses of Schofield's position when compared to that of late nineteenth-century conservative treatise writers, see Rosenberg (1986), pp. 203–4.

117. Schofield (1921), p. 515; see also pp. 521–22, 534–35.

118. Ibid., p. 523.

119. Ibid., p. 524.

120. Ibid., pp. 524, 532.

121. Ibid., p. 536. Schofield also suggested that states had the power to forbid all forms of political activity by public employees and to require that persons explicitly state all their reasons for recommending or objecting to candidates. See ibid., p. 514, n. 11 (questioning the holding of *Louthan v. State*, 79 Va. 196 [1884] and *Ex Parte Harrison*, 212 Mo. 88 [1908]).

122. Schofield (1921), p. 524.

123. The full text of the Espionage and Sedition Acts is quoted in chapter 3, nn. 2–3. Some clauses of the Sedition Act would probably be unconstitutional under Schofield's definitions.

124. *Schenck*, at 47, 52. The full text of the leaflet is reprinted in the record of that case. "Transcript of Record," *Schenck v. United States*, pp. 4a–b.

125. The Supreme Court also handed down *Frohwerk v. United States*, 249 U.S. 204 (1919), on March 10, 1919. Although that decision rejected a free-speech claim, the result might be explained by the defendant's failure to place the full factual record of the case before the Court. *Frohwerk*, at 206, 209. See Bogen (1982), pp. 164–65.

126. *Debs*, at 213, 216. The full text of Debs's speech is reprinted in the record of that case. "Transcript of Record," *Debs v. United States*, pp. 3–15.

127. Chafee (1941), p. 86.

128. See *Fox v. Washington*, 236 U.S. 273 (1915); *Burt v. Advertiser Newspaper Co.*, 154 Mass. 238, 242 (1891) (Holmes, J.); *Commonwealth v. Davis*, 162 Mass. 510 (1895); *Patterson v. Colorado*, 205 U.S. 454 (1907). See also *McAuliffe v. Mayor of New Bedford*, 155 Mass. 216 (1892) (states can fire policemen who participate in political campaigns). For general discussions of Holmes's prewar views, see chapter 1, nn. 46, 101.

129. *Lochner v. New York*, 198 U.S. 45, 76 (1905) (Holmes, J., dissenting). See R. Smith (1985), p. 85 ("one problem was that the dominant strain in the triumphant *Lochner* opposition was a relativistic pragmatism which lent itself most readily to support for majoritarian democracy").

130. See Rogat and O'Fallon (1984), p. 1383; Cover (1981), p. 373.

131. *Abrams*, at 628–29 (Holmes, J., dissenting).

132. While Holmes asserted that "the defendants had as much right to publish [their leaflets] as the Government has to publish the Constitution of the United States," *Abrams*, at 629 (Holmes, J., dissenting), his opinion clearly indicated that he thought Abrams could have been punished if the Sedition Act had outlawed verbal attempts to interfere with American intervention in the Russian Revolution. See *Abrams*, at

628 (noting that Abrams did intend to interfere with that facet of American foreign policy).

133. *Abrams*, at 630 (Holmes, J., dissenting).

134. Chafee (1920b), 771. See generally Polenberg (1987), p. 241 (citing other laudatory remarks).

135. Lerner (1943), p. 306. See Rogat and O'Fallon (1984), p. 1387; M. White (1957), p. 238; Bogen (1982), p. 187; Kalven (1988), p. 156; Rogat (1962–63), pp. 3–4, nn. 1 and 4 (citing sources).

136. As Yosal Rogat noted, it is difficult to find other areas of law in which Holmes defended civil liberties. Rogat (1962–63). For the standard view of Holmes as the liberal hero, see Chafee (1941), p. 509; Rogat (1962–1963), pp. 3–4 (citing sources).

137. Rabban (1983), pp. 1305–17; Gunther (1975), pp. 720, 741–43; Kalven (1973), pp. 238–39; Ginsburg (1973), pp. 243, 246–47; Kalven (1988), p. 146; D. Smith (1986), p. 31; Konefsky (1956), p. 193; Ragan (1971); G. White (1976), p. 170; Kelly, Harbison, and Belz (1983), pp. 528–29; Bollinger (1983), p. 461; Rogat and O'Fallon (1984), p. 1378; Corwin (1952), pp. 326, 331–34, 356–57.

138. Bogen (1982), p. 99, 173–87; Bowen (1944), p. 390; Murphy (1972), p. 250.

139. Rabban (1983), pp. 1305–6 and n. 634 (citing Holmes's correspondence).

140. *Abrams*, at 627 (Holmes, J., dissenting). See Holmes and Pollack (1941), p. 32.

141. Holmes never explicity stated why he concurred in *Gilbert*. On Brandeis's proposed dissent he merely scribbled, "I think you go too far." Rabban (1983), p. 1319. To Sir Frederick Pollak, Holmes wrote, Brandeis "had one ground worthy of serious consideration and others I thought all wrong." Holmes and Pollak (1941), p. 61. This ground may have been the claim that federal sedition laws preempted state sedition laws, a ground that Chafee urged Brandeis to emphasize. See D. Smith (1986), p. 288, n. 3. Holmes also dissented in *Meyer v. Nebraska*, 262 U.S. 390 (1923), a case that held states could not ban the teaching of the German language.

142. Holmes and Pollak (1941), pp. 32, 162.

143. Rabban (1983), p. 1319; Bogen (1982), p. 107, n. 515. If Holmes was unwilling to be the sole dissenter in *Pierce*, there is good reason to think that he would have been unwilling to be the sole dissenter in *Schaefer v. United States*, a case that raised similar constitutional issues.

The inspiring language of Holmes's free-speech dissents did not necessarily measure the depth of Holmes's convictions. As Yosal Rogat observed, Holmes was capable of writing stirring opinions on both sides of an issue. Rogat (1962–1963), p. 267.

144. Holmes and Laski (1963b), p. 320.

145. Holmes (1920), pp. 157–58; *Lochner*, at 76 (Holmes, J., dissenting); *Gitlow*, at 673 (Holmes, J., dissenting).

146. *McDonald v. Mabee*, 243 U.S. 90, 91 (1917); Holmes (1920), p. 310. See generally E. Wilson (1962), pp. 762–63; M. D. Howe (1963), pp. 174–75; Rogat (1964), p. 255; Ragan (1971), p. 26; Rogat and O'Fallon (1984), p. 1362.

147. Holmes (1963), p. 37; Holmes (1920), p. 314. See Holmes (1963), pp. 40–41; Gunther (1975), pp. 756–57. Holmes wrote to Harold Laski, "My thesis would be (1) if you are cocksure, and (2) if you want it very much, and (3) if you have no doubt of your power—you will do what you believe efficient to bring about what you want—by legislation or otherwise." Holmes and Laski (1963a), p. 116.

148. Holmes and Laski (1963a), p. 85. See Holmes and Laski (1963b), p. 220; Holmes and Pollak (1941), p. 36; Rogat (1964), p. 252, n. 194 ("Dewey's main objective was to keep us talking in order to find a way of avoiding fighting. But no one . . . stresses more than Holmes that soon it will be necessary to stop talking and start fighting").

149. *Northern Securities Co. v. United States*, 193 U.S. 197, 409 (1904) (Holmes, J., dissenting); Holmes (1963), p. 54. See *Swift v. United States*, 196 U.S. 375, 396, 402 (1905); *Commonwealth v. Peaslee*, 177 Mass. 267, 272 (1901). Holmes thought courts could use evidence of intent when determining the probability that an act would be "followed by harmful consequences." Holmes (1963), p. 56.

150. Bogen (1982), pp. 100 (quoting Holmes's letter to Chafee), 154–63; Rogat (1964), pp. 215–17; Chafee (1941), pp. 81–82; Rabban (1983), pp. 1265–75; Rogat and O'Fallon (1984), pp. 1361–66.

151. *Abrams*, at 629 (Holmes, J., dissenting); *Gitlow*, at 673 (Holmes, J., dissenting). See Holmes and Laski (1963b), p. 37 (the *Gitlow* dissent defended "the right of an ass to drool"); Corwin (1952), pp. 340–41 ("de minimis . . . was the root-stem of [the *Gitlow* dissent]") Konefsky (1956), p. 206; Kalven (1988), p. 143; Lustig (1982), p. 119; G. White (1971), p. 75; Rabban (1983), pp. 1312–13; Bogen (1982), pp. 172–74, 182–84.

152. *Gitlow*, p. 673 (Holmes, J., dissenting).

153. Compare *Gitlow*, at 658–59, n. 2 with *Gilbert*, at 327.

154. Holmes and Laski (1963b), p. 37; Morlan (1955).

155. Holmes and Laski (1963a), pp. 55, 67, 105; Holmes (1934), p. 59. See also M. D. Howe (1963), pp. 100–101 ("I think small beer of any man who does not commit himself to his crowd").

156. Holmes (1936), p. 137.

157. Goodrich (1921), p. 500.

158. Ibid., pp. 496, 493. Goodrich (p. 495) also declared that the punishment meted out in *Pierce v. United States* "was very harsh."

159. Ibid., p. 500.

160. Holmes (1920), p. 173; E. Freund (1921), p. 344.

161. E. Freund (1921), pp. 344, 345. In 1921, Freund still hoped that courts might declare unconstitutional laws punishing advocacy of peaceful anarchy, a matter not yet considered by the Supreme Court.

Freund's earlier Fourteenth Amendment defense of free speech may have stemmed from the Supreme Court's willingness to use the due process clause to protect substantive freedoms, rather than from Freund's personal belief that free speech was a due process right. See chapter 3, nn. 100–104 (noting that Brandeis made similar arguments).

162. See chapter 1.

163. E. Freund (1921), p. 344; E. Freund (1973), pp. 239–40.

164. E. Freund (1973), pp. 239–40; E. Freund (1921), p. 345.

165. *Masses Publishing Co. v. Patten*, 244 F. 535, 540 (S.D.N.Y. 1917). See Kalven (1988), pp. 125–28.

166. *Masses Pub. Co.*, at 538.

167. *Gilbert v. Minnesota*, at 325, 338–42 (Brandeis, J., dissenting).

168. *Schaeffer*, at 483 (Brandeis, J., dissenting).

169. *Pierce*, at 269–70 (Brandeis, J., dissenting).

170. *Masses Pub. Co.*, at 540. See E. Freund (1973), p. 239.

171. Pound (1954), p. 66.

172. *Gitlow*, at 654–55.

173. Hand (1953), p. 278; Hand (1963), p. 56.

174. *Dennis v. United States*, 341 U.S. 394, 539–40 (1951).

175. Brandeis and Frankfurter (1986), p. 320.

176. *Whitney*, at 373–74 (Brandeis, J., concurring).

177. Ibid., 376 (Brandeis, J., concurring).

178. Ibid., 373 (Brandeis, J., concurring). Thus, though he never suggested that Anita Whitney had advocated criminal conduct, Brandeis (at 379) claimed that she might have been constitutionally convicted because there was evidence "which tended to establish the existence of a conspiracy . . . to commit serious crimes" and "that such conspiracy would be furthered by the activity of the society of which Miss Whitney was a member."

179. Ibid., 377–78 (Brandeis, J., concurring).

180. Brandeis (1934), p. 51. See Brandeis (1942), pp. 5–6.

181. Brandeis and Frankfurter (1986).

182. See *Whitney,* at 373 (Brandeis, J., concurring) citing *Meyer v. Nebraska,* at 390 (states could not ban the teaching of German); *Pierce v. Society of Sisters,* 268 U.S. 510 (1925) (state could not require all children to attend public schools); and *Farrington v. Tokushige,* 273 U.S. 284 (1927) (the Constitution limits state regulation of private schools).

183. Lusky (1982), p. 1095.

184. *Near v. Minnesota,* 283 U.S. 691, 707 (1931). See *Herndon v. Lowry,* 301 U.S. 242, 255 (1937); *DeJonge v. Oregon,* 299 U.S. 353, 364 (1937); *Stromberg v. California,* 283 U.S. 353, 368 (1931).

Chapter Four

1. See D. Smith (1986), p. 1; Auerbach (1969), p. 531; Prude (1973), pp. 638–39, 655; Rabban (1981), p. 516; Meiklejohn (1960), p. 54; Kalven (1964), p. 206; Wright (1982), p. 634; Re (1981), pp. xxii–xxix.

2. Frankfurter (1961), p. 440; Auerbach (1969), p. 531 (quoting Arthur Garfield Hays, a prominent member of the ACLU in the 1920s); Frankfurter (1961), p. 443; M. D. Howe (1957), p. 183; Prude (1973), pp. 638–39, 653; D. Smith (1986), pp. 276–77.

3. Chafee (1919), p. 967 (quoting *Schenck v. U.S.,* 249 U.S. 47 [1919]).

4. Chafee (1919a), p. 967; Chafee (1941), pp. 81–82. There may have been another circumstance where Chafee protected less speech than a conservative treatise writer. Chafee believed that the Haymarket anarchists were constitutionally convicted; John Randolph Tucker argued that their free-speech rights had been violated. Chafee (1941), p. 145. Unlike Tucker, Chafee may have believed that the defendants in that case had actually advocated lawless conduct.

5. See Dewey (1927), p. 51.

6. Chafee (1949a), p. 895; Prude (1973), p. 652 (quoting Chafee). See Chafee (1949a), p. 901; Chafee (1956), p. 70; Gunther (1975), p. 773 (quoting Chafee).

7. Chafee (1956), p. 70; Chafee (1928b), p. 99. See Chafee (1928a), p. 132; Gunther (1975), p. 773 (quoting Chafee). See generally Gunther (1975), p. 746; Prude (1973), p. 641; Rabban (1983), p. 1299; D. Smith (1986), pp. 272–73.

8. Chafee (1919a), pp. 960–64; Chafee (1919b), pp. 380–81.

9. Chafee (1920a), p. 156; Chafee (1920b), p. 771.

10. Chafee (1919a), p. 967.

11. Rabban (1981), p. 594. See sources cited in chapter 3, n. 126.

12. Chafee (1919a), p. 944; Rabban (1981), especially pp. 589–90.

13. Chafee (1919a), p. 947. The accuracy of Chafee's claim that the framers intended to abolish seditious libel is the subject of an ongoing scholarly dispute. See Levy (1985); Rabban (1985); D. Anderson (1986).

14. Chafee (1941), pp. 506–7; Chafee (1919a), pp. 944–45.

15. Chafee (1941), p. 360.

16. Ibid., p. 294. See Chafee (1965), p. 33. For a discussion of conservative thought and state practice, see chapter 1.

17. For *Meyer v. Nebraska,* see 262 U.S. 390 (1923). For *Pierce v. Society of Sisters,* see 268 U.S. 510 (1925).

18. Chafee (1941), pp. 321–22.

19. The defense could not have cited *Pierce,* which was decided the week before *Gitlow v. New York* (268 U.S. 652 [1925]) was handed down.

20. Pollak and Nelles (1925), pp. 11–13, 76, 98–103.

21. For a discussion of these cases, see chapter 1.

22. Chafee (1941), pp. 295, 296 ("Justice Brandeis also suggests the possibility that liberty of speech is one type of 'liberty' of which under another clause of the Fourteenth Amendment no person can be deprived without due process of law").

23. Ibid., pp. 295–98. Similarly, Chafee's discussion of *Gitlow v. New York* did not defend Fourteenth Amendment protection for free speech. Chafee (1941), pp. 321–25; see also pp. 387–88 (failing to explain why the Fourteenth Amendment protected certain educational rights).

24. D. Smith (1986), p. 90 (Alexander Meiklejohn was the particular target of that criticism).

25. Chafee (1941), p. 322, n. 9.

26. Warren (1926), pp. 462–64.

27. Chafee (1949a), p. 900.

28. Chafee (1941), p. 360 (quoted below).

29. D. Smith (1986), p. 5. See Polenberg (1987), pp. 283–84; Prude (1973), p. 656; Auerbach (1969), pp. 518–22; Kammen (1986), p. 6.

30. Auerbach (1969), p. 519. See, e.g., Chafee (1941), p. 4.

31. Chafee (1941), p. 4; Chafee (1928b), p. 97. See Chafee (1941), pp. 497–509; Chafee (1965), p. 6.

32. Chafee (1941), p. 325; see also p. 136 (the *Abrams* dissent was a "magnificent exposition of the philosophical basis of" the First Amendment). Although Holmes frequently rejected free-speech claims, Chafee gave little or no explanation of those votes. He either implied that Holmes had since changed his mind or, as in the case of the first three Espionage Act cases, claimed that Holmes's vote was

part of a libertarian strategy designed to promote the clear and present danger test. Chafee (1941), pp. 86 (explaining *Schenck, Frohwerk v. United States*, 249 U.S. 204 [1919], and *Debs v. United States*, 249 U.S. 211 [1919]), 164 (no effort to explain Holmes's vote in *Fox v. Washington*, 236 U.S. 273 [1915]), 290 (explaining Holmes's vote in *Gilbert v. Minnesota*, 254 U.S. 325 [1920], in terms of state's rights, an explanation that is obviously wrong—see chapter 3), p. 321 n. 7 (no effort to explain Holmes's vote in *Meyer v. Nebraska*), p. 544 (implying that Holmes would no longer have voted to affirm *Mutual Film Corp. v. Ohio Industrial Commission*, 236 U.S. 230 [1915]).

33. Chafee (1941), p. 360.

34. Chafee (1956), p. 77. When Chafee listed modern heroes of free speech, he paired Hughes with Holmes more frequently than any other civil libertarian. Chafee (1941), pp. 4, 361–62, 437–38; Chafee (1956), pp. 81, 129. Chafee also included Justice Stone in this category. Chafee (1941), p. 360.

35. Chafee (1941), p. 360.

36. Ibid., pp. 348–49; Chafee (1956), pp. 65–77. See Chafee (1941), pp. 437–38 (not noting Brandeis in a shorter compilation of those who had influenced the development of the constitutional defense of free speech). Chafee did once credit Brandeis, along with Holmes, with developing "a group of arguments for toleration that may fitly stand beside the *Areopagitica* and Mill's *Liberty*." Chafee (1941), p. 325.

37. Chafee (1920a), p. 161. See D. Smith (1986), pp. 88, 301, n. 37.

38. Chafee (1941), p. 4; Chafee (1920a), p. 2.

39. D. Smith (1986), p. 264.

40. Chafee (1932), p. 44; Chafee (1928a), pp. 165, 185; Chafee (1949b), p. 270; Chafee (1941), p. 312; Chafee (1928a), p. 229.

41. Chafee (1928a), pp. ix–x; Prude (1973), p. 636, n. 14. Chafee did write extensively on other legal subjects and was particularly interested in the problems of equity. For a complete bibliography of Chafee's work, see Chafee (1981).

42. Chafee (1920b).

43. Auerbach (1969), p. 525 (quoting Chafee), pp. 518–19, 521–22 (citing other instances of similar statements); Chafee (1920a), p. 2; Chafee (1941), p. 4.

44. Richard Hofstadter emphasized the centrality of this theme in progressive thought. See Hofstadter (1955a), especially p. 328; Hofstadter (1973), pp. 266–367.

45. Chafee (1928a), p. 233; Chafee (1919b), p. 384; Chafee (1932), p. 44; Chafee (1949b), p. 278; Chafee (1956), pp. 295–96; Chafee (1965), p. 27.

46. Chafee (1949b), p. 270.

47. Chafee (1941), pp. 514–16; Chafee (1919b), p. 384; Chafee (1956), p. 76.

48. Chafee (1929), p. 84.

49. Ibid., pp. 84–85. See Chafee (1928a), p. 230 (unemployment).

50. Chafee (1956), pp. 60, 63 (quoting George Marshall); Chafee (1928a), pp. 224–25. See Chafee (1928a), pp. 8, 226.

51. Chafee (1956), pp. 264–66.

52. Chafee (1941), p. 195; Chafee (1965), pp. 24, 474–75; Chafee (1941), pp. 234–35 (endorsing cultural diversity); Chafee (1956), pp. 41, 266.

53. Chafee (1956), p. 45; Chafee (1965), p. 565.

54. Chafee (1928a), pp. 87, 15, 181 (asserting that the "general welfare of citizens is in charge of the state governments"), 200, 223 (state, church, and trade unions should not "become unduly centralized"); Chafee (1956), p. 52.

55. See D. Smith (1986), pp. 316–17, n. 39.

56. Chafee (1928a), pp. 27–28.

57. Chafee (1965), pp. 21–22.

58. Chafee (1941), p. 559.

59. Chafee (1965), pp. 27, 471, 474–75; Chafee (1928a), p. 167.

60. Chafee (1956), p. 61; Chafee (1928b), p. 113. See Chafee (1956), pp. 97–98.

61. Chafee (1928b), p. 113.

62. Chafee (1965), p. 545; Chafee (1956), p. 108.

63. See Chafee (1965), especially pp. 680–719.

64. Chafee (1941), pp.551–52, 559; Chafee (1965), pp. 472, 479, 706.

65. D. Smith (1986), p. 86. See Wigdor (1974), p. 201 (Pound's course "entirely changed my views of law").

66. D. Smith (1986), pp. 119–20.

67. See D. Smith (1986), p. 154.

68. Chafee (1932), pp. 39, 44; Chafee (1928a), p. 254, n. 1 (endorsing Cardozo's view of the judicial process); Chafee (1947), p. 419.

69. D. Smith (1986), p. 103 (quoting Chafee). See Prude (1973), pp. 651–52 (quoting Chafee).

70. Chafee (1947), p. 419. See Chafee (1932), pp. 38-39; Chafee (1928a), p. 261.

71. Chafee (1928a), pp. 36, 263. See Chafee (1936), p. 516; Chafee (1947), p. 420; Chafee (1932), p. 39 ("no single human being is wise enough to dispense with the wisdom of his predecessors").

72. Chafee (1936), p. 508.

73. Chafee (1949b), p. 278. See Chafee (1932), p. 44. See generally Chafee (1949a), p. 896.

74. Chafee (1941), p. 138.

75. See ibid., pp. 360–61; Chafee (1956), pp. 50–51, 167; Chafee (1928a), p. 69.

76. Chafee (1920b), p. 753.

77. Chafee (1919b), p. 382.

78. See chapter 3.

79. Chafee (1941), pp. 18–23, 499–506.

80. Ibid., pp. 29, 14. See Chafee (1928b), pp. 88, 94–95.

81. See chapter 2. Chafee also believed that the rule against prior restraints needed to be modified. Chafee (1919a), p. 939.

82. Chafee (1941), pp. 29–30.

83. Ibid., p. 509.

84. Ibid., p. 16.

85. Ibid., p. 32.

86. See chapter 4, nn. 68–71 and accompanying text.

87. Chafee (1941), p. 41.

88. Chafee (1919a), p. 959; Chafee (1941), pp. 33–34.

89. Chafee (1928a), pp. 67–68.

90. Chafee (1941), p. 149; Chafee (1965), p. 795. See Chafee (1919a), p. 939. See generally D. Smith (1986), p. 276.

91. Chafee (1941), pp. 34, 510.

92. Chafee (1919a), p. 932, n. 1. See Chafee (1941), p. 34 (quoting Holmes on the obligation of judges to consider social interests).

93. See Chafee (1941), pp. 31–32; Chafee (1949a), p. 900.

94. Chafee (1941), pp. 234, 312–13; Chafee (1920a), p. 283.

95. Chafee (1941), p. 137.

96. Ibid., pp. 33, 360–61.

97. Chafee (1956), pp. 106–7, 78–79, 266; Chafee (1949a), p. 900; Chafee (1941), p. 138.

98. Chafee (1949a), p. 900. See Chafee (1956), pp. 78–79. Chafee occasionally stated that the First Amendment covered subjects that "had no relation to self-government." See Chafee (1949b), p. 273; Chafee (1941), p. 138; Chafee (1956), pp. 106–7. However, even if Chafee believed that some nonpolitical speech was within the scope of the First Amendment, he clearly asserted that judicial activism on behalf of free speech was justified by the judicial obligation to police the democratic process.

99. Chafee (1956), p. 114.

100. Chafee (1941), pp. 31–35, 149, 158. See Chafee (1965), p. 6.

101. Chafee (1928b), p. 96. See Chafee (1965), p. 6; D. Smith (1986), p. 79, 274.

102. Rabban (1983), p. 1285 (quoting Chafee).

103. Chafee (1941), p. 35.

104. *Dennis v. United States*, 341 U.S. 494, 544–46 (1951) (Frankfurter, J., concurring).

105. Chafee (1941), p. 561. See chapter 4, n. 47. Chafee's approach seems to be what Martin Shapiro calls "preferred position balancing." Shapiro (1966), pp. 150–52. Chafee might have believed that Frankfurter's balancing approach was more appropriate when speech was not directly concerned with attaining truth on matters of public interest. See Chafee (1965), pp. 57–58.

106. For the classic discussions of the negative radiations of the commerce clause, see *H. P. Hood & Sons v. Du Mond*, 336 U.S. 525 (1949); *Gibbons v. Ogden*, 9 Wheat. 1 (1824).

107. Chafee (1928a), pp. 47–48. When *Gilbert* was before the Court, Chafee wrote Brandeis and urged him to rely exclusively on the preemption argument. See Rabban (1983), p. 1343 (quoting Chafee to Dean Acheson, who was Brandeis's clerk at the time); D. Smith (1986), p. 288, n. 3.

108. Chafee (1956), p. 29.

109. See Chafee (1941), pp. 508–9.

110. Chafee (1941), pp. 508–9; Corwin (1920a), p. 55. Corwin's analysis is discussed in chapter 2.

111. Chafee (1941), p. 397. As discussed below, Chafee believed the free-speech claim in *Schenck v. United States* was properly denied. Chafee also asserted that he supported the Court's decision in *Frohwerk v. United States*, but only on the ground that an "inadequately prepared record" may have indicated that the "evidence might conceivably have been sufficient . . . [to] satisfy the clear and present danger test." Chafee (1941), p. 83. Chafee may have thought *Whitney v. California* was correct on technical grounds, but he clearly believed Anita Whitney's conviction in the trial court violated her constitutional free-speech rights. See Chafee (1941), pp. 345–51.

112. See chapters 1 and 2.

113. Chayes (1976), p. 1285.

114. Courts could consider the defendant's state of mind when determining the probability that the defendant's acts would have had harmful consequences. See chapter 3.

115. Chafee (1941), pp. 47–48, 82, 183; Chafee (1956), p. 82. When Chafee first attempted to draw an analogy between the First Amendment and the law of criminal attempt, he did not know that Holmes had made a similar effort in *Schenck*. Chafee first stated his analogy in 1920, two years before he learned that Holmes had also derived the clear and present danger test from the law of criminal attempt. Chafee (1920a), pp. 213–14. Bogen (1982), p. 100. Nevertheless, this similarity

was probably not coincidental. Chafee and Holmes were both familiar with the work of Walter Nelles, a prominent attorney who defended free-speech cases for the National Civil Liberties Bureau and the ACLU. In 1918, Nelles wrote a short book arguing that the Espionage Act incorporated the common law of criminal attempt. Nelles (1918), p. 77. See Chafee (1956), pp. 69–70.

116. Holmes used similar language in *Abrams*. However, Holmes believed that the trial court had to examine evidence of Abrams's intent in order to establish an otherwise weak connection between the speech in question and the possibility of lawless action; if Abrams had intended to cause lawless conduct, then this would have increased the probability that lawless conduct would have taken place. See chapter 3.

117. Chafee (1941), pp. 47–48, 82.

118. Ibid., p. 175.

119. 301 U.S. 242 (1937).

120. Chafee (1941), p. 397.

121. Ibid.

122. Ibid., pp. 395–97. See D. Smith (1986), p. 3 (quoting Chafee).

123. Chafee (1941), p. 398.

124. D. Smith (1986), p. 3. See Prude (1973), pp. 644–45.

125. Chafee (1941), p. 218.

126. Ibid., p. 319.

127. Ibid., p. 48.

128. Ibid., pp. 81–82.

129. See ibid., pp. 401–9.

130. *Whitney*, at 380 (Brandeis, J., concurring).

131. Compare Chafee (1941), pp. 349–50 with *Whitney*, at 379–80 (Brandeis, J., concurring). See generally Van Alstyne (1984), pp. 35–37.

132. See chapter 5.

133. Chafee (1941), p. 84. See chapter 3.

134. Chafee (1941), pp. 42, 44.

135. Ibid., p. 139.

136. Chafee (1956), p. 167; Chafee (1928a), p. 213. See Chafee (1956), p. 220 (Congress may compel testimony for any reason).

137. Chafee (1919a), p. 963.

138. Chafee (1941), pp. 6–7, 167; Chafee (1956), p. 17.

139. Chafee (1956), pp. 89–91; Chafee (1949a), p. 894; Prude (1973), p. 651 (quoting Chafee). See Chafee (1941), p. 177 ("the wisdom and policy of a federal sedition law" is "a much more fertile subject of discussion"); Chafee (1965), p. 35; Chafee (1956), p. 180. See generally Prude (1973), pp. 641–42.

However, Chafee's policy arguments were usually legal arguments that had been unsuccessful in court. For example, in 1941, Chafee claimed that his discussion of deportation was based solely on policy considerations. In 1920, he had claimed that the identical positions were constitutional arguments. Compare Chafee (1920a), p. 284, with Chafee (1941), p. 232.

140. Chafee (1949a), p. 895. See Chafee (1941), pp. 170–71; Chafee (1920a), p. 200. For Holmes and Freund, see chapter 3.

141. Chafee (1941), p. 177. See also Chafee (1952), p. 1 (asserting that the First Amendment had little meaning before courts had interpreted it).

142. Chafee (1941), p. 139.

143. Chafee (1928a), p. 53. See Chafee (1949a), p. 894.

144. Chafee (1941), p. 564. See Chafee (1956), p. 101; Chafee (1928a), p. 107; Chafee (1965), p. 38.

145. Prude (1973), pp. 652–54 (quoting Chafee).

146. Chafee (1919a), pp. 957, 959.

147. Chafee (1928a), p. 69.

148. Chafee (1920b), pp. 771–72.

149. Chafee (1931), p. 338.

150. E. Freund (1904), p. 11; Dewey (1929a), p. 102; Frankfurter (1938), p. 51; Llewellyn (1919), p. 337. For similar observations, see Mason (1955), p. 129, n. 37 (citing sources).

151. Chafee (1928b), p. 98.

152. *Lincoln Federal Labor Union v. Northwestern Iron & Metal Co.*, 335 U.S. 525, 535 (1949).

153. *West Coast Hotel Co. v. Parrish*, 300 U.S. 379, 391 (1937).

154. *United States v. Carolene Products Co.*, 304 U.S. 144, 152–53 n. 4 (1938). The precise origins of the *Carolene Products* footnote are obscure. Most scholars agree that the footnote was probably written by Louis Lusky, Stone's clerk. Alpheus Mason claimed that "the groundwork had been laid in the earlier opinions of Justice Holmes, Justice Brandeis, and Chief Justice Hughes." Mason (1955), p. 129. However, as noted in chapter 3, none of these jurists justified judicial activism in that manner. It is more likely that speculations similar to the footnote were in the intellectual atmosphere at the time when it was written. For a discussion of the origins of the *Carolene Products* footnote, see Mason (1956), pp. 597–609, 612–27.

155. For *Board of Education v. Barnette*, see 319 U.S. 624 (1943). For *Minersville School District v. Gobitis*, see 310 U.S. 586 (1940).

156. Chafee et al. (1940), pp. 13–15, 22–26. For evidence that Chafee wrote these particular pages, see D. Smith (1986), pp. 203–4.

157. Chafee et al. (1940), pp. 14–15. For a summary of Chafee's activities promoting this two-tiered interpretation of judicial review, see D. Smith (1986), pp. 199–211.

158. Chafee (1941), pp. 360–61.

159. Ibid., pp. 360–61, 138–39.

160. See chapter 3.

161. Chafee (1941), p. 559.

162. Chafee (1941), p. 560.

163. Chafee (1965), p. 545.

164. Ibid., pp. 547, 471.

165. Chafee (1928a), p. 167.

166. Chafee (1956), p. 107.

167. Ibid., p. 108.

168. Ibid.

169. See chapter 4, nn. 62–64 and accompanying text.

170. Chafee (1965), pp. 500, 628, 545.

171. Chafee (1965), pp. 549, 563. See generally *United States v. Associated Press*, 326 U.S. 1 (1945).

172. Chafee (1965), pp. 628–29.

173. Ibid., pp. 627–28.

174. Ibid., p. 633. For his full argument against rights of access, see Chafee (1965), pp. 627–33. Because radio licenses were, by the nature of the industry, a scarce resource, Chafee believed that the FCC could require broadcasters to provide access to persons of differing views, although he believed that to be an unwise policy. Ibid., pp. 636–42, 693.

175. See chapter 5.

Chapter Five

1. See Frank (1931); Arnold (1962); Arnold (1937).

2. Bell (1988), p. 405. See Purcell (1973), p. 236.

3. See Purcell (1973), pp. 197–217, 235–66; R. Smith (1985), p. 80.

4. Hook (1940), p. 10; Shapiro (1984), p. 543. See Dahl (1956), pp. 22–27. For a general discussion of the various strands of democratic relativism, see Purcell (1973), pp. 205–10.

5. Lipset and Rabb (1978), p. 5; Bell (1988), p. 406. See generally Purcell (1973), pp. 237–39.

6. Parsons (1955), pp. 138–39. See Adorno et. al. (1950), especially pp. 654–726; Emerson (1966), p. 17. For examples of the behavioral disorders that intellectuals thought afflicted McCarthy's supporters,

see the essays collected in Bell (1955). For a cogent criticism of these claims, see Rogin (1967).

7. Hook (1940), p. 286; Dahl (1956), p. 66; Dahl (1970), pp. 106–7. See Lipset and Rabb (1978), p. xviii.

8. *Abrams v. United States*, 250 U.S. 616, 629 (1919) (Holmes, J., dissenting).

9. 376 U.S. 254.

10. See chapter 1.

11. 395 U.S. 444.

12. See especially, *Buckley v. Valeo*, 424 U.S. 1 (1976).

13. Meiklejohn (1960), pp. 27, 20; Meiklejohn (1961), p. 264. See Meiklejohn (1960), pp. 57, 72.

14. Emerson (1970), p. 5; Emerson (1977), pp. 739–40, 760. See Emerson (1966), p. viii.

15. Emerson (1970), p. 631; Emerson (1966), p. 115. See Emerson (1970), p. 4.

16. Emerson (1966), p. 26; Emerson (1970), pp. 4–5.

17. Meiklejohn (1960), pp. 19–20; Meiklejohn (1961), p. 260.

18. Ibid., p. 76. See Meiklejohn (1961), pp. 255–56; for a discussion of the absolute standard of free speech protection, see pp. 255–66.

19. Meiklejohn (1960), pp. 59–60.

20. Emerson (1981), p. 802.

21. Emerson (1966), p. 59. For Emerson's full protection doctrine, see Emerson (1970), pp. 16–20; Emerson (1966), pp. 59–62; Emerson (1980), pp. 477–80.

22. Meiklejohn (1960), p. 57.

23. Emerson (1966), p. 59.

24. Meiklejohn (1961), p. 255; Meiklejohn (1960), p. 75. See Meiklejohn (1961), pp. 253–54; Meiklejohn (1960), pp. 57–60, 79.

25. Meiklejohn (1960), pp. 79, 37, 42.

26. Emerson (1966), pp. 3, 4–15; Emerson (1970), pp. 6–7; Emerson (1977), pp. 740–45; Emerson (1980), pp. 423–28.

27. Emerson (1966), p. 4.

28. Chafee (1949), p. 900. See also Kalven (1960), pp. 15–16.

29. See, e.g., Meiklejohn (1960), p. 42.

30. Chafee (1949a), p. 900; Meiklejohn (1961), pp. 263, 257, 262.

31. Emerson (1966), pp. 14, 59.

32. Emerson (1980), p. 423.

33. See Chafee (1941), p. 149 (discussed in chapter 4).

34. Emerson (1970), p. 489.

35. Emerson (1966), pp. 31, 32.
36. Meiklejohn (1961), p. 256; Meiklejohn (1960), pp. 107–8. See Meiklejohn (1960), pp. 19–20, 86.
37. Emerson (1966), pp. 4–5.
38. Meiklejohn (1960), p. 87.
39. Emerson (1970), pp. 663, 666.
40. Ibid., p. 668.
41. Ibid., pp. 634, 639. See also Emerson (1966), p. 105.
42. Emerson (1970), pp. 638–39.
43. Ibid., pp. 639–40.
44. Levy (1963), p. 309.
45. Cahn (1960), p. 8; Shapiro (1966), p. 93. See also Meiklejohn (1961), pp. 263–64; Emerson (1970), p. 99. For a summary of reaction to *Legacy of Suppression*, see Levy (1985), pp. xiv–xix.
46. Shapiro (1966), p. 116; Kalven (1988), p. 28; Cahn (1956), p. 480. See McKay (1959), p. 1188; Rostow (1952), pp. 210–24; C. Black (1960), pp. 103–4 ("in many cases, moreover, the wrong complained of is one that amounts to an exclusion from the political process"). See also Kalven (1964), p. 221 (generally endorsing Meiklejohn's interpretation of the constitutional meaning of free speech). See generally R. Smith (1985), pp. 103, 106.
47. Rostow (1952), p. 202; McKay (1959), pp. 1184–85, 1191, 1198. Rostow (1952), pp. 202–3. For endorsements of the *Carolene Products* footnote, see Shapiro (1966), pp. 58–59, 113–17; Mason (1956), pp. 625–28; Lusky (1942), pp. 19–21; C. Black (1960), pp. 110–12, 90–99, 217–21. See generally R. Smith (1985), pp. 81, 89.
48. See generally Lange (1973), pp. 2–3, n. 5 (citing articles discussing mass-media and free-speech problems).
49. See Shiffrin (1983), pp. 1212–13.
50. 341 U.S. 494 (1951).
51. *Thornhill v. Alabama*, 310 U.S. 88, 102 (1940); *Thomas v. Collins*, 323 U.S. 516, 543 (1940) (Jackson, J., concurring); *Thomas*, at 529–30. See *Schneider v. State*, 308 U.S. 147, 161 (1939) (quoted in chapter 4); *Board of Education v. Barnette*, 319 U.S. 624, 639 (1943); *Murdock v. Pennsylvania*, 319 U.S. 105, 115 (1943). See generally McKay (1959), pp. 1223–27 (quoting judicial opinions defending free speech).
52. See especially *Dennis v. United States*, 341 U.S. 494 (1951); *Scales v. United States*, 367 U.S. 203 (1961). For general summaries of the Supreme Court's attitudes toward free speech from the 1920s to the 1960s, see Mendelson (1952); Shapiro (1966).

53. *Dennis v. United States*, at 494, 584 (Douglas, J., dissenting). See *Poulos v. New Hampshire*, 345 U.S. 395, 423 (1952) (Douglas, J., dissenting); Douglas (1958), p. 41.

54. *Breard v. Alexandria*, 341 U.S. 622, 650 (1951) (Black, J., dissenting); Hugo Black (1968), p. 49.

55. *Garrison v. Louisiana*, 379 U.S. 64, 82 (1964) (Douglas, J., concurring); Hugo Black (1968), p. 45.

56. Powe (1974).

57. *United States v. C.I.O.*, 335 U.S. 106, 107 n. 1, 123 (1948); *United States v. International Union United Automobile Workers*, 352 U.S. 567 (1957). See also *United States v. C.I.O.*, at 106 (Rutledge, J., concurring) (claiming statute was void for vagueness).

58. *United States v. International Union United Automobile Workers*, at 567, 596, 598 n. 3 (Douglas, J., dissenting); Douglas (1958), pp. 31–32.

59. *New York Times Co. v. Sullivan*, 376 U.S. 274–75 (1964); Brennan (1965), pp. 18, 10; Kalven (1964), p. 221.

60. *New York Times Co. v. Sullivan*, at 397 (Black, J., concurring).

61. Ibid., at 301 (Goldberg, J., concurring). See generally R. Smith (1985), p. 198.

62. See Kalven (1964), p. 221.

63. *Cohen v. California*, 403 U.S. 15 (1971); *Tinker v. Des Moines School District*, 393 U.S. 503 (1969); *New York Times Co. v. United States*, 403 U.S. 713 (1971). See also *Watts v. United States*, 394 U.S. 705 (1969); *Bond v. Floyd*, 385 U.S. 116 (1966). But see *United States v. O'Brien*, 391 U.S. 367 (1968) (First Amendment held not to protect persons who protested the draft by burning their draft cards).

64. See *Shuttlesworth v. Birmingham*, 394 U.S. 147 (1969); *Gregory v. Chicago*, 394 U.S. 111 (1969); *Brown v. Louisiana*, 383 U.S. 131 (1966); *Cox v. Louisiana*, 379 U.S. 536 (1965); *Edwards v. South Carolina*, 372 U.S. 229 (1963). These and similar cases are analyzed at length in Kalven (1965). For other instances where the Court upheld the First Amendment rights of civil rights organizers or protestors, see *Street v. New York*, 394 U.S. 576 (1969); *NAACP v. Button*, 371 U.S. 415 (1963); *Wood v. Georgia*, 370 U.S. 375 (1962); *NAACP v. Alabama*, 357 U.S. 449 (1958). But see *Adderly v. Florida*, 385 U.S. 39 (1966) (First Amendment held not to give persons the right to protest on prison grounds).

65. See *Brandenburg v. Ohio*, 395 U.S. 444, 447, 449 (1971) (overruling *Whitney v. California*); *Watts*, at 705, 711–12 (Douglas, J., concurring) (noting that the decision had implicitly overruled several lower federal court decisions handed down during World War I). In these earlier cases, courts held that persons had no constitutional right to

insult the president. See also *Brandenburg,* at 452 (Douglas, J., concurring) (suggesting that the Court should overrule *Schenck v. United States*).

66. 385 U.S. 116 (1966).

67. See also *Watts,* at 705, 711–12 (Douglas, J., concurring) (noting that persons had been punished for similar hyperbolic threats during World War I).

68. *Brandenburg,* at 447.

69. Nimmer (1984), p. vii.

70. Kalven (1964), p. 221, n. 125; Emerson (1968), p. 988. See Dorsen and Gora (1983), pp. 28–29.

71. See Cox (1981), p. 6.

72. See Dorsen (1988), pp. 483–84.

73. See, e.g., Downs (1985).

74. See, e.g., *Texas v. Johnson,* 491 U.S.———, 105 L. Ed. 2d 342, 371 (1989) (Rehnquist, C. J., dissenting).

75. The most famous work in this genre is Charles Beard's *An Economic Interpretation of the Constitution* (1913), which claimed that concentrated wealth had triumphed over democratic interests from the very beginning of the republic.

76. See, e.g., Jacobson (1980); Burnham (1982); Wolfinger and Rosenstone (1980); Ferguson and Rogers (1986); Drew (1983); Edsall (1984); Verba and Nie (1972); Piven and Cloward (1989).

77. Lindblom (1977), pp. 5, 194, 202, 356. Robert Dahl expressed similar concerns in *Democracy and its Critics.*

78. Winter (1973), pp. 27, 3–5. Winter (1971), p. 53. Some conservative scholars praise unregulated campaign spending for less egalitarian reasons. Brice Clagett and John Bolton ([1976], p. 1335) insist that "the wealthy need means to exercise their financial power to defend themselves politically against the greater numbers who may believe that their economic interests militate toward leveling."

79. 391 U.S. 308 (1968).

80. Chafee (1941), p. 23.

81. *Amalgamated Food Employees v. Logan Valley Plaza,* 391 U.S. 308, 326 (1968) (Douglas, J., concurring).

82. *Logan Valley Plaza,* at 332–33 (Black, J., dissenting); *Bell v. Maryland,* 378 U.S. 226, 325 (1964) (Black, J., dissenting).

83. Emerson (1970), p. 679; Shapiro (1966), pp. 148–49 (this comment was not made in the precise circumstances of *Logan Valley Plaza*).

84. See Fiss (1986), p. 1407; Powe (1983), pp. 243–44.

85. Dorsen and Gora (1983), p. 44; Van Alstyne (1980), pp. 67–68; R. Smith (1985), p. 114; Fiss (1986), p. 1407; *Clark v. Community for*

Creative Non-Violence, 468 U.S. 288, 314 n. 14 (Marshall, J., dissenting).

86. *Buckley*, at 1, 256–57 (Burger, C. J., concurring). See *Gitlow*, at 673 (Holmes, J., dissenting).

87. *Buckley*, at 19. See *FEC v. National Conservative PAC*, 470 U.S. 480, 493–94 (1985).

88. *Buckley*, at 48–49. See *Citizens Against Rent Control v. Berkeley*, 454 U.S. 295–96 (1981); *First National Bank v. Bellotti*, 435 U.S. 790–91 (1978);*Pacific Gas and Electric Company v. Public Utilities Commission of California*, 475 U.S. 1, 14 (1986).

89. See *Wooley v. Maynard*, 430 U.S. 705, 713–15 (1977); *Board of Education v. Barnette*, at 624, 633–42.

90. The relevant portions of the Federal Election Campaign Act Amendments of 1974 are:

(b)(1) . . . no person shall make contributions to any candidate with respect to any election for Federal office which, in the aggregate, exceed \$1,000.

(2) No political committee (other than a principal campaign committee) shall make contributions to any candidate with respect to any election for Federal office which, in the aggregate, exceed \$5,000. . . .

(3) No individual shall make contributions aggregating more than \$25,000 in any calendar year. . . .

(c)(1) No candidate shall make expenditures in excess of —

(A) \$10,000,000, in the case of a candidate for nomination for election to the office of President of the United States. . . .

(B) \$20,000,000, in case of a candidate for election to the office of President of the United States;

(C) in the case of any campaign for nomination for election by a candidate for the office of Senator or by a candidate for the office of Representative from a State which is entitled to only one Representative, the greater of—

(i) 8 cents multiplied by the voting age population of the State . . . ; or

(ii) \$100,000;

(D) in the case of any campaign for election by a candidate for the office of Senator or by a candidate for the office of Representative from a State which is entitled to only one Representative, the greater of—

(i) 12 cents multiplied by the voting age population of the State . . . ; or

(ii) \$150,000;

(E) \$70,000, in the case of any campaign for nomination for election, or for election, by a candidate for the office of Representative in any other State. . . .

(e)(1) No person may make any expenditure . . . relative to a clearly identified candidate during a calendar year which, when added to all other expenditures made by such person during the year advocating the election or defeat of such candidate, exceeds $1,000.

(a)(1) No candidate may make expenditures from his personal funds, or the personal funds of his immediate family, in connection with his campaigns during any calendar year for nomination for election, or for election, to Federal office in excess of, in the aggregate—

(A) $50,000, in the case of a candidate for the office of President or Vice President of the United States;

(B) $35,000, in the case of a candidate for the office of Senator or for the office of Representative from a State which is entitled to only one Representative; or

(C) $25,000, in the case of a candidate for the office of Representative. . . .

88 Stat. 1263–66 (1974). In addition, Congress required that contributions and expenditures be publicly disclosed, established a system of partial federal funding for presidential elections, and set up a commission to monitor compliance with the statute. See 88 Stat. 1263–1304 (1974).

91. *Buckley*, at 44–45, 24–25, 245 (Burger, C. J., concurring) ("if such restraints can be justified at all, they must be justified by the very strongest of state interests"); *National Conservative PAC*, at 480, 493; *Citizens Against Rent Control*, at 290, 294; *Consolidated Edison Co. v. Public Serv. Comm'n*, 447 U.S. 530, 540–41 (1980); *Bellotti*, at 765, 786.

92. *Buckley*, at 25–28. See *National Conservative PAC*, at 496–97; *FEC v. National Right to Work Committee*, 459 U.S. 197, 206–11 (1982); *California Medical Assn. v. FEC*, 453 U.S. 182, 194–95 (1981); *Citizens Against Rent Control*, at 297.

93. *Buckley*, at 28.

94. Ibid., at 39–59.

95. Ibid., at 47, 48–49, 55.

96. Ibid., at 49.

97 *Bellotti*, at 765, 777. See *Consolidated Edison Co.*, at 530.

98. *Bellotti*, at 788 n. 26. See *Austin v. Michigan Chamber of Commerce*,———U.S.——— 58 U.S.L.W. 4371 (1990) (limitations on nonprofit corporate expenditures on behalf of political candidates held constitutional as applied to a nonprofit corporation that solicited funds from for-profit corporations); *National Right to Work Committee*, at 197 (limitations on corporate expenditures on behalf of political candidates held to be a constitutionally adequate means of preventing corruption). But see *FEC v. Massachusetts Citizens for Life*, 479 U.S.

238 (1986) (states cannot regulate the expression of nonprofit corporations formed solely for ideological purposes if they do not accept contributions from for-profit corporations).

99. *Citizens Against Rent Control*, at 290, 297.

100. Ibid., at 297–99.

101. *National Conservative PAC*, at 480, 495. But see *California Medical Assn. v. FEC*, at 182 (sustaining limitations on contributions to a multicandidate political committee).

102. *National Conservative PAC*, at 498.

103. *Red Lion Broadcasting Co. v. FCC*, 395 U.S. 367 (1969).

104. *Columbia Broadcasting v. Democratic Comm.*, 412 U.S. 94 (1973) (opinion of Burger, C. J.).

105. Ibid., at 148 (Douglas, J., concurring). Justice Douglas did not take part in the *Red Lion* decision.

106. *Miami Herald Publishing Co. v. Tornillo*, 418 U.S. 241, 256 (1974).

107. *Lloyd Corp. v. Tanner*, 407 U.S. 551, 568–69 (1972); *Hudgens v. NLRB*, 424 U.S. 507 (1976) (overruling *Logan Plaza*).

108. See *Lloyd Corp.*, at 578 (Marshall, J., dissenting).

109. *Pruneyard Shopping Center v. Robins*, 447 U.S. 74, 97 (1980) (Powell, J., concurring).

110. Ibid., at 83; see at 94 (Marshall, J., concurring). See also *CBS, Inc. v. FCC*, 453 U.S. 367 (1981) (upholding a statute that required broadcasters "to permit purchase of reasonable amounts of time . . . by a legally qualified candidate for Federal elective office on behalf of his candidacy").

111. *Pacific Gas*, at 14.

112. See *Pruneyard*, at 99–101 (Powell, J., concurring); see also at 95 (White, J., concurring).

113. *Hague v. C.I.O.*, 307 U.S. 496, 515 (1939) (opinion of Roberts, J.). See *United States v. Grace* (affirming the constitutional right to hand out political pamphlets on the sidewalk outside the Supreme Court). But see *Heffron v. International Society for Krishna Consciousness*, 452 U.S. 640 (1981) (states have the right to restrict a religious group handing out literature to a specific area on the state fairgrounds).

114. *Perry Ed. Assn. v. Perry Local Educators' Assn.*, 460 U.S. 37, 45–46 (1983).

115. Ibid., at 49. See *Greer v. Spock*, 424 U.S. 828 (1976); *Cornelius v. NAACP Legal Defense & Ed. Fund*, 473 U.S. 788 (1985); *Lehman v. Shaker Heights*, 418 U.S. 298 (1974); *U.S. Postal Service v. Greenburgh Civic Assns.*, 453 U.S. 114 (1981); *City Council v. Taxpayers for Vincent*, 466 U.S. 789 (1984).

116. See *Cornelius*, at 832–33 (Blackmun, J., dissenting); *Perry*, at 63–66 (Brennan, J., dissenting).

117. See especially *U.S. Postal Service*, at 144 (Marshall, J., dissenting); *Cornelius*, at 815 (Blackmun, J., dissenting).

118. *Buckley*, at 256; *Austin*, at 4383 (Scalia, J., dissenting). Indeed, Justice Scalia's speech-protective opinions in traditional free-speech cases suggest that he accepts the conservative libertarian interpretation of the First Amendment. See especially *Texas v. Johnson*, 491 U.S. —— (1989) (Scalia, J., concurring) (endorsing the constitutional right to burn the flag).

119. *Buckley*, at 265 (White, J., dissenting).

120. *Bellotti*, at 823 (Rehnquist, J., dissenting).

121. For libel, see *Dun & Bradstreet, Inc. v. Greenmoss Builders, Inc.*, 472 U.S. 749 (1985) (Brennan, J., dissenting); *Gertz v. Robert Welch, Inc.*, 418 U.S. 323 (1974) (Brennan, J., dissenting). For obscenity and offensive language, see *FCC v. Pacifica Foundation*, 438 U.S. 726 (1978) (Brennan, J., dissenting); *Miller v. California*, 413 U.S. 15 (1973) (Brennan, J., dissenting); *Paris Adult Theater I v. Slaton*, 413 U.S. 49 (1973) (Brennan, J., dissenting). For public forum, see *Perry*, at 37 (Marshall, J., dissenting); *U.S. Postal Service*, at 114 (Marshall, J., dissenting); *Greer v. Spock*, at 828 (Brennan, J., dissenting); *Community for Creative Non-Violence*, at 288 (Marshall, J., dissenting). See also *Richmond Newspapers, Inc. v. Virginia*, 448 U.S. 555 (1980) (Brennan, J., concurring) (First Amendment grants citizens a right to know certain information); *Connick v. Myers*, 461 U.S. 138 (1983) (the First Amendment should bar the firing of a governmental employee who passed out questionnaires concerning working conditions in her department); *Board of Education v. Pico*, 457 U.S. 853 (1982) (the First Amendment limits the right of school boards to remove books from the school library); *Wayte v. United States*, 470 U.S. 598 (1985) (Brennan, J., dissenting) (the First Amendment should bar the governmental practice of prosecuting only persons who publicly objected to draft registration). See generally Powe (1982), pp. 271–73.

122. See *Lloyd Corp.*, at 551 (Marshall, J., dissenting); *Hudgens*, at 507 (Marshall, J., dissenting); *Pruneyard*, at 74, 97.

123. Compare *Bellotti*, at 765 with *Consolidated Edison Co.*, at 765. Compare *Pacific Gas and Electric Company v. Public Utilities Commission of California*, 475 U.S. 1 (1986) with *Hudgens*.

124. Justice Brennan did contribute a one-paragraph addendum to *Miami Herald* (signed only by Justice Rehnquist!), which asserted that newspapers might have to print replies from persons who proved defamatory falsehood. *Miami Herald*, at 258–59 (Brennan, J., concurring).

125. *Massachusetts Citizens for Life,* at 264; *Austin,* at 4376.

126. *Massachusetts Citizens for Life,* at 257–58.

127. See *Austin,* at 4379–80 (Scalia, J., dissenting); Nicholson (1988), p. 605. Although Justice Scalia's criticisms were specifically aimed at Justice Marshall's majority opinion in *Austin,* Marshall dissented in *FEC v. National Conservative PAC,* the case holding that individuals could spend unlimited sums of money on behalf of political candidates. Justice Brennan, however, voted with the majority in that case.

128. Ely (1980), p. 101 (quoting Hans Linde).

129. Ibid., p. 87.

130. Ibid., pp. 106, 76.

131. Ibid., p. 104.

132. Ibid., pp. 110–11.

133. Ibid., pp. 108–9.

134. Ibid., pp. 105–16 (primarily discussing the relationship between free speech and lawless conduct).

135. For other contemporary theorists who emphasize the relationship between judicial review and democratic processes but fail to discuss the constitutional relationships between free speech and private property, see Bork (1971); Lusky (1975).

136. Dworkin (1978), p. 126. See generally Graber (1989), pp. 88–89.

137. Michelman (1979).

138. See Dworkin (1985); Dworkin (1978); Perry (1982).

139. See Gunther (1985), p. lxiv.

140. See, e.g., Blasi (1977), pp. 637–38, 645–46; Van Alstyne (1984), pp. 126–27, n. 90; Redish (1984), pp. 112–13.

141. Karst (1975), pp. 64–65; Baker (1978), p. 1040.

142. See Schauer (1982); Bollinger (1986); Kalven (1988); Downs (1985); Greenawalt (1980); Lewis (1983); Neubourne (1988).

143. Blasi (1985), pp. 449–50, 477–80.

144. Emerson (1980), p. 461.

145. Emerson (1981), p. 795; Emerson (1980), p. 461.

146. Emerson (1980), pp. 480–81.

147. Ibid., p. 481.

148. Emerson (1981), p. 799.

149. Ibid., p. 810.

150. Ibid., p. 827. For similar thoughts, see Carter (1984); Pool (1983).

151. Emerson (1981), p. 823.

152. See Powe (1987a), pp. 250, 281 n. 3; Fleishman and McCorkle (1984), pp. 237–38; Nicholson (1988), pp. 590–92, 606–7; Wright (1982), pp. 637, 642.

153. Dorsen (1988), p. 492; Dorsen and Gora (1983), p. 44.

154. Dorsen and Gora (1983), pp. 43–44.

155. Haiman (1981); Neubourne (1988), pp. 576–77.

156. See Dorsen (1984); American Civil Liberties Union (1985).

157. Dorsen (1984), p. xv (quoting Paul Freund). See American Civil Liberties Union (1985), pp. 288, 292.

158. Creating a judicially enforceable minimum standard of living, for example, would not resolve all the problems that are created by limited access to expensive communications technology.

159. See Powe (1987a), p. 253; Fiss (1987), p. 785; Fiss (1986), pp. 1407, 1410.

160. Powe (1987b), p. 382 (quoting D. Anderson [1983], p. 522); Pool (1983), p. 3; Kalven (1967), p. 23.

161. Powe (1987b), p. 363; Fleishman and McCorkle (1984), p. 238. See Powe (1987a), p. 250.

162. Baker (1982), p. 651.

163. Fleishman and McCorkle (1984), p. 242; Redish (1971), pp. 910–11.

164. Powe (1983), p. 281. See also Winter (1973), pp. 18–19; Winter (1971), p. 60.

165. Redish (1971), p. 915; Fleishman and McCorkle (1984), p. 242. See Kalven (1967), p. 47. See also Powe (1987b), pp. 374–80 (suggesting some doubts about the chilling effect argument).

166. Polsby (1977), p. 43; Powe (1987a), pp. 6, 256. See also Winter (1973), p. 13; Winter (1971), pp. 45–46, 61.

167. Baker (1982), p. 651; Powe (1983), p. 281; Fleishman and McCorkle (1984), p. 217. See Redish (1971), pp. 900–901.

168. Powe (1983), p. 281; Redish (1971), p. 933. See Fleishman and McCorkle (1984), p. 238.

169. Powe (1983), p. 282. See Fleishman and McCorkle (1984), pp. 275–78; Polsby (1977), p. 42.

170. Powe (1983), p. 283; Baker (1982), p. 651; Fleishman and McCorkle (1984), p. 296. See Dorsen (1988), p. 493.

171. Fleishman and McCorkle (1984), pp. 294–95. See Powe (1983), pp. 282–83; Redish (1971), p. 903.

172. See Chevigny (1981), pp. 225–26; Fiss (1987), p. 792.

173. Emerson (1981), p. 818; *Buckley,* at 292–94 (opinion of Rehnquist, J.). See Fleishman (1975), p. 897.

174. Wright (1976), p. 1005; Cox (1981), p. 86; Nicholson (1988), p. 606; Wright (1982), pp. 635–36, 609; Carter (1984), p. 604. See Leventhal (1977), p. 373; Fiss (1986), p. 1424; Barron (1967), p. 1678.

175. Rosenthal (1972), p. 21. See P. Freund (1972), p. 72; Cox (1981), pp. 76–77; Wright (1976), p. 1019.

176. Nicholson (1974), p. 828; Wright (1982), pp. 621–22 (quoting Rosenthal [1972], p. 40). See Leventhal (1977), p. 371; Barron (1967), p. 1647.

177. Nicholson (1988), pp. 597–98; Fiss (1986), p. 1413; Barron (1967), p. 1643; Wright (1982), p. 625. See Chevigny (1981), pp. 219–20; Carter (1984), p. 582.

178. Wright (1976), p. 1007.

179. Meiklejohn (1960), p. 26. See Barron (1967), p. 1653; Leventhal (1977), p. 360; Wright (1982), p. 639.

180. See Rosenthal (1972), p. 12; P. Freund (1972), p. 71; Wright (1982), pp. 639–40; Cox (1981), p. 720.

181. P. Freund (1972), p. 72; Nicholson (1974), p. 845. See Wright (1982), p. 639; Leventhal (1977), pp. 361–62.

182. *Kovacs v. Cooper,* 336 U.S. 77, 102 (1949) (Black, J., dissenting).

183. *Kovacs,* at 104 (Black, J., dissenting); Dorsen and Gora (1983), pp. 43–44.

184. For similar objections, see Karst (1975), p. 40.

185. Winter (1971), p. 52.

186. Bell (1988), p. 105 (quoting Nicholas Biddle).

187. Wright (1982), p. 631.

Chapter Six

1. See chapters 4 and 5.

2. Shapiro (1978), pp. 197, 201–2; Shapiro (1983), p. 223; Truman (1962), pp. 479, 494–97; Peltason (1955), pp. 43–54; Vose (1972), pp. 329–39. See also Stumpf (1984), p. 536.

3. Chafee (1941), pp. 357–60. See Rabban (1981), pp. 557–59; Murphy (1972), pp. 25, 30–37.

4. Shapiro (1978), pp. 192–93.

5. Skinner (1974), p. 299; J. White (1984), p. 6.

6. Skinner (1974), p. 300. See Gordon (1984), p. 101; R. Smith (1988), p. 88; Tulis (1987), pp. 15–17.

7. Levinson (1988), p. 156 (citing Geertz [1973]). See R. Smith (1988), p. 98 (quoting Gordon [1984], p. 101).

8. Skowronek (1982), p. 285.

9. Rorty (1989), p. 56; see also pp. 41–42.

10. See R. Smith (1988), p. 91.

11. Skinner (1974), p. 287. See J. White (1984), pp. 278–84; Flathman (1989), pp. 29–30.

12. Of course, pragmatism and sociological jurisprudence were themselves fashioned out of the intellectual resources of late nineteenth-century conservatism. See Eric Goldman (1955).

13. See, e.g., Tribe (1985); Perry (1982); Dworkin (1986); Ackerman (1984); Posner (1977); Epstein (1985); Michelman (1973).

14. Graber (1988), pp. 339–40 n. 34.

15. See Graber (1989).

16. See chapter 5.

17. Rae (1981). For a more general attack on the use of "gross concepts" in political thought, see I. Shapiro (1989).

18. Rawls (1971); Dahl (1989).

19. Walzer (1984), p. 321.

20. See Walzer (1983), pp. 86–91, 97–108, 135–48, 236–37.

21. See Fishkin (1984), pp. 757–58.

22. Hamilton, Madison, and Jay (1961), p. 354.

23. See chapter 5.

24. Arendt (1965), p. 12. See Arendt (1958), pp. 26–27.

25. J. White (1984), p. 282; Rorty (1989), p. 67. See Rorty (1989), pp. 51–52, 60–61; Habermas (1979), p. 186; W. Wilson (1981), p. 144. See also R. Smith (1989), p. 75 (noting that both proponents and skeptics of moral reality may "aspir[e] to create a community of rationally inquiring and self-governing citizens").

Obviously, I will have to defend this point at length in the future work promised above.

26. Walzer (1983), pp. 304–5.

27. Ibid., p. 309.

28. Walzer (1984), p. 321.

29. Ibid., p. 318; Walzer (1983), p. 304.

30. See *Cohen v. California*, 403 U.S. 15 (1971).

31. See chapter 3.

32. See chapter 4.

33. Walzer (1981), pp. 396–97.

34. I would similarly argue that unions and foreigners have no constitutional free-speech rights, although the Constitution prohibits legislation that discriminates among citizens who wish to use unions or foreigners as vehicles for their own speech. Thus, while a Russian scholar may have no right to give a speech in the United States, an American group may have a First Amendment right to invite such a person to give a talk.

Minors and aliens qualified for citizenship have some free-speech rights by virtue of their entitlement to a share of political power in the future. Because they are not yet citizens, however, they may not enjoy the full protection of the First Amendment. This is not to say that minors and aliens have the same free-speech rights.

35. Actually, the last clause of this standard might read "as long as *all* members of the community can afford to make a similar investment in politics." However, this would give elected officials the power to regulate virtually all political activities because some members of our community cannot afford to make any investment in politics. The interpretive principle that best justifies an "average member of the community" rule is the same used by the Fairy Queen in *Iolanthe* when she declared, "But I cannot slaughter the whole company" after discovering that all her minions had incurred the death penalty by marrying mortals.

The need for this modified standard reveals the fundamental unconstitutionality of poverty in any affluent democratic society.

36. See *Buckley v. Valeo*, 424 U.S. 1 (1976); *FEC v. National Conservative PAC*, 470 U.S. 480 (1985).

37. This rule might be modified if, because of scarcity, a similarly sized group had no access to the airwaves.

38. See *Dombrowski v. Pfister*, 380 U.S. 479 (1965).

Bibliography

Ackerman, Bruce A. 1984. "The Storrs Lectures: Discovering the Constitution." *Yale Law Journal* 93: 1013.

Adams, Henry Brooks. 1968. *Democracy: An American Novel.* New York: Airmont Publishing Company.

———. 1958. *The Great Secession Winter of 1860–61 and Other Essays.* Edited by George E. Hochfield. New York: A. S. Barnes.

———. 1930. *Letters of Henry Adams.* Edited by Worthington Chaucey Ford. Boston: Houghton Mifflin Company.

———. 1918. *The Education of Henry Adams.* Edited by Ernest Samuels. Boston: Houghton Mifflin Company.

———. 1886. "Shall We Muzzle the Anarchists." *Forum* 1: 445.

Addams, Jane. 1965. *The Social Thought of Jane Addams.* Edited by Christopher Lasch. Indianapolis: Bobbs-Merrill Company.

———. 1964. *Democracy and Social Ethics.* Edited by Anne Firor Scott. Cambridge, Mass.: Belknap Press of Harvard University Press.

———. 1961. *Twenty Years at Hull-House.* New York: New American Library.

———. 1945. *Peace and Bread in Time of War.* Morningside Heights, N.Y.: King's Crown Press.

———. 1930. *The Second Twenty Years at Hull-House.* New York: Macmillan Company.

———. 1907. *Newer Ideals of Peace.* New York: Macmillan Company.

Adorno, T. W., et al. 1950. *The Authoritarian Personality.* New York: Harper & Brothers.

American Bar Association. 1918. "Report of the Committee to Oppose Judicial Recall." *A.B.A. Journal* 4: 400.

American Civil Liberties Union. 1985. *Policy Guide of the ACLU: 1981.* Rev. ed.

————. 1970. "The Fight for Free Speech." *American Civil Liberties Union: Annual Reports.* Vol. 1. New York: Arno Press and The New York Times.

Anderson, Alexis J. 1980. "The Formative Period of First Amendment Theory, 1870–1915." *Journal of Legal History* 24: 56.

Anderson, David A. 1986. "Levy vs. Levy." *Michigan Law Review* 84: 777.

————. 1983. "The Origins of the Press Clause." *U.C.L.A. Law Review* 30: 455.

Arendt, Hannah. 1965. *On Revolution.* New York: Penguin Books.

————. 1958. *The Human Condition.* Chicago: University of Chicago Press.

Arnold, Thurman Wesley. 1962. *The Symbols of Government.* New York: Harcourt, Brace & World.

————. 1937. *The Folklore of Capitalism.* New Haven, Conn.: Yale University Press.

Atkinson, Edward. 1871. *Inefficiency of Economic Legislation.* Cambridge, Mass.: Riverside Press.

Auerbach, Jerold S. 1969. "The Patrician as Libertarian: Zechariah Chafee, Jr., and Freedom of Speech." *New England Quarterly* 42: 511.

————. 1967. "Woodrow Wilson's 'Prediction' to Frank Cobb: Words Historians Should Doubt Ever Got Spoken." *Journal of American History* 54: 508.

Avrich, Paul. 1984. *The Haymarket Tragedy.* Princeton, N.J.: Princeton University Press.

Baker, C. Edwin. 1982. "Realizing Self-Realization: Corporate Political Expenditures and Redish's *The Value of Free Speech.*" *University of Pennsylvania Law Review* 130: 646.

————. 1978. "Scope of the First Amendment Freedom of Speech." *U.C.L.A. Law Review* 25:964.

Baldwin, Roger Nash. 1961a and 1961b. *The Reminiscences of Roger Baldwin.* Parts I and II. New York: Oral Research Office, Columbia University.

Barron, Jerome A. 1967. "Access to the Press—A New First Amendment Right." *Harvard Law Review* 80: 1641.

Beard, Charles A. 1986. *An Economic Interpretation of the Constitution of the United States.* New York: Free Press.

Beisner, Robert L. 1985. *Twelve against Empire: The Anti-Imperialists, 1898–1900.* Chicago: University of Chicago Press.

Bell, Daniel. 1988. *The End of Ideology: On the Exhaustion of Political Ideas in the Fifties.* Cambridge, Mass.: Harvard University Press.

Bell, Daniel, ed. 1955. *The New American Right*. New York: Criterion Books.

Beth, Loren P. 1971. *The Development of the American Constitution, 1877–1917*. New York: Harper & Row.

Black, Charles L., Jr. 1960. *The People and the Courts: Judicial Review in a Democracy*. New York: Macmillan Company.

Black, Henry C. 1927. *Handbook of American Constitutional Law*. 4th ed. St. Paul: West Publishing Co.

———. 1910. *Handbook of American Constitutional Law*. 3d ed. St. Paul: West Publishing Co.

———. 1895. *Handbook of American Constitutional Law*. St. Paul: West Publishing Co.

Black, Hugo. 1968. *A Constitutional Faith*. New York: Knopf.

Blackstone, Sir William. 1773a and 1773b. *Commentaries on the Laws of England* (Books Three and Four). 5th ed. Dublin: Exshaw et al.

Blasi, Vincent. 1988. "The First Amendment and the Ideal of Civic Courage: The Brandeis Opinion in *Whitney v. California*." *William and Mary Law Review* 29: 653.

———. 1985. "The Pathological Perspective and the First Amendment." *Columbia Law Review* 85: 449.

———. 1977. "The Checking Value in First Amendment Theory." *1977 American Bar Foundation Research Journal* (1977): 521.

Blum, Jeffrey M. 1983. "The Divisible First Amendment: A Critical Functionalist Approach to Freedom of Speech and Electoral Campaign Spending." *N.Y.U. Law Review* 58: 1273.

Bogen, David S. 1982. "The Free Speech Metamorphosis of Mr. Justice Holmes." *Hofstra Law Review* 11:97.

Bollinger, Lee C. 1986. *The Tolerant Society: Freedom of Speech and Extremist Speech in America*. New York: Oxford University Press.

———. 1983. "Free Speech and Intellectual Values." *Yale Law Journal* 92: 438.

Bork, Robert H. 1971. "Neutral Principles and Some First Amendment Problems." *Indiana Law Journal* 47: 1.

Bourne, Randolph S. 1977. *The Radical Will: Selected Writings, 1911–18*. Edited by Olaf Hansen. New York: Urizen Books.

———. 1964. *War and the Intellectuals: Collected Essays, 1915–1919*. Edited by Carl Resek. New York: Harper & Row.

Bowen, Catherine Drinker. 1944. *Yankee from Olympus: Justice Holmes and His Family*. Boston: Little, Brown and Company.

Brandeis, Louis D. 1975. *Letters of Louis Brandeis* (Vol. IV). Edited by Melvin I. Urofsky and David W. Levy. Albany: State University of New York Press.

————. 1942. *Brandeis on Zionism: A Collection of Addresses and Statements by Louis D. Brandeis*. Edited by Dr. Solomon Goldman. Washington, D.C.: Zionist Organization of America.

————. 1941. *The Brandeis Guide to the Modern World*. Edited by Alfred Lief. Boston: Little, Brown and Company.

————. 1934. *The Curse of Bigness: Miscellaneous Papers of Louis D. Brandeis*. Edited by Osmond K. Fraenkel. New York: Viking Press.

————. 1932. *Other People's Money: And How the Bankers Use It*. New York: Frederick A. Stokes Company.

————. 1933. *Business—A Profession*. Boston: Hale, Cushman & Flint.

————. 1908. "Brief for Defendant in Error." *Muller v. Oregon*, 208 U.S. 412.

Brandeis, Louis D., and Felix Frankfurter. 1986. "The Brandeis-Frankfurter Conversations." Edited by Melvin I. Urofsky. *Supreme Court Review* 1985: 299.

Brannon, Henry. 1901. *Treatise on the Rights and Privileges Guaranteed by the Fourteenth Amendment*. Cincinnati: W. H. Anderson.

Brennan, William J. 1965. "The Supreme Court and the Meiklejohn Interpretation of the First Amendment." *Harvard Law Review* 79:1.

Brewer, David J. 1899. *The Spanish War: A Prophecy or an Exception*. Buffalo, N.Y.: Liberal Club.

————. 1886. "Libel." *Central Law Journal* 22: 363.

Brooks, John Graham. 1915. "Freedom of Assemblage and Public Security." *Publications of the American Sociological Society*. Vol. 9. Chicago: University of Chicago Press.

Brown, Bernard Edward. 1951. *American Conservatives: The Political Thought of Francis Lieber and John W. Burgess*. New York: Columbia University Press.

Brown, Henry Billings. 1900. "The Liberty of the Press." *American Law Review* 24: 321.

Brown, Ray A. 1927. "Due Process of Law, Police Power, and the Supreme Court." *Harvard Law Review* 40: 943.

Burgess, John W. 1934. *Reminiscences of an American Scholar*. New York: Columbia University Press.

————. 1927. *The Sanctity of Law*. Boston: Ginn & Company.

————. 1923. *Recent Changes in American Constitutional Theory*. New York: Columbia University Press.

————. 1916. *The Administration of President Hayes*. New York: Charles Scribner's Sons.

————. 1915. *The Reconciliation of Government with Liberty*. New York: Charles Scribner's Sons.

———. 1908. "The Chief Questions of Present American Politics." *Political Science Quarterly* 32: 383.

———. 1904. "Present Problems of Constitutional Law." *Political Science Quarterly* 19: 545.

———. 1902a. *Reconstruction and the Constitution, 1866–1876.* New York: Charles Scribner's Sons.

———. 1902b. "The Election of United States Senators by Popular Vote." *Political Science Quarterly* 17: 650.

———. 1900. "The Relationship of the Constitution of the United States to Newly Acquired Territory." *Political Science Quarterly* 15: 381.

———. 1899. "How May the United States Govern Its Extra-Continental Territory?" *Political Science Quarterly* 14: 1.

———. 1898. "Private Corporations from the Point of View of Political Science." *Political Science Quarterly* 13: 201.

———. 1895. "The Ideal of the American Commonwealth." *Political Science Quarterly* 10: 404.

———. 1890a and 1890b. *Political Science and Comparative Constitutional Law.* Vols. I and II. Boston: Ginn & Co.

———. 1886. "The American Commonwealth: Changes in Relation to the Nation." *Political Science Quarterly* 1: 9.

Burke, Edmund. 1973. *Reflections on the Revolution in France.* Edited by Conor Cruise O'Brien. Middlesex, England: Penguin Books.

Burnham, Walter Dean. 1982. *The Current Crisis in American Politics.* Oxford: Oxford University Press.

Cahn, Edmond. 1960. "How Limited Were Our Early Civil Liberties." 37 *New York Herald Tribune Book Review* October 16, p. 8.

———. 1956. "The Firstness of the First Amendment." *Yale Law Journal* 65: 464.

Campbell, J. A. 1873. "Plaintiff's Brief." *Slaughter-House Cases.* 16 Wall. 3.

Cardozo, Benjamin N. 1921. *The Nature of the Judicial Process.* New Haven: Yale University Press.

Carnegie, Andrew. 1908. *Problems of Today.* New York: Doubleday, Page.

Carroll, Thomas F. 1919. "Freedom of Speech and of the Press in War Time: The Espionage Act." *Michigan Law Review* 17: 621.

Carter, Stephen L. 1984. "Technology, Democracy, and the Manipulation of Consent." *Yale Law Journal* 93: 581.

Chafee, Zechariah, Jr. 1981. *Freedom's Prophet: Selected Writings of Zechariah Chafee, Jr., University Professor, Harvard Law School.* Edited by Edward D. Re. London: Oceana Publications.

———. 1965. *Government and Mass Communications.* Hamden, Conn.: Archon Books.

————. 1956. *The Blessings of Liberty.* Philadelphia: J. B. Lippincott Company.

————. 1952. "Thirty-Five Years with Freedom of Speech." *Kansas Law Review* 1: 1.

————. 1949a. "Book Review." *Harvard Law Review* 62: 891.

————. 1949b. "Charles Evans Hughes." *Proceedings of the American Philosophical Society* 93: 267.

————. 1947. "Do Judges Make or Discover Law." *Proceedings of the American Philosophical Society* 91: 405.

————. 1941. *Free Speech in the United States.* Cambridge, Mass.: Harvard University Press.

————. 1936. "Some New Ideas about Law." *Indiana Law Journal* 11: 503.

————. 1932. "Mr. Justice Cardozo." *Harper's Magazine* 165: 34.

————. 1931. "Liberal Trends in the Supreme Court." *Current History* 35: 338.

————. 1929. "Prosperity." *Nation* 129: 84.

————. 1928a. *The Inquiring Mind.* New York: Harcourt, Brace and Company.

————. 1928b. "Law and Liberty." *Freedom in the Modern World.* Edited by Horace M. Kallen. New York: Coward-McCann.

————. 1920a. *Freedom of Speech.* New York: Harcourt, Brace and Howe.

————. 1920b. "A Contemporary State Trial—The United States versus Jacob Abrams et al." *Harvard Law Review* 33: 747.

————. 1919a. "Freedom of Speech in Wartime." *Harvard Law Review* 32: 932.

————. 1919b. "Legislation Against Anarchy." *New Republic* 19: 379.

————. 1918. "Freedom of Speech." *New Republic* 17: 66.

Chafee, Zechariah, Jr., et al. 1940. "Brief of the Committee on the Bill of Rights, of the American Bar Association, as Friends of the Court." *Minersville School District v. Gobitis*, 310 U.S. 586.

Chamberlain, John D. 1915. "Freedom of Speech in Public Streets, Parks and Commons." *Case and Comment* 22: 461.

Chayes, Abram. 1976. "The Role of the Judge in Public Law Litigation." *Harvard Law Review* 89: 1281.

Chevigny, Paul G. 1981. "The Paradox of Campaign Finance." *N.Y.U. Law Review* 56: 206.

Clagett, Brice M., and John R. Bolton. 1976. "Buckley v. Valeo, Its Aftermath, and Its Prospects: The Constitutionality of Government Restraints on Political Campaign Financing." *Vanderbilt Law Review* 29: 1327.

Clarke, John H. 1923. "Judicial Power to Declare Legislation Unconstitutional." *A.B.A. Journal* 9: 689.

Coben, Stanley. 1963. *A. Mitchell Palmer: Politician*. New York: Columbia University Press.

Commager, Henry Steele. 1950. *The American Mind: An Interpretation of American Thought and Character Since the 1880's*. New Haven: Yale University Press.

Connor, Henry Groves. 1920. *John Archibald Campbell, Associate Justice of the United States Supreme Court, 1853–1861*. Boston: Houghton Mifflin Company.

Cooley, Thomas M. 1893. "Grave Obstacles to Hawaiian Annexation." *The Forum* 15: 389.

———. 1880. *The General Principles of Constitutional Law in the United States of America*. Boston: Little, Brown and Company.

———. [1871] 1878. *Constitutional Limitations*. 4th ed. Boston: Little, Brown and Company.

———. 1873. "Notes and Editions." In *Commentaries on the Constitution of the United States* edited by Joseph Story. 4th ed. Boston: Little, Brown, and Company.

Corwin, Edward S. 1952. "Bowing Out 'Clear and Present Danger.' " *Notre Dame Lawyer* 27: 325.

———. 1941. *Constitutional Revolution, Ltd.* Claremont, Calif.: Claremont College.

———. 1938. *Court Over Constitution: A Study of Judicial Review as an Instrument of Popular Government*. Princeton: Princeton University Press.

———. 1934. *The Twilight of the Supreme Court: A History of Our Constitutional Theory*. New Haven: Yale University Press.

———. 1920a. "Freedom of Speech and Press under the First Amendment: A Resume." *Yale Law Journal* 30: 48.

———. 1920b. "Constitutional Law in 1919–20." *American Political Science Review* 14: 635.

Cover, Robert M. 1981. "The Left, the Right, and the First Amendment: 1918–28." *Maryland Law Review* 40: 349.

Cox, Archibald. 1981. *Freedom of Expression*. Cambridge: Harvard University Press.

———. 1980. "Foreword: Freedom of Expression in the Burger Court." *Harvard Law Review* 94: 1.

Crews, Kenneth D. 1985. *Edward S. Corwin and the American Constitution: A Bibliographical Analysis*. Westport, Conn.: Greenwood Press.

Crick, Bernard R. 1959. *The American Science of Politics: Its Origins and Conditions*. Berkeley: University of California Press.

Croly, Herbert. [1909] 1965. *The Promise of American Life*. Reprint. Indianapolis: Bobbs-Merrill Company.

Croly, Herbert, et al. 1919. "Freedom of Speech: Whose Concern?" *New Republic* 18: 102.

———. 1918a. "Editorial Notes." *New Republic* 16: 239.

———. 1918b. "The Issue and Our Critics." *New Republic* 16: 339.

———. 1917a. "Editorial Notes." *New Republic* 11: 314.

———. 1917b. "Editorial Notes." *New Republic* 12: 227.

———. 1917c. "Public Opinion in War Time." *New Republic* 12: 255.

———. 1917d. "A War Program for Liberals." *New Republic* 10: 249.

———. 1917e. "War Propaganda." *New Republic* 12: 204.

Curtis, Michael Kent. 1986. *No State Shall Abridge: The Fourteenth Amendment and the Bill of Rights*. Durham, N.C.: Duke University Press.

Dahl, Robert A. 1989. *Democracy and Its Critics*. New Haven: Yale University Press.

———. 1970. *After the Revolution?: Authority in a Good Society*. New Haven: Yale University Press.

———. 1961. *Who Governs? Democracy and Power in an American City*. New Haven: Yale University Press.

———. 1956. *A Preface to Democratic Theory*. Chicago: University of Chicago Press.

Damico, Alfonso J. 1978. *Individuality and Community: The Social and Political Thought of John Dewey*. Gainesville: University Presses of Florida.

Darrow, Clarence S. 1895. "Brief and Argument for Petitioners." *In re Debs*, 158 U.S. 564, 571.

Dawson, John B. 1915. "Brief and Argument of Appellees." *Mutual Film Corp. v. Industrial Commission of Ohio*, 236 U.S. 230.

Debs v. United States. 1919. Transcript of Record. 249 U.s. 211.

Dewey, John. 1969. "The Ethics of Democracy." *John Dewey: The Early Works, 1882–1898*. Carbondale: Southern Illinois University Press, Fefler and Simons.

———. 1950. *Reconstruction in Philosophy*. New York: Mentor Books.

———. 1939. *Freedom and Culture*. New York: G. P. Putnam's Sons.

———. 1935. *Liberalism & Social Action*. New York: Capricorn Books.

———. 1934. *A Common Faith*. New Haven: Yale University Press.

———. 1929a and 1929b. *Characters and Events: Popular Essays in Social and Political Philosophy*. Vols. I and II. Edited by Joseph Ratner. New York: Henry Holt and Company.

———. 1928. "Philosophies of Freedom." *Freedom in the Modern World*. Edited by Horace M. Kallen. New York: Coward-McCann.

———. 1927. *The Public and Its Problems*. Chicago: Swallow Press.

———. 1916. *Democracy and Education*. New York: Free Press.

Dewey, John, and James H. Tufts. 1913. *Ethics*. New York: Henry Holt and Company.

Dickson, William H. 1907. "Brief of Defendant in Error." *Patterson v. Colorado*, 205 U.S. 454.

Dillon, John F. 1881. *Commentaries on the Law of Municipal Corporations*. 3d ed. Boston: Little, Brown.

Donohue, William A. 1985. *The Politics of the American Civil Liberties Union*. New Brunswick, N.J.: Transaction Books.

Dorsen, Norman. 1988. "The Need for a New Enlightenment: Lessons in Liberty from the Eighteenth Century." *Case Western Law Review* 38: 479.

———. 1984. "Introduction." In *Our Endangered Rights*, edited by Norman Dorsen. New York: Pantheon Books.

Dorsen, Norman, and Joel Gora. 1983. "The Burger Court and the Freedom of Speech." In *The Burger Court: The Counter-Revolution That Wasn't*, edited by Vincent Blasi. New Haven: Yale University Press.

Douglas, William O. 1958. *The Right of the People*. Garden City, N.Y.: Doubleday & Company.

Dowell, Eldridge Foster. 1939. *A History of Criminal Syndicalism Legislation in the United States*. Baltimore: Johns Hopkins University Press.

Downs, Donald Alexander. 1985. *Nazis in Skokie: Freedom, Community, and the First Amendment*. Notre Dame, Ind.: University of Notre Dame Press.

Drew, Elizabeth. 1983. *Politics and Money: The New Road to Corruption*. New York: MacMillan Publishing Company.

Drinnon, Richard. 1961. *Rebel in Paradise: A Biography of Emma Goldman*. Chicago: University of Chicago Press.

Dworkin, Ronald. 1986. *Law's Empire*. Cambridge: Harvard University Press.

———. 1985. *A Matter of Principle*. Cambridge: Harvard University Press.

———. 1978. *Taking Rights Seriously*. Cambridge: Harvard University Press.

Edsall, Thomas Byrne. 1984. *The New Politics of Inequality*. New York: W. W. Norton & Company.

Ely, John Hart. 1980. *Democracy and Distrust: A Theory of Judicial Review*. Cambridge: Harvard University Press.

Emerson, Thomas I. 1981. "The Affirmative Side of the First Amendment." *Georgia Law Review* 15: 795.

———. 1980. "First Amendment Doctrine and the Burger Court." *California Law Review* 68: 422.

———. 1977. "Colonial Intentions and the First Amendment." *University of Pennsylvania Law Review* 125: 737.

———. 1970. *The System of Freedom of Expression.* New York: Vintage Books.

———. 1968. "Freedom of Expression in Wartime." *University of Pennsylvania Law Review* 116: 975.

———. 1966. *Toward a General Theory of the First Amendment.* New York: Random House.

Epstein, Richard A. 1985. *Takings: Private Property and the Power of Eminent Domain.* Cambridge: Harvard University Press.

Faulkner, Harold U. 1959. *Politics, Reform and Expansion.* New York: Harper & Row.

Ferguson, Thomas, and Joel Rogers. 1986. *Right Turn: The Decline of the Democrats and the Future of American Politics.* New York: Hill and Wang.

Fine, Sidney. 1956. *Laissez-Faire and the General Welfare State: A Study of Conflict in American Thought 1865–1901.* Ann Arbor: University of Michigan Press.

Fishkin, James S. 1984. "Defending Equality: A View from the Cave." *Michigan Law Review* 82: 755.

Fiss, Owen M. 1987. "Why the State?" *Harvard Law Review* 100: 781.

———. 1986. "Free Speech and Social Structure." *Iowa Law Review* 71: 1405.

Flathman, Richard E. 1989. *Towards a Liberalism.* Ithaca, N.Y.: Cornell University Press.

Fleishman, Joel L. 1975. "The 1974 Federal Election Campaign Act Amendments: The Shortcomings of Good Intentions." *Duke Law Journal* 1975: 851.

Fleishman, Joel L., and Pope McCorkle. 1984. "Level-Up Rather Than Level-Down: Towards a New Theory of Campaign Finance Reform." *Journal of Law and Politics* 1: 211.

Frank, Jerome. 1931. *Law and the Modern Mind.* New York: Brentano's.

Frankfurter, Felix. 1965. "Memorandum on 'Incorporation' of the Bill of Rights into the Due Process Clause of the Fourteenth Amendment." *Harvard Law Review* 78: 746.

———. 1961. "A Legal Triptych." *Harvard Law Review* 74: 433.

———. 1938. *Mr. Justice Holmes and the Supreme Court.* Cambridge: Harvard University Press.

Freund, Ernst. 1973. "The *Debs* Case." *University of Chicago Law Review* 40: 239.

―――. 1928. *Administrative Powers over Persons and Property.* Chicago: University of Chicago Press.

―――. 1921. "Freedom of Speech and Press." *New Republic* 25: 344.

―――. 1916. "Principles of Legislation." *American Political Science Review* 10: 1.

―――. 1904. *The Police Power, Public Policy and Constitutional Rights.* Chicago: Callaghan & Co.

Freund, Paul A. 1972. "Commentary." In *Federal Regulation of Campaign Finance: Some Constitutional Questions,* edited by Albert J. Rosenthal. Princeton, N.J.: Citizens' Research Foundation.

Friedman, Lawrence M. 1985. *A History of American Law.* 2d ed. New York: Simon & Schuster.

Gamer, Robert E. 1965. "Justice Brewer and Substantive Due Process: A Conservative Court Revisited." *Vanderbilt Law Review* 18: 615.

Garrett, G. P. 1919. "Free Speech and the Espionage Act." *Journal of Criminal Law and Criminology* 10: 71.

Geertz, Clifford. 1973. *The Interpretation of Cultures: Selected Essays.* New York: Basic Books.

Ginger, Ray. 1958. *Altgeld's America: The Lincoln Ideal Versus Changing Realities.* Chicago: Quadrangle Books.

Ginsburg, Douglas H. 1973. "Afterword." *University of Chicago Law Review* 40: 243.

Gleason, Philip. 1982. "American Identity and Americanization." In *Dimensions of Ethnicity,* edited by Stephen Thernstrom. Cambridge: Belknap Press of Harvard University Press.

Godkin, E. L. 1900. "Our Conquests and the Constitution." *Nation* 70: 104.

―――. 1890. "The Rights of the Citizen: IV.—To His Own Reputation." *Scribner's Magazine* 8: 58.

―――. 1899a. "Incendiary Literature." *Nation* 68: 346.

―――. 1899b. "Suppression." *Nation* 68: 388.

―――. 1893. "Naval Politics." *Nation* 56: 173.

―――. 1887. "The Execution of the Anarchists." *Nation* 44: 366.

Goedecke, Robert. 1965. "Justice Field and Inherent Rights." *Review of Politics* 27: 198.

Goldman, Emma. 1982. *Red Emma Speaks: An Emma Goldman Reader.* Edited by Alix Kate Shulman. New York: Schocken Books.

―――. 1932. *Living My Life.* London: Duckworth.

Goldman, Eric. 1955. *Rendezvous with Destiny: A History of Modern American Reform.* Rev. ed. New York: Alfred A. Knopf.

Goldstein, Robert. 1978. *Political Repression in Modern America: From 1870 to the Present.* Cambridge, Mass.: Schenkman Press Co.

Goodrich, Herbert F. 1921. "Does the Constitution Protect Free Speech?" *Michigan Law Review* 19: 487.

Gordon, Robert W. 1984. "Critical Legal Histories." *Stanford Law Review* 36: 57.

————. 1982. "New Developments in Legal Theory." In *The Politics of Law: A Progressive Critique*, edited by David Kairys. New York: Pantheon Books.

————. 1981. "Historicism in Legal Scholarship." *Yale Law Journal* 90: 1017.

Graber, Mark A. 1989. "Our (Im)Perfect Constitution." *Review of Politics* 10: 86.

————. 1988. "The Transformation of the Modern Constitutional Defense of Free Speech." Ph.D. diss., Yale University.

Graham, Otis L., Jr. 1967. *An Encore for Reform: The Old Progressives and the New Deal.* London: Oxford University Press.

Greenawalt, Kent. 1989. "Free Speech Justifications." *Columbia Law Review* 89: 119.

————. 1980. "Speech and Crime." *American Bar Foundation Research Journal* 1980: 645.

Grimes, Alan Pendleton. 1953. *The Political Liberalism of the New York Nation, 1865–1932.* Chapel Hill: University of North Carolina Press.

Gunther, Gerald. 1985. *Constitutional Law.* 11th ed. Mineola, N.Y.: Foundation Press.

————. 1975. "Learned Hand and the Origins of Modern First Amendment Doctrine: Some Fragments of History." *Stanford Law Review* 27: 718.

Gutfeld, Aaron. 1968. "The Ves Hall Case, Judge Bourquin, and the Sedition Act of 1918." *Pacific Historical Review* 37: 163.

Guthrie, William D. 1898. *Lectures on the Fourteenth Article of Amendment to the Constitution of the United States.* Boston: Little, Brown.

Guthrie, William D., and Bernard Hershkopf. 1925. "Brief on Behalf of Appellee." *Pierce v. Society of Sisters*, 268 U.S. 510.

Habermas, Jürgen. 1979. *Communication and the Evolution of Society.* Translated by Thomas McCarthy. Boston: Beacon Press.

Haig, Alfred Roland. 1891. "The Right of Criticism and Faire Comment." *American Law Register* 39: 517.

Haiman, Franklyn Saul. 1981. *Speech and Law in a Free Society.* Chicago: University of Chicago Press.

Hall, James Parker. 1921. "Free Speech in War Time." *Columbia Law Review* 21: 526.

———. 1917. *Constitutional Law.* Chicago: LaSalle Extension University.

Hallam, Henry. 1847. *The Constitutional History of England from the Accession of Henry VII to the Death of George II.* New York: Harper & Brothers.

Hamilton, Alexander, James Madison, and John Jay. 1961. *The Federalist Papers.* New York: New American Library.

Hand, Learned. 1963. *The Bill of Rights.* New York: Atheneum.

———. 1953. *The Spirit of Liberty: Papers and Addresses of Learned Hand.* Edited by Irving Dillard. 2d ed. New York: Alfred A. Knopf.

Hartz, Louis. 1955. *The Liberal Tradition in America.* New York: Harcourt Brace Jovanovich.

Higham, John. 1978. *Strangers in the Land: Patterns of American Nativism, 1860–1925.* New York: Atheneum.

Hilton, Clifford L., and James E. Markham. 1920. "Brief and Argument for Defendant in Error." *Gilbert v. Minnesota,* 254 U.S. 325.

Hilton, O. A. 1951. *The Minnesota Commission of Public Safety in World War I, 1917–1919.* Stillwater: Oklahoma Agricultural and Mechanical College.

———. 1948. "Freedom of the Press in Wartime, 1917–1919." *Southwestern Social Science Quarterly* 28: 346.

———. 1947. "Public Opinion and Civil Liberties in Wartime, 1917–1919." *Southwestern Social Science Quarterly* 58: 201.

Hofstadter, Richard. 1973. *The American Political Tradition and the Men Who Made It.* New York: Vintage Books.

———. 1955a. *The Age of Reform: From Bryan to F.D.R.* New York: Vintage Books.

———. 1955b. *Social Darwinism in American Thought.* Rev. ed. Boston: Beacon Press.

Holmes, Oliver Wendell, Jr. 1963. *The Common Law.* Edited by Mark DeWolfe Howe. Boston: Little, Brown.

———. 1936. *Justice Oliver Wendell Holmes: His Book Notices and Uncollected Letters and Papers.* Edited by Harry C. Shriver. New York: Central Book Co.

———. 1934. *Speeches.* Boston: Little, Brown.

———. 1920. *Collected Legal Papers.* New York: Harcourt, Brace and Company.

Holmes, Oliver Wendell, Jr., and Harold J. Laski. 1963a and 1963b. *Holmes–Laski Letters.* Vols. I and II. Edited by Mark DeWolfe Howe and abridged by Alger Hiss. New York: Atheneum.

Holmes, Oliver Wendell, Jr., and Sir Frederick Pollock. 1941. *Holmes-Pollock Letters: The Correspondence of Mr. Justice Holmes and Sir Frederick Pollock, 1874–1932.* Volume Two. Edited by Mark DeWolfe Howe. Cambridge: Harvard University Press.

Hook, Sidney. 1940. *Reason, Social Myths, and Democracy.* New York: John Day Company.

Howe, Mark Anthony DeWolfe. 1932. *Portrait of an Independent, Moorfield Storey, 1845–1929.* Boston: Houghton Mifflin Company.

Howe, Mark DeWolfe. 1963. *Justice Oliver Wendell Holmes: The Proving Years, 1870–1882.* Cambridge: Belknap Press of Harvard University Press.

———. 1957. "Zechariah Chafee, Jr. (1885–1957)." *Nation* 184: 183.

Huntington, Samuel P. 1981. *American Politics: The Promise of Disharmony.* Cambridge: Belknap Press of Harvard University Press.

———. 1968. *Political Order in Changing Societies.* New Haven: Yale University Press.

Hurst, James Willard. 1956. *Law and the Conditions of Freedom in the Nineteenth-Century United States.* Madison: University of Wisconsin Press.

Hyman, Harold M. 1960. *To Try Men's Souls: Loyalty Tests in American History.* Berkeley: University of California Press.

Hyman, Harold M., and William M. Wiecek. 1982. *Equal Justice under Law: Constitutional Development, 1835–1875.* New York: Harper & Row.

Jacobs, Clyde E. 1954. *Law Writers and the Courts.* Berkeley: University of California Press.

Jacobson, Gary C. 1980. *Money in Congressional Elections.* New Haven: Yale University Press.

Jaffa, Henry V. 1970. "On the Nature of Civil and Religious Liberty." In *American Conservative Thought in the Twentieth Century,* edited by William F. Buckley, Jr. Indianapolis: Bobbs-Merrill Company.

Jefferson, Thomas. 1975. *The Portable Thomas Jefferson.* Edited by Merrill D. Peterson. Middlesex, England: Penguin Books.

Jensen, Joan. 1968. *The Price of Vigilance.* Chicago: Rand McNally & Company.

Johnson, Donald. 1963. *The Challenge to American Freedoms: World War I and the Rise of the American Civil Liberties Union.* Lexington: University of Kentucky Press.

Johnson, John G., William Gooch, Herbert C. Smyth, and Frederick Scofield. 1908. "Brief for Plaintiff in Error, Albert G. Twining." *Twining v. New Jersey,* 211 U.S. 78.

Jones, Alan. 1967. "Thomas Cooley and 'Laissez-Faire Constitutionalism': A Reconsideration." *Journal of American History* 53: 751.

Judson, Frederick N. 1913. *The Judiciary and the People*. New Haven: Yale University Press.

———. 1891. "Liberty of Contract Under the Police Power." *American Law Review* 25: 871.

Kaczorowski, Robert J. 1985. *The Politics of Judicial Interpretation: The Federal Courts, Department of Justice and Civil Rights, 1866–1876*. Dobbs Ferry, N.Y.: Oceana Publications.

Kairys, David. 1982. "Freedom of Speech." In *The Politics of Law: A Progressive Critique*, edited by David Kairys. New York: Pantheon Books.

Kallen, Horace Mayer. 1977. "Zionism and Liberalism." In *The Zionist Idea: A Historical Analysis and Reader*, edited by Arthur Hertzberg. New York: Atheneum.

———. 1928. "Why Freedom Is a Problem." In *Freedom in the Modern World*, edited by Horace M. Kallen. New York: Coward-McCann.

———. 1924. *Culture and Democracy in the United States: Studies in the Group Psychology of the American Peoples*. New York: Boni and Liveright.

Kalven, Harry, Jr. 1988. *A Worthy Tradition: Freedom of Speech in America*. Edited by Jamie Kalven. New York: Harper & Row.

———. 1973. "Professor Ernst Freund and *Debs v. United States*." *University of Chicago Law Review* 40: 235.

———. 1967. "Broadcasting, Public Policy and the First Amendment." *Journal of Law and Economics* 10: 15.

———. 1965. *The Negro and the First Amendment*. Chicago: University of Chicago Press.

———. 1964. "The New York Times Case: A Note on the Central Meaning of the First Amendment." *Supreme Court Review* 1964: 191.

———. 1960. "The Metaphysics of the Law of Obscenity." *Supreme Court Review* 1960: 1.

Kammen, Michael. 1986. *A Machine That Would Go of Itself: The Constitution in American Culture*. New York: Vintage Books.

Karst, Kenneth L. 1975. "Equality as a Central Principle in the First Amendment." *University of Chicago Law Review* 43: 20.

Keller, Morton. 1977. *Affairs of State: Public Life in Late Nineteenth Century America*. Cambridge: Belknap Press of Harvard University Press.

Kellor, Frances A. 1918. *Neighborhood Americanization: A Discussion of the Alien in a New Country and of the Native American in His Home Country*. New York: National Americanization Committee.

————. 1916. *Straight America, a Call to National Service.* New York: Macmillan.

Kelly, Alfred, Winfred A. Harbison, and Herman Belz. 1983. *The American Constitution: Its Origins and Development.* 6th ed. New York: W. W. Norton & Company.

Kennedy, David M. 1980. *Over Here: The First World War and American Society.* Oxford: Oxford University Press.

————. 1970. *Birth Control in America: The Case of Margaret Sanger.* New Haven: Yale University Press.

Kimball, Day K. 1920. "The Espionage Act and the Limits of Legal Toleration." *Harvard Law Review* 33: 442.

King, Willard L. 1967. *Melville Weston Fuller: Chief Justice of the United States, 1888–1910.* Chicago: University of Chicago Press.

Knowlton, Hosea M., and George C. Travis. 1897. "Brief of Defendant in Error." *Davis v. Massachusetts,* 167 U.S. 43.

Kolko, Gabriel. 1963. *The Triumph of Conservatism.* New York: Macmillan.

Konefsky, Samuel Joseph. 1956. *The Legacy of Holmes and Brandeis: A Study in the Influence of Ideas.* New York: Macmillan.

Kraines, Oscar. 1974. *The World and Ideas of Ernst Freund: The Search for General Principles of Legislation and Administrative Law.* University: University of Alabama Press.

Lamson, Peggy. 1976. *Roger Baldwin.* Boston: Houghton Mifflin Company.

Lange, David L. 1973. "The Role of the Access Doctrine in the Regulation of the Mass Media: A Critical Review and Assessment." *North Carolina Law Review* 52: 1.

Lasch, Christopher. 1965. *The New Radicalism in America (1889–1963): The Intellectual as a Social Type.* New York: Vintage Books.

Law, Sylvia A. 1984. "Economic Justice." In *Our Endangered Rights,* edited by Norman Dorsen. New York: Pantheon Books.

Lawrence, Thomas A. 1974. "Eclipse of Liberty: Civil Liberties in the United States During the First World War." *Wayne State Law Review* 21: 33.

Lerner, Max. 1943. *The Mind and Faith of Justice Holmes: His Speeches, Essays, Letters and Judicial Opinions.* Boston: Little, Brown.

Leventhal, Harold. 1977. "Courts and Political Thickets." *Columbia Law Review* 77: 345.

Levinson, Sanford. 1988. *Constitutional Faith.* Princeton: Princeton University Press.

Levy, Leonard W. 1985. *Emergence of a Free Press.* New York: Oxford University Press.

———. 1963. *Freedom of Speech and Press in Early American History: Legacy of Suppression.* New York: Harper & Row.

Lewis, Anthony. 1983. "*New York Times v. Sullivan* Reconsidered: Time to Return to 'The Central Meaning of the First Amendment,' " *Columbia Law Review* 83: 603.

Lindblom, Charles E. 1977. *Politics and Markets: The World's Political-Economic Systems.* New York: Basic Books.

Lippmann, Walter. 1922. *Public Opinion.* New York: Free Press.

Lipset, Seymour Martin, and Earl Raab. 1978. *The Politics of Unreason: Right-Wing Extremism in America, 1790–1977.* Chicago: University of Chicago Press.

Livermore, Seward W. 1966. *Woodrow Wilson and the War Congress.* Seattle: University of Washington Press.

Llewellyn, Karl N. 1919. "Free Speech in Time of Peace." *Yale Law Journal* 29: 337.

Loewy, Arnold H. 1989. "The Flag-Burning Case: Freedom of Speech When We Need It the Most." *North Carolina Law Review* 68: 165.

Lusky, Louis. 1982. "Footnote Redux: A *Carolene Products* Reminiscence." *Columbia Law Review* 82: 1093.

———. 1975. *By What Right?: A Commentary on the Supreme Court's Power to Revise the Constitution.* Charlottesville, Va.: Michie Co.

———. 1942. "Minority Rights and the Public Interest." *Yale Law Journal* 52: 1.

Lustig, R. Jeffrey. 1982. *Corporate Liberalism: The Origins of Modern American Political Theory, 1890–1920.* Berkeley: University of California Press.

Madison, James, 1973. *The Mind of the Founder: Sources of the Political Thought of James Madison.* Edited by Marvin Meyers. Indianapolis: Bobbs-Merrill Company.

March, James G., and Johan P. Olsen. 1978. "The New Institutionalism: Organizational Factors in Political Life." *American Political Science Review* 78: 734.

Marshall, Burke. 1987. "Book Review: On Learning to Love Vituperation." *Yale Law Journal* 96: 1687.

Martin, Charles H. 1976. *The Angelo Herndon Case and Southern Justice.* Baton Rouge: Louisiana State University Press.

Mason, Alpheus Thomas. 1956. "The Core of Free Government, 1938–1940: Mr. Justice Stone and 'Preferred Freedoms.' " *Yale Law Journal* 65: 597.

———. 1955. *Security Through Freedom: American Political Thought and Practice.* Ithaca: Cornell University Press.

McCloskey, Robert Green. 1951. *American Conservatism in the Age of Enterprise, 1865–1910*. New York: Harper & Row.

McClosky, Herbert. 1964. "Consensus and Ideology in American Politics." *American Political Science Review* 58: 361.

McClosky, Herbert, and Alida Brill. 1983. *Dimensions of Tolerance: What Americans Believe about Civil Liberties*. New York: Russell Sage Foundation.

McCurdy, Charles W. 1979. "The *Knight* Decision of 1895 and the Modernization of American Corporate Law." *Business History Review* 53: 304.

McKay, Robert B. 1959. "The Preference for Freedom." *N.Y.U. Law Review* 34: 1182.

Meiklejohn, Alexander. 1961. "The First Amendment Is an Absolute." *Supreme Court Review* 1961: 245.

————. 1960. *Political Freedom: The Constitutional Powers of the People*. New York: Oxford University Press.

Mendelson, Wallace. 1952. "Clear and Present Danger—From *Schenck* to *Dennis*." *Columbia Law Review* 52: 313.

Michelman, Frank I. 1979. "Welfare Rights in a Constitutional Democracy." *Washington University Law Quarterly* 1979: 659.

————. 1973. "In Pursuit of Constitutional Welfare Rights: One View of Rawls' Theory of Justice." *University of Pennsylvania Law Review* 121: 962.

Mill, James. 1913. *On Liberty of the Press*. New York: Free Speech League.

Miller, Loren. 1967. *The Petitioners: The Story of the Supreme Court of the United States and the Negro*. Cleveland: Meridian Books.

Minor, John Barbee. 1882. *Institutes of Common and Statute Law*. Richmond: Privately printed.

Moley, Raymond, Jr. 1966. *The American Legion Story*. New York: Duell, Sloan and Pearce.

Morlan, Robert Loren. 1955. *Political Prairie Fire: The Nonpartisan League, 1915–1922*. Minneapolis: University of Minnesota Press.

Murphy, Paul L. 1979. *World War I and the Origin of Civil Liberties in the United States*. New York: W. W. Norton & Company.

————. 1972. *The Meaning of Freedom of Speech: First Amendment Freedoms from Wilson to FDR*. Westport, Conn.: Greenwood Press.

Murray, Robert K. 1955. *Red Scare: A Study in National Hysteria, 1919–1920*. New York: McGraw-Hill Book Company.

Nash, George H. 1976. *The Conservative Intellectual Movement in America Since 1945*. New York: Basic Books.

Nelles, Walter. 1940. *A Liberal in Wartime: The Education of Albert DeSilver.* Edited by Louis Gannett. New York: W. W. Norton & Company.

———. 1918. *Espionage Act Cases—With Certain Others on Related Points.* New York: National Civil Liberties Bureau.

Neuborne, Burt. 1988. "Notes for a Theory of Constrained Balancing in First Amendment Cases: An Essay in Honor of Tom Emerson." *Case Western Law Review* 38: 576.

Nicholson, Marlene Arnold. 1988. "Basic Principles or Theoretical Tangles: Analyzing the Constitutionality of Government Regulation of Campaign Finance." *Case Western Law Review* 38: 589.

———. 1974. "Campaign Financing and Equal Protection." *Stanford Law Review* 26: 815.

Nimmer, Melville A. 1984. *Nimmer on Freedom of Speech: A Treatise on the First Amendment.* Student ed. New York: Matthew Bender.

Noble, David W. 1981. *The Progressive Mind, 1890–1917.* Rev. ed. Minneapolis: Burgess Publishing Company.

Note. 1931. "Previous Restraints Upon Freedom of Speech." *Columbia Law Review* 31: 1148.

Note. 1916. "Constitutional Law—Freedom of Speech and of the Press—Recent Decisions." *University of Pennsylvania Law Review* 65: 170.

Page, George T. 1919. "Government." *A.B.A. Journal* 5: 527.

Paper, Louis. 1983. *Brandeis.* Secaucus, N.J.: Citadel Press.

Parker, Alton B. 1914. "The Citizen and the Constitution." *Yale Law Journal* 23: 631.

———. 1904. "Reply." In *Anti-Imperialism: The Great Issue.* Boston: New England Anti-Imperialist League.

Parrington, Vernon Louis. 1930. *The Beginnings of Critical Realism in America, 1860–1920.* New York: Harcourt, Brace & World.

Parsons, Talcott. 1955. "Social Strains in America." In *The New American Right,* edited by Daniel Bell. New York: Criterion Books.

Paschal, Joel Francis. 1951. *Mr. Justice Sutherland: A Man Against the State.* Princeton: Princeton University Press.

Paul, Arnold M. 1960. *Conservative Crisis and the Rule of Law.* Ithaca: Cornell University Press.

Paxson, Frederick L., Edward S. Corwin, and Samuel B. Harding, eds. 1918. *War Cyclopedia: A Handbook for Ready Reference on the Great War.* Washington, D.C.: Government Printing Office.

Peltason, Jack W. 1955. *Federal Courts in the Political Process.* New York: Random House.

Pencak, William. 1989. *For God and Country: The American Legion, 1919–1941.* Boston: Northeastern University Press.

Perry, Michael J. 1982. *The Constitution, the Courts, and Human Rights: An Inquiry into the Legitimacy of Constitutional Policymaking by the Judiciary.* New Haven: Yale University Press.

Peterson, H. C., and Gilbert C. Fite. 1957. *Opponents of War, 1917–1918.* Madison: University of Wisconsin Press.

Pickering, James F. 1897. "Brief for Plaintiff in Error." *Davis v. Massachusetts,* 167 U.S. 43.

Piven, Frances Fox, and Richard A. Cloward. 1989. *Why Americans Don't Vote.* New York: Pantheon.

Polenberg, Richard. 1987. *Fighting Faiths: The Abrams Case, the Supreme Court, and Free Speech.* New York: Viking.

Pollak, Walter H., and Walter Nelles. 1925. "Brief for Plaintiff in Error." *Gitlow v. New York,* 268 U.S. 650.

Polsby, Daniel D. 1977. "Buckley v. Valeo: The Special Nature of Political Speech." *Supreme Court Review* 1976: 1.

Pomeroy, John Norton. 1870. *An Introduction to the Constitutional Law of the United States.* New York: Hurd and Houghton.

Pool, Ithiel de Sola. 1983. *Technologies of Freedom.* Cambridge: Harvard University Press.

Posner, Richard A. 1977. *Economic Analysis of Law.* Boston: Little, Brown.

Pound, Roscoe. 1954. *An Introduction to the Philosophy of Law.* New Haven: Yale University Press.

———. 1916. "Equitable Relief Against Defamation and Injuries to Personality." *Harvard Law Review* 29: 640.

———. 1915. "Interests of Personality." *Harvard Law Review* 28: 343, 445.

———. 1910–11. "The Scope and Purpose of Sociological Jurisprudence." Parts 1, 2. *Harvard Law Review* 24: 591; 25: 140, 489.

———. 1909. "Liberty of Contract." *Yale Law Journal* 18: 454.

———. 1908a. "Mechanical Jurisprudence." *Columbia Law Review* 8: 605.

———. 1908b. "Editorial Notes." *Illinois Law Review* 3: 38.

———. 1908c. "Common Law and Legislation." *Harvard Law Review* 21: 383.

Powe, L. A., Jr. 1988. "Tornillo." *Supreme Court Review* 1987: 345.

———. 1987a. *American Broadcasting and the First Amendment.* Berkeley: University of California Press.

———. 1987b. "Scholarship and Markets." *George Washington Law Review* 56: 172.

————. 1983. "Mass Speech and the Newer First Amendment." *Supreme Court Review* 1982: 243.

————. 1974. "Evolution to Absolutism: Justice Douglas and the First Amendment." *Columbia Law Review* 74: 371.

Preston, William. 1963. *Aliens and Dissenters*. Cambridge: Harvard University Press.

Price, David E. 1974. "Community and Control: Critical Democratic Theory in the Progressive Period." *American Political Science Review* 68: 1663.

Prude, Jonathan. 1973. "Portrait of a Civil Libertarian: The Faith and Fear of Zechariah Chafee, Jr." *Journal of American History* 60: 633.

Purcell, Edward A., Jr. 1975. *The Crisis of Democratic Theory: Scientific Naturalism and the Problem of Value*. Lexington: University Press of Kentucky.

Quandt, Jean B. 1970. *From the Small Town to the Great Community: The Social Thought of Progressive Intellectuals*. New Brunswick, N.J.: Rutgers University Press.

Rabban, David M. 1987. "The Free Speech League and the Origins of the ACLU." Paper presented at the meeting of the Organization of American Historians, Philadelphia, Pa.

————. 1985. "The Ahistorical Historian: Leonard Levy on Freedom of Expression in Early American History." *Stanford Law Review* 37: 795.

————. 1983. "The Emergence of Modern First Amendment Doctrine." *University of Chicago Law Review* 50: 1205.

————. 1981. "The First Amendment in its Forgotten Years." *Yale Law Journal* 90: 516.

Radosh, Richard. 1975. *Prophets on the Right*. New York: Simon and Schuster.

Rae, Douglas et al. 1981. *Equalities*. Cambridge: Harvard University Press.

Ragan, Fred. 1971. "Justice Oliver Wendell Holmes, Jr., Zechariah Chafee, Jr., and the Clear and Present Danger Test for Free Speech: The First Year." *Journal of American History* 58: 24.

Re, Edward D. 1981. "Preface." In *Freedom's Prophet: Selected Writings of Zechariah Chafee Jr., University Professor, Harvard Law School*, edited by Edward D. Re. London: Oceana Publications.

Redish, Martin H. 1984. *Freedom of Expression: A Critical Analysis*. Charlottesville, Va.: Michie Company.

————. 1971. "Campaign Spending Laws and the First Amendment." *N.Y.U. Law Review* 46: 900.

Roalfe, William R. 1977. *John Henry Wigmore: Scholar and Reformer*. Evanston, Ill.: Northwestern University Press.

Roche, John P. 1964. *Shadow and Substance: Essays on the Theory and Structure of Politics.* London: Collier-Macmillan Ltd.

———. 1963a. *The Quest for the Dream: The Development of Civil Rights and Human Relations in Modern America.* Chicago: Quadrangle Books.

———. 1963b. "Civil Liberties in the Age of Enterprise." *University of Chicago Law Review* 31: 103.

Rogat, Yosal. 1964. "The Judge as Spectator." *University of Chicago Law Review* 31: 213.

———. 1962–63. "Mr. Justice Holmes: A Dissenting Opinion." *Stanford Law Review* 15: 3, 254.

Rogat, Yosal, and James M. O'Fallon. 1984. "Mr. Justice Holmes: A Dissenting Opinion—The Speech Cases." *Stanford Law Review* 36: 1349.

Rogin, Michael Paul. 1967. *The Intellectuals and McCarthy: The Radical Specter.* Cambridge: M.I.T. Press.

Root, Elihu. 1958. "Experiments in Government." In *Great Issues in American History.* Vol. II. Edited by Richard Hofstadter. New York: Vintage Books.

Rorty, Richard. 1989. *Contingency, Irony, and Solidarity.* Cambridge: Cambridge University Press.

Rosenberg, Norman L. 1986. *Protecting the Best Men: An Interpretive History of the Law of Libel.* Chapel Hill: University of North Carolina Press.

Rosenthal, Albert J. 1972. *Federal Regulation of Campaign Finance: Some Constitutional Questions.* Princeton, N.J.: Citizens' Research Foundation.

Ross, Edward Alsworth. 1915. "Freedom of Communication and the Struggle for Right." In *Publications of the American Sociological Society.* Vol. 9. Chicago: University of Chicago Press.

Rossiter, Clinton. 1962. *Conservatism in America: The Thankless Persuasion.* 2d. ed. New York: Vintage Books.

Rostow, Eugene. 1952. "The Democratic Character of Judicial Review." *Harvard Law Review* 66: 193.

Salomon, M., W. P. Black, Roger A. Pryor, and J. Randolph Tucker. 1887. "The Petition for Writ of Error." *Spies v. Illinois*, 123 U.S. 131.

Schauer, Frederick. 1982. *Free Speech: A Philosophical Enquiry.* Cambridge: Cambridge University Press.

Scheiber, Harry N. 1960. *The Wilson Administration and Civil Liberties, 1917–21.* Ithaca: Cornell University Press.

Schenck v. United States. 1919. Transcript of Record. 249 U.S. 47.

Schick, Marvin. 1970. *Learned Hand's Court.* Baltimore: Johns Hopkins University Press.

Schofield, Henry. 1921. *Essays on Constitutional Law and Equity.* Edited by The Faculty of Law, Northwestern University. Boston: Chipman Law Publishing Company.

Schroeder, Theodore. 1942. *Conservatisms, Liberalisms and Radicalisms & the New Psychology.* Cos Cob, Conn.: Next Century Press.

———. 1916. *Free Speech for Radicals.* Enlarged ed. New York: Free Speech League.

———. 1911. *"Obscene" Literature and Constitutional Law: A Forensic Defense of Freedom of the Press.* New York: Da Capo Press.

———. 1910. "The Meaning of Unabridged 'FREEDOM OF SPEECH.' " In *The Fight for Free Speech*, compiled by Alden Freeman. New York: Free Speech League.

———. 1908. "The Scientific Aspect of Due Process of Law and Constructive Crimes." *American Law Review* 42: 373.

———. 1906. "Paternal Legislation: A Study in Liberty." Reprinted from *Mother Earth* 1: 27 (May) and 1: 38 (June).

Schuckers, Jacob William. 1874. *The Life and Public Service of Salmon Portland Chase, United States Senator and Governor of Ohio; Secretary of the Treasury, and Chief Justice of the United States.* New York: D. Appleton and Company.

Schumpeter, Joseph A. 1950. *Capitalism, Socialism and Democracy.* New York: Harper & Row.

Schurz, Carl. 1913. *Speeches, Correspondence and Political Papers of Carl Schurz.* Vol. VI. Edited by Frederic Bancroft. New York: G. P. Putnam's Sons.

———. 1893. "Manifest Destiny." *Harper's Magazine* 87: 737.

Shapiro, Ian. 1989. "Gross Concepts in Political Argument." *Political Theory* 17:51.

Shapiro, Martin. 1984. "Recent Developments in Political Jurisprudence." *Western Political Quarterly* 36: 541.

———. 1983. "Fathers and Sons: The Court, the Commentators, and the Search for Values." In *The Burger Court: The Counter-Revolution That Wasn't*, edited by Vincent Blasi. New Haven: Yale University Press.

———. 1978. "The Supreme Court: From Warren to Burger." In *The New American Political System*, edited by Anthony King. Washington, D.C.: American Enterprise Institute.

———. 1966. *Freedom of Speech: The Supreme Court and Judicial Review.* Englewood Cliffs, N.J.: Prentice-Hall.

———. 1964a. *Law and Politics in the Supreme Court: New Approaches to Political Jurisprudence.* London: Free Press of Glencoe.

———. 1964b. "Political Jurisprudence." *Kentucky Law Journal* 52: 294.

Shattuck, Charles E. 1891. "The True Meaning of the Term 'Liberty' in Those Clauses Which Protect 'Life, Liberty and Property,' " *Harvard Law Review* 4: 365.

Shepard, A. G. 1915. "Freedom of Speech in Industrial Controversies." *Case and Comment* 22: 466.

Sherman, Carl, and Joab H. Benton. 1925. "Brief for Defendant in Error." *Gitlow v. New York*, 268 U.S. 650.

Sherman, Carl, W. J. Wetherbee, and Claude T. Dawes. 1925. "Brief for the State of New York." *Gitlow v. New York*, 268 U.S. 650.

Shiffrin, Steven. 1983. "The First Amendment and Economic Regulation: Away from a General Theory of the First Amendment." *Northwestern Law Review* 78: 1212.

Shulman, Alix Kate. 1982. "Bibliographical Introduction." In *Red Emma Speaks: An Emma Goldman Reader*, edited by Alix Kate Shulman. New York: Schocken Books.

Shumate, I. E. 1887. "Professional Responsibility." In *Report of the Fourth Annual Meeting of the Georgia Bar Association.* Macon, Ga.: Georgia Bar Association.

Siegan, Bernard H. 1980. *Economic Liberties and the Constitution.* Chicago: University of Chicago Press.

Skinner, Quentin. 1974. "Some Problems in the Analysis of Political Thought and Action." *Political Theory* 2: 277.

Skowronek, Stephen. 1982. *Building a New American State.* Cambridge: Cambridge University Press.

Smith, Donald L. 1986. *Zechariah Chafee, Jr.: Defender of Liberty and Law.* Cambridge: Harvard University Press.

Smith, John E. 1963. *The Spirit of American Philosophy.* London: Oxford University Press.

Smith, Rogers A. 1989. "The New Institutionalism and Normative Theory: Reply to Professor Barber." *Studies in American Political Development: An Annual.* Vol. 3. New Haven: Yale University Press.

———. 1988. "Political Jurisprudence, the 'New Institutionalism,' and the Future of Public Law." *American Political Science Review* 82: 89.

———. 1985. *Liberalism and American Constitutional Law.* Cambridge: Harvard University Press.

Smolla, Rodney A. 1988. *Jerry Falwell v. Larry Flynt: The First Amendment on Trial.* New York: St. Martin's Press.

Solomon, Martha. 1987. *Emma Goldman.* Boston: Twayne Publishers.

Spencer, Herbert. 1972. *On Social Evolution.* Chicago: University of Chicago Press.

———. 1902. *Facts and Comments.* New York: D. Appleton & Company.

———. 1896. *The Man Versus the State.* New York: D. Appleton & Company.

Steel, Ronald. 1980. *Walter Lippmann and the American Century.* Boston: Little, Brown and Company.

Stumpf, Harry P. 1988. *American Judicial Politics.* San Diego: Harcourt Brace Jovanovich.

———. 1984. "The Recent Past." *Western Political Quarterly* 36: 534.

Sumner, William Graham. 1982. *What Social Classes Owe to Each Other.* Caldwell, Idaho: Caxton Printers.

———. 1963. *Social Darwinism: Selected Essays of William Graham Sumner.* Edited by Stow Persons. Englewood Cliffs, N.J.: Prentice Hall.

———. 1958. "The Absurd Effort to Make the World Over." In *Great Issues in American History.* Vol. II. Edited by Richard Hofstadter. New York: Vintage Books.

———. 1934. "The Conquest of the United States by Spain." In *Essays of William Graham Sumner.* Vol. II. Edited by Albert Galloway Keller and Maurice R. Davie. New Haven: Yale University Press and Oxford University Press.

———. 1901. *The Predominant Issue.* Burlington, Vt.: F. A. Richardson.

Sutherland, George. 1919. *Constitutional Power and World Affairs.* New York: Columbia University Press.

———. 1917. "Private Rights and Governmental Control." *A.B.A. Report* 42: 197.

Taft, William Howard. 1920. "Mr. Wilson and the Campaign." *Yale Review* 10: 1.

Taft, Henry. 1921. "Freedom of Speech and the Espionage Act." *American Law Review* 55: 695.

Tanner, W. V., and Fred G. Remann. 1915. "Brief of Defendant in Error." *Fox v. Washington,* 236 U.S. 273.

Thayer, James Bradley. 1893. "The Origin and Scope of the American Doctrine of Constitutional Law." *Harvard Law Review* 7: 129.

Thomas, John L. 1981. "Nationalizing the Republic, 1877–1920." In *The Great Republic: A History of the American People.* 2d ed. Lexington, Mass.: D. C. Heath and Company.

Tiedeman, Christopher G. 1900. *A Treatise on State and Federal Control of Persons and Property in the United States.* Vol. I. St. Louis: F. H. Thomas Book Co.

————. 1894. *A Treatise on the Law of Municipal Corporations in the United States.* New York: Banks & Bros.

————. 1886. *Limitations of Police Power.* St. Louis: F. H. Thomas Book Co.

Tompkins, E. Berkeley. 1970. *Anti-Imperialism in the United States: The Great Debate, 1890–1920.* Philadelphia: University of Pennsylvania Press.

Tribe, Laurence H. 1985. *Constitutional Choices.* Cambridge: Harvard University Press.

Truman, David B. 1962. *The Governmental Process: Political Interests and Public Opinion.* New York: Alfred A. Knopf.

Tucker, John Randolph. 1899a and 1899b. *The Constitution of the United States.* Vols. I and II. Edited by Henry St. George Tucker. Chicago: Callaghan & Co.

————. 1899c. "Our New Colonial Policy." *Arena* 21: 84.

Tulis, Jeffrey K. 1987. *The Rhetorical Presidency.* Princeton: Princeton University Press.

Twiss, Benjamin R. 1962. *Lawyers and the Constitution.* New York: Russell & Russell.

Urofsky, Melvin I. 1975. *American Zionism from Herzl to the Holocaust.* Garden City, N.Y.: Anchor Press, Doubleday.

————. 1971. *A Mind of One Piece: Brandeis and American Reform.* New York: Charles Scribner's Sons.

Van Alstyne, William W. 1984. *Interpretations of the First Amendment.* Durham, N.C.: Duke University Press.

————. 1980. "The Recrudescence of Property Rights as the Foremost Principle of Civil Liberties: The First Decade of the Burger Court." *Law and Contemporary Problems* 43: 66.

Vaughn, Steven. 1979. "First Amendment Liberties and the Committee on Public Information." *American Journal of Legal History* 23: 95.

Verba, Sidney, and Norman H. Nie. 1972. *Participation in America: Political Democracy and Equality.* New York: Harper & Row.

Villard, Oswald Garrison. 1918a. "Sedition Laws and Juries." *Nation* 106: 562.

————. 1918b. "Our Ferocious Sentences." *Nation* 107: 504.

————. 1917a. "Notes." *Nation* 104: 410.

————. 1917b. "Bryce on the Real Prussian Menace." *Nation* 104: 481.

————. 1917c. "The Limits on Free Speech." *Nation* 105: 59.

————. 1917d. " 'Treason' on the Street Corners." *Nation* 105: 214.

————. 1917e. "Censorship of the Press." *Nation* 105: 361.

————. 1916. "Wilson, the Country, and War." *Nation* 103: 389.

————. 1912. "Centralization and Monopoly." *Nation* 95: 204.

Vose, Clement E. 1972. *Constitutional Change: Amendment Politics and Supreme Court Litigation Since 1900.* Lexington, Mass.: D. C. Heath and Company.

Wallace, M. G. 1920. "Constitutionality of Sedition Laws." *Virginia Law Review* 6: 385.

Walzer, Michael. 1984. "Liberalism and the Art of Separation." *Political Theory* 12: 315.

————. 1983. *Spheres of Justice: A Defense of Pluralism and Equality.* New York: Basic Books.

————. 1981. "Philosophy and Democracy." *Political Theory* 9: 379.

Ward, Harry F. 1921. "Book Review." *Columbia Law Review* 21: 498.

Warren, Charles. 1926. "The New 'Liberty' Under the Fourteenth Amendment." *Harvard Law Review* 39: 431.

————. 1917. "What Is Giving Aid and Comfort to the Enemy?" *Yale Law Journal* 27: 331.

Watson, David K. 1910. *The Constitution of the United States.* Chicago: Callaghan & Co.

Wechsler, Herbert. 1941. "Symposium on Civil Liberties." *American Law School Review* 9: 881.

Weinstein, James. 1968. *The Corporate Ideal in the Liberal State, 1900–1918.* Boston: Beacon Press.

Whipple, Leon. 1927. *The Story of Civil Liberties in the United States.* New York: Vanguard Press.

White, G. Edward. 1976. *The American Judicial Tradition: Profiles of Leading American Judges.* Oxford: Oxford University Press.

————. 1971. "The Rise and Fall of Justice Holmes." *University of Chicago Law Review* 39: 51.

White, James Boyd. 1984. *When Words Lose Their Meanings: Constitutions and Reconstitutions of Language, Character, and Community.* Chicago: University of Chicago Press.

White, Morton. 1957. *Social Thought in America: The Revolt Against Formalism.* Boston: Beacon Press.

Wiebe, Robert H. 1967. *The Search for Order: 1877–1920.* New York: Hill and Wang.

Wiesel, Elie. 1961. *Dawn.* Translated by Frances Frenage. New York: Avon Books.

Wigdor, David. 1974. *Roscoe Pound: Philosophy of Law.* Westport, Conn.: Greenwood Press.

Wigmore, John H. 1920. "*Abrams v. United States:* Freedom of Speech and Freedom of Thuggery in War-Time and Peace-Time." *Illinois Law Review* 14: 539.

Williamson, Harold Francis. 1934. *Edward Atkinson: The Biography of an American Liberal, 1827–1905.* Boston: Old Corner Book Store.

Willoughby, Westel W. 1910. *The Constitutional Law of the United States.* New York: Baker, Voorhis.

Wilson, Edmund. 1962. *Patriotic Gore.* New York: Oxford University Press.

Wilson, Woodrow. 1981. *Congressional Government: A Study in American Politics.* Baltimore: Johns Hopkins University Press.

Winkelman, Barnie F. 1942. *John G. Johnson: Lawyer and Art Collector, 1841–1917.* Philadelphia: University of Pennsylvania Press.

Winter, Ralph K., Jr. 1973. *Campaign Financing and Political Freedom.* Washington, D.C.: American Enterprise Institute for Public Policy Research.

————. 1971. "Money, Politics and the First Amendment." In *Campaign Finances: Two Views of the Political and Constitutional Implications.* Washington, D.C.: American Enterprise Institute for Public Policy Research.

Wolfinger, Raymond E., and Stephen J. Rosenstone. 1980. *Who Votes?* New Haven: Yale University Press.

Woods, Arthur. 1915. "Reasonable Restrictions upon the Freedom of Assemblage." In *Publications of the American Sociological Society.* Vol. 9. Chicago: University of Chicago Press.

Wreszin, Michael. 1965. *Oswald Garrison Villard: Pacifist at War.* Bloomington: Indiana University Press.

Wright, J. Skelly. 1982. "Money and Pollution of Politics: Is the First Amendment an Obstacle to Political Equality?" *Columbia Law Review* 82: 609.

————. 1976. "Politics and the Constitution: Is Money Speech?" *Yale Law Journal* 85: 1001.

Wyzanski, Charles E., Jr. 1947. "Judge Learned Hand's Contributions to Public Law." *Harvard Law Review* 60: 348.

Index

Compositor: Miller Freeman Publications
Text: 11/13 Caledonia
Display: Caledonia